The Things
I Wish They'd
Told Me as I was
Growing Up

The Things I Wish They'd Told Me as I was Growing Up

David Rankin

Matador
9 De Montfort Mews
Leicester LE1 7FW, UK
Tel: (+44) 116 255 9311 / 9312
Email: books@troubador.co.uk
Web: www.troubador.co.uk/matador

ISBN 978 1848760 936

British Library Cataloguing in Publication Data.
A catalogue record for this book is available from the British Library.

Typeset in 11.5pt Bembo by Troubador Publishing Ltd, Leicester, UK

Matador is an imprint of Troubador Publishing Ltd

Printed in Great Britain by the MPG Books Group, Bodmin and King's Lynn

To Audrey Mary Hansell and Nicholas John Rankin.

Contents

Foreword

I trust I have not misled you with the title of this book, 'The Things I Wish They'd Told Me As I Was Growing Up' is not a list of advice. It doesn't contain tips such as; remember to floss, look after your knees and your back, learn manners as they will open doors for you, never boil your woolies, don't eat yellow snow, and never trust a fart up until you're seven and after your sixty. No, although I would highly recommend you heed my warnings, this is advice you are likely to hear elsewhere.

So this book is a journey; a ramble in places but it's simply the way I see our place in the Universe. I share the thought with many others in thinking that we live in both dangerous and interesting times. As you read on we will talk about how our vibrational levels are rising and lifting our consciousness. More and more people are awakening and in the process seeing the structure we find ourselves trapped in for the falsehood that it is. I don't believe a soul has walked this earth that did not feel better when in a place of love. However we are denied this Eden, this place of utter joy and we can only visit this bliss when we escape the severe constraints of this delusion that we call reality. Instead we find ourselves in a world in which we survive but rarely thrive, the names change but the results are the same and we see the mistakes of the past repeated constantly. We worship the wrong gods and admire the incorrect masters and in the process have become manipulated into serving those who greedily feed from our energy. Each of us as individuals can collectively defeat the dark forces at work that are doing all within their power to keep us down all in an attempt to prevent and stilt our birthright towards enlightenment.

We not only accept but we ironically fund the massive resources which enable our imprisonment, were we released we would become enlightened and we then empower ourselves to live awesome, magnificent, loving lives. However as long as we remain trapped in servitude, unmindful of our dreams, programmed from our instincts, blinded by beliefs, then we remain bound to the very few that dictate the terms of our enslavement and we remain upon a cycle, a treadmill, the rat-race, which only enlightenment can break. But I'm getting ahead of myself because we need to go on a journey to discover how we are constrained, controlled and spellbound and so this book is essentially about communication, how it reaches us on all levels and the profound influence that it has upon us. Communication plays such a vital role in our lives that it would be difficult to envision how we could exist in the World without it. It is everywhere and we are equipped to both receive and transmit enormous amounts of information, however the vast majority of this information is beyond what we are capable of understanding whilst we are locked down within our five-sense 'reality.'

Communication comes to us in two basic forms; what we are aware of and what we are not, it comes to us by way of our summoning it but mostly it arrives uninvited and largely unnoticed. A large amount of what we recognise and process is on a conscious level but a far greater amount finds its way into our subconscious.

In essence this book only asks one fundamental question and that is – are we processing the best possible quality information to enlighten us as we progress on the journey we call life, or is that information corrupted with the result that we are deluded and guided to remain restricted and unfulfilled? To put this questions another way – are we really living the lives we were designed to live?

Although our genetic lineage will dictate the colour of our eyes and many other unarguable traits, we enter this realm relatively uncorrupted, we are born innocent, largely a blank slate, designed, enabled and fit to learn, equipped for most of what our life will throw at us. Without exception all communication comes to us in the form of vibration but we operate attuned to an extremely limited bandwidth mainly due to early childhood programming.

We are taught the development of the intellect but not the expansion of instinct and we are seriously robbed of something vital in the process.

We are constantly trying to understand and make sense of our place in the World from a mass of information such as our sight as it processes and converts light and from sound delivered to us in waves. Information is carried to us through non-verbal means such as writing and symbols and through auditory means such as speech and sound.

We talk, make gestures and give facial expressions and they all transmit messages. We absorb transmission by electrical impulses such as the television, the phone and the radio. We are influenced by E-mail, persuaded by advertising, touched by a funny feeling or a hunch regarding something or someone, the list is endless because as I will try to demonstrate as you read on, everything is communicating with everything else in the Universe. On a macro level the planets all demonstrate communication and affect one another, on a micro level we find that atoms, molecules and the smallest of organisms all affect one another. In a nutshell - communication is everywhere and it is linked by Consciousness.

As a result we act as gifted mediums in a benign Universe where we are invited in every moment to assimilate and make sense of abstract vibrations all in an attempt to understand ourselves, one another, what we are faced with and our place in the grand scheme of things. We cannot escape, even if we retire to the back of a cave and cut ourselves off from all contact with the world, we will still be swamped with information, from the breeze in the air to the snap of a twig and of course we are forever communing and trapped with our thoughts. We are communicating constantly with one another, our clothing, hairstyle, our cars, our behaviour and so on, all make a communicative statement to others who will in turn form conclusions. So whether your standing on stage plucking your shiny red Gibson Les Paul in front of an audience of 150,000 people or sitting in dull grey mac alone on a park bench, you are broadcasting and receiving.

Intrinsically this book is about communication on all its levels and that's what we are doing now as I broadcast and you receive. You have been programmed to understand these symbols; these letters forming words, as your gaze runs over them you convert them into meaning, into substance.

We should not underestimate the power of these and other symbols because they influence us emotionally, words can deliver love or fear, humour or pain, and dependant upon how we feel will entirely dictate the quality of life we will lead.

Communication is fundamental and essential to us but if I had communicated the title of this book to you as ... 'The Benefits and Vicissitudes of Communication,' then I doubt you would have bought it but again please be assured I am not trying to mislead you. As we will discuss there is quite enough of that going on all around us, but I am trying to communicate some different thought processes other than the ones we currently embrace because they don't seem to serve most of us very well in the present.

'Sticks and stones may break my bones but words can never hurt me ...' do you remember that saying when you were growing up? Whoever thought it up was deluded because words are powerful, magical tools and they have a profound effect upon us. Words of praise and comfort soothe and build a child's confidence, words of love fill us with warmth, conversely words of criticism will sadden or make us defensive, angry words will hurt us more deeply than we are prepared to admit to and ready to realise and we will carry these injuries forward into adulthood, for many of us these wounds will never heal. We are all damaged goods to a greater or lesser degree and one of my chief motivations in the writing of this book is to enable us to come to terms with these buried scars, these trauma based experiences, in order that our lives might become more fulfilling.

During the time it has taken me to write this book I have asked myself what else motivated me, I suppose we all want to be heard and communicate with one another and this is one of many ways of enabling us to form a bridge. Writing is more permanent than speech, words once uttered disappear into the ether although as we are aware, not without first having a profound impact upon us.

Perhaps the view we all take when we try and communicate with one another is, will anyone listen and what right do I have to express my opinion? Whether you agree with the content of this book or not, I can only say, this is my truth and instinct drove me to share it with you and instinct is the primary reason you find yourself reading this. I firmly believe that we would lead more beautiful, abundant and natural lives if we used more of our instinct and less of our intellect.

In the process of writing people have asked me what I was doing and when I mentioned that I was writing many of them said that they too had always wanted to write. It is said that we all have a book in us, this is the book that was in me.

Anyway, back to what motivated me to write - it could be just a desire to communicate my views because in conversation I get constantly interrupted and therefore my audience might find me boring or consistently wrong. It's possible they could all be suffering from an immense viral contamination of low attention span deficiency.

I am an ordinary man who has led an interesting life so as in much of what we do, I could simply be exercising my ego as I try to tell you – 'this is what I think I know.' It's not as if you know me, I am nobody, you have never heard of me. I am not famous and don't want to be and after you read this book you will understand why. Having said that, it is nice to get a bit of affirmation, a pat on the back always does wonders for my fragile ego. And despite the castigation I give to ego, it is impossible to live in the world without deploying it to some extent or another but I accept that it's an arrogance that I might think you would be interested in the things that interest me.

Possibly I am trying to earn a few quid from the proceeds of this books sale or after packing a lot of experience into what is after all just a life, then the truth might be that I am becoming more aware of my mortality as the summers race by I think I better get some of this written down prior to my demise and so I write for posterity.

There is also a selfish desire to write down some of my experiences accumulated over the years in order to vent my spleen, get it all off my chest, give me some closure, a bit like opening a valve to reduce the pressure, I admit in the process of writing and especially now that it's done, I have achieved a release.

But the most conscious thought that I cling to is the hope that you might just hit a cord with a few of the gems that I gathered as I staggered along the way.

Unscrambling the puzzle

Whenever we choose to communicate we give something of ourselves in the process. What is it that we are projecting as we encounter one another and furthermore will that encounter benefit the recipients or hinder them?

We have come to intimately understand our five-sense world; the sciences have enabled us to realise how we function. The organs that allow us to see, smell, taste and touch hold no further mystery, indeed physically we are very much a known quantity.

Beyond our five-senses there are forces that have a massive influence upon us and although we are able to witness the effects of some of these forces, such as the power of the Sun with its life giving light and heat and the Moon which pulls our oceans and enables the tides, but we know so little beyond these effects which manipulate and form this vast Universe that we are such a tiny part of.

Powerful minds such as Einstein have shown us that we live in a Conscious Universe where everything is in flux, subjected to change and flow. Matter is everything that we might consider to be solid, but in fact this is an illusion from our five-sense perspective because there is nothing that is solid in that everything vibrates to a pulse and that includes ourselves and through Consciousness this vibration runs throughout the entire Universe.

We know that energy converts to matter as it slows in vibration and this is part of the natural order and there is nothing in existence that is not affected by this principle. This is how energy finds the form that we call matter and we would be better served to realise that there is no distinction between matter and energy until we come to observe and discern it.

One of the main arguments on these pages is to try and demonstrate that a variety of man-made manipulations influence us on a grand scale, this is against nature and most certainly against ourselves both individually and collectively. This is not a particularly controversial or original idea but perhaps it is time to fully realise the scale of what is happening.

Within this so-called reality we influence others by our actions but in the world that exists beyond our senses we are both transmitting and receiving as part of an exchange. Our senses might be sophisticated but they are also limiting, they are able to pick up on much information and we convert and process these findings as we try to make sense of our environment, but there is so much more going on.

In the lives we have made for ourselves we find ourselves heavily grounded and largely separated from Universal Consciousness. The process begins as soon as we enter this realm, for example a baby will receive vaccines some of which contain mercury, the second most toxic metal in existence, this poison breaks down our brains synapses. Other compounds such as the addictive food flavourer monosodium glutamate is introduced everywhere in our food and causes a frightening list of problems including allergies, obesity and lethargy. More toxins come our way as pesticides and fluoride are both introduced to us and sold to us with the concept that they will improve our lives, but at what cost to our physical and mental functioning? And unless we become aware of these and the many other factors which serve to harm us and dumb and numb us, then we are destined to turn on the wheel in a never-ending cycle from one generation to the next repeating and manifesting the same problems, making the same mistakes.

Every apprentice begins with a master and he learns the master's style before going onto develop his own. Most of the meanings ascribed to the word 'master' infer a person who has knowledge and therefore power and a master uses power to influence others in a variety of ways.

A master has power over – an animal such as a dog – a person such as a worker – a child such as a pupil.

However one more definition of Master is a title given to a male up to the time that he enters his teens, thereafter he will be known as Mister. Master used in this context indicates that there is still much to learn and that maturity and knowledge is yet to come.

It is very confusing because in one word we are being offered two almost directly opposed meanings; does the master have great knowledge and power (therefore he is old) or does the Master have great naivety and much to learn (he is young)?

As we journey through our lives the relevance and meaning of why we are here is a puzzle we are constantly trying to solve, as young Masters we are compounded to be influenced by older masters because we have no choice, therefore a child growing up will encounter many masters and they will all mould that child and leave their mark.

They will include parents and guardians, aunts and uncles, teachers and headmasters, in fact anyone and everyone who is older is an influence and can therefore perform mastery over a child. These masters do not have to come into direct and personal contact with the young Master; the celebrity, the model, the newscaster, the sportsman, the priest, the politician and everywhere our Master turns he will be influenced by everyone and everything.

From all these influences the Master will receive instructions on how to act, how to perform and what to believe in. The boy will have his name chosen for him, what religion he will be, patriotism will be instilled, manners, respect, political persuasion, the language he will use to communicate and the accent he will use to speak, his sense of right and wrong, his tastes and his values; the list is vast and the road before him long, but the old masters will see to it that all of this is firmly in place well before the Master becomes a Mister and it is worth noting that neither the young Master nor the eventual Mister he will become will have had much of a say in the construction of what will define, govern and guide him for the rest of his natural life.

We are therefore made, formed, instilled, groomed and moulded in a series of encounters that will go on to be our beliefs. However these beliefs are not yours - they are not You – they are in fact a conglomeration of other people's ideas, theories, imprints and instructions.

Therefore we become a long way removed from being the masters of our own destinies and as a result we become reflections and projections of what others expect of us and would want us to be.

The obvious gulf and direct contradiction between old master and young Master is demonstrated on the one hand - the old master is an individual who is full of knowledge, he is the possessor of consummate skills and he is prepared to share, instruct, programme and initiate. On the other hand - a young Master is a novice with a lack of skill and is both raw and defenceless and he is therefore largely a blank slate.

Our Masters defence might be an attempt at rebellion however as we will go onto learn, this is not a realistic option.

The very word master is indicative of one who subjugates or defeats another and when you are a slave you have a master.

Master - the same word defining very different roles - most confusing.

As children growing in our formative years we are at our most vulnerable. If we are being guided by benign forces or influenced by those who love us and care for our well being, we shouldn't have a problem but what if those that guide us are wrong, even if they are wrong with the best of intentions?

Are we being taught the correct skills that will empower us as we set out on our life's journey? One of the main arguments on these pages is that we are not and not by a long way.

And if we are not then why not, where are we going wrong, what are the forces that are at work, what is the agenda and finally what can we do about it? Based on the assumption that we should want to consider all of the options rather than the ones we are force-fed in a never-ending cycle from one generation to the next as it passes its baton of belief on down the generational line.

We have an inbuilt desire to learn because we are naturally curious beings and we are only halted by our attention being diverted elsewhere. These diversions are invariably enforced upon us, as a result for example; 'high-ho-high-ho - it's off to work we go.'

Are we so distracted by outside influences and manipulated into a set of beliefs that resign us into the acceptance of a life far less fulfilling with limited potential and as a result we are therefore consigned to live an 'ordinary' life because of the successive corruption of old masters?

Have we reached a stage in our development and evolution where we have become so imprinted, manipulated and programmed that our expectations have become limited, where we find ourselves little more than puppets groomed to do the bidding of others as our strings are pulled by those who ultimately control our lives and in the process we serve men who stand in the shadows and despise us but need us for their survival?

I trust this is one of the uncomfortable points that will be dealt with as you read on. Another of the points made in these pages is the proposal that we have come so far 'off road' with our lives that many of us are lost and we continually search for the elusive but genuine article in our lives; valid and truthful with meaning and substance, a life of love and joy, that is not just the promise of a life containing a dream which we are regularly sold but seems to constantly evade us, with the result that we live little more than a tough existence where we occasionally glimpse and constantly reach for the proverbial pot of gold but never actually achieve it.

Perhaps we conclude that we are fated and that our destiny is mapped out for us and 'what will be will be,' or alternatively we consider that right now we are just too busy to do what we feel is instinctively 'right' and the distractions that inhibit and prevent us are therefore self-imposed and we put our desires off and as a result we place them into the vague mists of the future.

We are here to learn and to create and when we are denied we become frustrated. This frustration then manifests itself as we embrace our lives. Lives that are full of compromise and often difficult to accept. We may bandage these painful frustrations with the intake of drugs or we may endure a breakdown, a catharsis or a spiritual emergency, (which are all basically the same thing).

We may simply accept our lot and manage to function in spite of feeling somewhere between sad or downright depressed.

I can find no other reason for our manifestation and presence on this planet than to exploit the inbuilt desire to learn, but is this inherent ability used against us? As we learn we grow and expand and although we might find it difficult to recall where we left those house keys or the name of the person we just met - we have not forgotten, we simply find we are unable to recall. We cannot 'unlearn' anything. Learning then allows us to create and as we create we continue to grow, we alter and we change.

What was right for us once no longer holds good.

As a child my parents took me to see West Side Story. I guess I would have been about eleven years old and I can remember being mesmerised by the film. I drove my parents crazy to see it again, in short I loved the music, the story, the dancing; the film blew me away. (It's based on the story of Romeo and Juliet, updated and set in New York). I have watched this film a few times over the years and every time I watch it I find something profoundly new.

The film obviously has not changed, but I have.

As we change physically we are able to watch the changes we undergo. These changes are more obvious than our mental or spiritual growth. Change can be witnessed in those we know; you see a friend you haven't seen in a while and the changes are more marked. A bit like the brakes on your car, you're quite happy driving it and then someone else drives it and remarks, 'your brakes are poor,' you hadn't noticed because the decline was gradual and you lived with it every day. As our lives pass however we are less able to see emotional transitions and spiritual growth.

As human beings (or humans becoming), we seek to avoid pain. This is understandable; who would actively seek pain?

For those that do, pain and pleasure are closely linked in that they both release chemicals such as serotonin, endorphins and dopamine, as they say; there is a fine line between pain and pleasure.

The brain produces endorphins, which resemble the effects of the opiate drugs and produce a sense of well-being. Dopamine is also naturally produced by the body and is picked up by receptors in the brain. Serotonin is nicknamed 'the happy molecule' and it plays an important role in the regulation of our anger, aggression, body temperature, sexuality and appetite.

Low levels of serotonin are associated with several disorders including; clinical depression, obsessive-compulsive disorder and migraine.

So if your bag is a wrap-up in Mistress Fifi's dungeon while she performs mastery over your person and proceeds to give you a good hiding, then perhaps you are not going to agree with me.

However those that are urged to enact in this drama are no different to the rest of us, because pain delivered in childhood produces trauma. This trauma is often buried so deeply in the mind that the person is not consciously aware of it and as we will go on to discuss, these buried traumas (or altars) are the root of all of our maladies and if left to slumber will always return to resurface and affect us at some stage of our lives because what we don't deal with will come back to haunt us. The results are there to see in depression, eating disorders, self-harming, behavioural difficulties, disfunctionality and a whole cartel of negative manifestations.

As we witness our own becoming and the unfolding of others we realise pain seems non-selective. Some people receive loads of it while others seem to get through their lives unscathed. This may seem unfair but as we know; bad thing happen to good people every day. That is the deal but it is our ability to handle what comes our way that remains important and it is said, 'what doesn't kill you makes you stronger.' Indeed the best of steel is forged over the strongest of fires and we humans have overcome incalculable and unbelievable odds in order to survive and to prosper.

Much of what is contained here has been written down on bits of paper scattered around over a period of twenty-odd years.

I wasn't conscious I was ever going to do what I am trying to do here which is to pull all those bits of paper together and go on a backwards and forwards journey: filling in the spaces as it were.

I apologise in advance if I do not cover a subject properly but this is for two reasons; there just isn't enough room on these pages and because should the subject interest you then there is much more information out there and perhaps there is a spark or two on these pages that will encourage you to seek further and better information. Secondly, because not everything is discussed to its fullest conclusion you must therefore be allowed to make up your own mind. The ability to do this is often denied us as we get presented with another 'fact' which we are coerced into believing is true or we find ourselves governed by yet another law and are told that it is for the common good, I hope by the end of reading this book you might consider how we are controlled and manipulated, in what I propose is a very poor deal as far as we as individuals are concerned.

If I use the male 'he' or 'his' in terms of a story, it is not because I seek to define gender. My opinion (for what it's worth) on the subject is that we enter our bodies (or spacesuits) as androgynous: that is as none sexual beings, thereafter our upbringing and largely external forces will go on to define our sexuality.

Boys are given soldiers and girls are given dolls; this is overly simplistic but you get my drift.

I think that's why many people get confused and express themselves outside of what the 'normals' would call normal behaviour, but since I have never met anyone who is actually normal I have no yardstick on this and therefore conclude; we really should not care what someone's sexual leanings are about and I therefore invite you to consider in this instance and throughout all of our lives and in every situation that we will encounter, the following might be a good principle to use before we judge or condemn anyone …

You can do anything you want in this life, providing it is appropriate to you and it does not hurt anyone else.

And as we will go on to discuss; since we all come from Oneness we are therefore all One, there is no duality, there are no opposites except those that we have constructed by the act of separation that brought us to this matter-based realm.

One equals One – therefore 'he' means all of us.

I hope I live long enough to regret that I didn't call this book something else like; 'Lets All Just Go And Claim Our Birthright,' however I have no idea how you will receive the stories I am about to tell, but here is where you are and something brought both of us to this point, and I can't help but be exceedingly pleased about that and since you have invested time and perhaps money in an effort to reach this point, then it is my humble suggestion you continue your (much appreciated) visit to these words and the meanings that they carry and I hope by the end you feel that you might be empowered to do just that – go claim your birthright – go and claim what is rightfully yours.

Either that or at least you'll discover – just who is kidding who.

I thought I would write this book in alphabetical order for my own convenience. I have jumped back and forward, taking bits out here and adding bits there.

I trusted at the end a better layout or formula would become obvious to me but it hasn't so I'm stuck with the original plan.

I hope you read this book from start to finish, but if you're like me – it helps you to skip.

Advertising

In an experiment done by Dr. I. A. Mirsky and Dr. R. E. Miller of the University of Pittsburgh School of Medicine in 1959, a monkey was subjected to conditioning by showing him a symbol and at the same time giving him an electric shock. The monkey soon learned to avoid the shock by pressing a lever as soon as he saw the symbol. Since the monkey's heart beat faster whenever the shock was applied, it also was conditioned to beat faster when only the symbol was presented. The researchers then shortened the time the symbol was flashed to the monkey to thousandths of a second. They found that the animal's heart would beat faster but it failed to press the lever. The monkey was now not consciously aware of what it subconsciously perceived but its reaction on a subliminal level was demonstrated by its heartbeat.

In 1957, a drive in theatre used a tachistoscope to flash the words 'Drink Coca Cola' and 'Eat Popcorn' for $1/3000^{th}$ of a second every 5 seconds. In this six-week experiment Coke sales rose by 58% and popcorn sales rose 18%. This was the brainchild of New York market researcher James Vicary and although he refuted some of what he had done early in the 1960s there is much evidence that shows advertisers use subliminal messages in their advertising to this day.

The evidence is with us in flashing messages, in sound, image, and repetition; the assault on our senses is unrelenting.

A subliminal message is a communication below the conscious level of perception. By its nature you will not be aware of receiving it, but the message can be embedded in any picture or noise transmitted to us.

The extent of these messages in our everyday life is disturbing. For example, in America a programme called Iron Chef, a food cookery programme was televised where a MacDonald's advertisement was flashed for $1/30^{th}$ of a second.

The Disney Corporation is notorious for subliminal messages, which are even more heinous and sinister when one considers that they are targeted mainly towards children and are often of a sexual nature.

There are subliminal messages in every form of advertising and if we realised how many of these messages we received in any given day most of us would be very shocked.

If advertising did not work and have the desired effects upon us, then why would manufacturers and institutions pay fortunes to advertising, media and marketing companies in order to sell their products or their services?

Those that support this highly controversial form of programming say that the benefits of this experience can be used to eliminate negative personality traits. Positive subliminals can be used to change bad habits, remove depression, and alleviate imposed feelings of hate, anger and fear for example.

Consumers in America spend over 50 million dollars every year on these subliminal self-help products.
Dennis Love, Journal of Advertising Research, 2000.

This radical treatment is a double-edged sword because the same technology can be used to make us think and act in a way that can be against our better interests.

Used in the wrong hands it is clear we would become nothing more than robots moving to the whim of those that seek to control us. Subliminal messaging exists in our every day lives through the subtle use of symbology. However the few that are caught out using it are not brought to task, it is always stated as being an accident but these 'accidents' just keep on happening.

Advertising has to be the most expensive form of human communication. When we sit back and relax to watch TV we are at our most receptive and therefore at our most vulnerable. The clever adverts that we watch cost more – second by second – to produce than any major blockbuster film. These adverts are carefully constructed in the finest of detail, so for those responsible for making them to come out later, having been caught out, and state – 'it was just an accident,' is not only unbelievable it is wholly unacceptable.

Supermarkets invite us to 'save as we spend.' We have the simple but very effective, 'buy one-get one free,' Adverts are full of hooks to draw us in and work to hone us in on the seller's products.

We turn on the TV there's Carol Vorderman, 'our thinking man's bit of crumpet,' informing us how easy it is to get a loan and in the following advert we are informed how to embrace debt management when we cannot afford to make the payments.

There are many who will judge and say 'you shouldn't take out loans you can't afford to pay back,' but for the many who are trapped in poverty this is the only way out or more precisely, not a way out but a temporary escape – a quick fix.

The *'people who can't afford to pay back loans shouldn't take them out in the first place,'* lobby, may well have a point but it is hardly a fair or an even playing field.

In the society we have constructed for ourselves we have given away so much of our power to those who control and manipulate us. Those people are to be found heading governments, the media, banks, corporations and so on, they are the same people who push us into aspiration and desire, programme us into want and haul us happily into debt and they do not have our best interests at heart. For the few that prosper and profit from the consumerism of the many there will be casualties. Many of those casualties are decent people and as we know; bad things happen to good people every day.

If you still doubt me then perhaps by the end of this book, I might have softened your hard heart.

On with the programming

On the commercial television stations we watch programmes that have little or no continuity. We settle down to watch half an hours worth of programme, it's bang on ten 'o' clock and the moment is ours as we wait in anticipation for the adverts to end, they finish and the opening title credits roll then there is a little catch up sequence, just in case you missed last weeks episode. The actual programme gets started at about 10 minutes past the hour.

We see about five minutes of actual programme, the adverts come on again then we get an advertising trailer for the programme that follows this one, a plug for the new series that starts tomorrow, a quick word from our sponsor and then it's back to our programme, there is a long winded explanation just in case we were not paying attention to the five minutes we saw before the break, then four minutes of actual programme until the next adverts.

In half an hours worth of programme you will be fortunate to see ten minutes of actual content. Television has become an endless stream of advertising and even the programmes themselves are trying to sell us something. The principals now adopted are obvious; consume, work, buy, keep up with your neighbour or better still; burst a gut, raise your blood pressure all in an attempt to be ahead because then he will have to buck his ideas up because you have upped the anti.

Obey, don't ask questions and pay your licence fee for your TV because the BBC is the only place where you can avoid adverts, not all adverts of course but the more obvious ones. So be prepared for the new hidden advertising, it's called 'product placement.' it is here to stay and it is thriving big-style, here's a demonstration of it.

In an episode of an American sci-fi series about alien abduction, a group of people go out for a few beers to toast a comrade they have just buried. They remember fondly how they used to drink Budweiser together by the crate. One of the mourners raises his can, which also happens to be a Bud. In fact, the whole table is covered in Budweiser.

'Look at the can,' the character says, 'it's just like it was back then.'

Is this entertainment or a shameless plug for a product? Either way, it is the wave of the future in Britain especially now that the European Union has loosened hitherto strict rules on product placement – or as it is euphemistically know in US marketing speak, 'brand integration.'

Product placement is a deal that has everything to do with commerce and nothing to do with art. Producers acquire free props and often-significant financial help. In exchange advertisers can count on the attention of their target audience.

'V for Vendetta,' is a film that contains a message for the true power that we the people really have, it also makes a profound statement for how badly governments throughout the world have gone wrong. It demonstrates how fear is used against us. The film speaks for itself, my only criticism is; why does this film use product placement? I appreciate this is a growing trend but it had no place in a film with such a powerful and alternative message.

I'm not suggesting that you will see this film and become a hard-core conspiracy theorist or a Marxist-quoting revolutionary, but you may see what politics are ultimately all about.

Comic book stuff? I don't think so.

Lucifer's dreambox

It has been shown that as we watch television our brains enter an alpha-wave condition, as we become relaxed we go onto autopilot, this altered state of consciousness is similar to what a hypnotist will achieve when accessing your subconscious.

Alpha waves are oscillating electrical voltages in the brain. Alpha waves occur in relaxed states such as meditation and under hypnosis. They are not a measure of peaceful thinking because they can also occur under other conditions, but they are indicative of a lack of visual processing and focus.

Subliminal messages are images and sounds embedded within a medium that evades normal perception. A person will not consciously realise they have been shown a subliminal message, however the hidden messages will influence the brain subconsciously and will alter our behaviour.

The brain emits electrical signals that correspond with our different states or levels of consciousness. Scientists and researchers recognise four basic kinds of brainwave and they measure these frequency patterns by cycles per second (cps) as follows;

Beta (14 – 40 cps) this is our normal waking or conscious state. We are awake and able to focus and concentrate.

Alpha (8 – 13 cps) we are relaxed but remain in an alert medative state. This vibration is good for internal visualisation and creativity.

Theta (4 – 8 cps) this is the state of deep meditation and is related to intuition, creativity, and sleep and dreaming.

Delta (0 – 4 cps) the deepest reaches of sleep, and conducive to our healing process.

This next subject has little to do with advertising but like much advertising, it comes into our lives uninvited and is fired into our minds through the tube.

We have seen massive growth in quizzes (they are the cheapest form of TV to produce) and as corporations and companies have cut back on their advertising budgets, quizzes have proven to be a most lucrative replacement as they raise vast revenue for all involved.

And hey, lets not be too unkind, you might win £500 although the odds against you are massive – and wait for it – here is today's quiz question;

What colour is the Hulk?
A. Green.
B. An invisible Yorkshire pudding.

Channel Five has been fined £300,000 for faking winners on its Brainteaser quiz show.

The Sun July 2007.

An investigation concluded that the company behind the Richard and Judy premium rate telephone quiz on Channel 4, found millions of viewers were urged to call in after the quiz had ended and the winner had been selected. Just to confirm everything was above board Tony Blair the then PM, featured and participated in the quiz.

Icstis (the regulator) said almost five million viewers entered the competition at a cost of £1 per call. But 47% of calls were received after the shortlist of winners was already chosen. Production Company, Cactus was responsible for choosing potential winners.
BBC News report. July 07.

Premium rate services regulator slapped a £150,000 on Eckoh UK. Ltd. It also ordered a sanction to provide refunds to all those affected.

The company was punished after an inquiry into allegations that the 'You Say, We Pay,' telephone quiz on Channel 4's Richard and Judy show urged viewers to call in even though potential winners had already been chosen.
thisismoney.co.uk Aug2007.

Icstis says the fraud goes back to 2004.
Telegraph.co.uk

Speaking about ITV. Its biggest shows, including Ant and Dec's 'Saturday Takeaway,' and the 'X Factor,' were found guilty of deceiving millions of viewers.

The phone line and faking scams will cost £18 million. It could still face a fine from watchdog Ofcom. Last night ITV refused to comment.
The Sun. Thursday 25th Oct 2007.

BBC One's Blue Peter, a programme aimed at children, had to apologise for featuring a fake contestant after a 'technical glitch' hit a phone in competition.
BBC News report July 07.

Media watchdog Ofcom has imposed an unprecedented £50,000 fine on the BBC over the Blue Peter phone-in scandal in which a young studio guest posed as a fake competition winner.
thismoney.co.uk Aug 2007.

Whilst admitting we are moving away from the point here but thought it worthy of a mention, since the fine is levied against the BBC with the money going to the Treasury and since the BBC is publicly funded through licence payers, it transpires that the culprits are not paying the fine in any event.

Uncomfortable thought time; you don't watch the quiz – you don't pick the phone up – you don't even have to turn on your TV – but you're paying.

Congratulations! A quiz you never entered and a deception you played no part in – *you* – the licence payer will foot the bill.

There is nothing new in these frauds. On American TV in the 1950's, when ratings were high because TV was a new medium and there were only a handful of stations to watch, shows called 'The 64,000 Dollar Question,' 'Twenty-One,' and others, created a national scandal when it was shown that popular contestants had been coached or given the answers in advance. From the scandal that ensued for twenty years thereafter this format essentially disappeared from American TV.

Because fraud in these cases is difficult to prove we will never know how much has been scammed from people. I am not suggesting that the individuals involved in these popular television shows have any knowledge of what is going on but these deceits are practiced with distain against a vulnerable public, a public that has placed their trust in a medium that would have us believe in their credibility.

Even if the odds against are long, surely when we pick up the phone and enter a contract to pay, we at least deserve to feel we actually stand a chance to win?

Banks, broadband Internet firms and other abusers of expensive 0870 and 0871 phone numbers pursue another ploy. These companies keep customers hanging on, racking up profits that are shared with phone companies.

thisismoney.co.uk

Government agencies are still raking in millions of pounds from premium-rate 0870 phone numbers despite being told more than two years ago to switch to standard charges.

Ibid.

ITV has confessed to yet another quiz show gaffe after allegedly cheating hundreds of callers to a show broadcast on Freeview.

Ibid.

If you are fed up with being ripped off by these expensive phone calls there is a web-site that attempts to give you an alternative or a non-premium rate number for you to call. In some cases it gives freephone numbers if they are available. The website is www.saynoto0870.com. Safe in the knowledge that your not being charged for your enquiry just might help to bring your stress levels down – as you wait forever to be spoken to by a robot.

'Sell the benefits' type advertising is understandable however the favoured method of pushing your product and peddling your wares recently is the disturbing; 'if you don't buy our produce you will be injured, suffer or die policy' – it's a kind of advertising gangsterism.

Margarine that actually lowers your cholesterol – okay so I've got high cholesterol – so what's the proposal here – am I going to eat a tub of grease twice a day?

Bleach, we are informed that kills 99.9% of germs – I start to worry I mean can someone look into what the other .01% that it doesn't kill does to us? The .01% survival germ that saw 99.9% of its friends die must be very powerful and could conceivably be very annoyed.

Another example is the; 'if you don't take out this particular life policy, you are totally irresponsible and you really don't love your family because when you've gone what will their broken lives be like without you?'

The fundamentals of advertising seem to have become much that is wrong with this medium and the fashion that has taken over the world, that is to say the spread of fear.

So come on you marketing people out there, those of you who are responsible for these adverts – is hidden symbolism and fear all you can muster?

Answers on a postcard please, for some strange reason I don't fully understand – I really want my second tub of margarine – about now.

Incidentally in the late 1940's, margarine was not at all popular. Consumers had no interest in buying it because it was white. In America a marketing man named Louis Cheskin coloured it yellow, wrapped it in foil (suggesting quality) and called it Imperial Margarine and the rest as they say, is history.

The power of imagery cannot be underestimated.

Allowing

The phone rings and you pick it up. The person at the other end is someone you haven't spoken to in ages. You say, 'this is really bizarre, I was just thinking about you.' This is the most powerful law in the Universe being demonstrated. It is the law of attraction. The law of attraction is a law of nature. It is as impartial as the law of gravity. Whatever you think about will be drawn to you.

Nothing can come into your experience unless you summon it through persistent thought.

To know what you are thinking, ask yourself how you are feeling. Emotions are valuable tools that instantly tell us what we are thinking and how we are feeling. It is impossible to feel bad and at the same time have good thoughts. Your thoughts determine your frequency, and your feelings tell you immediately what frequency you are on.

The thoughts that affect our emotions are the ego talking to us through an earlier childhood trauma; 'you don't deserve this,' 'why bother you never finish things anyway,' or 'your not capable.'

When we were children growing up this is what the masters who programmed us made us believe; remember the negative, harmful, fearful poisons they spread into your mind? To some extent or another these viruses have touched us all.

However don't lets get too heavy with coming down on the programmers because they were programmed as well. We also do it to one other because it was done to us, we were programmed to do this – everything is cyclic – unless we break the cycle.

Forgive yourself instantly please.

Similarly you won't be reading this unless you have allowed it to come to you and so this is what you have been asking for – this is why we are here at this point – nice to meet you.

Secret emotional shifters, such as pleasant memories, nature, or your favourite music, can change your feelings and shift your frequency in an instant.

The feeling of love is the highest frequency you can emit. The greater the love you feel and emit, the greater the power you are harnessing.

Rhonda Byrne. The Secret.

The state of alignment with the Well-Being that flows from Source. The focusing of your attention upon things that cause you to offer a vibration that 'allows' your connection to your natural source of Well-Being. Tolerating is very different from allowing. Tolerating is seeing what is not wanted, feeling the vibrational evidence of that perspective but deliberately taking no action. Allowing is deliberately giving your attention only to that which causes a vibration of alignment with Source. When you are in the state of allowing, you always feel good.

Ask and it is Given. Esther and Jerry Hicks.

This gives such credence to the old adage 'be careful what you wish for, it just might happen.' The truth is we get what we think about whether we want it or not

When you wish upon a star
Makes no difference who you are
Anything your heart desires
Will come to you.

Ned Washington.

Age

Age should not be seen as a barrier, age is just another one of those labels we place upon one another. Age is a unit of time and since time is a human notion perhaps we should pay less attention to it. Those who act without the prejudices of age and pay less attention to what others might think will often prove how irrelevant age in fact is.

- Alfred Tennyson wrote his first volume at eighteen.
- Alexander was in his youth when he rolled back the Asiatic hordes that threatened to overwhelm European civilisation almost at its birth.
- Napoleon had conquered Italy at twenty-five.
- Byron, Raphael and Poe died at age thirty-seven having made names for themselves that would make them immortal.
- Newton made some of his greatest discoveries before he was twenty-five.
- It has been said that no English poet equalled Chatterton at age twenty-five.
- [a] Jim Morrison the lead singer of the Doors died aged twenty-eight.
- Jimi Hendrix demise, aged just twenty-seven heralded the finish of the sixties and the end of the love and peace attitudes that influenced so many.
- Mozart, the famous composer, died aged thirty-five .
- Bob Marley, the great reggae musician was thirty-six when he left his legacy.
- Victor Hugo wrote a tragedy at age fifteen. St Joan of Arc was nineteen when she was burned at the stake.
- Many people regarded as genius today died before they were forty.

You know you're not thirty-nine any more when it takes you more time to recover than it does to tire you out.

Jack Benny.

Any man who celebrates being a year older is a fool.

F. Shepherd.

There is no old age, there is, as there always was, just you.

Betty Friedan.

If you want to capture your youth, just cut off his allowance.

Al Bernstein.

I have enjoyed greatly the second blooming that comes when you finish the life of the emotions and of personal relationships; and suddenly find − at the age of fifty say, that a whole new life has opened before you, filled with things you can think about, study, or read about … it is as if a fresh sap of ideas and thoughts was rising in you.

Agatha Christie.

We do not grow absolutely, chronologically. We grow sometimes in one dimension, and not in another; unevenly. We grow partially. We are relative. We are mature in one realm, childish in another. The past, the present, and the future mingle and pull us backward, forward, or fix us in the present. We are made up of layers, cells, and constellations.

Anais Nin.

There's no pleasure on earth that's worth sacrificing for the sake of an extra five years in the geriatric ward of the Sunset Old People's Home, Weston-Super-Mare.

Horace Rumpole.

Statistics might indicate that we will live to a ripe old age. Age is influenced by our lifestyle, our genes, our minds, the environment and by fate. But the gamble that we call life should be enjoyed regardless of age. When we look around very few of us are truly enjoying ourselves, we are programmed to feel guilt about having fun. We stick plasters over emotional wounds; we find escape in the use of drugs that for a short time allow us to forget about the pain, until reality returns, time races by and we find ourselves looking back and reflecting on what might have been.

Don't wait − begin it now.

Anger

Anger is about loss.

Anger is just a cowardly extension of sadness. It's a lot easier to be angry at someone than it is to tell them your hurt.

Tom Gates.

'Some have great stories, pretty stories that take place at lakes with boats and friends and noodle salad. Just no one in this car. But, a lot of people, that's their story. Good times. Noodle salad. What makes it so hard is not that you had it bad, but that you're that pissed that so many others had it so good.'

As Good As It Gets. Mark Andrus.

All parents damage their children. It cannot be helped. Youth, like pristine glass, absorbs the prints of its handlers. Some parent's smudge, others crack, a few shatter childhoods completely into jagged little pieces, beyond repair.

The Five People You Meet in Heaven. Mitch Albom.

Ruby stood and Eddie stood, too. He could not stop thinking about his father's death.

'I hated him.' he mumbled.

The old woman nodded.

'He was hell on me as a kid. And he was worse when I got older.'

Ruby stepped toward him. 'Edward she said softly. It was the first time she had called him by his name. 'Learn this from me. Holding anger is a poison. It eats you from the inside. We think that hating is a weapon that attacks the person who harmed us. But hatred is a curved blade. And the harm we do, we do to ourselves.'

'Forgive, Edward. Forgive. Do you remember the lightness you felt when you first arrived in Heaven?'

Eddie did. Where is my pain?

'That's because no one is born with anger. And when we die the soul is freed of it.'

She touched his hand. 'You need to forgive your father.'

'The Five People You Meet in Heaven.' Mitch Albom.

Anger varies in its intensity from mild irritation to full on fury and rage. Anyone can become angry that's easy. But to be angry with the right person to the right degree and at the right time, for the right purpose and in the right way, that is not easy. Every day is likely to present events that are at odds with us, at odds with our supposed wants needs and requirements. Anger is an understandable reaction to the feeling that we are being wronged, criticised, attacked; physically or mentally, that something or someone we care for deeply should suffer some similar indignity will also naturally annoy us. There are many opportunities even in the average day where one can feel angry, but it is how we handle anger that matters and this falls roughly into five categories:

Accidental; there is no intention to harm.

Hostile; as it sounds – you just kick right off, shout, intimidate and upset all around you (including yourself). You are acting to cause harm.

Repressed; you keep it all in, anger then implodes upon you and the bitterness eats away within you and can make you depressed.

Instrumental; you delay your reaction allowing it to fester and consider when you will vent your point until a later or better opportunity comes along.

Controlled; the anger passes in and out and is acknowledged but is deflected; this then is the reflection of a well-adjusted person.

The above examples are born of psychologists who will try and treat the symptoms that cause us to be angry. Usually anger is the result of frustration and feelings of inadequacy, where anger rises the person is overwhelmed and defaults to earlier childhood programming, which is why an angry person will act in a childish way and adopt behaviour such as screaming and stamping their feet.

We make the mistake of treating a symptom and rarely its cause and foundation, although psychologists will try and access through counselling the emotions are difficult to mend and are part of a complicated web of beliefs which are in turn supported and fuelled by the formidable ego. We might be better served to understand how to handle our anger because with this comes a rapid realisation and resultant healing.

Regard every difficult situation as a test, if you loose your temper – you loose the test, but don't beat yourself up, just be aware and with practice you will realise anger is a waste of energy as it serves no purpose and you are not compounded to waste your energy.

There is one key to unlock this and allow enormous growth within you, that key is simple to talk about but difficult to deploy but it comes with practice; never judge and never condemn.

Although this is the key, it is difficult to unlock the source within you because you are undoing programming and taking on your ego, but when this can be understood, through practice and mindfulness, we enable ourselves to automatically default to forgiveness and we find there is nothing to get angry about.

Like all of our emotions anger is accompanied by physiological and biological changes. Anger will send your heart rate and blood pressure up and your energy hormones like adrenaline are increased.

The effects of anger continue to ruin countless peoples lives, but anger isn't 'out there' somewhere, it is contained within. Its only treatment has to be undertaken by the sufferer and the results are extraordinary beyond words.

The only upside of anger is the person you become. Hopefully someone that wakes up one day and realises they are not afraid of the journey. Someone that knows that the truth is at best, a partially told story. That anger, like growth, comes in spurts and sits and in it's wake leaves a new chance of acceptance and the promise of calm.
The Upside of Anger. Kevin Costner and Joan Allen.

Anger makes you smaller, while forgiveness forces you to grow beyond what you were.
Cherie Carter-Scott.

If you are patient in one moment of anger, you will escape a hundred days of sorrow.
Chinese proverb.

Do not speak harshly to any one, those who are spoken to will answer thee in the same way, angry speech is painful, blows for blows will touch thee.
Buddha, The Dhammapada (c BC 300)

Never get angry. Never make a threat. Reason with people.
Don Corleone. The Godfather, Mario Puzo.

Beware the fury of a patient man.
John Dryden. Oedipus, 1679.

The next time you find yourself stuck in a long line at an ATM machine, traffic jam, or supermarket checkout counter, resist your urge to react. Do not get angry.

The line is there to test you, and to give you an opportunity not to react. But if you do react, the situation becomes the cause and you the effect.
                    The Power of the Kabbalah. Yehuda Berg.

Once we begin to practice this mindfulness, we begin to see the whole world differently.

You are no longer the person who is seething and boiling as you stand in the queue, you are chilled and relaxed.

You then begin to observe others as they loose the battle with their emotions. This gives us great incite and we learn much more about ourselves. With practice we can come to regard situations that could provoke our anger as tests – we fail the test if we succumb to anger; we learn something about ourselves in its absence.

Any kind of an upset, from a mild discomfort to outright anger, is a warning sign. It tells you that your hidden guilt is rising up from the recesses of your unconscious mind and coming to the surface. Think of that discomfort as the guilt that needs to be released by forgiving the symbol you associate with it. The ego thought system is trying to put some distance in between yourself and the guilt, and any suitable object or person who comes along will suffice. Don't, hold to anger, hurt or pain. They steal your energy and keep you from love.

Projection always follows denial. People have to project this repressed guilt onto others, or correctly forgive it. Those are the only two choices that are available, no matter how complex the world may seem. If you want to outplay the ego and successfully turn the tables on it, you have to be alert for that warning sign of discomfort or anger, and then stop reacting and start forgiving. That's how you'll win.
                    Gary R Renard. The Disappearance of the Universe.

Beauty

Beauty without grace is the hook without the bait.

Ralph. Waldo. Emerson.

Think of all the beauty still left around you and be happy.

Anne Frank (1929-1945)
Diary of a Young Girl, (1952).

Anne Frank was a Jewish girl who hid from the Nazis in a cupboard within a warehouse for over two years until she was betrayed.

She wrote in her diary, 'nearly every morning I go to the attic to blow the stuffy air out of my lungs, from my favourite spot on the floor I look up at the blue sky and the bare chestnut tree, on whose branches little raindrops shine, appearing like silver, and at the seagulls and other birds as they glide on the wind. As long as this exists, I thought, and I may live to see it, this sunshine, the cloudless skies, while this lasts I cannot be unhappy.'

Anne had her diary posthumously published by her father; he was the only surviving member of her family. She died in Bergen-Belsen concentration camp days after her sister and just a few weeks before the end of the war.

To talk of and appreciate beauty in such oppressive and terrible circumstances is an example to us all.

Beauty is in the eye of the beholder.

Margaret Wolfe Hungerford.

People often say that 'beauty is in the eye of the beholder.' And I say that the most liberating thing about beauty is realising that you are the beholder. This empowers us to find beauty in places where others have to dared to look, including inside ourselves.

Salma Havek.

It's beauty that captures your attention, personality that captures your heart.

Anyone who keeps the ability to see beauty never grows old.

Franz Kafka.

Beauty is an experience, nothing else. It is not a fixed pattern or an arrangement of features. It is something felt, a glow or a communicated sense of fineness. What ails us is that our sense of beauty is so bruised and blunted, we miss all the best.

D H Lawrence. Assorted Articles.

When I'm working on a problem, I never think about beauty. I think only how to solve the problem. But when I have finished, if the solution is not beautiful, I know it is wrong.

Richard Buckminster Fuller.

I'm tired of all this nonsense about beauty only being skin-deep. That's deep enough. What do you want, an adorable pancreas?

Jean Kerr.

Beauty in the eyes of a misogynist.

Beauty is of course relative to us – what one might admire another would not.

We were playing a game of dominoes like the bunch of old farts we were becoming. There were six or so players and a couple of onlookers, all men. As I put my domino on the board a drop-dead gorgeous girl walked into the bar and past us. We all looked up and silently admired her beauty, one of our gathering who was always good for an adage or a pop at the opposite sex decided to speak:

'Aye, but just remember lads, there's some poor bastard sitting in the house looking after the kids, sick to death of the sight of her.'

Beauty is all very well at first sight, but whoever looks at it when it has been in the house three days?

William Shakespeare.

Beauty is not real. Beauty only exists in perception.

Belief

We feel most comfortable when we are in a truthful zone. The truth is so difficult as to be almost impossible to define because your truth and someone else's truth may well be very different.

Part of this truth is belief, for example; you might be a fantastic salesperson however if you know the product you are selling has no merit you will ultimately suffer. A relationship built on falsehood will be difficult to sustain and will ultimately fail.

The one simple truth we should embrace is genuine belief and this is very different to the beliefs that are imposed upon us. Believing in yourself and that you are worth what you have is vital. You should also believe that you deserve more and if you apply this principle you will improve your circumstances. This world that you are experiencing is abundant and anything is possible. Only the restrictions you place upon yourself will prevent you getting what you want from life.

Others place restrictions upon us as we are growing up. As children our formative years are vital because this is when the 'good-and-bad stuff' is programmed into us. If those that you look up to (that's nearly everyone because your small) make you feel that you are useless and worthless, then you will grow up believing this – it will become your truth.

We are being programmed from nipple to grave. Those we look up to have such an effect on us and we absorb like sponges because we are unable to do anything else. Our parents, guardians, teachers, uncles and aunties are our heroes – but whoever it is that we most look up to it is impossible that any of them can be 100% healthy in mind. We fail or succeed because we are programmed to do so and unless we believe in ourselves, we will always fail.

One of the main purposes of this book is to show that this Universe can provide you with anything you want, but you must allow this natural law. The one and only thing that is stopping you from having every success you want is your belief. Within the word itself is the truth … be-lie-f.

Your negative beliefs will prevent you from getting what you want; some of the following harmful beliefs stand in your way;

I am too old or too young to form a relationship with this person, he or she is too young or too old. What will my family and friends think? I cannot socialise with these people they will judge me because of my accent. I am so unlucky – I never get a break. I missed out on my education, if only I could have stayed on at school. It's difficult for me to do this because I am short/tall, black/white/, male/female, fat/thin, clever/stupid – my memory is bad – I am incapable – I am disorganised.

The list we present ourselves with is endless and the seeds of doubt were planted as we were growing up, as a result our beliefs are held by us as our self-image and they were put there because we were programmed.

We might pretend otherwise but we deeply care about what others think of us. The only solution is to change and change is difficult. Even the most simple of habits are hard to alter and although we regard ourselves as adaptable in many ways we are not. We resist change and this often results in disasters; we are both evolved and programmed to be creatures of habit and then along comes a massive change in our lives, such as the death of someone close to us or a job loss and we suffer a catharsis that might result in a depression, which has become the single most common mindset malady to affect millions of people all over the world.

If the unconscious mind were a department store, the conscience mind would be the corner shop.

In England within the square mile of the City of London there is an organisation called the Tavistock Institute of Human Relations. It was founded in 1946 just after the Second World War with the aid of a grant from the Rockefeller Foundation. According to the blurb on the website, it was set up for the specific purpose of actively relating the psychological and social sciences to the needs and concerns of society.

It goes on to say that the circumstances of World War Two brought together an unusually talented group of psychiatrists, clinical and social psychologists and anthropologists in the setting of the British Army, where they developed a number of radical innovations in social psychiatry and applied social science.

They became known as the Tavistock Group because the core members had been at the pre-war Tavistock Clinic. Though only some of them continued their involvement with the post-war Tavistock organisation, those who did built on wartime achievements to introduce a number of far reaching developments in several fields. This style of research related theory and practice in a new way.

The object of the Institute was to study human relations under conditions of well-being, conflict or breakdown in the family, the community and the work group, larger organisations and to promote the health and effectiveness of individuals and organisations.

At the conclusion of World War II, Tavistock began to establish a global network of psychiatric research centres, in order to influence the ideologies of mass populations. This subversive network, which was funded primarily by the Rockerfeller Foundation and large corporations, which include such establishments as the Stanford Research Institute, the Centre for Research in Group dynamics and the United States Office of Naval Research.

Brian Desborough.

It is known that government agencies have experimented on humans in mind control, with and without the consent of the subject's knowledge.

(Scheflin. 1998)

Those who can make you believe absurdities can make you commit atrocities.

Voltaire.

I would rather have a mind opened by wonder than one closed by belief.

Gerry Spence.

The thing always happens that you really believe in, and the belief in a thing makes it happen.

Frank Lloyd Wright.

We had no choice to accept our beliefs because when we were children we believed everything we were told from grown-ups. They too were similarly imprinted or programmed.

There was a time when we questioned and felt resistance but the waves kept coming. There was often a rebellion in our adolescence but that will soon get knocked out of you as you 'conform.' As a result we didn't choose our beliefs, they were already put in place.

Beliefs are notions that are *thought* to be true – beliefs are not *known* to be true.

As a result we suffer emotional poison by this programming because the vast majority of what we believe is locked into the vaults of our minds and these are largely falsehoods. They exist because people who also believed put them there in an act that is the same as brainwashing and so the lies are passed down from one generation to the next.

Where you were born, your name, your creed and most of what you were taught and led to understand, were not choices that you made of your own volition.

Not only did you have no say in the language you speak, even the accent that defines what village you come from is all imprinted.

When we cannot understand what makes those terrorists do what they do, it is simply because we were programmed to believe something different.

As tough as this may sound and as uncomfortable as it may make you feel, if you had been programmed from birth to agree to eradicating from your Country; the interloper, the threat, the terror, the Communist, the Catholic, the Christian, the Jew, the Muslim – you may well have become what it is you now so loathe and hate.

You are born into an environment and the forces of an upbringing will dictate that there is little chance you will not be instilled into that belief system. To believe is to have faith and this unconditional and uncalled for agreement controls the rest of our lives. And because a child can only rebel against himself to any real effect we have all, every single one of us, lost the rebellion.

As we were growing up we all conformed to some degree or another because as small individuals we could not hope to win the rebellion.

Everyone knows deep down that there is more to life than the ones we are leading and once we begin to consider the structure of our society and our lives within it, we don't actually feel that this is 'as good as it gets.'

This is one of the reasons why many avoid the pain of our reality by the use of the bandage of drugs – however those drugs might be delivered into our blood-stream and whether they be labelled chocolate or heroin, alcohol or caffeine, Prozac or cannabis – we seek to numb the pain of a programmed belief system that clearly doesn't work.

We don't choose the things we believe in – they choose us.

Minority Report.

I would never die for my beliefs because I might be wrong.

Bertrand Russell.

Anyone who seriously follows their intuitive 'knowing' rather than their indoctrinated, fearful, head/mind is going to face the ridicule and the condemnation of the psychological fascists. These are not only people in jackboots with silly moustaches; they are our parents, friends, colleagues at work, and, if you are in the public eye, 'journalists' and the public in general. Anyone, in fact, who makes it difficult or unpleasant to be different, Most of the human race is so utterly indoctrinated by the externally implanted 'norms' that bombard their mind from cradle to grave that they have no comprehension that their 'normal' thinking is their own individual and collective prison. Such is their bewilderment they not only contribute minute by minute to the building of their prison, they defend it ferociously from anyone who questions or challenges the foundations and assumptions on which it stands.

David Icke. Tales from the Time Loop.

Promise me you'll always remember. You're braver than you believe, and stronger than you seem, and smarter than you think.

Christopher Robin to Pooh. A A Milne.

Boxes

This one is about our compulsion to put *everything* into boxes, so just for a moment I want to put forward the following idea – without exception all boxes should be banned.

We sit in lounges and watch 'the box' called TV, this features game shows featuring boxes or football with formations played in boxes or boxing matches or dramas with police putting people in boxes with bars and court room drama's, the real drama all being played out by the (alleged) evil-doer in the witness box. Then it's the news at 6' or 10' or whatever and there sits reading from an autocue - a programmed individual who seeks to programme you as they tell us to fear everything - plague, war, famine, flood, interest rates going up, knife attacks, inflation, global warming, global dimming, each other, terror, virus, bird flu, pig flu, muggings, rape, etc, etc - 24/7 - but here is a happy little story at the very end about a lost bunny rabbit who finally found his way home - so everyone go to bed safely, sleep well, worship the Queen, believe that Obama is actually going to make a difference, (and will eventually come up with a birth certificate showing he is an American citizen thus proving he has not secured the Presidency of Wall Street ... er sorry ... of The United States of America by fraud), pay your taxes, conform and get up tomorrow bright and early - and go do it all over again.

You hope the kids are in bed and not playing on the 'X-Box' or watching TV on the upstairs goggle-box and look for the light under the door of Jimmy's room to check he's not on the boxes that make up his computer as we make our way upstairs to our box within a box.

The truth is that much in sport, business, politics etc, is corrupt and everywhere we look in the Western World we worship the wrong gods; boxes – they have got to be watched carefully. They are a global menace and a threat to the future of humankind.

Most of us are conceived in bed (it is estimated that 17% of all Europeans were conceived in a Ikea bed. Ikea; a big blue and yellow box selling boxes to its million a day world-wide customers, the guy who owns it even drives a box called a Volvo) we are conceived and thereafter born in a box and if we are fortunate we die in one – box to box. (A good bed even has boxes under it so you can put things in boxes inside them).

Our fate thereafter is to be placed in a box or burned and our ashes put into one; thus, caskets and coffins.

We live in a box called a house or a flat. Inside our homes are boxes called rooms and in those rooms are a variety of boxes. The so-called more fortunate amongst us have fences around our boxes, which in turn form boxes called yards and gardens (which have boarders).

On Sundays we run a lawn mower up and down a bit of grass and it has a box on the front to collect grass, which we empty into a box. The smallest of accommodation can have a window box but if your quite grand you may have a box-hedge.

On Mondays, unless it's a bank holiday which will have meant that on the previous Friday one of us or God forbid all of us, had to go to the Asda box and buy lots of things in boxes for the next few days and although we used to have dustbins that were circular, now we put about a third of the things we bought in the boxes from the Asda box on Friday into a box called a wheelie bin and about six days later, the men driving a big box arrive to take the contents of the little boxes in boxes away.

You bought something (anything) in a box and when you got home and opened it the box was full – that is not half or two thirds full. And the box didn't state on the side in very small print – *the contents might settle*. Of course the contents will settle, its just another scam we are supposed to think that the box was full in the first place.

On Mondays we leave our homes, get into a little box that we drive or we get onto a bigger box we call a train or a bus with mostly strangers as we set off for this ridiculous thing we invented called '*work*' … a crushing environment, a world full of boxes, of porta-cabins, lifts, offices, compartments, where we 'box-clever' or we 'box-something off.'

And further evidence that the lives we have made for ourselves are contained within boxes follows the statement to 'think outside the box,' it demonstrates that we are using our imagination.

'He is off his box,' demonstrates that his imagination might just be winning.

Well perhaps we just need a holiday, so let's hook up the car to the caravan – the box to the box and take a break.

And hey, if it all goes 'tits up' because we can't make the payments – well there's always the cardboard box on the embankment and at least there ironically there lies some hope of salvation because then we get to look back at the big open skies – where there are no boxes.

We are programmed to box, to segregate and to compartmentalise and therefore we are driven to evaluate where everything fits. When we can't fit things into boxes we become disturbed.

Meeting new people is a good way of demonstrating this.

Watch how others fight to place you in boxes as they automatically default to asking your – name, status, age, what do you do, what do you believe in, where do you live? All in a frantic desire to categorise you, where you belong, find out just where you fit.

Just as an experiment try this – it won't win you many friends but on meeting someone for the first time, try not to give out any information about yourself – it drives people crazy. It is because of their childhood programming, which is buried in their subconscious mind and the resultant need they have to access you in order to assess you. They want to classify you in order to feel safe and if they can't they feel fear.

Okay, if I haven't lost you with my rant I have hopefully made a point. I saw the film 'New World' recently, the story of the first English to set foot in America in the area that became Jamestown, history tells us that this was the first English settlement.

The savages, (or if you prefer, the noble-indigenous-spiritual-native-people that we variously; lied to, introduced alcohol to, presented them with new diseases that they had no immunity to, took their land which they didn't believe they owned but lived from and in harmony with and in exchange for beads and mirrors or, when the deal was hot – guns and alcohol – we took what we wanted) yes ... the savages ... well they were slaughtered and the survivors were subjected to our ways and our beliefs which included the re-education of their children, they were forced fed our religion and so on whilst separating them from everything they believed in, while having the gall to tell them it was for their good, we were after all 'civilising' them. Ironically, had the Native Americans not helped the invading task force, they would have perished. Since history is written by the winners it is doubtful we will be taught this important point as we are growing up.

... so the savages watched as three sailing ships pulled into paradise and the first meaningful job the English did was erect a box called a fort.

This inherent need of ours to put people into boxes; age, weight, colour, political persuasion, religion, etc, is a result of programming. Anything placed in a box has to then be labelled and this causes separateness, this is unhealthy because we all come from the same source, we are all the same.

The last thing (*honestly*) about the box business is represented by the contagious spread of the box, because from there the compartments just get bigger; my desk, my dog, my wife, my kids, my room, my house, my street, my town, my region, my country and so on. The box makes a statement; this is mine and this is yours.

Whichever way you look at it boxes cause division and mislead. Boxes are constructions built and constantly reinforced by our ego both separately and collectively. Perhaps it's the geometry of boxes that affect me so badly. I heard it said that there are no straight lines in nature. One thing consistent about nature is its flow and boxes stop flow, they define and separate us.

The old adage goes – 'divide and conquer' – and here is the bad news – we have become both.

Celebrity

In 2003, New Scientist magazine reported that one third of Americans were suffering from what it called 'celebrity-worship syndrome.'

What drives someone to want to be a celebrity? It's kind of showing off and getting paid for it; it is an ego thing. I can appreciate someone wanting to paint or make music, to act, to make pots, to build, partake in a sport, to aspire to do anything creative and to try and do that thing well should be encouraged and admired.

Inside all of us there is genius waiting to manifest and even the most disadvantaged of people, if allowed to express themselves will achieve remarkable feats. In turn we appreciate genius in others because it helps us all aspire to something greater. Often we are drawn to the underdog, the individual who breaks the mould and triumphs against all the odds.

Sport is similar and once again we all have our favourites and the individuals who excel are a joy to behold. I always loved football, I loved to play the game but now I know I will never play again, but I can project – I can imagine. We can with anything; we can all derive our pleasure through a third-party by projection and this dynamic plays a major role in our lives.

Fashion models are projected upon, although we might be better off admiring the clothes that are the new 'must have thing,' than the size zero bodies and the large egos they contain. Clearly if we have a high regard for their image and aspire to resemble what it is they are selling, then the price of this will be evident in the impressionable young who may diet to extreme, develop eating disorders and as a result risk serious health problems. Amongst the fragrant smells of perfume at many a fashion show one can often detect the scent of vomit emanating from the breath of the slender frames of those on the catwalk, what examples are being shown to our young masters? We should be mindful of the gods we worship.

Celebrities have frail egos that are fed and empowered as they fight with painted smiles to attract more money, greater power and more recognition as we transmit them energy – our energy.

If we collectively withdraw our energy – our attention – then we send them in a downward spiral crashing straight down the celebrity alphabet.

Always be yourself, express yourself, have faith in yourself; do not look for a successful personality and duplicate it.

Bruce Lee.

We should not dwell too much upon our idols; we should instead be looking to ourselves as individuals and attempt to fulfil our own potential.

We should all be allowed to live lives that can realise our own true value and be sure and safe in the knowledge that within us all is the potential for everyone of us – to be a star. After all – it is the stars where we all came from.

The fuel that drives anyone to want to be revered, worshiped and adored is a psychosis that is built in childhood and if you doubt this look at the lives of the stars, because if you could look behind their curtains you would be able to see damaged goods, chemical abuse to kill the pain and very often the inability to maintain one on one relationships, because one person cannot possibly fill the holes in their damaged subconciousness.

Monumental egos are standard because it was the ego that took them, fuelled them and sustained them on their journey. And we, the admirers of these flickering stars, not only give them what they need which is in essence a transference of energy called our attention, as we hold them up for as long as we choose.

We watch with fascination as they crash and burn as many of them do whilst the media that feeds upon them holds them in an uneasy alliance, because the monster that has become the media can destroy them in a heartbeat.

Coronation Street, Eastenders, Emerdale, Neighbours – the 'soaps' are endless; is there so much lacking in our lives that we feel the need to watch as other people live made-up catastrophic lives? Why not just pull our most comfortable chair out the front door, drag it across the road, settle ourselves down and stare through our neighbour's windows? – and be safe in the knowledge that truth is stranger than fiction.

And whilst I'm on a roll in alienating the 15 million people who watch these celebrities 'pretending' to be other 'ordinary' people – why is it we care so much about the personal lives of people we have never met? The reasons are complex however some psychologists think it is because we are bored and living through stars is a way of alleviating that boredom.

Another view is that we are hard-wired into searching for identity. There is also pleasure to be derived from looking at an object we admire. The brain therefore rewards us with a release of endorphins but then again – so does a sweet.

As family and community values are crushed by the growth of individualism and a powerfully influential media, perhaps we are finding that fantasy relationships are easier to maintain than real ones. One of the reasons the cult of celebrity exists is that we the worshippers imagine that our hero's are having a great time and getting everything that us 'normal' folk think we want. The truth is very often the reverse and we can witness that most obviously when they fall. For as long as we give celebrity its power we will continue to weaken ourselves.

We should not unnaturally celebrate the individual who is a celebrity but instead, admire and respect what many of these clever and very talented people produce and at the same time be more mindful in the recognition of the Creative Source from which that talent came. We should also know with absolute certainty that the source of this talent is available to us all.

We can be moved to our core by great acting, by actions, music and words. But do we really want to camp on the artist's doorstep for a glimpse of them as they pick up their milk? Should we not allow them to move through society with respect and without hindrance? Does it really matter if they just came out of rehab or if they are suffering the breakdown of a personal relationship, must the media think it needs to constantly invade the personal lives of people because it believes that 'it sells papers'? If there weren't the demand then the supply would dry up. If the supply dried up we wouldn't have to see more news coverage given for example to Stephen Gerard's toe and will he play football for England, than the horror of gentle Buddhist Monks being subjugated and slaughtered in the streets of Burma.

This demand and supply is a similar rational to witnessing the plight of sharks being hauled from the sea to have their fins hacked off and being thrown back still alive to die a tortured death. So some guy in China thinks it will get his dick hard, has he not heard of Viagra, it's the 21st century?

If there was no demand; for the sharks fin, the monkey torn from his slaughtered mother, the bear bled for its gall, the gorilla killed for its hands to make ornaments, the rhinos demise for its horn, the tigers head in the trophy room of the fool that ended its noble life, the elephant that had to die for its tusks, and yes even those bonny fish that swim in our aquariums and the pretty birds we keep locked up in cages or the millions of other injustices we dish out to animals every single second of every single day – for what – for something it is that we think we need?

If there was no demand – there could be no supply.

And whilst I'm on a rant, I might as well mention if there was no oil under the sands of the Middle-East, then I wonder how much our leaders and their partners in the oil business would be interested in the place? If we ran our vehicles on hydrogen fuel cells or another more environmentally friendly energy-source it follows that oil would be massively devalued.

Similar rational applies *everywhere* we place value to the cost and detriment of something else; diamonds from Africa, fur coats from animals or a shirt made in a sweatshop in Asia.

The results of not being interested in something means that the value and demand for it becomes dramatically less significant and our attention can be diverted elsewhere and into more constructive issues. If there were no market value for the 'precious' parts of an animal then it follows that those parts wouldn't be precious anymore and we would leave it alone, and this applies to everything that this beautiful earth has to offer whereby an animal or a fellow human has to die or to live and suffer in order to meet our values – what it is we think we want – what we think it is that we need – and what it is we think we require. The earth could survive, global warming could be addressed and the millions of people who live in conditions of slavery in order they might serve the desires of the few could be released to pursue better lives.

Anyway – back to celebrities. If values were diminished upon the people we perceive as celebrities, we wouldn't have to look at more pictures of celebrities with eating disorders or falling into rehab and therefore perhaps more attention to the diabolical horrors that people have suffered in *say* Iraq, Afghanistan, Burma, Tibet, New Orleans and elsewhere because needless suffering is all around us.

We could even begin to dare to wonder that if these and other injustices were not allowed to manifest and our minds were in the trim, that is to say not so programmed into needing, not so demanding and so wanting, just what the results might be because with heightened public awareness we could actually address the problems rather than participating or spectating.

Perhaps then we would just take from animals and from people that which we genuinely needed rather than anything we might just fancy.

They say I'm a dreamer but I'm not the only one.

John Lennon.

Celebrities are fascinating because they live in a sort of parallel Universe, one that looks and feels like ours yet appears beyond our reach.

On our TV screens stars cry to Trisha and Oprah etc, about their problems;

failed marriages, abusive upbringings, bad career decisions, in fact all the fears the ego will manifest and we relate. The paparazzi catch them falling out of a nightclub a little the worse for chemicals or with messy hair and a stained T-shirt and we are delighted. Look they're ordinary, just like us.

Stars appear to live in another world, one that makes our lives dull by comparison but we don't know their story, we are lead by assumptions and the lies of the media.

They may live in a world that seems to have abundance, however that same abundance is available to us all if we can break the chains of suppression that hold us back from fulfilling our true purpose and potential.

There is also reason to sympathise with celebrity because it shares a common theme with all so called 'success,' – politicians, gangsters, the boss – anyone and everyone who has assumed mastery and power over others, they are surrounded by people who are almost as deluded as they are because no one can deliver the truth to them anymore – if they told them the truth they'd be out of a job, so these sycophants also wear the masks and ride the wave.

Funny old thing the ego.

I had a epiphany a few years ago where I was out at a celebrity party and it suddenly dawned on me that I had yet to meet a celebrity who is as smart and interesting as any of my friends.

Moby.

To be able to do this job in the first place you've got to have a bit of an ego.

Gary Oldman.

An actress must never lose her ego – without it she has no talent.

Tom Lehrer.

When John Lennon outraged many by saying The Beatles were more popular than Jesus, perhaps he was onto something. As we look back in history and across the dynamics of culture, people have always revered and worshipped idols. With its myth, ritual and power, the immortalisation of celebrity could be filling a similar need.

So the next time we are caught worshipping Brad, Angelina, David, Victoria, George or Paris we could just smile and say its Darwinian and enjoy a little quality time with them.

Coincidences

Over the years I have written many coincidences down. A word I prefer to coincidence is synchronicity.

Synchronicity is described in the Oxford dictionary as;

'The simultaneous occurrences of events, which appear meaningfully related but have no discoverable casual connection.'

Synchronicity is the conscious mind penetrating into the unconscious mind and alludes to the world beyond the five-sense image of what we call reality. A remarkable man I know called Fred Robson who I can best describe as a healer says, *'there are no such things as coincidences.'* In other words, when we notice coincidence we are witnessing that there is more to life than the five-sense 'reality' we find ourselves locked into.

I have found that very often these coincidences happen more often and are more powerful when I am with certain people.

They indicate that being 'One Consciousness' defines and links us all and they are the Universe's way of demonstrating this.

Psychiatrist Carl Jung coined the word 'synchronicity' to describe the amazing coincidences that happen to us, which are thousands or millions of times beyond statistical chance. It is as if some 'force' was guiding such events. Well it is. In my view, synchronicity is the conscious mind observing what the subconscious has decided what will happen. 'Going with the flow,' is going with the will of the subconscious; fighting the flow is fighting the will of the subconscious. Do we really have free will? Yes, but not necessarily at the conscious level of the five-senses, except, that is, for what we chose to observe into holographic illusion from the thought fields placed before us.

David Icke. Tales from the Time Loop.

'That defender should be shot.'

A comment that Alan Hanson made whilst commentating on the footballer Escobar when he scored an own goal.

Escobar was shot in a restaurant shortly after the game.

A little bit of Annie's Story.

Annie was adopted as a baby and brought up in Newcastle by a doctor and his wife. Four years ago, she expressed a desire to try and find her birth parents. In the family that loved her and brought her up there was a natural brother Eamon and another boy called Michael, who was also adopted.

Annie's adoptive parents died within a short space of time when she was 14 and the three children went their own separate ways, Eamon went to Ireland and then Canada and became a doctor but Michael had a real tough time of it and after a gap of 25 years was reunited with Annie, but he was critically ill.

She deserved a saint-hood for what she did for Michael and it was her love and care that sustained him and kept him alive for a year.

Now this is a fascinating story in itself, but this is about coincidences so I'll get back to the point. When Annie mentioned she might like to find her blood mother and father, I started a journey that was peppered with incredible coincidences. I had put an advert in an Irish newspaper seeking the whereabouts of Annie's birth mother (the adoption agency had told me her mother was from Southern Ireland). I only got one phone call from Ireland to my home in Newcastle in response to the advert from a chap called Noel. After many conversations via telephone, text and email and many months of digging with many false dawns, this generous man seemed to be getting warm in this needle-in-the-haystack search.

He suspected he had found an area in Southern Ireland where Annie's birth mother might have lived in the past. He knew the headmaster of a school in the region and decided to start his enquiries with him. Noel made an appointment and met with the Headmaster who found a room where they could speak privately.

After exchanging pleasantries the Head asked Noel why he had come to see him. Noel was about to answer when the telephone started to ring; both men hesitated waiting for the switchboard to answer. The ringing persisted and the Headmaster glanced at Noel apologetically, crossed the room and answered it, he established the caller wanted to speak to someone and made the connection.

He turned to Noel and asked him to continue. Noel asked if he had heard of Ruth O'Leary, (I have changed her name) the headmaster hesitated and said that he had and, 'oh, by the way,' he added, 'that's Ruth on the phone now, speaking to her best friend – our assistant headmistress here at the school!'

Back in England I told Annie of the latest development and this powerful coincidence. She in turn had shared her story with only one close friend called Siobhan (Annie had met her on a ship going to New York about twelve years ago).

Siobhan and Annie live near to each other in London and had kept in touch since this first chance meeting. A few weeks later Siobhan told Annie that she had found her birth-father's brother and confirmed what we already knew; that her birth-father had been killed in an agricultural accident many years ago.

All that Siobhan had been given was his name and rough location but she had managed to track his family down. The next astonishing coincidence to reveal itself was that; Annie's father's family and Siobhan's family's farm in Southern Ireland both shared the same boarder, it transpired that the two independent family farms were right next to each other separated only by a fence.

The Barefoot Doctor and the synchronistic happening.

I wanted to write for as long as I can remember. I was not able to achieve this in any meaningful form in England because I had created too many obstacles, for example I am easily distracted and don't do stress well.

For many years I had written down anything that appealed to me from one-liners to adages and ideas. As the pile grew bigger, I realised I was becoming frustrated and wanted to put this into some form. To do this I needed to find solitude and so having read Paulo Coelho's latest book and the fact that he admits he needs solitude in order to write, this then started to influence my thoughts. Mr Coelho is from Brazil and is a well-travelled individual but admits that when he wants to write he retreats to South West France. He will not say too much more about his location because he does not wish to be found and disturbed.

There is a mention on the sleeve of one of his books that he has sold more than 75 million books. Now I have never had one word published, (although in my defence I have never tried – well apart from when I was 10 or 11 in 'Termtime,' the school magazine, but that story comes under 'programming' later) – so I got to thinking – if it's good enough for Mr Coelho, it's good enough for me.

I tried to get my affairs into some sort of order – miserably failed, moved from my home, gave away some of my possessions, stored some more, emptied my life into a van destined for France, crammed the car with various other detritus which seemed important to me for no apparent reason now – plus the dog (bless) and threw everything else into a skip.

So in the vague hope that you dear reader – (*very pleased to meet you by the way and thank you for buying this book for what I hope you will come to regard as an investment, I mean if for no other reason than you might get something from all of this and save lots of time not making the same mistakes as me*) – have bought this book and are therefore reading this, then I hope you admire my level of commitment.

And to Paulo Coelho, as I write this in the Dordogne area of South West France, my heartfelt thanks. You certainly don't need me to plug your wonderful books but if this one of mine doesn't work out then please rest assured – I am unable to find you to discuss why solitude for me does not agree.

Right I have managed to move away from the point I was trying to make – I told you how easily I am distracted so with your indulgence let's return to the point where my life is – in storage, given away, in a van or in a skip and I'm off to France with the puppy where I pen these words.

I went to bed in an empty house the night before my new adventure and was woken in the morning as a text came in on my phone, I was tempted to ignore it in favour of more sleep as I was still tired and plenty stressed. But I knew how much I had to do so I read the text on the phone as I got out of bed and the text said – 'are you up yet?' So I phoned the sender of the text. And it transpired it was from a friend, his name is Alan so I said, 'why do want to know if I'm up yet or not?' and whilst I accept that might sound a little rude, I should mention that many times a day but especially first thing in the morning – my ego wakes up before I do.

There was a silence so I said 'where are you?'

And Alan said 'put the kettle on – I'm sitting outside.' It transpired that he'd generously driven up to give me a hand with any loose-ends and there were enough loose-ends to make a ball of string that if you had kicked it, you would have seriously hurt your foot.

I went downstairs and the echoes of an empty house sounded under my feet. I put the kettle on and opened the back door. I glanced to see Alan sitting in his car looking chilled and reading the paper. But my legs were carrying me towards the overflowing skip. During the night I had thought of another book that I wanted to retrieve from the skip. I wanted to do this because that was the thought that was in my head when I had woken up.

(Which, when I think about it, is kind of impressive because it demonstrates that even when we are buried in stress, instinctive consciousness can still find a way).

I began to rummage through the skip at the part where I thought the book was. Alan walked past me and I confirmed 'the kettles on,' and he asked me what I was doing. I told him that I regretted throwing lots of books away but was trying to find one in particular by 'The Barefoot Doctor.' 'Oh,' replied Alan nonchalantly offering me a parcel wrapped in brown paper, 'I just brought you up his new CD set for you to take to France because I thought you might get something out of it.'

Alan and I have discussed many things but I swear we have never once mentioned 'The Barefoot Doctor.' It's strange how it works sometimes, when we are thinking right – then the right things seem to happen and we allow instinctual synchronicity to enter our lives

The problem remains however – just how many of us are allowed to think 'right' within the lives we have structured for ourselves?

If we want to witness synchronicity in nature, we can see it in a flock of birds, a colony of bats in flight, a school of fish as they shoal or fireflies flashing in bursts of rhythm collectively. Your heart beats in beautifully timed waves of contraction as millions of muscle cells draw together, and we demonstrate our own synchronised abilities when we applaud as part of an audience or move as one to music at a concert.

It is impossible to understand within our five-sense reality, (and therefore our constricted view of the Universe) just how thousands of individuals act as if they are one body. And yet this is precisely what they do. Clearly other forces are at work here and whilst there will be varied views on what these forces are, my way of trying to grasp this is to call this Universal Creative Source Energy or Consciousness, it is our life force and it flows through everything.

We become alienated from Source in the process of growing up; fear and its many relatives block this, but we can unblock ourselves, we just have to remember the truth of what it is we forgot in childhood, it is simple – everything is One but our conditioning deludes us into thinking otherwise.

A small wiggly meander

There is a caterpillar out there and he's called the processional caterpillar. They drop out of pine trees in Spain and kill you and you're dog regardless of any witnesses or not. (Your tongue can swell up and you suffocate).

Apart from that they are absolutely no bother, but they go on the move occasionally and that's where they get their name from – the Processional Caterpillar, sounds important and intimidating – the Processional Caterpillar is in town and beware he's on the move.

That would be the day I would stay in, maybe do a little tidying up, paperwork, sleep, think, something – anything rather than risk me and the dog, I mean I've just got the little sod to 'come here.' Yes, I would definitely give the processional caterpillar march a miss. Anyway my pal, who lives in Spain is the one who told me about the 'Killer-Katerpillars,' although I believe that they have walked (in procession?) all the way into France and are also a problem there.

As if Spain hasn't got its hands full enough already. I mean, apparently in many towns throughout the country and always in this circular arena, which is made from wood and concrete, a big black, full-of-hell bull, rocks up and proceeds to kick-off with a load of the local totally innocent, townspeople.

This must have been going on for years and I believe it happens regularly however, (as coincidence would have it) there are men who are constantly on standby and are ready and mounted on the backs of horses.

These men have suits of armour and to prove that they love the horses, they give them suits of armour as well.

These very brave men also have sharp spears about twenty metres long. Meanwhile the bull runs around frightening people and posturing as if to say '*if it wasn't for the fact you are all behind reinforced concrete walls and very high up, I would be amongst you and slap you lot about a bit.*'

Then the very brave-armoured men with spears on top of the horses creep up on the evil bull and about three of or four of these wonderful, shinning, noble knights take turns to stab the bull.

Then they have a little rest and then they stab him a bit more. When the evil bull has lost about four or five bathfuls of blood this guy comes in with a swollen crotch (how anyone can be so horny and yet so brave at the same time is genuinely beyond me). The bull is starting to wish he hadn't broken out of his field and he's just thinking back to '*how nice the weather was yesterday when he ate the lush grass in the field and kidded with his pals, the other vegetarian herbivores, whilst his big black bollocks were cooled as they swung in the soft embrace of a most pleasant breeze.*'

When all of a sudden, the rather annoying but very smart, recently arrived ponce goes and sticks a massive sword right in between his shoulder blades and all the way up to the hilt.

'*Ow,*' thinks the bull, '*that smarts a bit.*' But the townspeople are happy and they all applaud El Ponce'o (the skinny smart guy with the sweet butt-cheeks and embroidered jacket very fetching in gold but rather confusingly carrying a red towel).

'So praise be,' I say to the supporters of bullfighting and do not mess with these people because they are very well organised and extremely resourceful. They apparently prove this week in and week out by reacting immediately and very efficiently to any 'bull-in-the-middle-of-town' type problems.

Many years ago, when I was about nine or ten, my father *(who was also psychic because he knew just when and where a bull was going to turn up in a town where we were just sitting, minding our own business catching a few rays)* and I were having a Coca-Cola on my first trip abroad, and this lunatic bull turns up slinging his weight around, without so much as a by-your-leave trying everything possible to ruin our holiday.

After all the great heroes had dealt with this wicked creature by stabbing him and then hiding until after a while he died, I couldn't believe what happened next, exactly the same thing happened again and again about eight times more.

I mean how about that? What are the odds against it? – nine bulls simultaneously going crazy and trying to attack people in broad daylight in the middle of the town and in exactly the same area.

Those odds must be millions to one; I would bet those odds would be as much as – say – father and son being voted President of the United States of America *(Odds that are a little longer than 150 million to 1 – still I suppose its handy when your brother is helping out by counting the votes).*

I remember much later in life asking my Dad about how I reacted to the '*Cheek Of The Bulls and How They Properly Got What Was Coming to Them Big-Style Day.*' He said that I looked 'a little green,' well hell it was the least I could do – change colour out of respect for those brave townsfolk who have to put their lives on the line on a regular basis and the heroes who appear as if from nowhere to help. I can't believe they haven't made a film about it.

Just in case any of my Spanish friends think that I am having a go at their country, I am not, I am having a go at the mentality of the many people in general who are cruel to animals, therefore shooting small furry animals when they are trying to run away or small fluffy feathery type animals in flight is worthy of huge dollops of contempt and fox hunting's a proper load of bollocks too.

What did someone once say about it? 'The unspeakable in pursuit of the inedible.' I mean what is that all about, how the hell can anyone derive pleasure from it? And just in case I've alienated both the Spanish and the English gentry, and just to make my position totally clear as a bleeding heart liberal – *anything – any single thing* – that involves the use of animals when it involves their suffering and demise is entirely wrong.

This wrong includes the breeding of dogs for example, that can hardly breathe or walk because some 'expert' says, 'this is the standard for the breed.'

This wrong is clearly demonstrated in the way we are manipulating animals – witness the Belgian Blue Cow – 100 years in the making, manufactured in a laboratory, a double-muscled, one-ton, four-arsed cow which can scarcely walk and cannot breed except by artificial insemination. To see one is to realise this poor beast is not a freak of nature but a tragedy produced by man's own hand totally in the pursuit of profit.

It is wrong to abuse animals and as we wake from our slumber more and more people are realising this simple truth.

– Well anything that is apart from processional caterpillars – because they kill dogs. So back to synchronicity and processional caterpillars – when they go on the move they stretch out in single file and the row can be as much as twenty metres long.

If you're brave and remove the very last one in the line; the one at the front will stop and so will all the others.

Fantastic thing synchronicity.

A close to home coincidence

I watched a film called, 'Uncommon Valour,' back in the Eighties. One of the first 'bring the boys back from Vietnam,' and the film I suspect that Rambo II drew its theme from. (Another one of those glorious Hollywood productions that rewrite history in order to sanitise the wrongdoings of the past).

In the jungle before going into the prison where American prisoners are being held, the star of the film, Gene Hackman removes his hat and quotes a few words from Julius Caesar written by Shakespeare. He says something along the lines of; 'if we meet again, why we shall smile, if not then this parting was well made.'

Because these words touched a chord within me I wrote them down. The following day the words were still in my head and I vaguely remembered that somewhere in the house there was a copy of Julius Caesar by William Shakespeare, so I went in search of it. After much rummaging I found the book in a dusty box and for the first time in my life I opened it.

Leafing through the pages I found the words Hackman had quoted. In the margin, next to the words someone had written 'fine words these' and I thought, that's a bit scary someone else thinks like me!

I turned to the front of the book and realised from the date and signature inside the front cover, that the book had belonged to my mother, she had written this in 1950, before I was even thought of, she died when I was 14. I felt such a powerful connection with her again after such a long expanse of time had separated us.

Serendipity is the art of finding something by looking for something else. In practice Alexander Fleming might best demonstrate serendipity because he we simply cleaning up his laboratory when he discovered that penicillium mould had contaminated one of his old experiments? He was not looking for penicillin - he stumbled upon it.

Happenstance is described as a chance or accidental happening.

However they come to us, and whatever we choose to call them; coincidences, synchronicity, serendipity, chance, luck, good fortune, or happenstance, (they all share the same bed) these 'occurrences' happen all the time. Are we aware they are happening? Probably much less so when our heads are full of rubbish, definitely more so when we are freed by those encumbrances.

Perhaps they are simply pointers that come along and allow the Universe to give us a nudge and show us how everything is connected. Very often when we are talking about them another one seems to manifest before us. There is something extraordinarily powerful about coincidences and if they achieve nothing more than to show us that there is so much more going on in our lives than being locked into our prison of a five-sense reality – then I suggest they will have achieved their purpose.

Colour

Colour affects our senses and therefore our mood, primarily through our vision. It affects us every day of our lives. We emanate colour (it is recorded in every religious building where we see enlightened beings depicted by yellow light around their heads called a halo, it is a representation of an aura).

Advertisers, designers and retailers know the influence of colour and have been quick to capitalise on psychological research into the effects on our emotions, perceptions and thoughts. The adverts that bombard us use this knowledge to evoke feelings or memories that make us want the goods on display.

If a supermarket were to display for example, loaves of bread, packaged in different colours, it would be the red packs that would sell the best. Red draws our eye, the great painters knew this, for example Constable would often put a red object in his paintings to indicate the focal point of his pictures. Red is the colour most frequently used upon flags.

> *The colour of my soul is iron-grey and sad bats wheel about the steeple of my dreams.*
>
> Claude Debussy.

> *Speed kills colour … the gyroscope, when turning at full speed, shows up grey.*
> Paul Morand.

> *Mere colour, unspoilt by meaning, and unallied with define form, can speak to the soul in a thousand different ways.*
>
> Oscar Wilde.

The influence of colour is not exclusive to humans. The US Agricultural Service Centre showed that using red plastic sheeting under tomato and cotton plants produced a 15-20% higher yield that those that were grown with traditional black or clear plastic. They showed that turnips could have improved flavour by using blue sheeting they also demonstrated an increase in vitamin C.

We take colour for granted; it totally surrounds us and penetrates our bodies as light waves. We eat it in fruit, vegetables and in the artificial food colourings used to make our food look more desirable.

Colour and light are inextricably linked. You cannot have colour without light. Light consists of seven colour energies; red, orange, yellow, green, blue, indigo and violet. This is known as the spectrum.

These colours are also called the Chakras and come from the yogic teachings of India. The charkas store and distribute energy throughout the body. Chakra means wheel and when these chakras are blocked or there is a lack of flow the body feels the effects.

Colour/light is a vibrational frequency:

Red is note C, Orange is D, Yellow is E, Green is F, Blue is G, Indigo is A and Violet is B.

Colour affects us. We are living beings of light and as we process light it affects us at our core. Even though we may not understand this consciously, frequencies are our identity.

Everywhere we go we are bombarded with electromagnetic fields, a spectrum that includes electricity, radio and television frequencies, microwaves, x-rays and light. If we regard ourselves as solid then the assumption is that these waves simply bounce off our bodies. This is not the case, our bodies absorb all of these waves because we are not solid, in fact like all matter we are a mass of vibrating particles.

Most of these waves pass right through us but in the process they influence us, they alter us and they change us.

Our skin is a photoreceptor and it is argued that it absorbs more colour and light than our eyes.

Colour/light is used in medicine, some of its influences include; the treatment of jaundice in premature babies (blue light is used to eliminate the yellow of the jaundice), the treatment of disorders such as psoriasis, red light has demonstrated the ability to kill the HIV virus in blood, and it shows the ability to stimulate cell tissue and the regeneration of tissue.

Light cannot be seen it can only be known.

There is no such thing as darkness - just an absence of light.

Don't be afraid of your shadow - it just means that there is a light shining behind you.
Laura Siebert.

Colour is a living energy; it is a property of light. Light is an electromagnetic energy produced by the Sun and delivered to us in different wavelengths. The Sun delivers its light from 93 million miles away and it takes just over 8 minutes to reach us. The light from the sun hitting the moon and reaching us takes 1.3 seconds.

As light is absorbed or reflected we end up with different colours.

Every shade of colour vibrates to a frequency.

Vibration forms *everything* in life.

However it is we as individuals that define colour because as the light of different wavelengths hits our the retina, special cells are stimulated to produce a discharge along the optic nerve to the visual cortex which is at the back of the brain.

It is here that colour is interpreted; primarily red, blue and green are mixed. Thus colour is produced in the brain to help us identify objects in a world without colour. Light itself is invisible and colourless to the eye. We identify it when it strikes an object and radiates back to us. Without reflection we would see nothing. This is why everything we experience in our 'reality' is not real because we are interpreting everything within ourselves.

It doesn't matter how long my hair is or what colour my skin is or whether I'm a woman or a man.

John Lennon.

Control dramas

I first encountered 'control dramas' through a book called The Celestine Prophecy. The author James Redfield not only wrote a fine book but also started a wave of opinion about the content. In his book he points to four basic control dramas, they are; aloof, intimidator, interrogator and poor me. We learn these control dramas as children as a way of providing ourselves with energy. We carry these dramas into adulthood because they work for us and much more unconsciously rather that consciously; we deploy them in our dealings with others. It is said, where attention goes energy flows. The basic traits are are follows:

Poor me

Will concentrate on gaining energy through sympathy for their perceived ills. Poor me's will resort to guilt to draw energy from the listener. Attention sought by traits such as sighing or crying, complains about being busy or tired. They might try to make you feel guilty for not solving their problems.

Beware asking a 'poor me' how they are, we have all done it and had to listen to their story of how exactly they are. At the end of the conversation we feel drained by the energy they have 'stolen' from us. The poor me is the victim, they seek rescue, it seems a 'nicer' way of getting energy. So poor me's make us feel guilty and responsible to them.

Someone I was socialising with occasionally a few years ago was married to a girl who I felt was a classic 'poor me.' Every time we met up and pleasantries were exchanged the inevitable question was posed 'and how are you?' One was given a biblical rant on her current ailments.

The first couple of times perhaps I could be forgiven for lending her sympathy (attention equals energy) after all it's natural to be empathetic to a fellow humans suffering. But one evening having listened to her 'my spine has collapsed, my feet have exploded and I can't lift my arms' routine, I noticed that about two hours and a few drinks later, she was demonstrating her high-kicking dance routine all the way backwards and forwards over a railway bridge.

In that revelatory moment I unkindly nicknamed her Lazarus.

The Intimidator

Will try to bully you by using verbally assaults and through their body language. You will be reminded of your failings and the consequences of these failings. An intimidator is threatening, strict, inflexible, angry and self-centred and they will try to make you feel afraid. Your subsequent compliance is the passage through which they gain energy. The disempowerment of the person or people that the intimidator is drawing energy from in turn boosts their energy.

The bonus for the intimidator is that having intimidated everyone successfully, they do not get intimidated, (better to throw the punch than receive it).

In this process they are seeking to protect themselves from a threat or an attack that could be real or more likely be imagined.

They have determined that the best form of defence is attack and like all the dramas they act in a way that is part of their programming and often the behaviour is not appropriate to the occasion. The correlation between what protected them and gained them energy as a child and the circumstances in front of them right now invites the programming to kick in.

Men and women use this drama whilst repressing feminine traits because they have determined not to be perceived as weak, vulnerable and useless. Intimidators will find an enemy or someone to control, this is what gives them their energy and their enemy more likely will be imagined.

Aloof

As the name suggests the aloof person will be keep you at arms length. They are mysterious and unreachable and your energy is given because you're invited to know more. Aloof will use silence as a weapon and play coy. Other traits include secrecy and preoccupation. They might be away from home a lot and not too interested in you. This strategy is designed to avoid any future possible pain.

Aloof people also act this way to imply to interrogators and intimidators that they are no threat. Very often this behaviour was used to protect themselves from physical, emotional or sexual abuse.

The Interrogator

Shares with the intimidator some similarities, but uses constant and probing questioning as the tool to attract attention and therefore energy. You will be made to feel you are compelled to answer. The interrogator will probe, undermine and be sarcastic.

They seek perfection and are self-righteous. Their practice is to question, judge and therefore condemn, the first step to gain energy is to interrogate, then because they always know better, they go onto devalue the other party by inviting them to consider that they are wrong.

The interrogator parent will create an aloof child. The interrogator interrogates because he does not want to be interrogated because when this occurs he looses energy.

We are all a mix of these dramas and are inclined to lead with one – the one that works best for us. It is revelatory to see for the first time what we are and what those we know are about. As mentioned, we use what works and we can be forgiven that this manipulation stems massively from the unconscious child within us.

We act according to our needs and we learned in childhood how to satisfy those needs. We taught ourselves and those that brought us up conditioned us by their treatment of us. This behaviour worked for us and became part of us and we are not mindful of this because this is how the mind works. The mind wants to busy itself with what is in front of it and the memories become buried and habitualised and remain deep in the unconscious. A hypnotherapist I know likened this conscious – unconscious relationship to that of an iceberg. On the surface one sees an iceberg (conscious) however there is a massive amount more unseen (sub or unconscious) under the surface.

Once you start and observe you can see these dramas being played out constantly. How many times have you considered that a certain individual drains you? Conversely those you think are fun to be with are charismatic, generous, warm, and so on, are giving of energy and they lift our spirits and boost us.

The dramas learned and adopted in childhood block our ability to fully experience the mystical. As we try to control others we believe that if they would change their behaviour we would be more happy and so would they. When people do things we do not like or we do not get our own way we judge them as being 'wrong,' we then impose our beliefs upon them.

Those with big, more obvious control dramas are judged as 'difficult or troubled people.' However once you have looked at yourself as insightfully as you are able then you begin to see for the first time what you have been doing in your dealings with others.

This is really powerful and revelatory stuff, a total wake up in terms of realisation. Once grasped you start to perceive these dramas in others who you know and realise what they are about and more importantly this further shows you more about yourself.

I can't remember if James Redfield, the author of the Celistine Prophesy, offered any real conclusions on how to deal with control dramas that are unhealthy so the following are my own conclusions.

The more obvious the control drama then the more the individual was damaged in childhood and the deeper his trauma will be.

The cure should you wish to find it is to firstly identify which of the traits is most obvious in you.

You are unable to deal with any problem unless you identify it and become mindful of it.

Should you choose to ignore it you are destined to repeat the errors of the past. 'If you always do what you have always done you will always get what you have always got.' Having identified the drama and concentrated for some time on breaking the habit you are now in a position to change. You have to love and respect yourself and this for many is difficult and is knocked out of us when we are children, where all the crap happens. Be happy with yourself, you are conditioned into a belief that you are better than some people but worse than others. These beliefs are based upon lies that separate us. This is not the way it is, you have value, every man is equal and no one is better than anyone else. Someone living three doors down in your street may have more money, more hair, be able to run faster, appear to command more respect – but so what? If Mister Golden bollocks develops a terminal disease tomorrow or gets wasted in a car wreck then his problems are ... I humbly suggest ... more insurmountable than yours.

Your 'problems' are manifested by what you believe of yourself.

Many years ago I walked into the newspaper shop next to where we worked. It was a small vibrant shop stacked to the roof with something for everyone. The shop was owned and managed by a lovely couple. I was waiting in the queue for my turn in the shop one day and it quickly came around. Dina (one half of the couple) before I could open my mouth to order said; 'Hello David, you look glum today.' 'Well Dina,' says I, 'perhaps I am not paying attention and this glum face I am wearing worked for me when I was seven years old and standing in a shop not dissimilar to this shop and the lovely lady not dissimilar to you behind the counter noticed that I looked glum and gave me some sweets … for free.'

Dina politely smiled, busied herself in an attempt to measure the extent of my madness, gave me my order and I left the shop passing the three or four customers behind me who had expressions of awe and respect at my rhetoric (not).

Whatever this little incident serves to demonstrate is not how mad I am but to illustrate a control drama; we use what works and that's not always good. It's why bullies bully, it's why we moan, it's why we act the way we do and we learned these dubious skills as we grew in our formative years.

And it just might be true that my glum face as a child got me some free sweets, (which is classic poor-me).

It is important to see these manifestations and therefore be mindful of them just as it is important to forgive yourself for having them.

All control dramas are a way of taking energy and almost every human interaction steals energy from each other. Subconsciously your ego knows this and protects itself by its use. Energy follows attention, so in an attempt to feel loved, worthy and respected, we use what works. The ego performs in this way because we have given it power and control, because as children we could see no other way to survive and get by. If a child has not received the love that all children need, it will resort to naughtiness and bad behaviour in order to get attention and therefore energy. This works and it becomes entrenched forming part of us.

A child is forced to get energy; the ego demands this fuel to maintain it. Starve the ego of energy and it will use the most efficient method available, this search for energy can be positive or negative; it's all just energy but it is important that it comes and this is why a child will learn to accept negative attention when there is nothing else available. Remember the ego separates us and that is one of the primary reasons it requires energy.

Without energy the empire of the ego crumbles because there is no separation. We do not need to enter these dramas; we must learn to have no agenda in obtaining what it is we think we want. We can give our energy freely and realise that others are more likely to respond. Giving love and respect earns us love and respect. Be genuine when you show a smile, raise a laugh, give empathy and you will receive it.

If you are feeling restless you're not alone, there are many people who are starting to look for more meaning in life. We could start by paying closer attention to seemingly random or chance coincidences and strange occurrences. Following them will give us incite to spiritual truth.

Our culture has unfolded and developed so that the first half of the past millennium was spent under the control of the church, in the second half we became preoccupied with material comfort.

Now in the dawning of this new millennium we've just about exhausted that preoccupation. Many people seem to be waking up and ready to discover life's ultimate purpose.

A subconscious competition for energy underlies every conflict.

By dominating or manipulating others we get the energy we think we need. It might feel good at the time but both parties are damaged in the process.

The key to overcoming conflict in the world is to connect to Consciousness via instinct, this mystical experience is available to everyone, it builds our energy and is the natural thing to do.

Conversely to rob someone else of their energy is nothing but a temporary ego fix. The upside of connection to Consciousness is to be filled with a sense of love.

Due to our upbringings all of us are inclined towards one of four control dramas:

Intimidators – steal energy from others by threat.
Interrogators – steal it by judging and questioning.
Aloof – people attract attention (energy) to themselves by playing coy.
Poor me's – make us feel guilty and responsible for them.

All of these examples are about the distribution and acquisition of energy.

Become aware of the family dynamics that created your control drama and you can focus on your essential question, which is how to make of your life a higher-level synthesis of your parents' lives.

Once cleared of traumas, you can build through contemplation and meditation, focus on your basic life question, and start riding a steady stream of intuitions, dreams and synchronistic coincidences, all guiding you in the direction of your own evolution and transformation.

Technology will do most of our work for us. As we begin to value spiritual insight more and more, we will pay those who bring it to us, and this will eventually replace the market economy and our need for paid employment. We can connect to God's energy in such a way that we will eventually become beings of light, and walk straight into heaven.

Alan Atkisson. New Age Journal, August 1994.

Creation

The only reason someone is a genius, and knows things you do not know, is because he has opened his mind to contemplate the what-ifs, the outrageous thoughts, the thoughts of brilliance that go beyond the limited thinking of man. He has allowed himself to entertain and reason with these thoughts, whereas you have rejected them.

If any one thing can be conceived or pondered, it exists; for whatever is dreamed or imagined is already within the realm of existence. That is how all of creation came into existence.

Ramtha.

Contrary to what medical science is obsessed with telling us, the physical body is not the whole human being. It is the fantastic physical shell through which the eternal us experiences this physical world. There is far more to us than a body. Creation is the expression of one infinite mind and all life forms are aspects of that one mind: what many people call God. We are each other. We are all God, if you wish to use that term. At the heart of this mind is a consciousness I see as a blinding light- The Source Consciousness from which all has been thought into existence. Creation consists of an infinite number of dimensions, wavelengths, and frequencies, of reality.

David Icke. Introduction to 'And the Truth Shall Set You Free.'

It would seem we have a much bigger brain than we need, certainly studies over the years have pointed to the massive unused parts of it. An average brain contains between 10 to 15 billion neurons and up to ten times as many connecting cells (called glial from the Greek for 'glue' providing signal transmission).

It has been said we use only between 5% and 10% of our brain, but that's not to say we could lose 90% of it, it only needs a small amount of damage to deprive us of smell, taste, or sight.

Brain size is a poor indicator of intelligence. The brain of a sperm whale weighs 7800g, a dolphin 840g, ours 1500g and a mouse weighs in at 0.4d. If these rough figures were determining intelligence against mass then an

times as intelligent as a man, who is in turn twice as intelligent
, which in turn is 2000 times as intelligent as a mouse. If we rank
order of how large their brains are in relationship to their body
en the mouse wins with its brain comprising 3.2%. We humans come
in at _ .%, the dolphin less than 1%. The sperm whale is a miniscule 0.02%.

Neither absolute brain weight nor the relationship between brain weight and body size provide us with any sensible formula for the comparison of different species.

A typical adult male brain weighs three pounds, the heaviest brain weighed over 5 pounds (2.3kg), and it belonged to an American male and was reported by Dr T Mandybur of the Department of Pathology and Laboratory Medicine at the University of Cincinnati, Ohio, in 1992.

A Russian writer Ivan Turgenev, possessed a brain that weighed over 4 pounds, but by contrast a French novelist called Anatole France managed to win the Nobel Prize for literature with a puny sized brain of 2 pounds (1.017 grams). Just as we begin to grasp that the brain is underused and its capacity does not hinder intelligence – enter the spanner in the works; in the 1960's Professor John Lorber of the University of Sheffield published a paper. The paper 'Developmental of Medicine and Child Neurology' reported two children who literally had 'water on the brain. They had no brain they had fluid in its place. One of the children died early but a year later the other child continued to develop normally and quite capable of function.

This strange condition is known as hydrocephalus, and because it doesn't fit mainstream science it has largely been overlooked. Many suffer awfully, however in some cases individuals have well above average intelligence and to all other intents are normal.

One man has an IQ of 126 and achieved a 1st class honours degree in maths, economics and computer studies. And yet he only has a millimetre or two of cerebral tissue lining. The space where his brain should have been was filled with spinal fluid. He was bright, conventional in behaviour and appearance but he had no detectable brain.

In another case after the death of a similarly affected young man, the coroner tried to console his parents by suggesting it might be a relief that such a profoundly retarded man had finally found some peace. His dumfounded parents told the coroner that their son had been at work two days before.

Intelligent hydraencephalics make nonsense of neurological beliefs. The question this raises is well presented in the words of British naturalist A. R. Wallace, 'do we have an instrument that has been developed in advance of the needs of its possessor?'

One wonders what awesome power we might be capable of?

I see a future of unbounded potential, unbounded possibilities. Remember we're using, at most, 5 percent of the potential of the human mind. One hundred percent human potential is the result of proper education. So imagine a world where people are using their full mental and emotional potential. We could go anywhere. We could do anything. Achieve anything.

Dr. John Hagelin. The Secret.

We need to challenge our widely held beliefs and assumptions and build the case for the fact that everything is a form of conscious energy.

I repeat every single thing is a form of conscious energy and shaman and mystics have known and demonstrated this simple truth for thousands of years.

All matter is energy reduced to a lower vibration

It is the nature of the millions of misguided naïve 'realists' that they don't recognise anything beyond their 'realities' or beliefs. They consider themselves to have all of the facts about the way things are. This egoic belief system prevents us from understanding how this Universe, creation and how 'we' function and therefore how it all works. The essence and the very nature of things are beyond our five-senses.

Shaman or mystics assist the individual to become aware, certain drugs and meditation access and enable us to question our beliefs, despite what many think, this type of mysticism is a path of deep scepticism and rational enquiry, this modern world needs to remind itself of the meaning of these ancient simple truths.

Consciousness and intelligence are different but are related. The cases of the hydraencephalics demonstrate that consciousness is not located in the brain but is instead a function of the entire being. Consciousness is a universal phenomenon that underlies intelligence, but when matter is created then intelligence is allowed to form. When the simplest of forms are woven into being, consciousness is made evident. As the simple forms that interact to create more complex inner aspects, so do the inner aspects interact to create more complex inner aspects.

Particles create bodies and Universal Consciousness breathes in life. This creates an environment where intelligence is allowed to be present.

The real miracle of our creation is the knowing that arises when we look within and realise that our own consciousness is Universal Consciousness and it is this consciousness that animates everything. Once we access consciousness we make available the understanding that in essence we are all Universal

Consciousness then we know there is no separation and no distance between 'things.'

We are all One;

We are all one consciousness experiencing life subjectively

And if we are all One, then why are we being so mean to each other?

There is no such thing as death – life is but a dream

Have you ever thought that your world and all of its contents might just be a dream? Are you able to prove that this Universe is real? Which one of these can we know for sure? What is it you know with absolute certainty? It is possible this could just be a dream. To consider this one has to step outside of the prison that is our five-sense reality and in the doing we come to one of the most fundamental debates in philosophy; to analyse the true nature of the world. Are we presented with a ghostly plane of abstract sensations and ideas or is it a solid reality of atoms, energy and matter?

Solipsism is the theory that only consciousness exists and nothing else can be proven to actually exist. In other words Solipsism states nothing exists, it is all a dream. Solipsism and realism are totally opposite views of the world. Realism cannot be proven and Solipsism cannot be disproved.

Realism is easy to describe because realism is how virtually everyone experiences the world. Realism states the Universe exists as a stand-alone independent reality with its own laws and qualities, but this cannot be proven. Realism indicates we live in a world that we can experience through our five-sense reality.

Solipsism is demonstrated by the statement made by Rene Descartes known as the 'cogito ergo sum,' translated 'I think therefore I am.' It states that 'I am.'

I know I am because the thought that I might use to deny my existence proves that I exist. The only fact that we can know is that Consciousness exists. No individual thing can be proven to be real and real meaning cannot exist independently of Consciousness.

'*Consciousness is*,' demonstrates that consciousness exists and nothing else does. This bold statement has as yet to be disproved.

Solipsism is what is left after all belief and theory has been destroyed.

In essence the doctrines of philosophy state that we cannot know whether or not there is actually physical matter or just an experience that we are able to have of it. However we know that the physical world is ultimately a series of sensations taking place in Consciousness. The only thing we can know with certainty is that we are experiencing matter within our mind.

Without Consciousness we could not have physical sensation. All experience or sensation must involve a reference and that reference exists only because we process it, we make the decision.

All matter is energy condensed to its lowest vibration.
We are all one consciousness experiencing life subjectively.
There is no such thing as death; life is but a dream,
And we are the imagination of ourselves.

Bill Hicks.

... B-i-n-g-o ... the key to the secret of life!

Illusion recognised must disappear.

A Course in Miracles.

The survival of illusion is dependant upon us mistaking it for reality. One cannot know with certainty that any of this world is real. All experience is simply a dream and everything we receive is interpretations and copies of interpretations at that.

Whichever way we choose to look at it, our views are taking place in Consciousness. If you doubt this then it still remains that you possess logic and even if you disagree on whatever ideas of an inside self or an outside reality that happens to exist – it happens only in Consciousness. Even to the point where you imagine yourself to be – is imagined.

The self is only thoughts conceived of mind and then conceived as a person.

To be, or not to be: that is the question.

William Shakespeare. Hamlet.

Row, row, row your boat,
Gently down the stream.
Merrily, merrily, merrily, merrily,
Life is but a dream.

Creativity

Time is an invention.
Now is a reality.
So much creativity is happening for the simple reason that we have withdrawn ourselves from past and future.
Our whole energy remains blocked, either in the past or in the future.
When you chose to withdraw all your energy from past and future a tremendous explosion happens.
That explosion is creativity.

Bhagwan Shree Rajneesh.

The problem is never how to get new, innovative thoughts into your mind, but how to get old ones out. Every mind is a building filled with archaic furniture. Clean out a corner of your mind and creativity will instantly fill it.

Dee Hock.

Creative energy is the electrical current at the very basis of everything that exists. The Creative life force is defined in exactly the same way. A Creator is one who focuses creative energy and the resultant creative process, and this creative process is simply energy flowing towards ideas.

You are in this moment the creator of your reality.

You are the creator of your own experience whether you know that you are or not. Your life experience is unfolding in precise response to the vibrations that radiate as a result of your thoughts, whether you know this or not.

Ask and it is Given. Esther and Jerry Hicks.

We can predict with great accuracy what will occur under certain conditions in our matter-based dimension. Physics however has few logical answers for the paradoxes that exist in quantum objects.

We are starting to understand that in the Universe of the sub-atomic, there really is truth in the old saying; mind over matter. It is now that we should realise a basic truth that is withheld from us; that we are all intimately connected and are part of One Universal Source, and the realisation of this follows that our separation from one another ceases to be of any relevance.

Universal Source Energy or Consciousness, which, for the purposes of what is being said here is one step from what many of us call by the various names of god, this Consciousness is the agency that forms, moves and affects particles at a quantum level, then by harnessing this with the power of our minds and our thoughts it follows that mind can manipulate matter.

We are therefore all creators, but this is also the principle of how we are manipulated by others who use this knowledge to block us; because if we know what we will all know soon – yes we will – people are waking up all over the place – we will turn everything upside down. We won't fear anything anymore, death will be seen as a transition rather than an ending or a judgment to decide our everlasting fate, we will know by reconnecting to Consciousness that the brain does not house Consciousness because it was Consciousness that created the brain and everything else because Consciousness manipulates energy. We will then realise that; a particle, an atom, a letter, a word, a symbol, an emotion, a colour, a sound, a taste, etc, is just a vehicle that allows us to understand and interpret something as means of communicating to make ourselves understood with one another; everything isn't made up of atoms – everything is made up of Consciousness.

You are not separate from this Universe, you are in this Universe and therefore you are part of it, this knowledge will allow us to return to wholeness – to holiness – to Oneness.

Crime

The things we resist persist.

Carl Jung

The reason there is so little crime in Germany is that it is against the law.

Alex. Levin.

History is indeed little more than the register of the crimes, follies and misfortunes of mankind.

Edward. Gibbon.

Behind every great fortune there is a crime.

Honore de Balzac. (1799–1850).

Ed Koch, the former mayor of New York from 1982 to 1989, after being blamed for everything that had gone wrong under his regime was asked if he would stand again. He replied, *'the people threw me out – the people must be punished.'*

Crime butchers innocence to secure a throne, and innocence struggles with all its might against the attempts of crime.

Maximilien Robespierre.

Organised crime in America takes in over forty billion dollars a year and spends very little on office supplies.

Woody Allen.

I am convinced most of the current, topical, humorous texts we get, start in the vaults of the phone companies, a great way of getting extra revenue because they spread like a virus. When solving a crime always first suspect – those who benefit. History has proven you will normally be correct.

When I sell liquor, they call it bootlegging. When my patrons serve it on silver trays on Lake Shore Drive, they call it hospitality.

Al Capone

A crook is a crook, and there's something healthy about his frankness in the matter. But the guy who pretends he's enforcing the law and steals on his authority is a swell snake. The worst type is the Big Politician who gives about half his time to covering up so that no one will know he's a thief. A hard-working crook can buy these birds by the dozens, but he hates them in his heart.

Ibid.

Crooked bankers who take peoples hard earned cash for stock they know is worthless would be far better clients at penal institutions than the little man who robs so his wife and babies may live.

Ibid.

Crime is yet another one of those temperature gauges we have. Crime we are told is going up or going down. As with many ideas crime is nothing more than a matter of opinion.

The system wants 80,000 people incarcerated then this is what occurs. The jails get full and the courts are told to relax, as a result prisoners serve less of their sentences or get out early and are tagged, (and while we are on the subject, watch out for this one – they receive a bit off their sentences if they get micro-chipped) or the figures get massaged to show something else.

The valve is turned up or down on the boiler – the ducks on the water go paddling by – and the wheels go turning round.

Crime is predominantly reserved for poor and angry people. Very few 'suits and ties,' serve time, the occasional one gets sacrificed just so we believe that the rules are for everyone.

We have recently seen the messy ritual sacrifice of the speaker of the House and the hurried repayment of money stolen by fraud by a succession of our elected honourable Members of Parliament as they sought to extricate themselves from the mess they put themselves in. Interestingly in a wonderful demonstration of the ego at play, they have judged themselves and have obviously concluded that returning stolen property is sufficient punishment. In a court room this self inflicted compensation back in the rough direction of those you stole from originally, would be further evidence of guilt, if you were virtually anyone else who stole you would be readily convicted of a crime.

Your money that was stolen, endearingly called the public purse; your energy that you paid for with this thing that we so value but haven't really got a clue what it is worth until we are told by those that steal and profit from us, this meme we use to measure energy, we call it money.

The crimes being committed here include theft, deception, fraud, and tax evasion. Should the authorities choose, conspiracy could be thrown into the mix, the actual word conspiracy carries up to a fifteen-year jail sentence. Whereas you and I would risk incarceration, no harm will come to those you voted in, those who act as a shinning example to people especially when they are growing up. They serve up a crucial lesson in the process; life is unfair and the rules are not for everyone. It's best children learn this as soon as possible otherwise they might become confused, cynical even.

It not about chandeliers, various home improvements, the fraudulent avoidance of capital gains tax, the fiddling of VAT or the restoration of moats and drawbridges or the bright and shiny things your money has bought for them, it's about ego and power, because it's always about ego and power. With the mere stroke of a pen on a chequebook it's so comforting for us to observe, that they not only had the gall to seek to absolve themselves, but that they actually had the ability to pay for the results of their deceits in the first place.

But goodness, listen to me going against my own philosophy and judging and condemning our honourable members, our elected guardians. It is wrong; a fundamental flaw in our programmed enforced education to judge and condemn, and we will discuss this later. But please consider that one of one of our greatest failings is to judge and condemn an individual. Because I will try and convince you later, it's a total waste of energy; that which we dislike most in others is in truth what we fear within ourselves, that you don't fight anyone you fight yourself, and what we are actually doing is projecting guilt and embracing blame.

The cure against this malady is quantum forgiveness and a helpful tool is to automatically forgive. It helps if we understand what it is that made a person or people do something we find abhorrent (such as taking us to war on the back of a load of lies, or stealing from us when if we stole from them we would dealt with very differently). The answer lies on two levels, they did it to obtain power and they wanted power because of their ego. The second level is to take us ahead on our journey through this book, but I want to hoy this in so it doesn't come as too much of a shock when you get to this later … every single thing we do is a call for love.

Anyway I feel sure when all the dust has settled our governors will organise a survey; search every shoplifter to discover if they have the money to pay for their stolen food and if they have give them a receipt and let them go. Call it the 'Lets have an even playing field when it comes to crime campaign,' sounds a real vote catcher.

Of course the dishonest acquisition of thousands of pounds, (that would in fact be billions should there be a proper in depth historical investigation) would normally be viewed as a crime. However the real crime going on is that nothing meaningful will actually happen, and it takes your eye off whatever else is really going on in the world, oh, yes sorry, nearly forgot, it also sells papers.

My goodness on reading this back it would seem I'm suggesting that the law is applied vaguely, variously and varyingly dependant on where you are upon the greasy pole, which compartment you are imprisoned in within the pyramid. That where you are on the ladder of so called success will dictate whether your crime is viewed as an oversight or a felony.

To those of you reading this whose living is dependant on judging and condemning and the proliferation and maintenance of our utterly fair and untainted system, please rest assured, I suggest nothing of the sort. Finally might I just add how elated I felt and my confidence restored in the police, the CPS and the judicial system by the recent treatment of one Thomas Payne. Thomas aged 19 was fined, electronically tagged for four months and given 36 hours community service for dropping some mint imperials while riding his bike. As Thomas is now a criminal I assume he will also been relieved of his personal map; his DNA. And quite rightly so, I mean imagine if this behaviour isn't nipped in the bud, he could go onto commit even more serious crimes, next time it could be something far more serious like a bag of scones or horrors of horrors an entire battenburg cake.

In contrast not one of the MP's who have been caught stealing will be brought to trial. Not one of them will be branded a criminal. That must be a comfort to the blue pill takers because were the same laws enforced upon MP's that are enforced upon us mere mortals, we wouldn't have anyone left to govern us and tell us what is right for us, we would have no-one left because virtually all of them would be in jail.

After the echo of North Korea's second nuclear bomb test comes the reverberation of condemnation. But there is no mention where Kim Jong II bought the hardware. Clinton and Bush in successive administrations sold all the equipment and services in contracts worth billions. The USA leads the rest of the world in hypocrisy when it condemns a very small man with a very large ego for being shocked when the dangerous diminutive stands atop his highly stacked shoes and shouts in the World's nations playground.

'Hey look at me, I starved two million of my citizens in favour of a million strong army. And to his citizens, 'if you question my ethicacy you will visit one of my network of gulags and be tortured, raped and executed. The North Korean people are more obvious in their enslavement than we are. Food is used as a weapon, the West ships hundreds of thousands of tons of food directly to the dictatorship, and the food is distributed according to the level of allegiance to the state.

Is that not a crime I humbly ask you?

And if that is a crime is also engineering oil shortages to keep prices firm in the name of profit when even now, with technology as advanced as it is supposed to be, we still only glimpse alternative sources of energy to power our lives? Fixing the vote, taking the bung, spreading fear ahead of the virus to sell your pharmaceuticals, sponsoring all science to discover advances that never come into the public domain unless it's for profit and control. Is crime manipulating the masses with esoteric magic through knowledge held by the very few to control the very many. Being part of a system of religious belief that gives you power over children and then using that power to have sex with them. For planting the red screw driver with the suspects fingerprints at the scene of the crime because you just know he did it but the genuine evidence won't convict him, or these days the far more likely DNA shuffle?

Crime unfortunately is all around us; crime will always be around us as long as we exercise our egos in the search for power over one another. Crime will exist for as long as we aspire to false gods and worship the wrong idols. We cannot blame the individuals who commit crime because the agencies that define what crime is and is not, administer what they consider to be justice with such hypocrisy.

Crime is the symptom of a society dis-at-eased and as we humans have proven, we are at a loss to define it, perhaps in that case it might be time to dispense with crime altogether, and that utopia can only be achieved by our spiritual growth. That growth, that different mindset, that awesome power, is found on the road to enlightenment. However we are denied enlightenment, it is prevented by those that control us and in turn by ourselves.

That is humanities greatest crime.

We are quick to identify with crime and at the ready to feel fear at the mention of it but what is a crime? We should understand that virtually all crime is political and in its final analysis is not therefore criminal, this is a broad spectrum that involves power and ego and a sword that is welded for control. Then there is crime against the person which is the result of dysfunctionality which could be easily be prevented by a child's upbringing. So it is therefore important to qualify the issues of what is and what is not a crime because those boundaries are clouded, is crime about telling lies to lead a country to war or is it about noisy hooded youths hanging around shadowy corners, drinking and conspiring to break the law? Crime is about the breaking of those laws, like the burglar who breaks into a house and steals the TV and sells it to feed his heroin addiction, it is about smashing up the house, setting fires, muggings, knifings, shootings, this is what crime is all about in the pubic domain.

I feel there is a far greater crime and that is the neglect of our youth, the environments they are raised in and the examples we give them. If we addressed this and provided them with the tools of how to learn – not what to learn, gave them opportunity, realistic hope and belief in a better future, if we got them away from abusive households and demonstrated how the chain could be broken so the same old shit that was handed down from one generation to the next could finally stop. Once this cycle is broken the resultant happy people could raise more happy people – perpetually.

Behind those dark eyes under the hoodies hood is a frightened young man, he comes from a house where they shout all the time, he knows the threat of impending violence, he is surrounded by it, immersed in it, gets to bathe in it every day. He finds solace in his friends; they tease and bully one another to find the pecking order. They dare one another, they seek approval from one another, they are a gang, there is a bond, there is safety in numbers and we all want to belong to someone or something. One day the lager, the cannabis isn't enough when someone suggests they smoke heroin. But heroin is a needy drug, it costs and it is a hard habit to break. So it's a TV here and a computer there, a few quid and another bit of relief from the boredom and the pain.

Then it's the courts and the jails and yes, even if you're reformed with lessons learned you can't get a job because you've been to jail and the wheels go turning round.

Whatever our views might be on the rights and the wrongs of things, I am doing neither justification nor blame here, but the only solution seems to be the cry, 'lock them up' or 'give them national service.' Why could we not simply give them a better environment in which to grow?

Crime is the result of a problem – let's go fix the problem instead of treating the disease after it has broken out and infected everyone it touches, let's get to the source because prevention is always better than cure.

Depression

The West has the epidemic of depression and in the East there is the crime of poverty. Interestingly in the East where most people live a less material life the rates for depression are incredibly low.

For many people depression is a constant and something to live with on a daily basis. It's a bit like being in a bad mood but for a lot longer. Our parents, our grandparents and peers were not inclined to talk about it; depression was seen as a weakness and was swept under the carpet. They had been programmed to retain what we English would describe as 'a stiff upper lip.' Upon these masks were worn the ethics of fortitude, 'never say die,' 'children should be seen and not heard,' servitude, 'know your place,' 'don't question authority,' 'a woman's place is in the home,' all that sort of rubbish.

Behind those same masks was fear and programming on an awesome scale.

The consequences of this conditioning are seen in rebellion and the echoes of it still remain.

But there are signs things are improving on this front because finally we are talking about the subject. I have not had the pleasure of meeting Stephen Fry, but I congratulate him on admitting to suffering from one of depressions new words; bi-polarism and in fact he had the courage to make a documentary about it.

There is often a reward for courageous actions, I suspect Mr Fry found his journey a great personal help to him, certainly from a selfish point of view, I have felt that as I have typed, fretted, stumbled and fought to write this book, the experience for me has been massively cathartic. I didn't appreciate it would be when I started, but that's very often how life works, you go on a journey with no meaningful plan and you end up in a wonderful place.

So it's OK to be in a bad mood for a while and unlike a generation ago you are not made to feel as if you're alone, you can talk about it and even get a bit of help, but this is well overdue and will only scratch the surface of the problem because depression remains epidemic and is one of societies greatest problems especially in the West – in fact it can be a killer.

Estimates show that about 30 million Americans are affected by depressive disorders, that is well over 10% of the population.

In Britain, according to the Office for National Statistics, 10% of our 60 million population are depressed.

The rate of increase of depression among children is an astounding 23% per annum.
Harvard University Study Feb 2002

30% of women are depressed. Men's figures were previously thought to be half that of women, but new estimates are higher.
National Institute of Mental Health America.

80% of depressed people are not currently having treatment.
National Healthcare Quality Report USA. 2003.

92% of depressed African-American males do not seek treatment.
Ibid.

15% of depressed people will commit suicide.
Ibid.

By 2020 depression will be the second largest killer after heart disease, and ironically studies show depression is a contributory factor to fatal heart disease.
WHO report on mental illness released October 4th, 2001.

Standard antidepressants such as Prozac, Paxil and Zoloft have been revealed to have serious risks and are linked to suicide, violence, psychosis, abnormal bleeding and brain tumours.
Washington Post, Feb 2004.

So what causes or triggers depression? Short-term depression can be caused by loss or extreme trauma.

Chronic or life long depression is caused by trauma in childhood and this includes: emotional, physical or sexual abuse; veiling or threats of abuse; neglect; criticism; inappropriate or unclear expectation; maternal separation; conflict especially within the family; divorce; family addiction; violence, racism, bullying and poverty.

There may be a genetic predisposition to depression, but even so it must be triggered by the above events.

Trauma prevents development of certain parts of the brain such as the hippocampus and frontal lobe, where decisions are made. Depression is expressed in the body. Studies show illness manifesting because of depression these include: osteopororosis, diabetes, heart disease, some forms of cancer, eye disease and back pain.

80% who see physicians are depressed.
The Journal of the American Medical Association.1995.

Everyone will feel low at some point. A death of a loved one, a let down at work or the loss of a relationship. Grief and sadness are normal reactions but over time we are inclined to heal. But when the sadness will not pass we can become depressed. Very often it goes unrecognised because it may manifest itself in different ways. Someone who is depressed will feel any or all of the following emotions: anger, fear, anxiety, shame, confusion, worthlessness, fatigue and irritability.

A person who is depressed may be more prone to illness and in that weakened state sleeping patterns may be erratic. Depression affects our thoughts, our feelings and our relationships with others.

Left untreated as it very often is, the depressed person may choose escape through self-medication using drugs such as alcohol. They may also try to relive their emotional pain by overeating, physically harming themselves, being sexually promiscuous or other self-destructive behaviour.

Most people still think depression is a personal weakness. Of the many names that depression goes under, from a person who is troubled all the way to full on madness, the fact remains depression is a very real illness and 'cheering up' or 'snapping out of it' is not an option.

In some ways it was a typical breakfast meeting. The waitress was pleasant, the eggs were average, and the restaurant was full of busy people. We shared a cup of black; coffee-like substance, and the first few times my client took a sip he managed to spill quite a bit of it. His trembling hand was just one of the symptoms of his burnout. That's why we were meeting. He wanted to know if I could help him.

I picked up a fork and explained that as long as I used it for eating, the fork would last indefinably. However, if I began to use it to drive nails or dig trenches, it would soon break. The key was to use it for what it was designed to do.

The look in his eyes told me he got it, but I still went on to say that people are like the fork. When they do what they are not designed to do, they eventually break.

Henry Neils. Founder of assesment.com

Most of us can relate to this. With the signs of depression growing more and more evident and people being affected by it are growing into plague proportions.

You not depressed because trouble has come to you, but trouble has come to you because you are depressed.
You can change your thoughts and feelings and the outer things will come to correspond, and indeed there is no other way of working.

Emmet Fox.

Or put another way with a similar message, you're not happy because you are well. You are well because you are happy.

If you suffer from depression, anything that makes you feel has to be the most important thing in your life, because it is the only thing that can save you.

Siobhan Fahey.

Some famous people with mood disorder or bipolar disorder included; Beethoven, Vincent Van Gogh, Winston Churchill, Robert Louis Stevenson, John Kats and Virginia Woolf.

I thought depression was the part of my character that made me worthwhile. I thought so little of myself; felt that I had such scant offerings to give to the world, that the one thing that justified my existence at all was my agony.

Elizabeth Wurtzel.

Why are so many of us depressed? Why has it become the plague of the Western world?

Deep down we know that there is so much more to life and we are not living the lives that we were designed to live. It's why teenagers rebel; it's their last kick before we break them into our system of life and into a belief system that we ourselves have been programmed into.

There is a correlation between depressed mood and low social status. Evolutionary psychology suggests that depression is part of a genetically adaptive coping process. Depressive behaviour involves the passive submission to a prolonged or uncontrollable stress, and the truth is that many of us worry too much and unnecessarily. The simple certainty is that this growing epidemic could be largely cured overnight, not by counselling or pills but by simply not worrying. If we felt happiness we would be massively empowered and this would spread from the individual.

Happiness however is subversive to those who seek to control us, a motivated population, in contrast to the learned helplessness and behavioural despair many of us feel, can be made available to us by the raising up of our consciences, both individually and collectively. A happy plague is not only an exciting proposition … it is *the* solution to all of our problems.

DNA

Deoxyribonucleic acid or DNA is the basis for all life on earth; it is the blueprint or the instructions to construct cells, such as proteins and RNA molecules. Your genes, which decide what colour eyes you will have and how those eyes will see the world are carried in your DNA. The DNA strand is shaped like a spiral staircase and is referred to as a double helix.

Damage can be caused in many different ways: Oxidizing agents such as; chlorine, iodine, peroxide compounds, ozone, etc. Electromagnetic radiation such as: ultraviolet light, x-rays and free radicals. (Which are loosely described as; what rust is to steel, free-radicals are to us).

There is an obsession to grab samples of our DNA. Certain elements in the police force regard themselves as little more than DNA collectors.

More than one million people's genetic fingerprints have been added to the police DNA database in only ten months. This 'Big Brother' system is already the biggest in the world; it now permanently stores the details of more than 4.5 million individuals. The rise is the equivalent of 150 entries every hour.

The database covers one in thirteen of the population; around 7.5 per cent. As this astonishing pace of growth has intensified, concerns that the Government plans to create a universal genetic database by stealth grows. They are building a system that treats every citizen as a potential criminal from the day they are born.

Although the database is sold to us a crime-fighting tool, around a third of the entire DNA stored is taken from individuals who were not charged with any offence and have no criminal record.

Critics have raised particular concerns over the huge rise in the number of children on the database. It now includes 150,000 under-16s.

The DNA records, which are taken regardless of whether a youngster has committed a crime or not, are to be held on file until the day they die.

Critics believe the system is open to sinister forms of abuse, and that the dangers are growing as the database expands.

Claims include that the data has been used for genetic research without the consent of the individuals involved, including controversial attempts to predict 'ethnic appearance' from DNA profiles.

Children as young as 15 months should be screened for high cholesterol in an attempt to cut the number of Britons suffering from heart disease, is one of the excuses used to extract DNA from us.

A national screening programme, which would involve a blood test for babies, possibly at the same time as routine vaccinations such as MMR, could help to slash the number of people in the UK with heart disease caused by hereditary high cholesterol, according to the doctors, who publish their work online in the British Medical Journal.

The Guardian. Sarah Boseley, health editor, Sept 14th 2007.

Some recent Russian DNA discoveries documented by Grazyna Fosar and Franz Bludorf in their book Vernetzte Intelligenz have been summarised by Baerbel. 'The human DNA is a biological Internet,' with evidence that DNA can be 'influenced and reprogrammed,' by word and frequencies. This suggests that 'our DNA is not only responsible for the construction of our body, but also serves as data storage and communication.' The Russian scientists and linguists have found that the genetic code 'follows the same rules as all our human languages.' In effect, human language did not appear coincidentally but is a reflection of our DNA.

The Canadian. Sunday 16th September 2007.

By Mary Rodwell (excerpted).

Scientists constantly probe for answers but their egos prevent them from admitting they just don't know the answer to the question of what our DNA does, they understand 3 – 4% of our DNA but to call the rest 'junk' really isn't good enough.

It might be that parts are redundant but because we don't know what its function is does not make it useless. A more honest view is given by molecular biologists Chris Calladine and Horace Drew by saying; 'the vast majority of DNA in our bodies does things that we do not presently understand.'

One question that needs to be addressed is what would happen if these strands were activated?

This is a fascinating subject and we are just starting to learn that DNA receives and transmits signals or vibrational waves. Put another way, DNA is communicating and if we stilt it, we revert to living within ourselves but if we open our minds, it provides us with the ability to communicate with Creative Consciousness.

Shaman all over the planet access other frequencies by methods such as the ingestion of drugs. DNA was first isolated in 1869 by Friedrich Miescher, he called it nuclein. Debate continues as to who actually 'discovered' it, the fundamental credit goes to James Watson, Francis Crick and Maurice Wilkins who received the Nobel Prize in the early 1950's. There are many who believe Rosalind Franklin should receive a great deal more credit for her work on the subject.

When Watson and Crick produced the model of DNA that we are all familiar with, it demonstrated a double twisted helix, the two twisted strands run in opposite directions. When the double helix is unzipped it replicates itself, this then is how it multiplies and forms life. The following is an article, which is self-explanatory. (This article is reproduced by kind permission of the Mail on Sunday)

NOBEL PRIZE GENIUS CRICK WAS HIGH ON LSD WHEN HE DISCOVERED THE SECRET OF LIFE
By Alun Rees. Mail on Sunday. August 8th 2004.

Francis Crick, the Nobel Prize-winning father of modern genetics, was under the influence of LSD when he first deduced the double-helix structure of DNA nearly 50 years ago.

The abrasive and unorthodox Crick and his brilliant American co-researcher James Watson famously celebrated their eureka moment in March 1953 by running from the now legendary Cavendish Laboratory in Cambridge to the nearby Eagle pub, where they announced over pints of bitter that they had discovered the secret of life.

Crick, who died ten days ago, aged 88, later told a fellow scientist that he often used small doses of LSD, then an experimental drug used in psychotherapy to boost his powers of thought. He said it was LSD, not the Eagle's warm beer that helped him to unravel the structure of DNA, the discovery that won him the Nobel Prize.

Despite his Establishment image, Crick was a devotee of novelist Aldous Huxley, whose accounts of his experiments with LSD and another hallucinogen, mescaline, in the short stories 'The Doors Of Perception and Heaven And Hell,' became cult texts for the hippies of the Sixties and Seventies. In the late Sixties, Crick was a founder member of Soma, a legalise-cannabis group named after the drug in Huxley's novel 'Brave New World.' He even put his name to a famous letter to The Times in 1967 calling for a reform in the drugs laws.

It was through his membership of Soma that Crick inadvertently became the inspiration for the biggest LSD manufacturing conspiracy the world has ever seen, the multimillion-pound drug factory in a remote farmhouse in Wales that was smashed by the Operation Julie raids of the late Seventies.

Crick's involvement with the gang was fleeting but crucial. The revered scientist had been invited to the Cambridge home of freewheeling American writer David Solomon a friend of hippie LSD guru Timothy Leary who had come to Britain in 1967 on a quest to discover a method for manufacturing pure THC, the active ingredient of cannabis.

It was Crick's presence in Solomon's social circle that attracted a brilliant young biochemist, Richard Kemp, who soon became a convert to the attractions of both cannabis and LSD. Kemp was recruited to the THC project in 1968, but soon afterwards devised the world's first foolproof method of producing cheap, pure LSD. Solomon and Kemp went into business, manufacturing acid in a succession of rented houses before setting up their laboratory in a cottage on a hillside near Tregaron, Carmarthenshire, in 1973.

It is estimated that Kemp manufactured drugs worth £2.5 million an astonishing amount in the Seventies before police stormed the building in 1977 and seized enough pure LSD and its constituent chemicals to make two million LSD 'tabs.'

The arrest and conviction of Solomon, Kemp and a string of co-conspirators dominated the headlines for months. I was covering the case as a reporter at the time and it was then that I met Kemp's close friend, Garrod Harker, whose home police had raided but who had not been arrested. Harker told me that Kemp and his girlfriend Christine Bott, by then in jail, were hippie idealists who were completely uninterested in the money they were making.

They gave away thousands to pet causes such as the Glastonbury pop festival and the drugs charity 'Release.'

'They have a philosophy,' Harker told me at the time. 'They believe industrial society will collapse when the oil runs out and that the answer is to change people's mindsets using acid. They believe LSD can help people to see that a return to a natural society based on self-sufficiency is the only way to save themselves.

'Dick Kemp told me he met Francis Crick at Cambridge. Crick had told him that some Cambridge academics used LSD in tiny amounts as a thinking tool, to liberate them from preconceptions and let their genius wander freely to new ideas. Crick told him he had perceived the double-helix shape while on LSD.

'It was clear that Dick Kemp was highly impressed and probably bowled over by what Crick had told him. He told me that if a man like Crick, who had gone to the heart of human existence, had used LSD, then it was worth using. Crick was certainly Dick Kemp's inspiration.' Shortly afterwards I visited Crick at his home, Golden Helix, in Cambridge.

He listened with rapt, amused attention to what I told him about the role of LSD in his Nobel Prize-winning discovery. He gave no intimation of surprise.

When I had finished, he said: 'Print a word of it and I'll sue.'

This amazing revelation is incredible on its own merits, but when one marries it to the work of others such as Daniel Pinchbeck (Breaking Open The Head and more recently his 2012, The Year of the Mayan Prophecy) and Terence McKenna (True Hallucinations), who approach the subject from a totally different direction, there is a further series of revelations which are beyond the realms of coincidence.

If this subject interests you then I would urge you to read a book in a similar vein written by Jeremy Narby, it is called 'The Cosmic Serpent, DNA and the Origins of Knowledge.' Narby writes eloquently and has been there and done it, he spent much time with the shaman who eventually invited him to ingest the vine.

One of the questions he poses to his readers is, how was it possible that these people found the process to enlightenment and how in a jungle filled with endless varieties of plants did they discover the process of amalgamating not one drug but two? Because ayahuasca taken by itself cannot affect the person as there is an enzyme in the stomach which blocks it entering the system, so another drug has to be mixed in to enable the effects.

One day while inquiring about these matters he was told that if he wanted to know the true answers to his many questions he would have to take ayahuasca and see for himself. He accepted this offer and after drinking ayahuasca he had a life changing experience. His view on himself and reality shifted from an intellectually superior know-it-all to a mere human being with the realisation that he had no real understanding of reality at all.

In his altered state two giant snakes telepathically presented these thoughts to him. There was more to his ayahuasca experience, but these are the elements that had an important impact on him. In 1986 Narby returned to civilization to write his dissertation and two years later he became a doctor of anthropology. Following this he travelled around the Amazon working with indigenous people to earn them official governmental recognition for their territories. He also did fund-raising work in Europe. To appeal to benefactors Narby emphasized the practical knowledge of these Amazonian people, but he deliberately left out the controversial mention of ayahuasca. Narby returned to write about the mystery of ayahuasca. His research led him to many different topics including shamanism, the study of plants, serpent myths, DNA, quantum physics and more. As those who study mythology, mysticism and occult traditions already know; the symbol of the serpent as the creator of life is ever-present in what is called the axis mundi or axis of the world. This has been symbolised as the world tree, the pillar of the worlds, the ladder connecting the earth to the upper and lower realms, Jacob's ladder, the ladder in Freemasonry and so on.

Often this central axis of the macrocosm is mirrored in the central axis of the microcosm of the self in the form of the twin serpents. The kundalini snakes that spiral up the spine in eastern mysticism or the spiralling snakes of the ancient Greek caduceus that are still used today as the symbol of the medical profession.

These symbols are found in Sumerian, Babylon, Egypt, among Siberian shamans, (who incidentally have never seen a 'real' snake in their lives). Symbolised by Quetzalcoatl, the serpent-god of the Aztecs. The rainbow serpent and creator god of the Australian aborigines, the Midgard serpent of Nordic myths wound about the world tree, the serpent and the Tree of Knowledge in the Judeo-Christian mythology and so on. Through chance and synchronicity Narby encountered many uncanny connections between this symbol and DNA. He recognised that to the inhabitants of the jungle, the forest means everything, it is their home, larder, medicine cabinet and their television and it provides them with everything they need.

Fuelled by his own meeting with the two serpents he encountered in his ayahuasca experience years earlier in the jungle Narby developed the hypothesis that somehow, through what Eliade called 'archaic techniques of ecstasy,' the shaman receives information from DNA in the form of visions.

Indeed, in altered states a shaman gains his unique view of the world beyond our senses by travelling up and down the axis mundi of the macrocosm or the microcosmic axis of the self. (They don't have telescopes and microscopes). Through his studies, Narby became engrossed in the molecular biology of DNA and he gives us many correlations between DNA and the shamanic worldview. Narby explains his hypothesis as follows,

'I began my investigation with the enigma of plant communication. I went on to accept the idea that hallucinations could be the source of verifiable information. And I ended up with a hypothesis suggesting that a human mind can communicate in defocalised consciousness with the global network of DNA-based life. All this contradicts principles of Western knowledge. Nevertheless, my hypothesis is testable. A test would consist of seeing whether institutionally respected biologists could find biomolecular information in the hallucinatory world of ayahuasqueros ... my hypothesis suggests that what scientists call DNA corresponds to the animate essences that shamans say communicate with them and animate all life forms. Modern biology, however, is founded on the notion that nature is not animated by an intelligence and therefore cannot communicate.'

What Narby and others are saying is; that the knowledge of DNA and its purpose is *known* to those who have penetrated the veil of alternate reality all over the globe with the use of mind-altering substances. If we marry this to the information, learned from loose lips of one the two men credited with the discovery of the DNA molecule in the early 1950's – we are presented with an historical, uncomfortable but amazing dilemma -

Watson and Crick's famous revelation was known by wise men for thousands of years before we in the West 'discovered' it and furthermore, both revelations were enabled through the ingestion of a mind-altering substance!

If we consider this further it is yet another of the many examples that go on to prove what we already know; that people who access Universal Consciousness become privileged to both feeling and knowing so much more than our own locked-down existence here on planet-psycho or this so called reality that we have created.

Through the flow of Universal Consciousness and via their attuned DNA, wise men all over the planet were receiving and transmitting information, it follows that each and every one of us has that same ability should we chose to access it.

This is demonstrated wherever we go in the world and find profound common similarities, (in art, myth, knowledge and so on) unless of course we are to subscribe to the slightly more improbable idea – that everyone was meeting everyone else on the planet by physically travelling there, and since that seems highly unlikely *(I mean this was years before easyJet)* then we are left to ponder at the only other conclusion that we can draw – people all over the planet were mentally attuning themselves to this higher consciousness and communicating with one another.

The world that we function in is a small bandwidth and is largely a reflection of the egoic mind, this remains a delusion and is a world largely made manifest by fear. Shaman were in direct communication with each other and perhaps the virus of language that spread throughout the world (assisting us in the process to find yet another vehicle or box to place ourselves in – thus more separation) served to prevent or hinder our powers of telepathy.

No, of course that sounds just plain crazy – but I had this funny *feeling*.

Radio waves from mobile phones do harm body cells and damage DNA; a laboratory study has shown,

But the European Union-funded Reflex Research did not prove such changes were a risk to human health.

BBC News 24. 21 December 2004.

- '*Phew what a relief,*' – well that's all right then, I was worried for a second.

It's proven that we, the 1.5 billon or so of us who use mobile phones, are having our DNA altered – but its not doing us any harm.

However the discomfort of the dilemma remains – DNA *is* a vibrational field.

It's all in the DNA

I was due to attend my Great Aunt Lily's funeral and had arranged to collect my father on the way. The drive would take about an hour and my father lived about halfway on the journey. As the density of the City gave way to rolling countryside I realised that I had an hour to enjoy a drive that would take me parallel with the river that runs through Newcastle and therefore up the Tyne Valley.

I picked my father up and we arrived at the little rural church, where the ceremony was to take place, in good time.

Auntie Lily was the matriarch of the family and all due respect was afforded. My father and I, dressed in black like the rest of the mourners and family, stood outside the small church with heads bowed in deference as our family and the coffin filed past us.

My father gave me the slightest of nudges and whispered as the procession of elders had passed.

'You should look after yourself son,' as he nodded towards the line of elders.

'Why's that Dad?' I asked.

'Well,' he said, 'when you get a look at the stock you came from you might just live an awful long time.'

I just wish I had listened but I have adopted this motto as a result; if you can't be a good example – at least be a terrible warning.

Dreams

It's called the American dream because you have to be asleep to believe it.

George Carlin

All men dream; but not equally. Those who dream by night in the dusty recesses of their mind's wake in the day to find it was vanity; but the dreamers of the day are dangerous men, for they act their dream with open eyes to make it possible.

T E Lawrence. Lawrence of Arabia.

What dreaming does is give us the fluidity to enter into other worlds by destroying our sense of knowing this world.

Carlos Castaneda.

Yesterday is but today's memory; tomorrow is today's dream.

Kahlil Gibran.

There are some people, who live in a dream world, and there are some who face reality, and then there are those who turn one into the other.

Douglas H Everett.

… you choose your dreams, for they are what you wish, perceived as if it had been given you. Your idols do what you would have them do, and have the power you ascribe to them. And you pursue them vainly in the dream, because you want their power as your own.

Yet where are dreams but in a mind asleep? And can a dream succeed in making real the picture it projects outside itself? Save time, my brother; learn what time is for.

A Course in Miracles.

The purpose of time is to forgive. That is the only viable answer to life. Act accordingly, child of God.

The Disappearance of the Universe. Gary R Renard.

Drugs

As with everything we return to opinions. Why is it that some drugs are revered in society whereas they are repressed, ridiculed and made illegal in others? The answer is simple; we are programmed into the acceptance or rejection of a drug.

In the West we coined the word 'psychedelic' in the 1950's. Psychedelic in literal translation means; mind manifesting, but further back in time 'psy' meant soul. Therefore the literal meaning is different to the modern interpretation, the manifestation of the mind and the development of the soul represent two different journeys.

When looking to define drugs the West has two basic categories; medicine or narcotics.

In the random substances listed here I accept for example, that fluoride and sugar are not drugs in the conventional definition, in the 'good drugs – bad drugs,' debate. However, drugs cover an enormous spectrum. As mentioned a drug broadly speaking is a substance used as either a medicine or a narcotic.

The doctor, chemist, individual, policeman, government official, etc, dependant on their opinion can all describe a drugs role differently. For example, beer could be described variously as a food, a drug, a toxin or a medicine.

Throughout history people such as artists, musicians, politicians and writers have used drugs. Sometimes we hear about it, more often we don't.

A drug is only a drug by definition and a definition is an opinion. Opinions are like arse-holes – everyone has got one.

Just as a weed is a weed and a flower is a flower, just as something is good or bad, all purely formed by opinion.

Weeds are flowers too, once you get to know them.
A A Milne.

A highly enlightened Buddhist teacher said that if you observe people in conversation they devote the vast majority of the time giving of their individual opinions (*I'm doing it now*). If we could prevent ourselves from doing this we would conserve an enormous amount of energy.

Like me when I first heard this perhaps you think, but I like talking to people and giving my opinion and hearing others views, it enables us to build bridges and form or improve relationships.

This of course is true and one would struggle to survive in the society that we have constructed without conversation that gives voice to our opinions. I just invite you to think about this because to be mindful of something is to recognise it and to recognise something is to be able to deal with it in a way we choose.

When Howard Marks was asked about his philosophy on drugs he replied, 'The self, the setting and the substance.'

This is worth remembering because our view of drugs is most viable when we make a decision to ingest them.

I don't pretend to know what he was saying when he uttered these words however for me they translate thus;

The self, if your decision is to go out and get hammered on alcohol for example, then having achieved a mortal state you break down in a well of tears or want to pick a fight with someone, then you are allowing a problem within you to surface through the use of alcohol, therefore it might be considered wise to avoid drinking, your clearly not at peace with yourself and your angst will spoil other peoples evening who you encounter. You should therefore be in a fit mental state before you go and get plastered, the position is however, if you are in a fit and rounded state you will probably not want to go out and get hammered.

You may also have a low tolerance to certain chemical changes the drug will enable in your consumption of it and this could include an allergic reaction.

The setting, is all important because if you again make the decision to have a few too many then the company you're in and where you are is vitally important, those you are with will affect your mood on your journey, and if you do not share a common bond then perhaps restraint is advisable.

The substance, well at least make sure your drug is of some quality, if your popping a pill at least know who your supplier is and get a reference for the effects that the pill will produce and the fact that it is, as much as your able to discern, not cut to pieces with shit.

I have listed and discussed some drugs so now, with your indulgence we can tiptoe over the lily-pads with the following:

Alcohol

Alcohol is often not thought of as a drug largely because it has been around for so long and its use is common for both religious and social purposes in most places in the world. However it is a drug and the compulsion for many to drink to excess is one of today's societies most serious problems.

Anyway I am not commenting on grapes, potatoes, wheat, barley, or any of the many of ways the ingenuity of man has demonstrated his ability to ferment and extract alcohol. The consumption of grapes and so on has clear benefits … I am commenting on alcohol and it is bad for humans.

Alcohol, it was pointed out to me recently by a close friend is a gateway drug. When we are 'in our cups,' we are far more likely to be drawn into all sorts of behaviour that when sober we might otherwise not be drawn into. Speaking for myself however as a man who has led an entirely blameless, suppressed, clean, decent, kind, good, religious, moral, upstanding, pillar of the community, kind, tolerant, loving, innocent, scrupulous, unblemished, principled life … had no idea what he was talking about.

One of my friends and like me no stranger to alcohol, recons that it's mostly down to the function of the liver. Therefore those that hold and process alcohol well have good functioning livers, it occurs to me that I might have to get mine checked out – either that or chuck drinking.

One of the ways to define alcoholism is the idea that an alcoholic drinks to change the way they feel.

One of the more positive events of the twentieth century occurred in Akron, Ohio, in 1935. Two alcoholics founded Alcoholics Anonymous and began the self-help movement and a real community of support.

These are the words of an adult under treatment talking about his childhood with alcoholic parents. 'In our family there were two very clear rules: the first was there is nothing wrong here, and the second was, don't tell anyone.'

Always do sober what you said you'd do drunk. That will teach you to keep your mouth shut.

Ernest Hemingway.

When I read about the evils of drinking. I gave up reading.

Henny Youngman.

Alcohol may be man's worst enemy, but the Bible says, love your enemy.

Frank Sinatra.

I drink in order to relax; however I become so relaxed that I fall over.

George William Coulson.

I don't drink these days. I am allergic to alcohol and narcotics – I break out in handcuffs.

Robert Downey Junior

Amphetamines

Physically your teeth start grinding, and your blood pressure and heart rate will rise.

Mentally you begin to feel confident and you're whole central nervous system is stimulated. Users are inclined to be more alert and talk incessantly and usually what falls from their mouths is a load of shit.

There are three main types;

Speed that is notoriously impure,

Dextroamphetamine,

Methamphetamine, was supposed to have originated in Hawaii. It is highly addictive. It's also known as ice or crystal meth, it will more than likely seriously mess you up.

Aspartame

Is a sugar substitute. In the United States in September 2004, a $350 million lawsuit was filled against NutraSweet and the American Diabetics Association. This litigation saw Donald Rumsfeld named in the suit for his role in getting aspartame approved by FDA. (The Food And Drug Administration is an agency of the United States Department of Health and Human Services).

Equal, Nutrasweet, Equal Measure, Spoonful, Canderal, can be referred to as E951

All contain aspartame … *sweet pills … bitter results.*

Aspartame was not approved until 1981 in dry foods. For over eight years the FDA refused to approve it because of the seizures and brain tumours this drug produced in lab animals. The FDA continued to approve it until President Regan took office (a friend of Searle) and fired the FDA commissioner who wouldn't approve it. Dr. Arthur Hull Hayes was appointed as commissioner. Even then, there was so much opposition to approval that a Board of Inquiry was set up. The Board said: 'Do not approve aspartame.' Dr Hayes overruled his own Board of Inquiry.

Shortly after Commissioner Arthur Hull Hayes, Jr., approved the use of aspartame in carbonated beverages, he left for a position with G.D.Searle's Public Relations firm.

Long-term damage: It (aspartame) appears to cause slow, silent damage in those unfortunate enough to not have immediate reactions and a reason to avoid it. It may take one year, five years, ten years, or forty years, but it seems to cause some reversible and some irreversible changes in health over long-term use.

David Oliver Rietz' DORway to Discovery.

Ayahuasca

Has been used for thousands of years in sacred religious and healing ceremonies.

Ayahuasca is a way of accessing Universal Consciousness; it enables healing of the physical body and is used in cases of emotional or psychological problems.

Cactus, mescaline

San Pedro cactus is native to the high Andes. Fast growing and can reach highs of 40 feet. It was supposedly named after St Peter because, it, like him was thought to hold the keys to Heaven. There is evidence to suggest that it was cultivated as long ago as 2200BC. It is a natural source of mescaline

Peyote is a spineless cactus found in South-western America and Mexico. Its crown is used to produce mescaline.

The chemist Sasha Shulgin said after his first experience with mescaline, 'the world amazed me, in that I saw it as I had when I was a child. I had forgotten the beauty and the magic and the knowing-ness of it and me.' His realisation was that a tiny amount of white powder ingested could not cause profound visions, and that it had revealed what was already inside of him around him and flowing through him. He understood that, 'our entire Universe is contained in the mind and the spirit.' We may choose not to find access to it, we may even deny its existence, but it is indeed there inside us, and there are chemicals that can catalyse its availability.

A world in which everyone took mescaline would be a world with no wars, but it would also be a world in which there is no civilization, for we just couldn't be bothered to build it.

Aldous Huxley.

Cannabis

Banned by U.S federal government in 1937. It has been estimated that 15 million Americans use marijuana or roughly the population of Calcutta in India. Marijuana is the buds and leaves of the Cannabis sativa plant. It contains delta-9-tetrahydrocannabinol (THC), the plants main psychoactive chemical.

The most commonly used illicit mind-altering drug in the world. It is described as mind-expanding, a painkiller and a minor hallucinogenic with depressant qualities.

It's been used since prehistory. The user becomes relaxed although first time users find little or no effects. It can give you the 'munchies,' a yearning for anything sweet.

It is not called 'dope' for nothing as the after effects can leave you a little groggy. The toxicity of cannabis is low but this is heightened when smoked with tobacco. Taken as a food the effects take longer to hit but are more profound.

The use and cultivation of cannabis goes back thousands of years. Mostly used medically it was referred to in Chinese records dating from 28BC and traces of THC were found in an Egyptian mummy almost 3000 years old.

Hashish is more powerful than cannabis and is made from the resin of the flowers.

There are many ways of absorbing cannabis, as with all drugs the user needs to get it into the blood stream. The most popular is by smoking but it can be eaten.

44% of 16 to 29 year-olds have tried cannabis at some point in their lives.

In 1998, 76% of people arrested for drug offences in Britain were charged with possession of cannabis.

Smoking marijuana is more popular in America than surfing the Internet.

Ganja, marijuana, weed, puff, smoke, pot, herb, dope, resin, grass, there are hundreds of words to describe it. But, call it what you want, the recreational use of cannabis is still illegal in Britain, although that hasn't stopped around half of all young people trying it.

bbc.co.uk.16th November 2004.

They lie about marijuana. Tell you pot smoking makes you unmotivated. Lie! When you're high, you can do everything you normally do, just as well.
You just realise that it's not worth the fucking effort. There is a difference.

Bill Hicks.

I think people need to be educated to the fact that marijuana is not a drug. Marijuana is a herb and a flower. God put it here. If he put it here and He wants it to grow, what gives the government the right to say that God is wrong?

Willie Nelson.

Why is marijuana against the law? It grows naturally upon our planet. Doesn't the idea of making nature against the law seem to be a bit … unnatural?

Caffeine

Caffeine is found in coffee, tea, cola, chocolate and many pain killers, including over the counter Solpadine.

Around 90 per cent of Americans consume caffeine on a daily basis making it the USA's most popular drug. Known medically as trimethyixanthine, it is used as a cardiac stimulant and a mild diuretic (it increases urine production). It tastes bitter in pure form but recreationally it acts to boost energy.

Caffeine uses the same principals as cocaine, heroin and amphetamines to stimulate the brain and it is addictive. It acts to promote neuron firing in the brain, your pupils dilate, breathing tubes open, your heart beats faster, blood pressure rises, blood flow to the stomach slows, the liver releases sugar, and your muscles tighten. Caffeine also increases dopamine levels.

Chlorine

Again the official line is that chlorine destroys bacteria. It is a highly efficient disinfectant and combats water borne diseases such as cholera.

This however comes at a price. The list of damages are many and include asthma, eczema, bladder cancer, heart disease, birth defects and miscarriage. It is obviously much cheaper to add it to our water than have to actually clean up our water supplies.

Cigarettes

Why are cigarettes over £5 in England and less than 4 euros 22 miles away in France? We pay almost a third more for the privilege and we are led to believe we are part of a union.

Like many of our identical consumer goods there are anomalies in pricing. Ranging from for example, cars to food and drink. Imagine how many people would have to look for alternative employment if prices were brought in line.

The Government would lose millions in taxes and many customs officers would be unemployed, after all they are in jobs to confiscate mountains of cigarettes every year.

The anti-smoking lobbies can say that cigarettes are responsible for many deaths and burden an already stretched health service but this is not the point, it is simply unfair but it continues because it raises money and keeps people in jobs. Those that are working contribute financially to the system that exploits them.

We are subjected to adverts (which are paid for by us) that inform us that cigarette smuggling is a crime and it finances crime.

Okay, make prices the same – this would defeat the criminals involved and save the taxpayer (us) a fortune in the process. If a guy wants to hire a white van in Scotland, then drive it on an eight hundred mile round trip to France to buy and sell on the slim margin he can make to feed the habits of a few people who wish to harm themselves by inhaling the 4000 harmful chemicals we are told are in the product, well is that not democracy and freedom?

I am not saying cigarette smoking is right because it is provably harmful; only let us have an even playing field.

Let us experience the 'freedom' we are reminded about all the time.

We might also remember that the 'tobacco' that we smoke no longer resembles the natural product. It is unlikely that the original leaf would cause a great deal of harm. The smoker of the massively tainted product he consumes might argue that by the time he needs medical treatment (having puffed a pack a day for thirty years) he has paid over £40,000 in taxes.

Cocaine

Is a powdered drug that comes from the leaves of the coca plant and primarily originates from South America. It has been used for centuries and was made illegal in America in 1914. Widely used as an appetite suppressant and for medical purposes.

The name Coca-Cola comes from two of its original ingredients, the coca leaf and the kola nut. From 1886 until 1905 Coca-Cola contained cocaine.

When Coca-Cola was first introduced as 'a valuable brain tonic and cure for all nervous afflictions,' it contained 60mg of cocaine.

The effects are mentally you feel alert, a sense of well-being and like speed your inclined to talk a lot of shite.

Cocaine was sold over the counter until 1916. You could even buy it from Harrods.

Alleged famous users include Robert Louis Stephenson, who wrote Dr

Jekyll and Mr Hyde in six days and nights whilst on a coke binge, also Sigmund Freud and Stephen King (who claimed it saved him from alcoholism however that doesn't seem too good of a deal to me).

It has been said that cocaine is God's way of telling you that you have too much money. No one feels contented after a couple of lines of cocaine, they just want more. Crack cocaine processed with baking powder and is smoked; it is a much harder hit. It's called crack because that's the sound it makes when it is lit. Put simplistically cocaine is a 'selfish' drug although ironically it makes people more generous with words.

Dimethyl Tryptamine

Active ingredient of this powerful hallucinogenic is found in Ayahuasca otherwise known as DMT.

It has been used to explore the nature of reality. To delve deeply into the labyrinths of human psyche. It has been shown to heal psychological trauma, allow the person to awaken to other spiritual dimensions and even to voyage there.

Ecstasy

The chemical name for ecstasy is MDMA. It was invented in the early 1900's by a company called E.Merck and was intended to be a dietary supplement.

As soon as our killjoy politicians found out that people were actually enjoying themselves and having a good time on ecstasy – they went ahead and banned it. (Presumably, they did this some time in-between dumping nuclear waste into the Irish Sea and shagging their secretaries in Parliament while securing an arms deal selling land mines to some tin-pot dictator in the Middle East.) As a result of making ecstasy illegal, it has made the pills more dangerous and has put the supply into the hands of organised criminals.

Clubbers Guide to Ecstasy.

MDMA is one of the most intensely studied recreational drugs in history. But despite thousands of research papers and studies, scientific evidence on the side effects remains inconclusive. With no doubt a large dose of ecstasy can lead to the body overheating, in turn in rare cases this can trigger fatal heat-stroke.

As with all drugs there are contributing factors to the effects; the strength of the drug, whether other drugs have been taken such as alcohol, body weight, and the individuals state of mind. 'The self, the setting and the substance,' as Howard Marks so eloquently put it.

The bulk of fatalities related to ecstasy around the world have been young women. Users fearing they are overdosing have been panicked into drinking too much water. According to recommendations, a pint of water per hour is advised. Hyponaetraemia is the medical term for water poisoning; this has in some cases proven fatal.

Fluoride

Fluoride is added to the water supply that we drink. Wal-mart put it in its nursery water, which is the leading fluoridated water sold for babies in America. On November 9th 2006, the American Dental Association (ADA) issued alert-advising parents to avoid fluoridated water when reconstituting infant formula (people buy it to put into formula and other infant foods). As is usual the media largely ignored this.

According to the findings of the ADA, consumption of fluoridated water puts a baby at high risk for dental fluorosis (a defect of teeth that causes staining and sometimes corrosion of the enamel).

It makes brittle bones and is linked to cause cancer. It accumulates in the brains pineal gland, which is an important hormone control centre. Modern science only told us of the existence of the pineal gland relatively recently, the ancients knew of its existence and its function, in children it is more open however it shrinks into adulthood, Descartes described it as the seat of the soul.

Fluoride is a poison and yet we add it to our water, toothpaste, mouthwashes, processed food, some vitamin tablets and beverages. It has no nutritional value but the official explanation for adding it to water is that it prevents tooth decay. The recommendation level for artificial fluoridation was established in 1945 and it has not been changed since even though we also consume it by the methods above.

The use of fluoride for 'health reasons,' is yet another of the insanities of our time. Is it a coincidence that both the German and Russians used fluoride to make prisoners docile, passive and stupid or that the USA government faced legal action over the toxic effects of this nuclear waste product?

Studies have shown that girls reach puberty quicker and there is a direct link to thyroid disease.

The pineal gland is a pearl the size of a grain of rice, it sits in the centre of our brain and one of its functions is to produce melatonin.

Melatonin is a hormone that helps regulate the onset of puberty and assists the body in protecting itself from cell damage caused by free radicals.

Due to the meticulous work of Dr Jennifer Luke we know that the pineal gland is the primary target of fluoride accumulation in the body.

The pineal gland is also known as our third eye – our spiritual eye.

Heroin

A fast acting class 'A' drug derived from the Asian poppy plant. It is processed from morphine and comes in the form of a white (pure) or brown (cut) powder.

Heroin is a natural opiate and is addictive although this has been overstated. The opiate family includes, opium, morphine and codeine.

It is a painkiller and the poppies are grown in Afghanistan, Iran, Pakistan and Turkey. In the US it is more likely to come from Mexico, Columbia, the Dominican Republic and the Golden Triangle or SE Asia.

Ibogaine or Eboga

Is the product of an African plant. It enables us to get back in touch with the child within, our Consciousness, in that it dissolves the ego for a short period of time. Eboga's consumption is a movement towards wholeness on all levels. It releases emotion pain temporarily, the healing process cannot be undertaken by taking a pill and the healing process can take a long time dependant on the person and the problems. But the rewards are nothing short of divine.

It is thought to be the 'Tree of Knowledge,' as named in the Biblical Garden of Eden. The wellness we seek can be found elsewhere but if addiction is an attempt to numb us against overwhelming pain then although this is not a magic bullet, it is a massive help in dealing with the problem.

This is the drug taken by Bruce Parry in his excellent documentary, Tribe. Parry shows great courage in living amongst the indigenous natives and gives us fascinating and well overdue incite into their lives. The openness, empathy and understanding that he shows is in stark contrast to way our history demonstrates our relationship with other indigenous peoples. History tells of levels of abuse and genocide that were summed up by the expression, 'there is no inhumanity like man's inhumanity to man.'

Witness our occupation and subsequent treatment of Native American Indians, Aborigines, and everywhere else we have soiled with our bloodstained boots. In our search for gain in the past we have eradicated the cultures to which we now find ourselves returning. What we overlooked in the past were the conditions that men like Bruce Parry are discovering, that these people really do have something from which we can learn. Wherever these now largely scattered tribes live, be it in the jungles of South America, the tundra of Siberia, the mountains of Tibet, the expanses of the African Continent and many other places, the story remains consistently the same and we find people who are none grasping who lead lives of respect for the land that sustains them. They own little by way of possessions but they possess qualities and values that we have largely left behind and as a result we (consciously or unconsciously) mourn for.

We feel an indefinable emptiness of spirit and a longing for the knowledge of something lost. We may yet find in the culture and structure of these ancient societies what it is that we now so sadly lack, and we might start by no longer considering them to be primitive savages.

Ketamine

Is called a dissociative anaesthetic with analgesic properties; it numbs the body and creates the effect of removing users from their sense of reality. Common effects include 'out of body experiences,' hallucinations and can lead to temporary paralysis.

As with all hallucinogens the effects of taking ketamine are influenced by the user's mood and environment.

Methadone

Is an opioid, which is a painkiller. It works by mimicking the actions of our naturally occurring pain reducing chemicals (endorphins). Its primary use as a painkiller is to wean people away from heroin.

Mushrooms

Magic mushrooms or 'shrooms.' Amanita Muscaria, this highly visible and strikingly beautiful mushroom is also known as the Fly Agaric. It is yellow to red in colour and speckled with white. It is probably humanities oldest entheogen (a drug with hallucinogenic effects) and is associated with Shamanic and magical practices.

As long as we have history we have different mushrooms used, not to feed bodily hunger but to feed spiritual hunger. Represented as the Alice in Wonderland mushroom, and often seen in fairy tale books. There is a mystical quality about mushrooms, they provide visions of the beyond when ingested and they appear anywhere and for no apparent reason.

In Siberia, the mushrooms were rare and extremely valuable — apparently one mushroom could cost the same as a reindeer. Ibotenic acid and the other active ingredients of the mushroom concentrate in urine, and up to seven or eight people can share the intoxication by passing along their piss. Many Siberian tribesmen even preferred ingesting the piss as it caused less gastric distress. Reindeer also loved to drink the mushroom-scented piss. All a Siberian nomad had to do was pour a bit of the piss on the ground and reindeer would come galloping over from miles around. This archaic, symbiotic relationship — reindeer, red and white capped beings bringing gifts from another world, the frozen tundra — was incorporated, consciously or not, into he story of Santa Claus.

Daniel Pinchbeck. Breaking Open the Head.

Although the modern image of Santa Claus was in part the creation of Coca-Cola, his appearance, clothes, companions and actions all demonstrate that he was a revival of the earlier mushroom gathering shamans.

Santa has rosy cheeks that are a side effect of eating the mushrooms and his 'ho-ho-ho,' is the same euphoric laugh made by someone who has eaten of the magical fungus.

The Shaman would dress in the same manner as Santa, wearing long black boots and red and white fur trimmed coats.

The natives lived in dwellings called 'yurts' similar to a tepee, the central smoke hole was often used as an entrance, climbing down the chimney they would share out the mushrooms gifts within. The mushrooms needed to be dried and the mushrooms would be strung along the hearth that is central to the story of Santa.

It was common practice for the Shaman to consume the fly algaric because there were toxins in the first consumption that were neutralised after the first consumption. The active ingredient giving the 'trip' however could be passed in the urine over many times over. Since the practice of consuming the mushroom predated alcohol by thousands of years it is suggested that the expression 'to get pissed,' started with the drinking of urine carrying the fly algaric.

Pinchbeck goes onto tell the following story about a friend called Robert, a gardener who in the past had worked for the Kennedy family:

He explains that Robert dried the mushrooms and he and a friend ate three each. Time passed and there were no effects until Robert went into the kitchen. As he turned around he saw three mushrooms of different sizes. They were animated and stared at him until the biggest mushroom spoke to him.

'Why did you eat us?' it asked.

He thought for a moment. 'I was just following my dream.'

The mushrooms conferred with each other. Finally they seemed satisfied by his answer. 'But are you prepared to follow this path?' the tallest Fly Agaric asked.

Robert answered intuitively and without hesitation. 'Yes I am.'

Whereupon the mushrooms vanished. Fifteen years passed before Robert realised that the path that he had agreed to follow was plant shamanism. He told me a story about a friend who ate Fly Agarics years later. The mushroom spirits showed up in the same surprising manner, and asked the same question: 'Why did you eat us?' His friend said, 'I was trying to get high.'

The mushrooms said, 'Well if you ever do this again, we're going to kill you.'

Daniel Pinchbeck. Breaking Open the Head.

The five foot tall spokes-mushroom may have worried Richard in this story but a more benign representation of these Fly agarics can be seen elsewhere. They are drawn in caves at Tassili, Algeria and are dated to around 5500 years ago. More recently they feature in the cartoon characters, the Smurfs, Disney's film Fantasia and the video game Super Mario Bros.

In the 1960's, Carlos Castaneda wrote of how he became an apprentice of Don Juan Matus, a shaman that he met in Nogales, Arizona.

In 1970, John Allegro wrote his controversial book, 'The Mushroom and the Cross.' The main theme of the book asserts that Christianity and Judaism were based on a secret cult whose god was Amanita muscaria, but was represented in the person of Jesus Christ. The cult eventually died out, but Christianity and Judaism remained as religions. 'Amanita muscaria' is the scientific name for the fly agaric.

R G Wasson wrote 'Soma, Divine Mushroom of Immortality,' in which he states the idea that Fly Agaric was the Soma described in Rig Veda (the holy book of the Hindu) and was the hallucinogen used for religious ceremonies until the identity of Soma was lost.

There are hundreds of varieties of psilocybin mushroom or 'magic' mushroom. Those that fall into this category contain the psychedelic or active ingredients psilocybin and psilocin.

The effects they have upon us when consumed depend on the species, dosage, and our individual physiology.

As for the over the counter legal drugs – the best sellers chart looks as follows,

Solpadine.

Sydol

Feminax
Co-codamol
Nurofen plus
Do-do chestEze tablets
Sudafed
Nytol tablets
Codeine linctus/ Galcodne linctus
J.Collis Browne's mixture.

We are spending more on painkillers than ever before. According to the market research company Euromonitor, the British painkiller market was worth £398m in 2003, it has grown from £309m since 2001, an increase of 30% in four years. Euromonitor predicts 2006 will see the market further expand to £483m. This is yet another indication that the numbers of people in pain are growing and that the pharmaceutical companies are happy to treat this expanding market. Is it enough to know that at least our addictions are legal?

Of course, pharmaceutical companies sponsor most pharmaceutical research and they are reluctant to explore the negatives. But what research there is suggests that analgesics, when used frequently chronically reduce levels of serotonin, and increase levels of pain-signalling molecules.

Earlier this year, the New York Times reported that a German study had found that even a two-week course of Tylenol (an American brand of paracetamol), 'caused a drop in serotonin-receptor density in rat brains,' an effect that is reversed when the rats are taken off the painkillers.

If you keep fooling your brain into not feeling pain, your body will eventually fight back and make you feel more pain. And then you'll want more painkillers; it's a vicious circle.

Imagine this as a business proposition. You buy a cardboard tub of white powder for around £100. You then turn the powder into a quarter of a million pills, which you sell at 10p per pill. Every cardboard tub you buy makes you a profit of £24,900. The powder is pure ibuprofen. The pills are painkillers. The company is Boots, which owns a subsidiary called Crookes Healthcare, which manufactures Nurofen.

What does the future hold? More painkillers. More pain pathways becoming desensitised. Packaging that looks more and more attractive. New pill shapes. Fast-acting pills. And then what? A big marketing push in the developing world, domestic advertising restrictions, and health warnings appearing on packets. There may come

a time when people will be wearing patches to wean them off painkillers, or chewing
low-dose ibuprofen gum – and what a marketing opportunity that would be.
Extracted from Guardian Unlimited, Special Reports. April 26, 2003

It is worth noting that codeine, which is a narcotic is converted like heroin in the body into morphine, thus many of the withdrawal effects suffered by users are similar to those of heroin. 10 per cent of the value of codeine is thus converted in the brain to pure morphine.

We seek to avoid pain. Now that is scary but think about this and watch how we operate in this five-sense dimension that we refer to as our reality. Nevertheless we will spend an inordinate amount of time in fear of the 'what if's.'

I am aware there are a lot of seemingly unfeeling people out there and we encounter them everyday, but when you get to know them they are in most cases just as scared as we are. We all have similar needs, wants and requirements but we have very different ways of meeting them, what would send one person into depression might stimulate another. For most the use of drugs is a quest to nullify our pain, however this raises an important question, why can we not treat the source of our pain?

'I took Benzedrine – I got clairvoyance. With Benzedrine you can have a very wide view of the world, like you can decide the destiny of man and other pressing problems, such as which is the left sock?'

Mort Shall.

If we could sniff or swallow something that would, for five or six hours each day, abolish our solitude as individuals, atone us with our fellows in a glowing exaltation of affection and make life in all its aspects seem not only worth living, but divinely beautiful and significant, and if this heavenly world-transfiguring drug were of such a kind that we could wake up next morning with a clear head and an undamaged constitution-then, it seems to me, all our problems (and not merely the one small problem of discovering a novel pleasure) would be wholly solved and earth would become a paradise.

Aldous Huxley.

LSD

Those who use (LSD) frequently or chronically almost inevitably withdraw from society and enter into a solipsistic, negativistic existence. These individuals, colourfully described by their confreres as acidheads, engage perpetually in drug-

induced orgies of intro spection and are no longer constructive active members of society…

Testimony from a Senate Subcommittee hearing. 1966.

A break from reality.

I experimented with LSD in the seventies; it is a very powerful drug.

I was inclined to take a tab when in the company of others. The deal between us was that we would watch out for each other, this arrangement worked reasonably well until one night I was going to a party and elected to take a tab by myself before leaving the house. I walked a couple of miles to the party and paused to go into the off-licence to get a bottle of wine. I remember feeling pretty good but I noticed the affect of the tab had begun to kick in.

There was a person in the shop being served so I started to chat to the other assistant who was at the side of the counter and thought she was really attractive she but wouldn't look at me or reply – she seemed very aloof.

The other customer had now been served and gave me a very odd look as he left and I engaged the other assistant who was behind the counter. Again a strange look, but I was given the wine I asked for and as I left I glanced at the other assistant who had previously ignored me. Reality must have kicked back in momentarily because I realised the other assistant wasn't an assistant at all … but a life sized cardboard cut-out presenting some sort of drink.

I remember leaving the shop quite quickly.

I walked another couple of streets and arrived at my destination. This area, a suburb of Newcastle, is called Jesmond and there are many large Victorian houses that contain flats. Arriving at the door I took my selection from a choice of bells with plastic covers and names or numbers next to them.

I pressed the bell and could hear noise and music playing above me. The speaker above the bells enquired who I was and I told them and the buzzer went releasing the front door, I walked in and up two or three flights of stairs and into the kitchen, (because that's what everyone seems to do when they go to a party).

Opening my wine and pouring a glass, I sauntered into the lounge feeling just fine about my place in the world. I took a seat on the end of a long couch at the far end of the lounge and tried to nod and smile at the only other occupant of the couch; a decent looking sort of a guy I mused. Scanning the room, I guessed the place was about two-thirds full.

I wondered was it early or late, had people come and gone or were there still others to arrive? I pondered deep and hard but as I looked at my watch for answers I realised it couldn't help me as it had melted all around my wrist. My seating companion must have noticed my dilemma as he called out to me 'it's 10 'o' clock,' I acknowledged his help and we started to chat, building of bridges stuff.

Pleasantries exchanged and with me just managing to hang onto reality, I scanned the room again looking for a friendly face or two, perhaps even the presence of my host, Tim my friend who had asked me here in the first place.

Nothing, it seemed to take about a day for me to decide I did not actually know anyone in the place, not one sinner and my newest best friend at the end of the couch, John was talking to me again as his face started to alter in a kind of morph. John and the rest of the room had *normalish* bodies, but they all had acquired lizard's heads.

And then the penny dropped – I am in the wrong party.

Now I'm thinking how do I get out without anyone noticing? Especially good old John here who has now grown horns and is talking about who knows what – because it's some sort of reptilian language and I can't quite understand.

A cunning plan was beginning to form – I turned to John whilst patting my sides and chest in a false self-pat-down type drama. John's head was changing colour quite a lot now but I persevered and said to him that I'd forgotten something.

John asked what it was that I had forgotten?

I told him that I had forgotten my address book – or lost it and I would have to leave the party to retrieve it from my imaginary car parked outside, very pleased with myself the way my errant wit and guile would enable my escape.

I could even visualise the imaginary address book.

'What colour was it?' Pressed John the pest.

'Black,' I lied quickly, '*you will have to get up early to catch me out buddy,*' I thought.

'Well,' he said, 'you had it when you came in.'

'*No!*' I thought my bubble burst, '*how can John know of my imaginary, made up address book?*'

Now John is on his feet and he's interviewing most of the room and nearly all the reptiles with the flashing coloured heads are talking to each other and to John and some of them are hissing 'no, we don't know,' and others are nodding and agreeing that I had the imaginary address book when I first walked in.

And all I can do for the moment is think '*some reptiles tell made up stories.*'

I don't recall how I finally extricated myself from the lizard party, but I never did find Tim's bash, frankly it never got a mention the next time I saw him so I assume it was a good do.

I remember getting home but unfortunately the front door of my house had shrunk and was far too small to admit me. As a result I must have fallen asleep in a bus stop and when I woke up there was an owl talking to me telepathically. (He told me he was single and had problems with relationships and I told him that I thought he didn't have the wit-to-woo).

Sometime later at the back of the house, I managed to get through the back door but like my watch earlier, it had severely melted.

This then is one of my experiences with LSD.

The question you have to ask yourself is simple; if you haven't already popped one will you? Here is one answer to the taking of all 'mind-altering substances.'

> 'You have seen it for yourself. This is your last chance. After this there is no turning back. You have to take the blue pill, the story ends you wake up in your bed and believe whatever you want to believe. You take the red pill, you stay in Wonderland, and I show you how deep the rabbit hole goes.
>
> Remember all I am offering is the truth, nothing more …'
>
> Morpheus, The Matrix.

The invitation made in The Matrix is not really about pills. The question being asked is whether or not you wish to change your perception of the world. The blue pill will leave us unchanged and we remain where we are in a life consumed by habit and of all the things we *be-lie-ve* we know.

Go to work, brush your teeth, eat, shit, sleep, consume, conform and behave yourself. The red pill invites a different proposition but you take it at your peril, your world will change, there is risk and things will never be the same. But we are curious and we pursue truth even though it may be fraught with danger and the journey may be tough.

There are many reasons to take either pill and only you know which one you would prefer and whatever you decide – is right for you.

The promise of the red pill is the truth, so we might ask the blue pill-takers … what is the point of an ignorant existence?

If we simply exist without meaning then there is no purpose to our lives. As Trinity says to Neo in the film of the same title, *'The Matrix cannot tell you who you are.'*

We are living in a matrix of our own making. This entrapment will continue as long as we are prepared to take the blue pill. But the question raised is – why, if are trapped would we not seek to free ourselves? – we are cunning – we can escape? However unless we accept that there is a problem then we will not do anything about it. If this is just the way it is or this is 'as good as it gets,' then we will never seek to escape – why should we?

My argument is not that we should ingest copious amounts of drugs but the fact remains, many of us embrace a temporary escape from the pain of this existence. We take the blue pill on weekdays ('normal') and pop a red one ('lets enter the other world please – we don't really like this one') on Saturday night for example.

I don't think it's a coincidence that I have often heard people (from my native North-East of England) when they have had a few drinks too many, issue the statement, 'I am mortal,' in acceptance and acknowledgement of the life force within us and a realisation that one can step through a temporary escape hatch and visit another realm.

And since many alcoholic drinks are called 'spirits,' are we asking once again to temporarily visit the divine?

The red pill taker will come back from his journey changed because he has learned something. So what are the 'red pills' that release us from our five-senses and send us on these journeys?

They include; the drugs that alter our perception, meditation, catharsis, nervous breakdown, hypnosis, out of body or near death experiences, dreams, self-mortification (not recommended but many of us are inclined to beat ourselves up on a regular basis), dancing into a trace-like state, reading of sacred texts and even a dip into nature can give us remarkable incites. And the one quality that all these experiences share is the reduction of the ego.

If God dropped acid, would he see people?

Stephen Wright.

There are three side effects of acid: enhanced long-term memory decreased short-term memory, and I forget the third.

Timothy Leary.

Ritalin

Prozac for kids. According to published figures in 2007 the National Health Service spending more than £1 million on mind-altering drugs designed to help to calm hyperactive children. Doctors now write almost 7,500 prescriptions a week for Ritalin tablets, otherwise known as 'chill pills.'

They cost about £200 a year per child and are likely to cost taxpayers a total of £12.5 million this year, figures obtained under the Freedom of Information Act have revealed.

Ritalin or similar pills are given to children diagnosed with Attention

Deficit Hyperactivity Disorder, a condition that affects mainly boys and includes problems focusing, controlling their actions and remaining still or quiet, the consequences have been likened to turning children into drones. Doctors wrote nearly one hundred thousand prescriptions for these controversial drugs in the last three months of 2006.

This is startling when there is no medical test for ADHD. Diagnosis is based upon monitoring problem behaviour, which is severely and persistently inattentive and disorganised, not just naughty or defiant.

Many are sceptical about the success of ADHD drugs and question whether the condition actually exists.

Professor Steve Baldwin, who died in the 2001 Selby train crash, had concluded from his research that Ritalin was being used as a 'quick fix' for children being used as 'guinea-pigs.

He believed ADHD as a biological brain disorder did not exist and that symptoms were caused by a number of social and psychological problems that could be treated with pills.

He considered the massive rise in Ritalin prescriptions 'a public heath scandal.

Research released today raises questions about the long-term effectiveness of drugs used to treat attention deficit hyperactivity disorder (ADHD).

A team of American scientists conducting the Multimode Treatment Study of Children with ADHD (MTA) has found that while drugs such as Ritalin and Concerti can work well in the short term, over a three-year period they brought about no demonstrable improvement in children's behaviour. They also found the drugs could stunt growth.

Guardian Unlimited. 4th December 2007.

Salvia diviner

'The diviners sage,' it is one of about 2000 varieties of sage. Used for centuries by the Mastic Indians to heal the sick and to induce visionary states. Found by the West in 1962. Salvia is most a powerful drug.

The use of plants to induce trance states is an ancient and worldwide practice. It is not the only way of seeking visions – dancing, fasting, meditation, self-mortification are other ways – but it seems to be the sure-fire method. Discoveries in archaeology and anthropology clarified this...

Daniel Pinchbeck, Breaking Open the Head.

Sugar

It's a great trick – the sugar trick.

Sugar was discovered by the West as a result of the Crusades in the 11th century. History says that sugar came originally from Polynesia and spread to India. It was used extensively throughout the Arab countries.

Columbus in 1493 took sugar cane plants to grow in the New World where the climate made its production easy. It was called 'white gold' because of its ability to make vast profits for both those that manufactured it and the governments that raised taxes on its back. The benefits of sugar to the consumer are difficult to argue because there are none.

The end result is that the customer is the end user and the consumer gets to ingest a toxin that he has been programmed to want. A sweet tooth is programmed into us in virtually everything we eat. We are genetically predisposed to like sugar, however not the processed sugar used throughout our commercially produced foods.

We are programmed into this habitual desire early in life as sugar is put into baby foods and processed foods and later in life we are encouraged to add it to our tea, coffee. It is found in soft drinks that we happily quench our thirst with. So we get to receive the dubious privilege of paying to be poisoned while everyone else from the pinnacle that precedes its consumption, does very well financially on the back of it.

Thomas Jefferson, the third and much revered President of the United States of America and the author of the Declaration of American Independence wrote, *'I have sworn upon the altar of God eternal hostility against every form of tyranny over the mind of man.'* This powerful advocate of liberty was obviously not including the hundreds of slaves he owned and put to work on his vast sugar plantation. In another example of hypocrisy he wrote; *'the amalgamation of whites with blacks produces a degradation to which no lover of his country, no lover of excellence in the human character, can easily consent.'* This prejudice however did not prevent him fathering children by one of his slaves.

He stated, *'We hold these truths to be sacred and undeniable; that all men are created equal and independent, that from that equal creation we derive rights inherent and inalienable, among which are the preservation of life and liberty, and the pursuit of happiness; that secure these ends, governments are instituted among men, deriving their just powers from the consent of the governed; that whenever any form of government shall become destructive of these ends, it is the right of the people to alter or abolish it, and to institute new government, laying its foundation on such principles and organising its powers in such form, as to them shall seem most likely to effect their safety and happiness.*

(Professor J Boyd's reconstruction of Jefferson's original draught of the Declaration of Independence.)

The average American consumes between two and three pounds of sugar a week. Sugar is found in baby food, bread, breakfast cereal (before we sprinkle it with more sugar), tinned food, microwave food, mayonnaise, sauces, the list is endless – sugar is in virtually all processed food.

Problems with sugar consumption are that it raises the individual's insulin levels; this inhibits the release of growth hormones, which in turn depress the immune system. Assuming you want to avoid disease this is not the way forward.

Every day 1,000 Americans are operated on for gallstones.

In Africa, there have been only 2 cases reported in the last 20 years. The incidence of kidney stones in the U.S. has doubled in the past 20 years. (The cause, in 75% of the cases is thought to be related to our high sucrose (white sugar) consumption).
Dorway. 18th January 2008. You Are What You Eat.

Sugar is a poison that we have become reasonably tolerant to, we are told not to give it to dogs as it's a poison to them as well but they have not built up any tolerance to it.

Your body's principle way of getting rid of sugar is to burn it. The sugar your body cannot burn will be stored as glycogen, when these reserves are filled then sugar is stored as fat. If you eat sugar your body will burn it and stop burning fat. I can't find any figures but in the West however there are millions of people, (many of them undiagnosed) with diabetes and high levels of insulin. High levels of insulin cause many problems, high blood pressure being one. High blood pressure is linked with heart attacks and strokes.

Consuming sugar causes insulin resistance, which leads to osteoporosis because insulin is a master hormone, which controls many anabolic hormones such as growth hormone, testosterone and progesterone. When these hormones are reduced side effects reduce the amount of bone being built.

Insulin increases cell proliferation, which helps cancers to grow. Other side effects of insulin resistance include fatigue, poor memory, cardiovascular disease, the lack of ability to focus, learning difficulties. Sufferers feel agitated and moody but once food is eaten relief comes immediately this in turn leads to increased weight and fat storage. In males the result is a large abdomen, in females it's prominent buttocks.

If this doesn't make you think then it is possible your depressed – which is another attributed side effect.

Sugar aggravates asthma, manifests mood swings, provokes personality changes, musters mental illness, nourishes nervous disorders, hurries heart disease, grows gallstones, hastens hypertension, aids arthritis, damages your dentals, can cause kidney damage, can speed aging process, can increase cholesterol levels, increases the risk of Crohn's disease and ulcers in the colon, it causes food allergies and has no benefits other than to sweeten food for our programmed habitualised tastes. Sugar can cause eczema in children; can increase our body's fluid retention and cause headaches and migraines. It alters delta, alpha and theta brain waves. The more sugar you eat the more elasticity and body function you lose.

Come on now – sit down now, relax – let's have a nice cup of tea – two lumps or three?

Yopo

Is a hallucinogenic snuff taken from the Anadenanthera tree found in South America. This tree is known as the visionary plant of ancient South America. It contains serotonin and DMT and was used extensively by shaman to induce visions.

When the western world found the Andean world, we rapidly embraced their foodstuffs such as potatoes and corn. But the mind-altering substances received little attention. We are now showing well overdue interest in exploring beyond our so-called reality.

Zoloft or Prozac

Prozac and its cousin Paxil go under the banner of SSRI's, (selective serotonin reuptake inhibitor). Other SSRI's include Zoloft, Celexa, Lexapro, Luvox, and many others.

These are antidepressants and are used to treat depression, anxiety, personality disorders and obsessive-compulsive disorders. General side-effects include, nausea, headaches, vivid dreams, changes in sexual behaviour, tremors, liver damage and in a rather ironical twist increased depression and anxiety. Over 30 million Americans currently consume antidepressants such as Zoloft or Prozac. Part of the hypocrisy of our society, induced by government, allow these conscious changing substances to be freely doled out, while substances such as marijuana are largely outlawed. Far more destructive drugs such as alcohol and cigarettes are allowed.

We therefore condone banning plant compounds, which have been safely taken by us for thousands of years, whilst we allow selective reuptake inhibitors or other totally synthetic and more powerful mind altering drugs made in a laboratory by pharmaceutical companies, who are motivated by profit.

As for much in our life there are no rules on taking drugs (aside from the inconvenience of many of them being illegal).

In moderation a drug is unlikely to kill you. In rare circumstances it is possible that you might suffer an allergic reaction. However it is far more likely that the crap they put into the drug to cut it may have a toxin in it.

As long as drugs are driven underground for the suppliers to dilute in order to make more profit, this will always occur.

With regard to the illegality of drugs; what business is it of anyone else if a person chooses of their own volition to drink alcohol, drop acid, smoke marijuana or consume ibogaine, after all people have ingested drugs to alter their consciousness since time began.

The only person at risk is the individual.

I am tired of the structure that tells us what we should do in all things. In the case of drugs and many other situations we are subjected to programming and we find ourselves policed and we in turn police ourselves.

Drugs that create an altered mental state have an obvious usefulness in marking off sacred experiences from profane, and therefore many drugs, including alcohol and marijuana, play a role in religious rites in some cultures. However, there is something special about the phenethylamines the drug class that includes LSD and psilocybin. Drugs in this class, whether naturally occurring (as in psilocybin, mescaline, or yage) or synthesized by a chemist (LSD, ecstasy, DMT) are unmatched in their ability to induce massive alterations of perception and emotion that sometimes feel, even to secular (non religious) users, like contact with divinity, and that cause people to feel afterwards that they've been transformed.

The Happiness Hypothesis. Jonathan Haidt.

Reality is a crutch for people who can't cope with drugs.

Lily Tomlin

Two thousand pharmacologists and biochemists were subsidized. Six years later it was being produced commercially. The perfect drug. Euphoric, narcotic, pleasantly halucinant. All the advantages of Christianity and alcohol; none of their defects. Take a holiday from reality whenever you like, and come back without so much as a headache or a mythology. Stability was practically assured.

Aldous Huxley. Brave New World.

There are many ways to achieve a mystical altered state and break from reality; drugs, meditation, fasting and dance being some examples. Indeed those who refute the idea might consider that in any give moment we can find ourselves in an altered state, while we day-dream, meditate and when we sleep. Through dance, many people from all over the world achieve an altered state. Dancing has been an important component of many religious rituals. Rhythmical repetitive movement is thought essential to build towards an ecstatic union with the deity.

Sufism is the mystical sect of Islam. Sufis seek ultimate religious experience often by the use of dance; this is where we get the expression 'a whirling dervish.' They enter states of visionary ecstasy by the group chanting religious texts and by the repetition of dance. The object is to be freed from the body and lifted into the presence of God.

We are both receiver and transmitter and when we discover altered states we find our frequency altered. I have heard this compared to a radio or a television set; your TV is tuned to 'Eastenders' for example; when you press the remote and alter the channel you find your watching 'Coronation Street.' However 'Eastenders' has not disappeared somewhere, it is simply that your set is attuned to another frequency.

We are similar, what consumes us is what's in front of us but that does not mean that we are unable to change our frequency or what we are attuned to. Deep within every human psyche there exists higher mental and emotional centres capable of unimaginably sublime states of consciousness. Due to the influences of the reality we have constructed for ourselves these centres remain dormant in most people.

We are between two mysteries – the outer world and the inner world – and in order to be open to both of these worlds, man has to know himself, to know himself totally.
George Gurdjieff.

Gurdjieff said we are 'asleep,' due to the hypnotic power of worldly influences. Our potential can be accessed and awakened by proper guidance.

There are many ways in finding access past the muscular doormen of reality. In allowing ourselves access to the enormity of this expansion we come to realise we have formerly been wearing blinkers. We cannot find our soul we can only allow it to reveal itself to us. This access is granted through dream, meditation, and altered states that are allowed by conditions such as ritualised dance, consumption of drugs, chanting and so on. All the sacred books of all religions confirm this.

Myth, gurus, awe-inspiring cathedrals, art, nature, sounds, words and images, they all can provide us with insight.

Our soul is the true authentic 'you,' and you brought it with you when you elected to enter this psycho-planet and you will take it with you when you have completed your journey. People will be born and will die and will not be aware that this deep identity exists. It is sealed away through constructed walls and barriers, through communicated programming.

Drugs allow us a temporary glimpse of the ego-less Universe we came from and to which we are compounded to return. There is nothing new in this thought, wherever we go in this world and whichever part of our past we explore; the simple truth remains that humans have always sought to get high. Everywhere that there are people there is a choice of natural drugs growing to allow us, if we choose to get high. The laws that govern most people throughout the world make this illegal, if we were allowed access to consume what we choose to consume, we would see our entire lives differently.

It is therefore perhaps no coincidence that we are prevented from doing this.

The altered states that the usage of the right drug in the right setting and in the right frame of mind enable and allow us access to the light of the One Universal Consciousness which many of us call God.

The most beautiful and most profound emotion we can experience is the sensation of the mystical. It is the source of all true science. He to whom the emotion is a stranger, who can no longer wonder and stand rapt in awe, is as good as dead. To know what is impenetrable to us really exists, manifesting itself as the highest wisdom and the most radiant beauty, which our dull faculties can comprehend only in their primitive forms, this knowledge; this feeling is the centre of true experience.

Albert Einstein.

We are programmed to consider that many drugs are 'bad,' which is why we accept that they are illegal. Naturally if we consider the harmful effects of drug usage then it follows that those who rule us and enforce the severe penalties for consumption, do so because they care so much for our welfare. This then is what we are given to think but when one considers how much devastation is caused to us by so called legal drugs, it becomes apparent that profits come a long way before consideration of what is actually 'good' or what is 'bad' for us.

Legal pharmaceutical drugs that are supposed to have been through rigorous testing before we ingest them are responsible for some of the most outrageous crimes against us than any of the so-called illegal ones. In the United States, when paranoia ruled the land after the events of 911, in the aftermath, when laws removing more and more civil rights were introduced, giving more and more power to the government and their instruments, (army, police, coastguards, boarder patrols, etc) a boy who was interviewed in the ghettos of Los Angeles made a statement which is worthy of serious consideration. He pointed out the steep rise in security and said there was no way anyone was driving, flying or sailing down to South America to buy drugs to sell on the street. It was as he pointed out, virtually impossible and more risky than ever.

His question was simple, poised to the reporter who was interviewing him; *'how do the drugs get here?'*

And in that question he raised an inconvenient truth – governments and their agencies control drugs.

The possibility exists that if we recognised how to access the mystical and finally see that we are all One, we would no longer require bodies such as the judiciary, lawmakers, police or prisons.

Governments and the thousands of civil servants that we support would for the most part, become redundant.

I am not suggesting this transition would be easy as what people describe as crisis enters their lives, relationships may dissolve, careers would be lost and the participants would need to embrace the prospect of an identity crisis. Even though the changes would be painful we would reflect back and know we were forming a more healthy society, we would still require guidance, advice and the goodness of acts of kindness towards one another but this could be given rather than enforced.

We see this happening on a regular basis in many parts of the world but not in societies that are built on materialism – unless a disaster occurs, then people and communities come together and show acts of supreme compassion and generosity of spirit toward one another.

It proves how capable we are of putting our differences such as materialism with our own imaginary selfish wants and needs (ego) as we put them aside for the genuine needs of others.

Unfortunately once the disaster passes we largely return to our programmed ways and go back to the lives we have constructed.

Recently we have seen the world affected by earthquakes, hurricanes, floods and acts of terrorism. These appalling and disastrous occurrences, by default have pointed to our salvation in showing us what unity instead of division can achieve.

The people affected and those drawn to help have shown far more spirituality and love for their fellow man than any government has ever done.

Ego

Now this one is a tough one and it plays tricks with us all the time.

The ego fights to protect itself and we very often regard it as the force that makes us an individual. I cannot stress enough how important it is to understand the ego and see how it rules our lives.

Many of us seem to live our lives virtually oblivious to the presence of our ego and when we glimpse it, usually it is because we see it in others.

The ego at work is made more powerful because we are unaware of it and yet we witness it at the bottom of every single problem and every single division of man and furthermore until we become aware of it – we will encounter it on every step of our life's journey.

Once we become aware of ego, a shift in our consciousness happens because you begin to understand the ego and the emotional response we feed it and you will never see the world the same way. For this reason alone it is worth the journey.

The more you come to recognise the monster we call ego; who lives in you but cares nothing for you – it doesn't even appreciate the massive amounts of energy you feed it – the more you subdue the ego the more you will find your true self.

However there is also a most useful beneficial trade-off to the recognition of the ego and that is, once seen and even partially understood, it begins to diminish in size and in power.

The ego is a difficult animal to contain and difficult to define; the ego is an illusion of a contrary nature, it needs other people and it craves them but at its depth it hates and it fears them.

The fuel behind the ego is your energy, which it then converts it into fear and want as it strives to strengthen the image of who you think you are.

The ego needs control, it needs you to express your id … your identity … for you to be special … for you to be separate.

The ego is never content, he requires much food and much maintenance, he wants all the time and he is profoundly and deeply insecure.

The egos vunerability makes fools of us all.

His worst fear is his demise and his demise can only be enabled by his recognition. He lives within us all, both as individuals and collectively, he loves boxes, but in yet another ironic twist, he much prefers it when we are lost.

The needy ego loves; masks, control, delusion, role-play and conflict, because that takes us onto the battlefield and then he can show off, the fact you might come to harm is of little consequence.

Any problem that has ever been – is – or ever will be (either on the part of the individual or collectively) is a manifestation of the ego.

Our emotions are fuelled by the ego and emotions are not who you are.

The ego fights to protect itself and is a powerful tool. The ego loves to complain and it talks to us all the time provoking our thoughts in an effort to become stronger. The ego is a master illusionist, a faultfinder who seeks to make others small in order it can grow. The ego loves 'I' and hates 'we' although it will reluctantly form alliances and then becomes 'us' and 'them.'

Whenever you hear the word 'I' you are dealing with ego. The ego loves a good moan, that's as opposed to a genuine complaint, that's not the ego, unless you hear 'I'. The ego takes everything personally and continually diverts our attention by causing us problems. The ego does not want you to go home – it does not want you to return to Oneness because it has been recognised and destroyed. The ego cannot exist in Oneness. The ego is nothing more than a part of your belief about yourself.

In Britain we can now access AQA via our mobile telephones. We can now ask any question via text and receive an answer. A friend told me about the service and by way of demonstration pumped in and asked for the definition of ego and this was the reply.

'Ego' explains why a human being is often conceived as being in the illusion of individual existence, and separateness from other aspects of creation.

AQA.

The ego is your self-image; it is your social mask; it is the role you are playing. Your social mask thrives on approval. It wants to control, and it is sustained by power because it lives in fear.

Chopra.

The ego is the illusion of ones belief in his individuality.

A Rankin.

The ego must offer you some sort of reward for maintaining this belief. All it can offer is a sense of temporary existence, which begins with its own beginning and ends with its own ending. It tells you this life is your existence because it is its own.

Text. Course in Miracles.

The ego's voice is an hallucination. You cannot expect it to say 'I am not real,' yet you are not asked to dispel your hallucinations alone.

Ibid.

… the people of the world will never live in peace until the people of the world have inner peace. The problem must be solved on the level of cause. Not the level of effect. Many famous teachers teach that people are born innocent, with a clean slate, and are then messed up by the world. It is not true. People are born with the ego intact. If it then plays itself out. If the ego weren't already there, then they would never have to come here in the first place! Still every lifetime is an opportunity to undo the ego and break the cycle of birth and death. And in the meantime, if you want to have world peace, the only way to do it in a lasting and meaningful way is to bring about a condition of inner peace within the people who appear to be here.

Gary Renard. Your Immortal Reality.

Personality, selfishness, egoism – these are the things which inhibit the manifestation of the divine energies within us. These it is which cripple men, so that men do not give full expression even to the powers and facilities that they now have.

G de Purucker. The Inner God. From Golden Precepts of Evolution.

Both the ego and the Holy Spirit are still to be found in every mind; it is just that the Holy Spirit is being drowned out by the ego's voice because that's what you chose to listen to – and what you really are has been pushed out of your awareness. We said before you may have forgotten the truth, but it is still there – buried in your mind.

Gary R Renard. The Disappearance of the Universe.

Whilst I accept it's a little early in the writing of this book to throw ourselves in at the deep-end, my problem is that I have written this in alphabetical order and I would have like to have made this statement a little later. However my ego demands I say this now! … Every single thing that prevents our consistent, everlasting, permanent unequivocal happiness and the ability to live with peace and love, within ourselves as individuals and with one another collectively - the one and only block that exists - is the ego.

In my hands is everything you want and need and hoped to find among the shabby toys of earth.

I take them all from you and they are gone.

And shinning in the place where once they stood there

Is another gateway to another world

Through which we enter in the Name of God.

Helen Schucman. The Gifts of God.

Energy

Energy cannot be manufactured or destroyed. Albert Einstein's famous equation E=mc squared.

'E' stands for energy,

'M' stands for mass,

and 'c' squared is for the speed of light squared.

This equation is saying, that mass and energy have equivalence. They are two forms of exactly the same thing; energy is matter liberated, matter is energy waiting to happen.

The 'c' squared is an enormous number and basically states that in every material thing there is a massive amount of energy.

We are made up of matter, which means we are energy reduced to a lower vibration. We are a series of magnetic fields and so is everything that is matter. We perceive ourselves as solid because this is what we 'see' and this is what we are taught.

We are *not* solid; we are a vibrating mass of particles we call atoms that form into molecular structures. But that does not adequately describe you, these are just words to allow us to form some understanding.

The atom is a model on the physic's teacher's desk – it doesn't really look like that. Nothing is absolutely solid; its just some things are perceived as more solid than others. When I was trying to get my head round this I used water as an example; water is primarily three different substances at different temperatures or three different vibrational levels:

Gas, when it is heated into a vaporous form where the atoms that make it up are vibrating faster.

Liquid, where its presence is vital to virtually all life as we know it.

Ice, at a lower temperature where it becomes more solid but the atoms that make it up are still moving.

So water is energy reduced to lower and lower vibrations and dependant on the level of vibration its form is dictated.

Everything is the same – all matter is energy and the lower the vibration the more 'solid' the object appears to be.

Energy vibrates at a variety of frequencies therefore the more 'solid' the object the slower the rate of vibration.

The higher it vibrates the purer it is as it rises up a spectrum which includes; electricity, sound, light, ether and spirit.

Energy is not confined to the three-dimensional world where our bodies reside and the days are dawning when more and more people are realising that our thoughts direct it, or to put it more accurately – a thought is energy and energy is Consciousness in motion.

If we look down the microscope we realise the further we go in terms of magnification the more space there is between matter and the mistake we make is to consider that matter is solid, it is not, it is just energy vibrating on a lower scale.

This is how it we can be manipulated by forces such as sound.

Our senses perceive form as solid when in fact every form is made up of more than 99.99% of space. We think our learned picture of the atom gives us an idea of solidity however lets consider the perspectives here. Imagine an atoms nucleus to be the size of a marble – the protons in its orbit would be less than the size of a hairs width – and they would be approximately two miles away.

Another example of scale and perspective is to visualise a golf ball, if this were blown up to the size of the Earth then the particles that made this inflated form would be the size of the original golf ball. We are considering enormous amounts of space here; ten million atoms of carbon placed side by side would measure less than a millimetre in width.

Above and below there is an unbelievable amount of space and the further we look up the telescope and into the Universe, or down the microscope and into the world of the atom, the more we come to accept this. It's no wonder they call it space – there is so much of it.

Because energy cannot be manufacture or destroyed I always think it curious when someone asks is something 'real or fake?' I appreciate the question posed is valid and might be asking 'did an animal have to die for that?' However everything in the Universe is synthetic, because everything is made up of atoms that previously made up something else. The government must not find this out – we must keep this to ourselves – we might be taxed on the inheritance of atoms.

Railway workers exposed to low frequency magnetic fields may have an elevated risk of certain blood cancers so new study findings suggest.

In a study of more than 20,000 Swiss railway workers who were followed for 30 years, researchers found that certain workers risk of myeloid leukaemia and Hodgkin's lymphoma climbed in tandem with their exposure to very low frequency magnetic fields.

Train drivers, who had the greatest exposure, were nearly five times more likely to develop myeloid leukaemia than station managers, (the workers with the lowest exposure to magnetic fields). Drivers were also more than three times as likely to be diagnosed with Hodgkin's disease, a cancer of the lymph system. The findings appear in the Journal, Occupational and Environmental Medicine.

Electric and magnetic fields (Em's) are areas of energy surrounding electrical devices, including appliances, computers, electrical wiring and power lines.

Electric plugs could become things of the past after scientists have devised a way of recharging laptops and mobile telephones without the need for cables. For the first time electrical engineers have powered a light bulb from a source seven feet away without a cable using magnetic waves. They believe this Historicity technology (wireless electricity) could be developed to allow portable electronic gadgets to be charged wirelessly. It would also help the environment, dispensing with the long-term problems caused by battery disposal,

Scientists have long known that transferring electrical power does not require wires, but for years have struggled to make it work. A team from the Massachusetts Institute of Technology has unveiled its Historicity concept in Science Express, an online advance publication of the journal Science.

The method exploits an effect close to inductance, which is at work in transformers used to charge everyday appliances containing coils, which transmit energy to each other by electromagnetic induction. Up to now transferring energy this way over distances of more than a few inches has been inefficient.

Concerns have also been raised about a possible link between electromagnetic waves and cancer. However, Prof Marin Solace, who has led the research, said he believed the technology can be developed without posing any additional heath risks.

Instead of irradiating the environment with electromagnetic waves, a power transmitter could fill the space around the power waves with a non-radioactive electromagnetic field he said. Gadgets designed to 'resonate' with the field would only pick up energy.

Anything that resonates to a different frequency than us – is bad for us.

Nicola Tesla

According to an article in the MailOnline 23rd of June 2008, fourteen people living within a mile of a mobile phone mast that emits one of the highest levels of radiation in the country have died of cancer. Four of the deaths have been in a cul-de-sac yards from the site. A further 20 residents have developed tumours in the last seven years although to date they have survived.

Low wavelength electromagnetic waves such as X-rays and gamma rays cause cancer. Signals such as wireless signals are not from one point to another point; they are spread out or disseminated.

It is a bigger version of how your mobile phone, electric toothbrush or anything that sits on a pad can work. People who work and live around high-voltage switchgear suffer higher cases of leukaemia.

A few years ago in Wales, a chap produced a piece of art by putting hundreds of used fluorescent light tubes into the ground under overhead power cables. That is all he did, there were no wires just old tubes pushed into the ground vertically. The tubes lit up and glowed fed by 'invisible power' as they drew their energy from the pylons. The sight was spectacular as well as informative because it showed the incredible amount of energy pumped out by these blights on the landscape and curse upon ourselves.

Those who give permission and profit from houses built in and around these monstrosities include house builders and planners, but I wonder how many of them would live and bring up their families within the shadow of a row of pylons?

Everything in the material world contains energy.

Money is a form of energy. When we put petrol in our cars a transaction is involved whereby we give money (energy) for the fuel (energy).

If we work in a factory at the end of a given time we will be paid for our labour, the remuneration we receive is in exchange for what we produced. Our energy (labour) is paid with energy (money).

The energy of the mind is the essence of life.

Aristotle.

Emotions

Emotion is that which leads one's condition to become so transformed that his judgement is affected, and which is accompanied by pleasure and pain. Examples of emotions include anger, fear, pity and the like, as well as the opposites of these.

Aristotle (384–322 BC). Rhetoric.

Without emotion, man would be nothing but a biological computer.
Love, joy, sorrow, fear, apprehension, anger, satisfaction, and discontent provide the meaning of human existence.

Arnold M Ludwig.

Emotions are what we have the most of and yet remain the least understood. If you fall and break your leg it will be repaired and healed in the days ahead. We are told a mended break is actually stronger because the energy that went into its healing repaired and formed more bone around the break. But broken emotions in childhood rarely, if ever, get healed.

Talented psychologists (who are often talented because they themselves have gone through childhood trauma) are people who help us in an attempt to unravel implanted pain and do great work, but trauma always leaves a scar because a negative emotion is most difficult to mend. It is said that what we don't deal with will come back to haunt us, this is the source of most peoples problems; this is the source of our disorders, anxieties and addictions.

Everything has a vibrational frequency and we are no exception.

We *feel* the different vibrations of ourselves and of others.

Our emotions are the most massive influence on how we vibrate.

When we ask, why there is so much violence in the world? It is because violence and fear is all around us and it is a law of the Universe that what we fear we will draw to us however and because of the same principles, if we thought via love instead of fear the world would instantaneously become a very different place.

Emotions are described as 'that which moves.' The law of emotional response or the law of attraction is responsible for communication between Universal Conscious Source Energy and ourselves, this is the invisible field that unites and flows through everything and everyone.

When we can grasp this we can enter a whole new world and in the process rid ourselves of fear. Vibration is a principle we experience constantly. We pick up on people's feelings and dependent on how they are vibrating we feel a variety of feelings. We affect one other and we draw, manifest and have the ability to grow by what we think, but the emotions act like a temperature gauge, the nearer we are to love the better we feel, the nearer we are to fear the more cut off from Source we become and therefore the worse we feel.

Emotions are a set point from which we are sending out a clear message to Consciousness. This message is then interpreted and translated by a benign Universe.

The following is extracted from, 'Ask and it is Given,' by Ether and Jerry Hicks.

In the forward, Dr Wayne W Dyer explains to us that this is a Universe of vibration. As Einstein one observed, 'Nothing happens until something moves' – that is, everything vibrates to a particular measurable frequency. Break the solid world down to smaller and tinier components and you see that which appears to be solid is a dance – a dance of particles and empty spaces.

Go to the tiniest of these quantum particles, and you discover that it emanated from a source that vibrates so fast that it defies the world of beginnings and endings. The highest/fastest energy is called Source Energy. You and everyone and everything originated in this vibration and then moved into the world of 'things,' bodies, minds and egos.

It was in the leaving of this Source Energy in our body/minds that we took on our entire world of problems, illnesses, scarcities, and fears.

Dr Dyer goes onto say. 'The message here is quite startling and yet oh-so-simple, you came from a source of love and well-being. When your matched up to that energy of peace and love, you then regain the power of your source – that being the power to manifest your desires, to summon well-being, to attract abundance where scarcity previously resided, and to access Divine guidance in the form of the right people and precisely correct circumstances. This is what your source does, and since you emanated from that source, you can and will do the same.'

We can say that the different emotions have different vibrational frequencies, but a more accurate way of saying it would be: Your emotions are *indicators* of your vibrational frequency. When you remember that your emotions indicate your degree of alignment with Source Energy and that the better you feel, the more you are allowing your alignment with the things you desire, then it is easier to understand how to respond to your emotions.

Absolute alignment with Universal Source Energy means that you know the following:

You are free.

You are powerful.

You are good.

You are love.

You have value.

You have purpose.

All is well.

At any time that you are thinking thoughts that cause you to know your true nature, you are in alignment with who you really are, for this is the state of absolute alignment. And the way those thoughts *feel* is the ultimate emotion of connection. When you think in terms of a fuel gauge on a vehicle, this state of alignment would be the same as a fuel tank.

In other words, imagine a gauge or scale with gradations or degrees, which indicate the position of the (fullest) allowance of your connection with your Source Energy all the way to your (emptiest) most resistant disallowance of your alignment with your Source Energy.

A scale of your emotions would look something like this:

Joy/Knowledge/Empowerment/Freedom/Love/Appreciation

Passion

Enthusiasm/Eagerness/Happiness

Positive Expectation/Belief

Optimism

Hopefulness

Contentment

Boredom

Pessimism

Frustration/Irritation/Impatience

'Overwhelment'

Disappointment

Doubt

Worry

Blame

Discouragement

Anger

Revenge
Hatred/Rage
Jealousy
Insecurity/Guilt/Unworthiness
Fear/Grief/Depression/Despair/Powerlessness

Since the same words are often used to mean different things, and different words are often used to mean the same things, these word labels for your emotions are not absolutely accurate for every person who feels the emotion. In fact, giving word labels to the emotions could cause confusion and distract you from the real purpose of your *Emotional Guidance Scale*.

The thing that matters most is that you consciously reach for a feeling that is improved. The word for that feeling is not important.

Ask and it is Given. Esther and Jerry Hicks.

Esther and Jerry Hicks have written a series of remarkable books, they show that our emotions link in to consciousness.

Research has proven that laughing can:
1. Lower muscle tension
2. Help your respiration and blood circulation.
3. Combat stress levels
4. Release happy hormones
5. Release excess nervous energy
6. Massage our internal organs.

Laughter is the shortest distance between two people.

Victor Borge.

Although medical professionals have always recognised that states of the body affect states of mind – a simple proof is the way psychotropic (chemical) drugs alter mood, as indeed do foodstuffs, dancing, the weather, and everything else besides – and have also accepted the general belief that, somehow, the causal chain works in reverse too, in the direction mind-to-body, it is only now that proper research has begun into quantifiable questions about how this second and more mysterious direction works – and has started looking at the most unlikely places, viz. the three subtle and hugely complex communication networks of hormones, the nervous system, and the immune system.

The Reason of Things. A.C. Grayling. Living with Philosophy.

Every time we plug into the media and often when we engage one another we are reminded of a constant unchangeable and relentless list; of shootings in schools, murder, war, terror and so on.

In the pressure society we have created, these are the never-ending stories that bombard us; these acts are the steam let off by that pressure, the explosions of anger, desperation, and frustration.

When someone says they are worried sick, they are alluding to the fact we have that ability. Worry is a bedfellow of fear. Low-down vibrations equals ill at ease or disease, dis-ease. To be dis-at-ease is to be thinking about negativity and because we get what we ask for whether we want it or not, we bring dis-at-easement into our reality and into our lives.

We merely state that they (emotions) all are tantamount to setting up a magical world by using the body as a means of incantation.
Jean-Paul Sartre (1905-1980) The Emotions: Outline of a Theory.

Fear and love are basically the only two states you are able to experience and feel, all other vibrational levels or emotions fall between these two bookends on the scale. The scale is not exact science, but a sliding moveable measure of how you are feeling. The lower towards fear you are feeling then the lower you are vibrating because you are burdened with fear, stress and worry.

Conversely the higher towards love you are feeling the higher you are vibrating. The higher your vibration the nearer you are to Source Energy, Universal Consciousness, Love, Oneness or in other words to God. The lighter we are, the more en-light-ened we become. When we vibrate in the lower frequencies and are descending towards fear, everything is more ponderous, heavier and generally more difficult. The whole world feels a more difficult place to function and exist in.

We cannot go lower than fear because that state does not exist, but with some mental practice or through states of altered consciousness we can find our way back toward love. However the ego will always bring us back and the ego will act at odds with our desire to feel better. It will perform like a handbrake on our car, set to a few notches, binding, creating heat and slowing our progress.

Put another way – if you felt unconditional love all the time, the ego would become redundant and perish.

Where would we find ourselves without ego? – back where we first started with Oneness.

A human being is part of a whole, called by us the 'Universe,' a part limited in time and space. He experiences himself, his thoughts and feelings, as something separated from the rest – a kind of optical delusion of his consciousness. This delusion is a kind of prison for us, restricting us to our personal desires and to affection for a few persons nearest to us. Our task must be to free ourselves from this prison by widening our circles of compassion to embrace all living creatures and the whole of nature in its beauty.

Albert Einstein.

Emotional intelligence

Is the title of a book written about fourteen years ago by Daniel Goleman. As the title suggests the author helped me to understand the value of emotions and how they can easily overrule our intelligence. Emotions are the governing force in how we vibrate, they are our link to Consciousness and how we are feeling will dictate what we are drawing to us, what we are manifesting in our lives. This is clearly demonstrated in coincidences or shown by adages such as 'be careful what you wish for, it just might happen,' or thinking of someone who then phones you. These and a myriad of other examples happen to us every day and very often go unnoticed. If we can gain a degree of mastery over how we are feeling through our emotional responses then it follows we can draw what we want rather than what it is we would prefer not to have.

Goleman explains the architecture of our brains as follows. In humans the amygdala is an almond-shaped cluster of interconnected structures. We have two amygdala's, one on each side of the brain. He explains that the hippocampus and the amygdala are the two parts of the primitive 'nose brain' that in evolution, gave rise to the cortex and then the neocortex. These structures do most of the brain's learning and remembering, the amygdala is the specialist for emotional matters. If the amygdala is severed from the rest of the brain, the result is the inability to gauge the emotional significance of events. As a consequence life without the amygdala is a life stripped of personal meanings. All passion is dependent upon it.

He goes on to say that tears are an emotional signal unique to humans and are triggered by the amygdala and a nearby structure, the cingulated gyrus; being held, stroked, or otherwise comforted soothes these same brain regions Without an amygdala, there are no tears of sorrow to soothe.

We have used classical fear conditioning as a behavioural assay for studying emotional memories. In fear conditioning, the subject receives a neutral stimulus in connection with some unpleasant event. As a result of its past association with the unpleasant event, the neural stimulus acquires the capacity of illicit protective reactions in anticipation of danger. If you were being bitten by your neighbour's dog yesterday, the sight of the beast today (and for some time to come) will certainly put you on guard, causing you, for example, to freeze dead in your tracks, or perhaps to run away, and will also lead to a host of physiological responses.

Dr. Joseph LeDoux Laboratory.

In a follow up book called Working with Emotional Intelligence by Daniel Goleman, he demonstrates how a lack of emotional intelligence can cost us dearly.

When Mike Tyson bit off a chunk of Evander Holyfield's ear during their 1997 heavyweight boxing match; it cost him 3 million dollars which was the maximum penalty that could be taken from his 30 million dollar purse.

Goleman explains that the amygdala is the brain's memory bank for all our triumphs and failures, hopes, fears and frustration. It uses these stored memories in its role as a sentinel, scanning all incoming information – everything we see and hear from moment to moment – to assess it for threats and opportunities by matching what's happening now to the stored templates of our past experiences.

For Tyson, a head-butting by Holyfield flooded him with angry memories of him doing the same eight months earlier, in a match that Tyson also lost – and about which he had complained vociferously. The upshot for Tyson was a classic amygdala hijack, an instantaneous reaction with disastrous consequences.

The central nucleus of the amygdala is the portion responsible for sending out the signals to trigger the 'fight or flight' response. Once fear is imposed upon us, every time we; turn on the news, read the newspapers, talk to one another, listen to politicians, world leaders, religious leaders, marketing people via advertisements and so on, we are married to the fear that has been placed there by programming as we grew and we are presented with a monumental problem. This is the situation we find ourselves in, this is what we have allowed and this is what we are given by those who programmed us.

Dr. LeDoux and Daniel Goleman have both demonstrated that the amygdala is the central site of fear conditioning. And fear conditioning is believed to play a role in such anxiety disorders as phobias, post-traumatic stress disorder and panic disorder.

Goleman states that the memories that are stored in the amygdala are relatively indelible and there are far more cell circuits leading from the amygdala to the prefrontal cortex (the area of the brain which is most responsible for planning and reasoning) than there are going in the other direction. It is perhaps one of the reasons why it is so difficult to exert conscious control over fear.

Fear, once placed there is buried deeply but it is also extraordinarily difficult if not impossible to remove. And that is part of the trick played upon us because the fear that allowed us to successfully evolve, (such as the fear that motivated us away from a life threatening situation thus leading to our survival or the 'constructive' fear of realising that particular animal is too big and too tough to tackle and eat, so lets move on to a easier target), as opposed to the 'destructive' fear of; the war-monger, the terror, the protection insurers, the 'if you fall ill,' policy peddlers' (who pay us back about 1 billion of the 6 billion pounds they took from us three years ago), the advertisers with the 'if you don't eat this food you will die of high cholesterol,' the puppets that read from autocue's and deliver us the 'news,' the 'in-depth' journalists paid to pump the propaganda, the priests, the prophets and the purveyors of doom.

Each species is evolutionarily prepared and has a predisposition to be conditioned and we are no exception. We are built to be accepting of the imprint of fear.

As mentioned, fear and love are the bookends of how we are feeling and all other emotions fall in between; if these heavy members made up a corporation they would be the mutual chairmen of the board.

Of the many kinds of emotional problems we humans have, fear (and the resultant anxiety that follows) is the singularly most important and debilitating of emotions. I suggest we call ourselves civilised, when and only when we have eradicated all unnecessary fear from our planet. Goleman in the books he has written gives us insight and provides us with the tools to be mindful of our emotions and the most destructive emotion of them all is fear.

The effects of fear manifest themselves and are mirrored in the figures of the 40 million Americans that suffer from psychiatric problems. In truth there will be many more people all over the world, who will never seek or ever get close to the help that they so badly need. These people will not cost the system anything compared to the 'known' people whose problems are directly linked to fear. The cost of those known 40 million people will cost the American citizens an astounding 50 billion dollars a year.

Once again we find ourselves in a situation where we are trying to fix the symptom rather than the cause. In the society we have constructed we certainly would struggle to fund compensation for both the known and the unknown masses that need genuine help.

But these and the many other issues are the manifestation of a problem; the question is why do we not remove the cause? The causes are not removed because we serve in the mines and further the agenda of those that control us, they actually need us to behave the way we do, just imagine how many people would become redundant were our fears quelled.

If we did not feel fear we would be on the track, rising ever upwards to enlightenment and if we embraced enlightenment we would see this 'reality' very differently, more for the illusion it actually is, we would then realise how we are being controlled and manipulated and our thought processes would allow us to break from this lie, this prison, this matrix … this falsehood.

Fear is contagious; this is why it is used as a tool against us.
Fear is used as a political tool, fear is used as a marketing tool, and religions pivotal role is the installation of fear.

Fear, the guy in the bank that's selling you protected payments insurance plan which is costing you £20,000 over ten years and isn't worth the paper it's written on. Because if you do play football once a month and you fall and break your leg, the policy will be void because you didn't declare it on the policy.
'Yes, it's right there, look in the small print and if not, well it's in the rules.' Even if you argue and/or sue, they will only pay your one years interest anyway, 'yes, look, it's clear, you really should have read the small print.'

For the piece of paper you signed, that they bought for £450 from the insurance underwriter and sold to you for twenty large ones – thank you so much.

Or the insurance company that lured us in with a talking dog or a man with a parrot on his shoulder; to take out your house insurance with them and after paying them 12 grand over the next few years, your roof takes a leak because the wind dislodges some tiles. And then you meet with the 'insurance assessor,' a person who exists and his sole purpose is really to demonstrate to the insurance company that instructed him … that you Sir … are a fraudster and a liar. Because when his report goes in and the days roll into months and after several phone calls eventually, just at the point you're about to give up, the letter lands on your mat.

Dear Sir and Valued Customer,

It is with regret that our assessors and underwriters have rejected your claim of last year on the grounds that the tiles that were removed in the winds of last November were held by nails, and because these nails had rusted, they were unable to hold the tiles correctly onto the roof.

We would like to draw your attention to the fact that there is an excess of £350 on your policy and that is more than the £325 estimate you have produced to us. Therefore we have a least two reasons on this particular occasion; to regretfully decline your claim and consign it to the very big piles of other turned down claims.

These piles have become so big that we have to move to newer, bigger and more prestigious premises to house them.

In fact we would like to take this opportunity of inviting you to a privileged evening in our new purpose built conglomerate palace that you and the other turned-down claimants paid for, plus of course my wages.

Please don't be concerned, in order to keep the peace we will not be inviting any of the handful of successful claimants to our launch, we do not like to court controversy and nor do we welcome those who take from us. So please come along and enjoy a glass of fizzy warm wine and a dried cucumber sandwich, all with our complements and listen to the launch of our newest and some say most exciting product to hit the market yet.

Dominic Hargrove will be our speaker and Dominic is very excited about the product too - its protected payment insurance folks and it's a real must for you if you don't want - your home to be repossessed - your wife to leave you - your life to be destroyed in a cesspool of disgrace and ridicule and your children to be taken into care …

Sorry about that, I lost the plot again …
Funny old thing the emotions, as I prove on a regular basis they can really run away with you.

The point is; our young Masters intellect is being encouraged as he is growing up however his emotions go completely unrecognised and his instincts are never discussed. Furthermore if we removed the unnecessary fear by not programming it in the first place and demonstrate this to other individuals even if it is only by example, then each and every one of us that make up society can as a consequence, influence one another in a far more positive and beneficial way.

We are more sensitive and fragile than we would like to admit and we need to be mindful of our emotions.

I somehow managed to get through the first two-thirds of my life with a complete lack of emotional intelligence. I am not alone; we can see it in others all too regularly. We have all shown a lack of emotional intelligence (road rage for example). The price of snapping before we think rationally is enormous and incalculable; bodies lie in graves and are incarcerated in prisons for one moment of a lack of emotional intelligence.

Our emotions are the first reaction to a situation and as we can easily prove by casting our memories back, the emotions are not usually the best default we have. We cannot address any problem when we do not recognise it for what it is. But the emotions, once seen for what they are and the dangerous and destructive places they can take us, then it is best if they are harnessed, and the old adage of counting to ten will stand us in good-stead.

We are injured and hurt emotionally – not so much by other people or what they say or don't say - but by our own response.

Maxwell Maltz. Psycho-cybernetics.

Facts

Very concerning these ideas or statistics that are put forward as facts. The other area which we need to watch is what 'experts say.' And we should pay real attention if the two are combined as in 'experts today,' said 'that the facts are ... '

Usually 'the fact is' simply another spin being used to invite us to; do something, buy something, think something, that is not necessarily factual or more importantly in our best interests.

An example of this might be a statement saying 'Manchester United kick off their game today against Bolton at three o clock. Famous football pundit Bobby Hill, the designated producer of football-speak today, pointed out that according to the statistics Manchester United have only had four penalties awarded against them at Old Trafford in the last two seasons, so if Bolton are looking for any favours from the referee today it is unlikely they will come from the penalty spot.' Taking this statement at face value it would suggest that Manchester enjoy bias from referees because of their reputation, the fans vociferous support, etc. Whilst this and other factors may well have an influence and is worthy of debate, the statement does not represent the entire story. Manchester, because they play attacking football and will probably spend more time in the opponent's penalty box than their opponents will by proximity be more likely to be awarded a penalty.

We are hit with facts and statistics by 'experts' wherever we turn and usually to make us accept the concept of what it is we are being sold or how to think and therefore act. In a world where accountability for actions is diminishing, people should be more aware of factulalising events. It never ceases to amaze me that so many so-called pundits, experts, teachers, newsreaders, editors, journalists, etc, are prepared to quote lies without thought.

Why should they let the truth get in the way of a good story?

The only fact is that unless you tow the party line and repeat without question the words that you are given, well hell your just not going to progress or hold onto that career that you have spent the best part of your life building.

Nobody believes the official spokesman, but everybody trusts an unidentified source.

Ron Nesen.

One of the most concerning use of facts is when 'experts' make a statement and we are expected to follow their advice. These so called experts are responsible for everything ranging from the reasons we should go to war to why it is necessary to vaccinate our children.

Panels of experts announcing the experts of the past were wrong when they said the MMR vaccine (the measles, mumps and rubella combination jab) had side affects such as autism, brain damage, and many other suspected ailments.

Parents obviously want to do right by their children, the National Health Service wants to save money and one jab is cheaper than three. The arguments still rage; experts are accused of scare mongering. Ultimately can we trust the experts, the government, and medical or pharmaceutical industries spokesperson?

Unfortunately history proves we cannot.

In the American Museum of Natural History there exists a beautiful moment frozen in time. Many of us have become familiar with this image, it is recorded in film, shown in documentary and on show to visitors, it is a depiction of a couple of upright ape-like figures walking across a plain in Africa. The male figure has his arm in a around his partner. His arm touches her and the gesture of closeness and caring in turn touches our hearts. The entire scene is built upwards from the impression of footprints found in volcanic ash after it had hardened and preserved. The observer is being invited to believe in the accuracy of the scene, complete artistic licence is deployed. The only facts are the footprints exist and that is it; there are no other facts contained within this image.

The imaginations of the designers of this scene are left to run riot, we accept we are witnessing our ancestors as ape-like animals who will soon evolve into men-like apes, a glimpse of our ancient ancestors. We have little clue as to what they looked like and the flimsy evidence has no more foundation in truth than a cartoon, however this is just one more of the unbelievable amount of 'facts' we are invited to embrace and therefore make part of our belief system.

There are no facts, only interpretations.

Friedrich Nietzsche.

Christopher Columbus discovered America or so we were taught in skool.

Imagine how the people of Europe must have received this news in those times; 'The New World' beckoned anyone with the spirit of adventure who wanted a new life in paradise.

By this act the floodgates were opened and the acquisition of the New World and the destruction of the Native American Indians began. The story of Columbus is a good example of the rubbish we are programmed with in school and it is still going on in the present day. We were told as a fact of this heroic man, who found the 'New World,' brought back tobacco and corn and presented these new products. We were told he was Italian from a family of wool weavers in Genoa. In discovering America he also proved his theory that the World was round. We were even taught a little poem to ensure our memories would not falter. *'In Fourteen Hundred and Ninety-Two, Columbus sailed the ocean blue.'*

As time has passed this 'heroic' man has become an example to us all, the 'discovering' of America for Europe is testimony to many epic stories that surround him. This benevolent explorer befriended the native people wherever he encountered them, he demonstrated that heroes could come from any walk of life and achieve incredible good in the world for the benefit of us all.

Columbus is an example to us and demonstrates we can all make change if we are perfect, truthful, honest and noble.

In case his memory or the wonderful things he did and stood for be forgotten, we got a top up when two films and a centenary celebration was thrust upon us in 1992.

What you won't hear Miss telling the children.

Christopher Columbus was not his given name, his real name is unknown.

His chosen name was Colon. (Colon translated means 'member'). He was connected to Portugal's King John II through marriage prior to any epic voyages. His wife Filipa Moniz Perestrelo had members of her family who were part of King John II's court and household.

He lacked the status to marry nobility and there is no evidence to support that he had any connection to Italy, or could even speak the language.

His signature 'XpoFERENS Colon' would strongly indicate he was a member of the secretive Templar Military Order of Christ.

Christopher Columbus' reputation has not survived the scrutiny of history, and today we know that he was no more the discoverer of America than Mickey Mouse was the discoverer of Britain. Native Americans had built great civilisations with many millions of people long before Columbus wandered lost into the Caribbean.

Columbus' voyage has even less meaning for North Americans than for South Americans because Columbus never set foot on the continent, nor did he open it to European trade, Scandinavian Vikings already had settlements there in the eleventh century.

Contrary to our education, Columbus did not prove that the world was round; people had known that for centuries. There are many examples that prove this; the Great Pyramid has the dimensions of the earth encoded into its structure and the monastery of St. Catherine in the Sinai still has an icon, which shows Jesus ruling over a round earth, painted 500 years before Columbus. Nevertheless both Britain's and American's have fabricated many such legends around Columbus and he continues to be part of secular mythology for schoolchildren. School just would not be complete without the three little ships that Columbus sailed to America or without the drawings of Queen Isabella pawning her jewels to finance Columbus' trip.

This myth of the pawned jewels obscures the true and more sinister story of how Columbus financed his trip. The Spanish monarch invested in his excursion, but only under the condition that Columbus would repay this investment with profit, by bringing back gold, spices, and other tributes from Asia. The urgent desire to repay his debts is reflected in the frantic tone of Columbus' diaries as he raced from one Caribbean island to the next, stealing anything of value.

Columbus decided to pay for his voyage in the one important commodity he had found plentiful … human lives.

He took thousands of Indians and crammed as many onto his ships as would fit and sent them to Spain, the survivors who made it across the pond were paraded naked through the streets of Seville and sold as slaves. Columbus tore children from their parents and husbands from wives. On board Columbus' slave ships hundreds of slaves died. Columbus captured more Indian slaves than he could transport to Spain in his small ships and so he put the surplus to work in mines and plantations that he, his family and followers created throughout the Caribbean. His men hunted Indians for sport and for profit; they beat, raped, tortured and killed them.

Within four years of Columbus' arrival on Hispaniola, his men had killed or exported over a third of the original Indian population of 300,000. Within another 50 years the Taino Indian people had been made extinct, the first casualties in the holocaust of American Indians. The plantation owners then turned to the American mainland and thereafter to Africa for new slaves to follow in the tragic path of the Taino people.

This is the event America celebrates each year on Columbus Day.

The United States honours only two men with federal holidays bearing their names. In a memorable example of pure and unadulterated hypocrisy – every January they commemorate the birth of Martin Luther King Jr. His genuine, admirable struggle was to lift racial prejudice and break the remaining bonds of slavery in America.

Then later in stark contrast in October every year, they honour Christopher Columbus who opened up the Atlantic slave trade and launched one of the greatest waves of genocide known in history.

And we wonder why simple folk like me get a bit confused.

It is hard to determine exactly when the Old World 'discovered' the New. Columbus's voyages mark a watershed only of publicity and royal exploitation. Given that he seemed to know exactly where he was going and had fairly accurate sailing directions on how to get there (the maps are still used to this day), 'discovery' is hardly the correct term. In fact, the further back we go, the less of a distinction we find between the Old World and the New. One of the prime mysteries of the Bronze Age, (roughly 3000BC to around 800BC), is where did the enormous amounts of copper needed to plate whole buildings in bronze, such as we find in Minoan Crete, come from? The tin came from England and the coast of Cornwall, but there are no significant copper deposits in Europe or the Mediterranean basin.

> *In the five hundred years before Columbus, we find evidence of Vikings, Scottish and Welsh princes, and Irish monks all travelling to the New World. Indeed, the Vikings created a colony in North America. A twelfth-century pope even appointed a bishop to Vinland, and the remains of his church can still be seen today in Newport, Rhode Island. The Viking sagas show that they penetrated into the upper Midwest and the Great Lakes. The sagas also refer to the inhabitants of what is now New England as being Irish, labelling the region White Man's Land.*
>
> *In fact, New England has many Celtic and even megalithic-type stone structures whose closest analogs are found in Ireland and the west coast of Britain.*
>
> Jay Weidner and Vincent Bridges.
> The Mysteries of the Great Cross of Hendaye.

Columbus never set foot in America; he never even set eyes on the place. The closest he got was Puerto Rica. In the aftermath John Cabot sailed from Bristol in England, which in turn opened the way for the first colonisation in Jamestown, Virginia. As a result England claimed America as its own.

Columbus was allowed to go on a final voyage in 1502. He left with just four ships to voyage along the coast of South America, it was a disaster and he returned to Spain a beaten man with a tarnished and distrusted reputation.

In a book called 'Christopher Columbus, The Last Templar,' by Ruggero Marino, the author reveals his truth behind the official story. Marino exposes the flaws behind what we are taught in school and what we as Europeans believe, he points once more to the agenda that was being served as Columbus 'discovered' what was already known and his discovery allowed European's to claim the continent of the Americas.

Columbus was on a mission to claim America; he was a Knights Templar one of the last of his breed before absorption into Freemasonry.

… Thus these popes sailed even farther into the great beyond, painting the world. They were mariners and geographers. The books, charts, and maps of the Vatican were also in the Palazzo Venezia with all their secrets and mysteries. In those rooms, on a hot day – July 25, 1492 – Innocent V111 expired. Every July the Church celebrated the feast of St. Christopher. Innocent died with his eyes upon the world map, upon the new world soon to come. Seven days later, with the winds of Rome blowing in his sails, emblazoned with the eight-pointed cross of the Crusade, an unwitting beloved son set forth from Spain – on the most fascinating earthly adventure any human being has ever undertaken.

Ruggero Marino. Christopher Columbus, The Last Templar.

Marino suggests that Columbus was the son of Innocent VIII and whether was or whether he was not, he was without doubt his instrument.

Captain Cook claimed Australia for Britain in 1770. Another 'fact' we were taught in school. In a book entitled, Beyond Capricorn, its author Peter Tricket argues that a 16th century map, found in a Los Angeles library vault, proves Portuguese mariners were the first to find Australia. The map accurately details the geography of Australia's east coast and proves a Portuguese seafarer Christopher de Mendonca led a fleet of four ships into Botany Bay in 1522, that is almost 250 years before Cooks 'discovery.'

…It appears that the Portuguese Captain Christovao de Mendonca could have led his fleet of caravels down the east coast of Australia in 1522, sailing south as far as today's Warnambool and mapping the coast as he went …

McIntyre.K.G. (1982). The Secret Discovery of Australia.

Captain James Cook, R.N., the alleged adventurous navigator and cartographer is a myth of the colonial establishment. He holds, perhaps in the lands of the south

Pacific, the same mythological position as Columbus holds in the North Atlantic.
James Cook Unplugged or Cook-ing History.
By Jim Duffield. eniar.org

The native aborigines, who could trace their heritage back some forty thousand years, became the latest indigenous people to be usurped by their latest uninvited masters.

So we have Captain Cook 'discovering' Australia. This event was simply an effort to expand the British Empire. This coincided with circumstances surrounding the American War of Independence (1775-1783). Britain had lost this conflict and the thirteen 'United Colonies' overthrew its former rulers.

Previously Britain had disposed of many criminals into the New World however this practice could no longer continue. London was the biggest city in Western Europe and the divide between the rich and poor was profound. The numbers of criminals frightened the rich and the jails were bursting.

Britain claimed Australia and found a new land in which to dump those poor unfortunates. The story of these people would break any feeling heart and gives testimony to what would become the colonisation of Australia.

This is one of those stories.

From the age of ten Mary Wade spent her days sweeping the streets of London as a means of begging. Young Mary was one of a large family of a single mother living in poverty. With another child said to be 14 years of age, Mary stole clothes from a small 8-year-old girl and pawned them. Mary was arrested and brought in front of the court. Both children were found guilty and sentenced to death by hanging.

Mary spent 93 days in Negate Prison until her sentence was commuted to transportation to Australia for life. Mary arrived in Australia on the Lady Juliana after an 11-month voyage. It was 1789 and Mary was 11 years of age. The practice was for the sailors aboard to take a mistress from the female convicts for the duration of these voyages. Once in Australia they were assigned to free men, ostensibly they were used as house servants.

Through various relationships Mary bore 21 children. She had lived to survive her last husband and together they owned 62 acres in Illawarra. When she died in 1859 hers was the first funeral to be held in St Paul's Church of England built in Fairy Meadow on land donated by her son.

With some facts however there is no point in arguing. It is a little known fact that the name of the first Zulu to die at Rourkes Drift was 'Will.'

I know this to be unquestionably true because when I watched the fih Zulu, Michael Caine stood up and said to the British soldiers, 'fire at Will.'

Hardly a week passes without stories of shark attacks or sightings. We are constantly bombarded with 'facts' about the shark and we seem to have developed a real fascination with any shark related story. But I wonder how many lives the shark has saved?

Because of our dread of sharks there must have been many more people who through fear of the beast – did not enter the water and therefore saved themselves from the inconvenience of drowning.

Sit down before a fact like a little child, and be prepared to give up every preconceived notion, follow humbly wherever and to whatever abyss Nature leads, or you shall learn nothing.

T H Huxley.

Failure

Failure is very much a relative view. If you fall short of your aspirations you may be deemed a failure. Failure may be viewed as the opposite of success.

What would you attempt to do if you knew you could not fail?

Dr Robert Schuller.

Being defeated is often a temporary condition. Giving up is to make it permanent.

Marilyn Savant.

My will shall shape the future. Whether I fail or succeed shall be no man's doing but my own. I am the force; I can clear any obstacle before me or I can be lost in the maze. My choice; my responsibility; win or lose, only I hold the key to my destiny.

Elaine Maxwell.

Remember no man is a failure who has friends.

It's a Wonderful Life.

But there is suffering in life, and there are defeats. No one can avoid them. But it is better to lose some of the battles in the struggles for your dreams than to be defeated without ever knowing what you are fighting for.

Paulo Coelho.

A critic's life is a life without risk.

George Reynolds

It is not the critic who counts, not the man who points out how the strong man stumbled, or where the doer of deeds could have done better. The credit belongs to the man who is actually in the arena, whose face is marred by dust and sweat and blood, who strives valiantly, who errs and comes short again and again, who knows the great enthusiasms, the great devotions, and spends himself in a worthy cause, who at best knows achievement and who at the worst if he fails while daring greatly so that his place shall never be with those cold and timid souls who know neither victory nor defeat.

Theodore Roosevelt. (From a speech given at the Sorbonne. 1910).

In a world full of uncertainty, people rarely if ever fail but we do stop trying. Any project or idea requires a level of enthusiasm but it is patience and persistence that enable us to succeed.

We are programmed as we are growing up and, as a result, many believe the falsehoods imprinted that will lead to failure, in essence that we do not deserve success. In this abundant universe, everyone should get their living doing whatever it is that they love. For these circumstances to prevail, more of us need to eradicate much of the values we presently cling to so tightly.

Never feel your efforts are in vain, clearly intend what it is you want, visualise the outcome of those intentions because you create your own reality.

As in all things in life, it is important to learn as we travel towards success and if we can experience joy as we journey, then we cannot fail.

'You might as well wish you hadn't, as wish you had.'

Rob Coughlan.

Or put another way;

'I would rather regret something I have done, than regret something I haven't done.'
Gerald Robson.

Fear

Men fear thought more than they fear anything else on earth – more than ruin, more even than death. Thought is subversive and revolutionary, destructive and terrible; thought is merciless to privilege, established institutions, and comfortable habits; thought is anarchic and lawless; indifferent to authority, careless of the well- tried wisdom of the ages …

But if thought is to become the possession of many, not the privilege of the few, we must have done with fear. It is fear that holds men back – fear lest their cherished beliefs should prove delusions, fear lest the institutions by which they live should prove harmful, fear lest they themselves should prove less worthy of respect than they have supposed themselves to be.

> Bertrand Russell. Principles of Social Reconstruction.

To some extent or another we all live in fear.

Fear filters down from those who control us. Fear is the tool of manipulation; when you're in fear you're not paying real attention to anything else, you are not functioning as a spiritual human being, you cannot, it is impossible.

The system programmes us to fear or the system stumbles and it falls because it looses control.

Everywhere you turn fear is represented in case we ever forget.

Television is the greatest propaganda instrument ever invented and although powerful people 'own' the stations and channels, the government runs them. In turn, the people who control our world control these powerful people and those governments.

We are supposed to believe the government has a problem with something the BBC broadcasts, that is just a smokescreen so we are deluded into the believe that we are receiving unbiased reporting, there is *always* an agenda and that agenda is always the same – the promotion of fear.

In Britain the government has an option that dictates that at any time it can take over any and all broadcasts however it doesn't need to because it runs them anyway.

This is why, upon the invasion of another country; the first target is the media and once taken away the new propaganda can be spread.

We fear the past, present and the future. We fear our fellow man, we fear the unknown, we fear change and we fear not having enough and we fear loosing what we do have. We fear we will not be able to get what it is we think we want. We fear for those we love and we fear ourselves because deep down inside of us when the programming skips a beat and we escape it … we know deep down – this is not right.

Fear is an emotional response to impending danger. Fear is a survival mechanism, and usually occurs in response to a specific negative stimulus.

Wikipedia.

You can discover what your enemy fears most by observing the means he uses to frighten you.

Worry is like a rocking chair … it gives you something to do … but it doesn't get you anywhere.

Dorothy Galyean

'Quite an experience to live in fear, isn't it?
That's what it is to be a slave.'

Batty. Bladerunner.
From the book by Philip K Dick. Do Androids Dream of Electric Sheep.

We live in fear all the time; it is constant and unrelenting.

Most of our time is taken up between worrying about some impending doom that probably will not happen and further topped up with a diet of fear by all around us, by each other, the media, the politicians, the experts and so on, but the truth remains;

YOU CANNOT PROPERLY FUNCTION WHEN YOU ARE IN FEAR.

Fear is the baseline, the lowest possible negative emotion and when we are in fear we vibrate badly. Fear spawns all the negative emotions that hold us back, that prevent us from manifesting lives of awe and wonder.

The more time we give over to being in fear the more we attract negative circumstances into our lives.

It is said; 'be careful what you wish for, it just might happen.'

There is truth in this old adage because we get what we wish for, (or think about) whether we want it or not.

This is a basic law of the Universe.

When you are giving your attention to fear, you are giving fear power and drawing negativity towards you. The emotions spawned as bedfellows of fear include; grief, depression, despair, powerlessness, insecurity, guilt, unworthiness, jealousy, hatred, rage, anger, revenge, etc. All these emotional states are negative.

On the up side of the emotional scale we have joy, freedom, love, passion, appreciation, etc. The better you feel the better you vibrate ... the better you vibrate means you vibrate in conjunction with our Source Energy, the Creative Conscious Energy of the Universe.

Conversely the lower you feel ... the lower your vibrational level, the more cut off and isolated from Source you become.

Fear has become the tool of those who seek to control us.

It is the curse of humankind and within it we manifest all of our problems. Fear is a manifestation of the ego and therefore of the emotions. Fear binds the world whereas forgiveness sets it free. There is nothing to fear. To be free of fear is to be free.

We all see what we want to see.
Coffey looks and he sees Russians. He sees hate and fear.
You have to look with better eyes than that.

The Abyss. James Cameron.

You are a child of the Universe.
Your playing small doesn't serve the world.
There is nothing enlightening about shrinking,
So that other people won't feel insecure around you.
We are born to make manifest the glory of the Universe that is within us. It's not just in some of us: it is in everyone.
And as we let our own light shine,
We unconsciously give other people permission to do the same.
And as we are liberated from our own fear,
Our presence automatically liberates others.

Marianne Williamson

As a bee seeks nectar
From all kinds of flowers,
Seek teachings everywhere,
A quiet place to graze, seek seclusion to digest
All you have gathered

Like a madman
Beyond all limits,
Go wherever you please
And live like a lion
Completely free of all fear.

A Tantra of Zoggen.

The crowd neither wants nor seeks knowledge, and the leaders of the crowd, in their own interests, try to strengthen its fear and dislike of everything new and unknown. The slavery in which mankind lives is based upon this fear.

G Gurdjieff. (D. 1945)

For as long as anyone can remember we have focused on fear.

Our young Master lack fear, we instil fear into him; we are inclined to teach him what not to do … rather than what to do and slowly but surely we break him into our so-called normal way of life.

Our thoughts are our best friends and our worst enemies. Depending on what we think we will attract and we will become. It is very important that we understand this simple certainty.

Healthy constructive thoughts are more use to us than the skills of any doctor or the warmth of a close friend, genuine miracles can manifest themselves but we first have to believe or be shown.

We need to stop thinking about all the negativity that we are fed on in a daily diet. Thinking about terror and war will manifest terror and war. Think about death and disease and you will attract it to you. Think positively with confidence and your experience of life will be richer.

The more you think about your grievances or the misfortunes you may have suffered the more they will continue, your thoughts and your emotional set point is attracting and manifesting them.

If your thoughts are of success in life, of abundance and appreciation then this will follow; these are the qualities you are attracting.

You get what you think about whether you want it or not – it is the law.

Fear is spread like some unseen plague, when we are disturbed we in turn disturb others. For example when we watch television and see the never-ending war on terror on the news. The thought of war simply breeds more war and the ideas put forward by those that profit from war, become seductive.

We are asked to give our sanction by deceit and manipulation that this is a 'just' war and that 'they' are evil and as we have seen by events in Iraq, if we dissent and resist it goes ahead anyway.

There have been many Crusades and this is just the latest, a few profit, many die, hearts are broken and the wheels go turning around. If we think terror and warfare it follows we will manifest it because our emotions are the energy that secures this certain deal with the Universe.

Nothing can happen unless we think it first.

You cannot fight for peace it is a total contradiction in terms.

We have deep intuitive insight into the intelligence of the Universe and we cannot access this when in fear and so full of hatred.

Nothing in life is to be feared, it is only to be understood and once understood it holds no fear.

In the West, for the most part we fear death and so the truth is, we are largely unprepared for it. What works against us is simple; we live fearfully. However if we were to allow ourselves to live with joy and love, relaxed and open as a result, we would come to know that our demise was not an ending but a beginning of a new cycle the latest round of our journey that is without matter – spirit without a body.

My life has been full of terrible misfortunes, most of which never happened.
Michel de Montaigne.

Film

Because all life is in the movies.

> *The path of the righteous man is beset on all sides by the inequities of the selfish and the tyranny of evil men. Blessed is he whom the name of charity and goodwill shepherds the weak through the valley of darkness. For he is truly his brothers keeper and the finder of Gods children, and I will strike down upon thee with great vengeance and furious anger those who attempt to poison and destroy my brothers and you will know my name is the Lord when I lay my vengeance upon thee.*
>
> Pulp Fiction from the Bible.

Two brothers who are very different in nature are talking.

> *'Adventure and romance is what we seek,' says one.*
> *'There is no such thing as adventure or romance,' comes the other brother's reply.*
> *'There is only trouble and desire, funny thing is when you desire something your in trouble. Ironic isn't it?'*
>
> Dr Mabuse, der Spieler, film by Fritz Lang (1922) and in the film
> Simple Men.

> *'Those without swords can still die upon them.'*
>
> Two Towers.

> *'It's a funny feeling being taken under the wing of a dragon, its warmer than you think.'*
>
> Gangs of New York.

'I Heart Huckabees.' The underlying message in this film is you are responsible for and draw to you everything that occurs in your life. We create our own reality because of our thoughts.

'What do you call 500 lawyers lying on the bottom of the ocean?'
A good start.

Danny DeVito. The War of the Roses.

Drama is life with the dull bits left out.

Alfred Hitchcock.

You don't understand! I could've had class. I could've been a contender. I could've been somebody, instead of a bum, which is what I am.

Marlon Brando. On the Waterfront.

Get busy livin' or get busy dyin

The Shawshank Redemption.

I've seen things you people would not believe.
Attack ships on fire off the shoulder of Orion.
I watched C-beams glitter in the dark near the Tanhauser Gate.
All those moments will be lost in time, like tears in rain.
Time to die.'

Rutger Hauer. Blade Runner.

Remember, Ginger Rogers did everything Fred Astaire did, but she did it backwards and in high heels.

Faith Whittlesey.

I stand up on my desk to remind myself that we must constantly look at things in a different way. You see the world looks very different from up here... just when you think you know something you have to look at it another way. Even though it may seem silly or wrong, you must try...

...We all have a great need for acceptance, but you must trust that your beliefs are unique, your own, even though others may think them odd or unpopular, even though the herd may go that's baaaaa-d.

Robin Williams. Dead Poets Society.
(Extracted from D.Icke. Tales from the Time Loop.)

Forgiveness

Forgiveness is vitally important in our lives because if we do not forgive then we continue to judge and condemn.

In 1987 a bomb killed eleven people in Enniskillen in County Fermanagh in Northern Ireland. A further sixty-three people were injured. The device went off without warning at the town's cenotaph where on the 8th of November people had gathered to pay their respects to the war dead.

A young nurse called Marie died holding her father's hand. Gordon Wilson set an incredible example of forgiveness, when asked he said he could not hate his daughter's killers, he went on to say (as far am my memory serves) that he bore them no ill-will, any negative thoughts of that nature were not going to bring her back. But he wanted people to know what a wonderful person she was. Gordon Wilson had unwillingly seen his own daughter brutally taken from him, he chose to understand how this had happened and in the understanding was able to forgive, he did not judge and he did not condemn. He was an inspiration to his fellow man.

If you are at war with others you cannot be at peace with yourself. Only you can let go and forgive. It requires no strength only courage and wisdom. Life either expands or it contracts in your ability to forgive. For your own peace of mind – forgive. Because you either devote energy to holding a grudge or forgiveness.

Your choice is to move closer to what you desire or further away from it. Forgiveness brings closure for the person harbouring the resentment because hatred is a poison borne of anger and bitterness.

For 'give' ness, by its own definition is to 'give' something.

In the giving you are released of the poison, it ends the illusion of separateness and takes us back to love. To forgive and be compassionate at first may seem to be difficult. The more limited our perspectives are then it follows that the more overwhelmed we will be when asked to forgive. The place to start is with ourselves we need to forgive ourselves and not dwell on what has happened. When we are whole and healthy in mind nothing can disturb us. Thoughts and emotions, both positive and negative will rise and fall in our minds, but instead of allowing them to be believed or resisted we should wash them away with compassion and with love.

If we want to become more enlightened and enriched spiritually we only have to give mind to these conditions and slowly make them part of us as we begin to practice them, and there is a massive bonus; we save ourselves time and the inconvenience of splodging around – lost in the abyss.

There are those who will tell you why it is wise to never forget the pain of the past … but if you look closely at the anger, sorrow, bitterness that has hardened their faces, then you will also see why learning to forgive is the better of the two paths.

Guy Finley.

Our capacity to make peace with another person and with the world depends very much on our capacity to make peace with ourselves.

Thich Nhat Hanh.

Always forgive your enemies – nothing annoys them so much.

Oscar Wilde.

Forgiveness *is* freedom; freedom is not wielded or introduced to us by politicians. Freedom is not provided by another individual to be bestowed upon us, and this is one of the fundamental mistakes we accept from the programmers.

For freedom to exist without – freedom has to exist within.

Freedom from guilt, hate, envy and any of the many emotional meme's placed within our formative years. If you practice forgiveness, in place of where you would have normally got angry or fearful, then when a situation that would normally result in a negative or low vibrational state presents itself, the practicing of forgiveness will allow you to automatically default to it, the results will be so different than the ones we were programmed into.

If we are presented with a situation there are many ways of handling that situation. You may be upset about what someone has said about you; an injustice or a wrongdoing, however if you forgive then it follows that love will fill the void. Love will be revealed to you… because that is what you are … you are love.

Freedom

A word much vaunted by politicians. I do not subscribe to their views on freedom because of the way the option is presented.

Naturally we all would choose freedom against oppression; we were reminded by older generations that millions died in wars in order we might be free and because we are presented with this sterling argument, we do not argue as to do so would show disrespect to the memories of the millions of brave men who died giving their lives that we can be free, this then becomes part of our belief.

This is a very difficult subject and perhaps we should view it from a different angle; real freedom is having nothing to lose and to become who we really are. Real freedom is not thinking we are free, it is being aware that we are far from free.

Only when people realize that they have the power to use their thoughts to lift themselves from misery, only then will their freedom begin.
Dr. Thurman Fleet. Concept-Therapy

See we love – freedom. That's what they didn't understand. They hate things; we love things. They act out of hatred; we don't seek revenge, we seek justice out of love.
G W Bush.

And, yes, you have to even forgive this pure and unadulterated shite … you have to see it for what it is … realise the agenda, know that he is controlled by people who will dispense with him in the blink of an eye, just as they have done to others throughout history and although I might be inviting you to go a step beyond your comfort zone, especially if you dislike Bush, because and as hard as this sounds if you realised the full story of good old GW's life; the programmed trauma implanted in him as a child, the rituals that have changed the real person he originally was, the extent of his fears and all things considered, you might just end up feeling sorry for him.

If you want to be free, there is but one way, it is to guarantee an equally full measure of liberty to all your neighbours. There is no other.

Carl Schurz.

While the state exists, there can be no freedom. When there is freedom there will be no State.

Lenin.

The love of liberty is the love of others; the love of power is the love of ourselves.
William Hazlitt.

Real freedom is having nothing. I was freer when I didn't have a cent.
Mike Tyson.

If the possibility of the spiritual development of all individuals is to be secured, a second kind of outward freedom is necessary. The development of science and of the creative activities of the spirit in general requires still another freedom, which may be characterized as inward freedom. It is this freedom of the spirit which consists in the interdependence of thought from the restrictions of authoritarian and social prejudices as well as from unphilosophical routinising and habit in general. This inward freedom is an infrequent gift of mature and a worthy object for the individual.

Albert Einstein.

Perhaps freedom is best observed in animals or in children who before programming hits them, are free. In a child of less than four years old we can find a free human spirit. Most of the time they have a smile all over their faces, they are free from self-consciousness, they are having fun. They know they own the moment and don't care for the past or the future. Worry has not become part of their world, they are innocent and free to do and to say anything they want.

This then is the birthright of all of us, however along comes programming, a set of imposed beliefs, the dubious ability to judge and condemn, the so called rights and wrongs, the perceptions of good and of evil and there finally you have it – the misery of adulthood to face. A head full of transposed shit from those that brought us up.

You can't even blame those that educated you and programmed your innocent mind because the same happened to them, they knew no better.

The likely-hood is if you do ever get around to forgiving them you will probably end up blaming yourself and perhaps this is why we abuse ourselves or in extreme cases, we self-harm.

This terrifying position means that the majority of us are unaware of our condition because a lie repeated often enough becomes the truth, we believe we are free because we are told all the time, the truth is that we are free to do as we are told and many of us will be born and will die and never question this.

The first step towards personal freedom is awareness. As with everything you cannot and therefore will not, deal with a problem unless you recognise it. Then and only then can we solve the problem.

There is absolutely no reason for us to suffer. With practice we can change the beliefs that programmed us into habit, we can cleanse ourselves of the poison that we were fed, we can heal and we can realise that our past suffering was unnecessary and take responsibility and realise that unless we do, we will continue to repeat our mistakes until we die.

It was said in the sixties, 'tomorrow is the first day of the rest of your life,' it can therefore be another day just like all the others that you have had recently or you can change it by thinking, and therefore vibrating differently. And you do this when you embrace the moment – that's not the past – that's not the future – it is right now.

The more they damaged you are the more difficult it will be, but you and only you can do it. Imagine what you could be if you lived without fear, all that lost potential power waiting to be reclaimed. Not the genuine apprehension we feel for example; when we cross a busy road … but the rubbish implanted in our heads by the programmers.

To be YOU … without masks … without fear.

That is freedom.

I feel both of the following quotes reflect freedom. In a similar way they are both saying the same thing. These are the principles we need to go towards. Thinking not through those that manipulate us for their own ends, but for ourselves collectively and as individuals.

As a woman I have no country. As a woman my country is the whole world.

Virginia Woolf.

My heritage is the heritage of all humanity. The country of my ancestors is the planet Earth. I ain't no minority. I'm part of the human race.

Jim VanDenAkker.

Big Government and Big Business … will try to impose social and cultural uniformity upon adults and their children. To achieve this they will (unless prevented) make use of all the mind-manipulating techniques at their disposal and will not hesitate to reinforce these methods of non-rational persuasion by economic coercion and threats of physical violence. If this kind of tyranny is to be avoided, we must begin without delay to educate ourselves and our children for freedom and self-government. Such an education for freedom should be... first of all in facts and in values – the facts of individual diversity and genetic uniqueness and the values of freedom, tolerance and mutual charity, which are the ethical corollaries of these facts.

Aldous Huxley. Brave New World Revisited.

All those institutions that we have given our power away to – corporations, governments, churches, etc, – have largely enslaved us with our own power. The only path to true freedom is by reclaiming our power, responsibility and sovereignty, and doing it lovingly.

Wade Frazier.

The greatest gift we can give our children is the freedom to think for themselves, even if, outrage of outrage, we don't agree with what they believe; to encourage them to question, read, and come to their own conclusions, to respect their right to be different without felling the need to impose our beliefs because we know best. Of course, it has to be pointed out when their behaviour is unfairly and unpleasantly affecting others, but that's not what I mean here. I mean to encourage them to free their minds and to be open to all possibilities. Far too many parents are more concerned with what their neighbours, friends, and the teachers will think of their children, rather than what the children think of themselves and the world. We need to set the children free to think the officially unthinkable and question at every turn the officially unquestionable.

David Icke. Children of the Matrix.

The freedom we inherently yearn for is the freedom to be ourselves. Freedom is not something that can be imposed upon us because that is to contradict the very meaning of what it is to be free.

Freedom cannot be given to us no matter how many times politicians repeat the word.

The freedom we seek is to be ourselves and therefore to express ourselves. The sad truth is that we have lost sight of what real freedom is. The fact that most of the time we are acting to please others, parents, teachers, friends, everyone that is except ourselves. That small voice we heard as children merely whispers to us occasionally.

Now and for as long as we believe consciously that we are free, we are destined to remain stuck. As in all things, whatever they are, we need to be aware of a problem before we can act upon it. We live in dangerous times and we have given away our power to those that control us.

Our fear makes us sick and all the negative emotions we have hold us back from genuine freedom. Freedom is to be released from fear.

I'm the one that has to die when it's time for me to die, so let me live my life the way I want to.

Jimi Hendrix

You are the unchanging awareness in which all activity takes place. To deny this is to suffer, to know this is freedom. It is not difficult to realise this, because it is your true nature. Simple inquire, 'who am I? And watch carefully. Do not make effort and do not stir a thought. Look within, approach with all devotions and stay as heart. Keep vigilant and you will see that nothing will arise. This is the trick of how to keep the mind quiet and how to win freedom. This doesn't take time because freedom is always here. You simply have to watch: Where does mind arise from? Where does thought come from? What is the source of this thought? Then you will see that you have always been free and that everything has been a dream.

H W L Poonja (Papaji).

Let freedom ring!

Dr Martin Luther King.

Emancipate yourself from mental slavery,
None but ourselves can free our minds…

Bob Marley. Redemption Song.

Something about the enormity and beauty of nature makes the self, feel smaller and less important.

A walk on a quiet beach, a view of the sky away from all distraction, the magic of being in a forest, provide us with the opportunity to open ourselves up. In the doing we shrink the self; we reduce the ego.

'The only thing that burns in Hell is the part of you that won't let go of life, your memories, your attachments. They burn them all away. But they're not punishing you,' he said. 'They're freeing your soul. So, if you're frightened of dying and … and you're holding on, you'll see devils tearing your life away. But if you've made your peace, then the devils are really angels, freeing you from the earth.'

Jacobs Ladder 1990.

When your impurities are burned through suffering.

You will become more lustrous than a mirror in the sun, more pure than the most perfect of pearls.

Lalleshwari. Spiritual Poems by a Great Siddha Yogini.

We are informed that death is a transition; in religious terms life is everlasting. Without the soul dead is dead, other than the atoms in our bodies going on to create other *things* in the world.

The concept of soul cannot be proven in this five-sense reality however through spiritual practices, the quelling of the ego, the use of drugs, meditation, ecstatic states and the awe of nature can give us moments, glimpses and firm realisation of the genuine freedom that awaits us all.

Friendship

I no doubt deserved my enemies but I don't believe I deserved my friends.

George Bernard Shaw.

Any one can sympathise with the sufferings of a friend, but it requires a very fine nature to sympathise with a friend's success.

Oscar Wilde.

We cherish our friends not for their ability to amuse us, but for our ability to amuse them.

Evelyn Waugh.

He who has a thousand friends has not a friend to spare.
And he who has one enemy will meet him everywhere.

Ali ibn Abi Talib.

Don't walk in front of me, I may not follow; don't walk behind me. I may not lead;
Walk beside me, and just be my friend.

Albert Camus

It's much easier to turn a friendship into love, than love into friendship.

Proverb.

It is one of the severest tests of friendship to tell your friend his faults. So to love a man that you cannot bear to see a stain upon him, and to speak painful truth through loving words, that is friendship.

Henry Ward Beecher.

We sometimes encounter people, even perfect strangers, who begin to interest us at first sight, somehow suddenly, all at once, before a word has been spoken.

Dostoevsky. Crime and Punishment.

God

God does not play dice.

Albert Einstein.

God does not play dice with the Universe. He plays an ineffable game of his own devising, which might be compared, from the perspective of the players, (i.e. everybody), to being involved in an obscure and complex version of poker in a pitch-dark room, with blank cards, for infinite stakes, with a Dealer who won't tell you the rules, and who smiles all the time.

Neil Gaiman.

If God lived on Earth people would break his windows.

Jewish Proverb.

I imagine that God speaks to me, saying simply, 'I kept calling to you, and you did not come ..

And I answer quite naturally, 'I couldn't until I knew there was nowhere else to go.

Florida Scott Maxwell. The Measure of my Days.

God gives every bird its food, but He does not throw it in its nest.

J G Holland.

Perhaps the most common misconception is the concept of Ten Commandments! God does not command. And God does not dictate. Nor does God punish and reward. If one sticks their finger into a wall socket and electrocutes oneself, it's illogical to say that electricity punished the person.

The Power of Kabbalah. Yehuda. Berg.

Religion has actually convinced people that there's an invisible man – living in the sky – who watches everything you do, every minute of every day. And the invisible man has a special list of ten things he does not want you to do. And if you do any of these ten things, he has a special place, full of fire and smoke and burning and torture and anguish, where he will send you to live and suffer and burn and choke and scream and cry forever and ever 'til the end of time ... but He loves you!

George Carlin

Only the perfect, nondualistic oneness of god is real, and nothing else is real.

G R Renard. Your Immortal Reality.

Global warming

Planet Earth is 4,600 million years old.

If we condense this inconceivable time span into an understandable concept we can liken Earth to a person of forty-six years of age.

Nothing is known about the first seven years of this person's life and whilst only scattered information exists about the middle span, we know that only at the age of forty- two did the Earth begin to flower.

Dinosaurs and the great reptiles did not appear until one year ago when the planet was forty-five. Mammals arrived only eight months ago; in the middle of last week man-like apes evolved into ape-like men, and at the week –end the last ice age enveloped the Earth.

Modern man has been around for four hours; during the last hour man discovered agriculture. The industrial revolution began just a minute ago. During those sixty seconds of biological time, modern man has made a rubbish tip from paradise.

He has multiplied his numbers to plague proportions, caused the extinction of hundreds of species of animals, ransacked the planet for fuel, and now stands like some brutish infant gloating on his meteoric rise to ascendancy on the brink of the final mass extinction and of effectively destroying this oasis of life in the solar system.

Whilst it might have a few facts wrong and subsequent information puts a few holes in this piece, it is about 25 years old and was circulated by Greenpeace.

The frightening part is, that things in that short 25 years have become much worse.

The words of a 'savage' and a prophet.

'How can you buy and sell the sky?
We do not own the freshness of the air or the sparkle on the water.
How then can you buy them from us?

Every part of the Earth is sacred to my people, holy in their memory and experience.

We know the white man does not understand our ways. He is a stranger who comes in the night and takes from the land whatever he needs. The Earth is not his friend but his enemy, and when he has conquered he moves on.

He kidnaps the Earth from his children.

His appetite will devour the Earth and leave behind a desert.

If the beasts were gone we would die from a great loneliness of the spirit, for whatever befalls the Earth, befalls the children of the Earth.'

Chief Seattle 1854.

I can't read those words and not be filled with the awe of them. It is both poetry and prediction and I suppose that's why they fill me with sadness – until I have a word with myself.

Government

It is dangerous to be right when the government is wrong.

Voltaire.

We cannot keep blaming the government. They have taken our power only because we have given it away. There is a pyramid of power and at the top of that pyramid lies the majority of the tools that control us. These tools are wealth and information.

We have to remember that we hold this pyramid up and we have to realise that those in power will do everything they are able to retain their power.

We in turn are ruled on a diet of fear and have become preoccupied by our own material selves. We must aspire, keep our jobs and tow the line; the consequences for being truly individual are too onerous to comprehend.

Materialism has become a toxic fixation and the concept of nationalism is nothing more than materialism at its core, it is essentially a status symbol in our list of personal attachments, formed by our individual and collective egos in order that we might define ourselves. A division that separates mankind, ultimately for our salvation mankind needs to come together and know that …

We are all one consciousness, experiencing our individual lives subjectively (personally).

The true course of freedom is not to have it thrust upon us by those that really do not care about us. The true course of freedom is to work for a higher purpose. We must clear our muddled consciousness and stop segregation, and the resultant construction of boxes.

All men are equal, but I don't want to be told in a demonstration of pure hypocrisy, by a man who owned hundreds of slaves producing a toxin (sugar) that has no know benefit and in fact causes harm, upon which empires have been built and even if he was the third President of the United States of America, his arse, yours and mine point downwards and he was just a man like you and I, and your buying into a corrupted programme if you believe anything else to be true.

'All men are equal,' may be a great vote catcher but it's a lie that supports the structure we have made, words of truth distorted and used against us in the usual way.

Government decisions that take us to war on a foreign shore make this world no safer and we are fools to think what we destroy elsewhere in human life will not make its way back to us. The horror we watch on our TV screens is no less significant be it Baghdad, Beirut, Birmingham or Boston.

If we don't like what's happening at the very least we should see it for what it is. If we can and at last clear our minds and open them, it will help us to channel positive energy toward a higher purpose, we will then allow connection to Universal Consciousness and we advance on our miraculous journey, this thing we call our life.

Only you can do it, 'they' are not going to do it for you – 'they' are too busy riding on our backs, bless them.

Grace

Grace is a state of flow. A person in a state of grace has forgotten about the self, there is no nervous worry or embarrassment; they are lost in a moment and doing a task without effort.

Athletes know this state of grace as 'the zone' where excellence becomes effortless, where all distractions disappear.

Grace can be defined as the state of total immersion in a task.

The experience is a glorious coming together of joy, even rapture and it is available to us by ecstatic lovemaking. So if your partner mentions at a critical moment that your ceiling needs painting then perhaps they are not in the zone.

If you are depressed or anxious there is no chance of entering a state of grace.

Take a moment to consider before it's too late
What befell us men of the human state?
What of reason and of the dignity of grace
Where is it that we're going and will we like the place?

I knocked on a friend's door one day; we had decided to embark on an epic adventure – we had it all planned – we were off to the pub. My friend opened the door in response to my knock and I was ushered inside, as I stepped into the house his wife smashed a plate she was taking out of the sink.

'Janice be careful!' He shouted over his shoulder in the direction of the kitchen.

'She's always breaking the dishes,' he informed me.

'Perhaps she doesn't like doing the washing-up?' I offered.

I was ignored – I am used to it.

Anyway off we went on our adventure, the half-a-click walk to the pub (now come on we had to negotiate a road that can sometimes get a little busy).

We do something well when we like what we are doing and conversely we usually don't perform at our best when we hate the task. When we perform what we are doing brilliantly and without effort we become lost in that moment and that is a state of grace.

I saw the definition of grace well depicted in the film, 'A River Runs Through It.' The film was made in 1992 and is the story of the MacLean family set in the beauty of Montana in the early 1920's.

The father of the family is a pastor and uses his love of dry fly-fishing to bond with and teach his two sons. The two boys are very different in character, Norman, the eldest one is a cerebral, steady guy and the other, Paul, is played brilliantly by Brad Pitt, he is a rebel who lives life on the edge. In the film there are no special effects, it has breathtaking visuals and Robert Redford directs it wonderfully. The film is a journey measuring their lives as seen through the eldest brothers eyes.

Fly-fishing is the bond these three men share. The ritual of these artists shows that you cannot just start thrashing away at the water and hope for the best, you need to be attuned to your environment; you need to be in the moment.

There is a point in the film where Norman, the eldest brother, realises that although he and his brother have had the same teaching and indeed teacher in the art of fly-fishing (so they know the same principals and deploy their knowledge with similar style), however Norman acknowledges he will never be quite as good as his younger brother, in the knowledge and realisation that Paul has that magical ability, to not only place the fly upon the water and lure the illusive wild brown trout to take the hook, but that he enters that place referred to as a state of grace.

If part of your search is for inner peace then this is a helpful film. For me, the river represents the line that separates life from death and memories from reality. This is a film that touches your heart and moves your mind. It was taken from a short story by Norman MacLean and it closes with the following beautiful words.

'But when I am alone in the half-light of the canyon, all existence seems to fade to a being with my soul and memories. And the sound of the Big Black Foot River and a four count rhythm and the hope that a fish will rise. Eventually, all things merge into one, and a river runs through it. The river was cut by the World's greatest flood and runs over rocks from the basement of time. On some of the rocks are timeless raindrops. Under the rocks are the words, and some of the words are theirs. I am haunted by waters.'

A River Runs Through It.

Gracefulness has been defined to be the outward expression of the inward harmony of the soul.

William Hazlitt.

If we were free, really free to have choices, to try out new 'things,' we would all discover the things we really liked to do. And if we found something we really liked to do we would be good at that thing. If we were good at something within that something whatever that something might be – we would find success and we would perform that something with grace.

Grasping or Greed

Greed is a fat demon with a small mouth and whatever you feed it, it is never enough.

Janwillem Van De Wetering

Grasping is the source of many of our problems. Once again it is much more of a Western problem than Eastern. I have found that some of the loveliest and most gracious people in the World are those who are born and will likely die in what we would call poverty.

Our concept of poverty is to be poor but perhaps poverty or 'poorness' could also be applied to those who are bereft of any spirituality.

Surely to be unkind or cruel to someone or something is to be poor?

One of the essential doctrines of Buddhism expresses the idea that without exception everything is constantly in flux, that is to say it is changing. Our own lives demonstrate this change; we are born, we age, we die and on our journey we learn and we grow.

Impermanence is the word that describes this because *everything* is impermanent. Nothing stays the same; for each there is a season. Therefore attachment to anything is futile and to resist this will result in suffering. Since impermanence to us spells anguish, we greedily grasp onto things desperately, even though all things will change. We are terrified of letting go, terrified in fact of living at all because learning to live is learning to let go.

This then is the irony of our struggle as we seek to prevent the naturalness of flow, we find this is this impossible, ironically it brings to us the pain we are trying to avoid. The intention behind grasping is not necessarily bad, there is nothing wrong with us as we try to be happy and our desire to feel joy, but what we try to grasp onto is by its very nature *ungraspable*.

Nothing remains the same and we can use impermanence as a tool to understand reality and gain liberating insight.

We should not say that because things are impermanent there is suffering, because without impermanence life is impossible and our suffering would never end, our children could not grow up, the seasons could not change, nothing would seem 'new' and the world could not improve. How long would you seriously want to live in an unchanging world, in Groundhog Day?

Your suffering is not because things are impermanent it is because you believe things are permanent and you therefore grasp and resist change. If a flower dies, you will not morn it's passing because you recognise flowers are impermanent. But when a person dies who you loved you suffer deeply. Look into impermanence and know that you should do your best to make all around you and all involved with you, happy.

To be aware of impermanence is to become positive, loving and wise. Impermanence is not a curse, impermanence is the way things are and impermanence is the instrument for our liberation.

A Buddhist saying points out that you cannot wash the same dirty hand twice in the same running river.

To think upon impermanence is not enough. You have to practice and work with it in your life. Try an experiment; pick up a coin and imagine that it represents the object you are trying to grasp.

Hold it tightly in your fist and extend your arm with the palm of your hand facing the ground. When you open your hand or let go your grip you will drop what you are clinging onto.

That's why you grasp.

The alternative is to turn your fist upwards to the sky and open your fist. The coin still rests in the palm of your hand. You have let go, the coin is still yours and you still exert control over it.

Congratulations, you have accepted impermanence without grasping.

Greed drives us toward external objects, conquests, symbols, status or money, all in an attempt to fill a void within us: the emptiness of our egoism. This ego edifice we build, this grand construction of who we are, this false self-image, when pricked shows its true colours. Look just beneath its surface and you will see nothing there. We desperately try to assuage that insatiable emptiness in a futile attempt to mask our inner abyss with concrete material goods and symbols.

But that ego emptiness reflects the true emptiness inside us: the real void that opens to the depths through which the voice of God approaches us. Greed cannot console that void, nor even approach it. This points toward transforming our greed from grasping at external fulfilment to searching for inner fulfilment, the only real fulfilment, to open our channel to the depths, to a genuine love for those around us and for God.

But even here, the insidious temptation to grasp enters. Spiritual greed runs after states and experiences, wants spiritual status so that one can brag or preen in front of others or to oneself. Of course, this is just another absurd, ego-centered distortion of true spirituality. We cannot extract wages from God, like a day labourer. We seek a simple life in the spirit for its own sake; love is its own reward. Only the depths of the spirit can fill our emptiness and offer true contentment, as greed transforms into active service for the benefit of our neighbour.

Inner Frontier.

The form of grasping or not letting go is prevalent in many of us, (immediately forgive yourself – you were programmed).

Retaining the past and dwelling there will hold us back.

The past is written and gone, this moment, *right now* is all that we own, it is everything we have, everything else is an assumption, it is called 'the present,' because it is a gift to us. The future is open to conjecture and romance and only what we do in this moment can affect what will be. In any event, there is no such thing as the future because when we arrive there – it is now.

We would find much more of the positives in life if we could bind ourselves to the present and live in the moment, this is where children and animals live and we call them carefree.

As conditioning takes hold of us and as our ego grows, we find ourselves alternating between the past and the future.

Hanging onto the old ways, the beliefs, the habits, the guilt, the regrets and the heartaches can only hold us back. The only thing holding us back are the fears created and manifested in own minds.

When we stop grasping and let go new doors open, new sights and sounds, new friends and new opportunities, a whole Universe of awareness is made available. It is our birthright and we are robbed of what is ours by overwhelming conditioning, grooming, programming.

You can let go of feeling bad about yourself; guilt is a total bummer and such a negative form of programming. While we always do what we have always done a new door will never open to us and the past is destined to repeat itself.

Once we let go, not only do the doors come along but also we get to choose which one it is that we want to walk through.

We must let go of guilt and realise that no matter how much we suffer or feel the pain of a past wrongdoing there is absolutely nothing we can do about it.

It is time to grow from those mistakes and forgive others and ourselves and simply let go and move on.

So deal with guilt and all the other negative bedfellows that these emotions share because they make you vibrate badly, and in the process your sending out the wrong rockets of desire to a benign Universe and your reality is made worse and life in general is more difficult.

As long as we are prepared to beat ourselves up for a past deed or what someone we loved once did or said to us … as long as we feel this way we will individually and collectively destroy our progress. If we stop grasping onto negativity all that energy can be put to something of constructive value. Once you let go, you can heal. If you cannot see these facets in yourself, look at the lives of others around you. To put this into context remember that hating someone is like allowing them to rent space in your head – for free! That's a decent example of grasping.

Grasping takes many forms, it creates habit and tradition and that is not necessarily to our benefit. In order to grow spiritually we need to accept change however we are programmed to resist. Our ego centred self is the main obstacle to spiritual growth. It is our ego that presents us with trivial concerns and fears locking us into the material world of solidity and form. This is why we seek escape into other levels of consciousness where we vibrate differently. Release is available in many forms, through drugs, sexual ecstasy, meditation, dance and dream, to name a few.

Reality soon returns after our journey, bills to be paid, news to be absorbed, routine to be embraced, possessions to cling to and so our fears and worries return, preventing our transformation until the next time.

A spiritual path is tough, it requires time, dedication and self-denial. However it is left up to each of us as individuals to understand and it is highly unlikely, especially for those of us who live in the West, to be given the opportunity. Grasping is unhealthy in an ever changing environment because it is impossible. The motivating factor that generates the vast amount of energy we waste in the pursuit of grasping is our ego. Only when we see the ego for what it is can we permanantly escape and, until then, we are destined towards compromise.

Guilds and Clubs ... are we hung up on a word?

We are now fully programmed to view mention of words such as, cult or sect as evil.

Could we not just say 'an alternative collection of people who want something else?'

No, because the word cult has been repeated over and over again by the media to represent something we associate with evil.

No, guilds and clubs they are fine, they are 'good' they have nothing to do with cults, which by the way are bad, the same as sects, they are also bad.

Guilds are things that are attached to work, discipline and are places where a young master might join, become initiated through ritual, serve his apprenticeship and become a tradesman.

I wonder if the members of the Branch Davidian's had been named and tagged as a club or a guild – rather than a cult or a sect, the outcome might have been different and not have resulted in the slaughter of 80 or so innocent men, women and children on American soil with tanks and flamethrowers.

No, it is guilds and clubs because we all want to belong to something. It is strange how the assemblage of a few letters can communicate and provoke such powerful distinctions and represent such powerful meanings.

People are relentlessly guided by the drive to connect with others and that the majority of their thoughts, emotions, impulses and behaviours are at least rooted in that drive ... In that context, social exclusion or rejection is not simply one misfortune among many, nor just a sad bit of drama – it strikes at the very heart of what our psyche is designed for.

Prof R F Baumeister

Within Freemasonry, the French-Norman language is preserved in code words that remain in modern Masonry. There are many sources for proof that the persecuted Knights Templar evolved and hid as a trade guild.

That trade guild was Freemasonry. The term freemason was derived from the French *frere* meaning brother and *macon* is another word for knight.

The links that show freemasonry is an ancient brotherhood dating back thousands of years are irrefutable. Anyone investigating the structure quickly realises that even the most senior practitioners have virtually no idea of the significance of their practices and apparently weird rituals.

Freemasonry is structured into a series of degrees that serve to provide through initiation a knowledge of advancement as the initiate advanced from the first degree upwards.

It is suggested that there are 33 degrees in total, it has also been asserted that there are levels above 33 degrees but understandably in a secret society it follows that the further one looks up its pyramidal construction, the less one is likely to find out.

The knowledge and power of the world is held by a select few.

Power is knowledge. A doctor might demonstrate this; with his knowledge of medicine and the human body, he has the power to diagnose and heal others.

A man with great knowledge only retains the mastery of power if he retains that knowledge by keeping it to himself. If you are the only doctor in the village you have power, if everyone has your knowledge then everyone is a doctor and as a result the doctor becomes less important.

Power has been kept from us for as long as we can trace back in time, held in secret and used to control us.

Skull and Bones

In the early 1830's a Yale student named William H Russell showed great promise as a leader. He was sent to Germany to study for a year.

The origin of this society begins at Yale University. Elihu Yale was born near Boston, educated in London, and served with the British East India Company.

When a person is initiated into Skull and Bones they are given a new name. Fifteen juniors are inducted every year; they go onto be leaders in society. This is just one example of the many grooming schools that are in existence, the further the initiate rises the more powerful he becomes.

Habit

We are absorbed by habit.

D Goleman.

One of the most important things to remember is to use your imagination to the hilt. This is your intuitive force telling you to soar, and the more you use it the higher you will go with it. Most people don't have it. They get caught up with movies, TV and beer and get accustomed to habit. Habit is a very bad thing even if it's a good habit. For instance, in going to work every day, go by a different route, because adventure may be just around the corner. If you think anything can happen, it will.

Be an individual; think with your imagination.

Guru Rhh.

The Russian scientist Pavlov conducted one of psychology's most famous experiments in classic conditioning. The experiment was simple but it says much about programming and the resultant habits that are formed.

Pavlov rang a bell to signal to his dogs that food was ready. The dogs arrived in response to the bell and salivated in anticipation of their food. When the food was removed, the dogs still arrived on cue and still salivated whenever they heard the bell.

While writing this book I have unwittingly conducted a similar experiment. The front door of this house (in France where I'm writing this) has a bell that visitors ring. Luna, our dog, has learned quickly to bark on cue when a visitor rings the bell. Her hackles go up in response to the bell and she barks loudly at the inside of the door. Great, I was thinking, she is proving a good watchdog. However there is an old French clock standing in the hall and I thought I would wind it up as it hasn't had a run in a while.

So I turned the winder and lifted the lead weight up, the pendulum was kick-started and the old girl was brought back to life, she gives out a therapeutic 'tic-tock' which is soothing sound. But I had forgotten that once you wind the clock up it chimes every fifteen minutes, I mean it properly chimes and you're probably ahead of me here but every time the clock chimes, the dog barks her 'there-is-someone-at-the-door' routine. That's every fifteen minutes for the last three days, even (bless) fifteen minutes past five in the morning.

So Mr Pavlov and me have proven that dogs can be trained with bells. But what I desperately need to know now is how do I un-train them? Does anyone know if Mr Pavlov is still about and whether or not he takes personal calls?

This type of reflex process is what motivates the marketing executive, the advertiser and the retailer. They know associations can be made and fortified easily. The smell of coffee as you walk into a house for sale, gives one the feeling of relaxation and homeliness. The smell of baking may trigger thoughts of the kitchen at home in childhood and therefore of love and care. Our brain duly defaults to these images and we become more readily seduced.

'Old habits die hard,' as the old adage states. The disconcerting prospect is that these messages that go straight into our unconsciousness do not depend upon us doing anything. The simple scientific reason is this: the brain is a mass of millions of neural pathways, with each idea or memory moving along its own path. Whenever we do something new, we create a new neural pathway so we can re-access that experience again more easily. Each time we repeat a particular behaviour, we strengthen the associated neural pathway, just as when you walk down a path through a field it becomes a clearer path.

Research has shown that these neural pathways in the brain actually get physically larger through repetition of behaviour. That is how people become 'hard-wired' to certain automatic behaviours, such as smoking and overeating. We can use that same mental architecture to design pathways to success and happiness, and to create associations that allow us to 'switch on,' certain feelings whenever we want them.
Paul McKenna. Change Your Life in 7 days.

In short, habit is a double-edged sword and impossible to ignore. On one hand and because it is impossible to respond to each and every fragment of sensory information that we are bombarded with, it therefore provides us with freedom from sensory overload. But on the other hand, it can trap us into becoming set in our ways in a series of routines and ruts and once trapped into habit we embrace one of our greatest problems; a lack of mindfulness.

The reason a habit becomes a habit is more easily understood when one understands that the brain seeks to unclutter itself in order it might concentrate elsewhere. So habits become attached to us and manifest in essence, because it's easy.

Happiness

What fun it would be if one didn't have to think about happiness

Aldous Huxley. Brave New World.

If you depend on someone for your happiness you are becoming a slave, you are becoming dependent, you are creating bondage.

And if you depend on so many people; they all become subtle masters, they all exploit you in return.

Bhagwan Shree Rajneesh. The Book of the Books.

It was on the news this week (because a ventriloquists dummy with a tie on and a pretty lady with a face full of botox told me so – so that's official right): Pentecost Island is both one of the poorest and happiest places on the planet.

Penticost Island is in the Pacific, the people who live there have no money instead they use pigs teeth as a means of barter, The Chief runs the bank which stores the surplus. They have no police, no crime and no tax and they don't understand the concept of interest on the borrowing of pig's teeth when they need funds.

Please try and keep this to yourself – I don't really want to be disturbed by loads of tourists when I move there tomorrow.

Make happy those who are near, and those who are far will come.

Proverb.

St Paul quotes Jesus as having said that 'it is more blessed to give than to receive (Acts 20:35). One meaning of 'bless' is 'to confer happiness or prosperity upon.' Does helping others really confer happiness or prosperity on the helper? I know of no evidence showing that altruists gain money from their altruism, but the evidence suggests that they often gain happiness. People who do volunteer work are happier and healthier than those who don't; but as always; we have to contend with the problem of reverse correlation: congenitally happy people are just plain nicer to begin with, so their volunteer work may be a consequence of their happiness, not a cause.

The Happiness Hypothesis. Jonathan Haidt.

In his book, Jonathan Haidt also tells of a psychologist, Alice Isen, who has conducted more random acts of kindness than any other in her profession. Through the distribution of sweets, stationary and pictures that warm the heart, she has consistently demonstrated that happy people are kinder and more helpful.

Many years ago a survey shown on television showed shoppers being interviewed as they came out of a supermarket. All customers at the checkout were dealt with the same way, but with one exception – as the girl on the till handed shoppers their change she touched them on the hand.

At the exit those that were not touched reported a varying degree of satisfaction with their experience of shopping, but what became apparent when those that had been touched, (even though it was just a brush of the checkout-girl's finger on their hand) they reported that their shopping had been a more happy and pleasurable experience.

Too often we underestimate the power of a touch, a smile, a kind word, a listening ear, an honest compliment, or the smallest act of caring, all of which have the potential to turn a life around.

Leo Buscaglia.

I've learned that people will forget what you said, people will forget what you did, but people will never forget how you made them feel.

May Angelou.

Laughter is a state of mind. It is a victory over fear. It is an affirmation – a great big 'YES' for celebrating life.

Robert Holden. Of The Happiness Project.

I have now reigned about fifty years in victory or peace, beloved by my subjects, dreaded by my enemies, and respected by my allies. Riches and honours, power and pleasure, have waited on my call, nor does any earthly blessing appear to have been wanting to my felicity. In this situation, I have diligently numbered the days of pure and genuine happiness, which have fallen to my lot. They amount to fourteen.

Abd Er-Rahman III of Spain. (960 C.E).

Success is not the key to happiness. Happiness is the key to success. If you love what you are doing, you will be successful.

Albert Schweitzer.

Many of us pursue happiness and believe it is the ultimate goal. However happiness is an emotion, it is a state of mind; it is a form of awareness.

Happiness can be a mask and behind the mask there could be massive amounts of pain. Happiness on this level is not authentic, authentic happiness is to be in the moment … to be present, happiness can be found in

The sight of a flower,

The smell of the sea,

The touch of a friend.

But these three wonderful sensory gifts can also make someone else very miserable, because another individual might take these contradictory views;

– Flowers are to be avoided as they bring on my hay fever.

– My best friend was drowned in a boat at sea.

– I really did resent something my friend said the last time we met, until we are resolved, I don't want to be touched.

In other words happiness is there to be felt by all of us, but it is only yours to define.

We might think that material gain will bring us happiness, but the feeling soon diminishes and we are off again in pursuit of something else we believe will make us happy. There are many times you are happy and fail to be aware of it. Perhaps you have been working in the garden with no interruptions for a while, it is only when you are washing your hands that you realise you were happy and it had nothing to do with anyone else.

The only thing we actually own is this moment, right 'now,' this instant because whoever you are; rich man, poor man, beggarman or thief, you cannot even guarantee that you will draw your next breath.

And so to be happy in this moment is an emotion that often goes unnoticed and therefore passes us by.

Building the expectation that someone else can make you happy is a recipe for disaster. Happiness starts within, it is how you feel and it vibrates and emanates from inside and it affects, alters and touches everything and everyone around us.

You can't make someone else happy unless you're ok.

Two strangers were walking toward each other along a quiet country road. As they drew near to each other one stranger said to the other.

'What are the people like in the village you have just left behind you?'

'I didn't like them, they were miserable, they never smiled, they were aggressive, I felt intimidated and they kept taking behind my back,' the other stranger replied, 'tell me what were the people like in the village that you just left?'

'Oh,' replied the first stranger, 'I think you will find them just the same.'

This story shows how we create the circumstances that surround us. If you walk around with a frown you are projecting fear to others through a low vibrational frequency, conversely when you smile your vibration is more akin to love and you will experience very different feedback from the people that you encounter, as result your world will be a very different place.

Projection in the Freudian sense suggests for example, an individual who possesses malicious characteristics, but is unwilling or unable to see himself as the protagonist.

Being blind to seeing an undesirable, subconscious trait in ones-self could be shown in a person who accuses other people of being hostile when it is they who are the aggressor. Or someone who has problems with jealousy in their lives is projecting fear formed of his own self-doubts.

Projection represents placing onto others what is actually a trait manifested within ourselves and is buried in our subconsciousness.

Our hero's are what we would aspire to be because we admire and respect their attributes and are drawn to their qualities, that which we dislike or hate in others is prevalent and is rising in ourselves.

And when we go digging within our minds in this particular trench we are best advised, to take the honesty shovel with us.

Happiness is nothing more than good health and a bad memory.

The best remedy for those who are afraid, lonely or unhappy is to go outside, somewhere where they can be quiet, alone with the heavens, nature and God. Because only then does one feel that all is as it should be and that God wishes to see people happy, amidst the simple beauty of nature.

Anne Frank.

Remember that as a teenager you are in the last stage of your life when you will be happy to hear the phone is for you.

Fran Leibowitz.

Happiness is the meaning and the purpose of life, the whole aim and end of human existence.

Aristotle.

History

I wish they would teach real history as we are growing up, instead we teach a corrupted version because history is written by the winner. As a result we are taught and we teach a sanitised version.

History will be kind to me for I intend to write it.

Winston Churchill

The two comments above tell the truth of history, it is biased and it is largely untrue. The propaganda that runs through history alone is incredible. The truth of history is in absence if we only hear the winner's version. The inhabitants of the lands that have been conquered don't get to tell their stories ... they don't even get to tell their hi – stories.

It is sad fact that books are burned as a standard practice, a new religion is served up, new culture and even new language is taught as the new conquerors eradicate one civilisation in favour of their own. The history we learn in school and read in books is at best one-sided and is at worst, a blanket soaked in blood.

Read no history; nothing but biography, for that is life without theory.

Benjamin Disraeli.

Horoscopes

Isaac Newton wrote a book called Principia, I think he intended it to be difficult to read and understand, it contains his three laws of motion,

1/ An object pushed in a certain direction will continue to move in a straight line unless another force acts upon it to slow or deflect it.

2/ Every action has an opposite and equal reaction.

3/ Every object in the Universe has an effect upon something else and we call this universal law gravity.

We were taught in school that this last law was discovered when Newton sat under a tree and watched an apple fall to the ground.

These laws explain so much of how the Universe works. How our moon and sun pull the tides in and out for example. The force of the moon, the sun and the other celestial bodies, have a massive influence over us. As we are predominantly water this is not surprising, statistics inform us that suicide rates increase when there is a full moon, this is lunacy at work. The female menstruation cycle occurs in conjunction with the cycle of the moon.

Without doubt, the planets have an effect upon us, indeed we are affected, and therefore influenced, in many ways. But we know little about how we are affected at a quantum level where particles are influenced by one another regardless of distance. We have discovered recently what ancient shaman knew of; that our DNA receives and transmits information as it processes Consciousness.

'Hermetica' represents the forty-two sacred books of wisdom allegedly written by Hermes. The books combine the mythological wisdom and attributes of the Egyptian god Thoth and the Greek god Hermes.

These dual gods were considered inseparable, Thoth governed over all mystical wisdom, magic and writings, and he was also a healer. Hermes was the governor of universal wisdom and the patron of magic.

The combined myths of these two gods state that Hermes and Thoth revealed to mankind the gift of healing, magic, writing, astrology, philosophy and science.

The influence of these gods has been tremendous on the development of Western occultism and magic.

The books were originally written on papyrus, most of them are thought to have been burned in the royal libraries in Alexander. Rumour of surviving books say they lie buried in the desert, their location is only known to few initiates of the mystery schools and ancient secret cults.

The most famous remnant of these writings is called the Emerald Tablet, upon this tablet is one of the most thought provoking incites into how this Universe is constructed. It states the following;

'True, without falsehood, certain and most true, that which is above is the same as that which is below, and that which is below is the same as that which is above, for the performance of miracles of the One Thing. And as all things are from the One, by the meditation of One, so all things have their birth from this One Thing by adaptation. The Sun is its Father, the Moon its Mother, the Wind carries it in its belly, and its nurse is the Earth. This is the Father of all perfection, or consummation of the whole world. Its power is integrating, if it be turned into earth.'

The Emerald Tablets

'As above so below.'

Some believe that this phrase could be the revelation of all revelations. It is claimed that all systems of magic function by this formula. Macrocosmos is the same as microcosmos. The Universe is God – God is the same as man – man is the same as the cells that built us – the cells are made of atoms and so on.

Everything affects everything else, in other words we are all One and everything is connected.

We inhabit a frequency, a tiny range in a vast spectrum, this is where we live and we can easily lift that vibrational level and 'see' beyond the self-imposed prison we now find ourselves trapped in.

We look to the enormity of the heavens through the macro of telescopes and have come to realise that everything affects everything else. We look down a microscope to the micro and witness similar events.

No matter how much we magnify outwards or reduce downwards, we cannot see nor understand where it begins or ends. The more we probe outward or inward the questions just keep coming. Until that is, we go below the atom and engage the world of quantum physics, it is here that the rules change again.

We don't hear too much about quantum physics because it turns all conventional rules to nonsense. Once we start to understand the infitessimally small we will fully realise how mind affects matter, this realisation will be a quantum leap forward in our evolution and enlightenment. I honestly believe that day is coming soon because more and more people are waking up.

One of the most beautiful things about physics is its ongoing quest to find simple rules that describe the behaviour of very small simple objects. Once found, these rules can often be scaled up to describe the monumental systems in the real world.

Tim Berners-Lee. Weaving the Web.

'All things have their birth from this the One thing by adaptation,' is another way of saying that we are all One Consciousness.

Everyone has the ability to perform magic. Some are more proficient or adept than others, many are unaware they are performing it.

Wizards come in the most surprising garb.

When someone speaks to you and gives you a kind word that is a form of witchcraft, it has a direct effect and you will feel a transition.

That is all that magic is … manipulation.

When we gossip in a negative way about someone, that is also magic because there is an effect, an alteration and a transition. We are all capable of this and we all practice it, but we call those who we consider more practised, names like wizard, witch, magician, shaman and witchdoctor.

To perform a magical act is to cause an effect or a transformation without physical contact. This act is conjured in the mind as an act of will for it to allow it to occur, the practitioner needs the will to make it happen and the certainty that it will happen. Some might call this a miracle and be in awe of the outcome, however this is to fail to comprehend the power of external forces at work or in other words, magic.

Powerful magic is performed in ritual. People who perform magic are called masters because they have mastered themselves and the Universe. We can only hope we are not being abused by their power, which they draw from being attuned to Universal Source Energy or Consciousness.

They are acting synchronistically. To get in synchronicity with the creative force we all need to access the higher levels of spiritual function, the spiritual blocker is fear.

(We discussed this earlier, I hope your not skipping – I am joking – I am grateful we are communicating).

We are taught to believe that our progress on this earth has been gradual, the last fifty years have seen an acceleration in that process, with the invention of such things as flight and technical advancements, communications and so on.

50 years ago when Patrick Moore, first transmitted his programme 'The Sky at Night' on television there was not one satellite in operation, now there are thousands orbiting our skies. The sobering thought is that most of those satellites point inward – towards us.

The more we understand of ancient civilisations the more we realise they knew much more than the mainstream would have us believe. There are examples of wonderful ancient technology in evidence wherever we go in the world, very often these examples are in plain sight however when we cannot come up with explanations of the construction or use of these examples, we consign them to the point of ignoring them as we cannot make them fit into our version of history;

In an ancient city in eastern Lebanon called Baalbeck, there is a hewn block of granite that weighs an estimated 1,000 tons. In the Temple of Jupiter there are three stones raised in a wall estimated at about 800 tons each. The Nazca lines in Peru; many of the 300 figures are many kilometres long, and are etched into the surface but are only clearly visible from the air. The Great Pyramid at Giza, this 6.5 million ton construction covering 13 acres is the most discussed anomaly we have, it just defies description and we could not build it today, we have not got the technology.

In a groundbreaking book called 'Fingerprints of the Gods,' by Graham Hancock, the author shows some of the reasons why those that went before us on this planet knew a great deal more than we give them credit for.

Hancock shows us for example, that ancient man knew of the landmass under Antarctica. By combining, NASSA's satellite imagery, the results of modern seismology and copies of what became known as the Piri Reis maps, he demonstrates the ancients knew of this landmass hidden under the ice. The maps that were found in Iraq by Reis in 1545 were drawn on gazelle skins and are believed to be reproductions of much older charts.

From Hancock's findings we can only conclude that the land under the Antarctic, which showed riverbeds, rock formation and even palm trees, was either not covered in masses of ice or the unlikely proposition; that the ancients had some way of seeing through this covering.

This was the first book that gave me an interest in the Great Pyramid of Giza. This gave me the appetite to read more on the subject. The Great Pyramid is the last remaining of the Seven Wonders of the Ancient World and much has been written and postulated on the subject; how was it built, who built it, what was its purpose?

In another book entitled The Great Pyramid Decoded, by Peter Lemesurier, the author shows how a cycle known as the precession of the equinoxes takes place.

This is the one of the cycles of the earth, which covers a period of about 26,000 years; this massive time span was known by ancient people and is locked into the geometry of the Great Pyramid.

Through these and other books it is shown that, the ancient civilisations of Babylon, Egypt, and South America used this immense span of time and encoded it into their buildings. In this modern age, we only learned of this precession through the use of computers.

To understand precession we need to know that the Earth rotates on its axis but it also wobbles, this wobble is caused by the gravitational pull of the other celestial bodies upon it. The Sun and Moon are the most influential because of their size and proximity to us. The planets cause the Earth to wobble; with the result it sways clockwise, like the wobble on a spinning top as it slows down.

This wobble, or sway is called the precession of the equinoxes or 'The Great Year.' This phenomenon is difficult to visualise and there is much information out there for those who want to discover more about this 26,000-year cycle. Nevertheless the fact that ancient people knew of this incredible time span and encoded it into their buildings is something modern experts do not have a satisfactory explanation for.

Viewed from the Earth, the Sun moves around the ecliptic one full circuit every year. Twice a year, day and night are equal; we call this the equinox, the Sun rises exactly in the east and sets exactly in the west.

The ancients dissected the 26,000 precessional cycle into 12 houses, and … as above so below … we have the influence of energy upon the Earth shown as 2160 years (26,000 years divided by 12 houses).

These influences characterised by what we know of history reveal a pattern and this is the theory of horoscopes; where each of us is supposed to be born under a particular star sign when we divide out our 12 month year into 12 segments, from where astrologers assert we get out 12 star or sun signs.

I am unsure about the relevance of astrological sun signs as a method of ascribing traits to us as individuals, the subject is open to much conjecture and everyone will have their own opinions.

But it is important to understand that the constellations and the zodiac are not the same thing, the confusion that exists is because they share the same name.

The astrology that is being dealt with here is to do with World Ages.

And the qualities of each age of 2160 years are quite clear in the influences that are brought to bear on us collectively.

What is also incredible are the beliefs of ancient peoples who were capable

of measuring 26,000-year cycles and the traits that each age seemed
the Earth.

Anyone who has heard of the musical Hair from the 60's will recall
'This is the Dawning of the Age of Aquarius.' We now find ourselve ... that
changing period. We are passing from the 2160-year cycle of Pieces and into
the Age of Aquarius, which will last the same period of time.

Dependent on who you listen to; this new age could be anything from
cataclysm to enlightenment; world war to world peace. Massive earth changes
from physical destruction, massive spiritual awakening towards our inherent
Oneness. But one thing is clear; this is a critical transformative period. The
influences that are listed below indicate even more profoundly that an old world
is dying and that we should prepare ourselves for a new one being born.

Perhaps the most difficult concept to fathom is the processional cycle of
26,000 years determined by the axis of the Earth carving a great circular arc in
the heavens known as the 26,000-year precession. In looking at and trying to
analyse the Mayan 2012 prediction, it shows how the rising sun on December
21st, 2012 will align itself directly with the centre of the entire galaxy. The
movement of Earth's axis changes our orientation to the galactic centre and this
opens the way for the start of a new world age ... a re-birth into an entirely
new participation into the greater whole.

This 2012 solar galactic alignment offers all humanity the opportunity to
assimilate the complete understanding of our place in the Universe; the
vibrations are with us now as more and more people search and ask for
meaning.

Despite the fear, the chemicals, the programming and all the other
influences that enable us to vibrate badly we are still able to attune to Creative
Conscious Source Energy and in spite of all the negativity that we are bathed
in, we should congratulate ourselves in that it seems that many people are
waking up.

As we near this important date and pass through it and on into the Age of
Aquarius we will find within us a growing realisation of Oneness and an
opportunity to become vastly more enlightened.

The opening of our higher, spiritual minds will give us the potential to
finally break from the chains of slavery that we now find ourselves in.

Unfortunately those who control and feed from us are also acutely aware
of our rapidly developing and more healthy mindset and this is why the agenda
is being ramped up as more subjugation and more control is levered upon us.
Our understanding of the appalling deceit and the complete 'wrongness' of our
structure will be clear for many more of us to see.

One perhaps could take the view that humanity has always been fixated with some future impending doom, could the reason for this to be yet another corrupted programme to keep us suitably absorbed? The opportunity to change occurs now and not at some point in the future. December 21st 2012 is a date we will hear more and more of as we move closer to it.

(And you thought the millennium bug was a fuss please note – you ain't seen nothing yet).

We should prepare ourselves for a plethora of 'experts' telling us to do everything from 'the sooner you get your microchip implanted the better,' to 'it's time to start building an ark.'

However and much more sinisterly there are going to be massive changes in the coming few years as the men behind the curtains have their agendas revealed, as their New World Order collapses and their structure and existence is threatened.

They of course are not alone, change will devalue and alter the values of billions people who cannot envisage or accept what has to happen in order for us to survive and prosper. But a new vibrational level is being offered up to us and as more and more people awaken it spreads a happy plague and we lift one another up to what must prevail, as it becomes more and more about 'us' than about 'I.'

This is not a time that people need to fear, we have been made to fear for long enough, what is about to be revealed is what has been hidden from us for long enough – love conquering fear.

Now that is a major cause for celebration.

One precession is coming to an end as Pisces accedes to Aquarius. This is what happens every 26,000 years as each house of the Zodiac is 30 degrees wide and it takes 1/12th of that time to move from one age to another – about 2160 years. Each of these periods seems to have typical traits when (just as the similarly and confusingly named horoscopes) the people of that age seem influenced to act in certain ways. 'As above so below.'

Leo to Cancer – the period of time over one precession of 2160 years when the sinking of the great Atlantic islands took place.

Cancer to Gemini – the next precession was the presumed striking of the earth by a comet or the catastrophic arrival of Venus took place. The age of Cancer lasted until Gemini entered.

Gemini (the heavenly twins) to Taurus – the beginning or regeneration of new civilisations in the ancient East.

Taurus (The Bull) started around 4400 BC – Aries – about 1875 BC –

A new series of floods and catastrophic earth changes. In the age of Taurus, when the Ancient peoples who lived in the lands we now call Egypt, the Pharaohs encouraged the people to worship the bull, which is the symbol of Taurus.

There was a massive conflict in the transitory period that led to the age of Aries. So started a period of conflict as the sheep took power away from the bull.

Aries (the Ram) started around 2300 BC – this age was influenced by Mars, the god of war, to Pisces (The Fishes) – the spread of Christianity.

Pisces (fish) began roughly in 1AD – the Age of Aquarius (the Water Carrier)

Heralded in by Jesus, in the age that followed Pisces took over, fishers of men turned to Jesus; the leader of the Piscean age with all the elements of individuality.

Much of the symbology surrounding this age included:

The fish symbol we see denoting a Christian placed on the back of cars.

The bishop's hat or mitre, which is a fish head, and the crook, he carries denoting the shepherding of his flock.

The parables of Jesus, many of which involved water. We have walking on water, water into wine, baptism and anointing with water.

The actions of the crossing of Aries into the Piscean age are clearly demonstrated. Jesus is the Lamb of God, in one of the stories from this time Jesus was said to have turned to the fishermen (Pisces) and invited them to leave their jobs and become disciples or fishers of men.

The age of the last three precessions represent the Holy Trinity; Aries the Age of the Father, Pisces the Age of the Son and Aquarius the Age of the Holy Spirit and reassuringly the Holy Spirit is all about love we just have to allow the wisdom of the Spirit to guide us, so this then is the dawning of the Age of Aquarius – the Age of Love should we attune to it.

Right now as Pisces accedes to Aquarius, we enter this new age. Aquarius traits are love, truth and brotherhood.

We are going to need all these qualities.

Aquarius then leads to Capricorn (the Goat) and that age will begin shortly after 4000 AD.

Listed here are the 2160 precessional years that are to come thereafter;

Sagittarius (the Archer)

Scorpio (the Scorpion)

Libra (the Scales)

Virgo (the Virgin)

Leo (the Lion).

Every civilisation sought to measure time, and since they lived under a blanket of stars they were consumed by the skies. Through the movement of the celestial bodies they saw how everything 'out there' influenced everything else and they knew that everything 'out there' affected them collectively and individually. They also knew that this same principle worked at a quantum level. They understood the world we now know of as quantum physics and they had knowledge of the DNA helix, which they demonstrated in their art, scripture, and fable, they knew far more than we are taught they knew.

They used the movement of everything 'out there' to measure time and to predict the arrival of the coming seasons and they used this ability to portend the future. The Mayan calendar, (the Long Count which measures The Great Year) stops in 2012. The critical midpoint between the age of Pisces and the Age of Aquarius is December 21st 2012. For some interpreters this is the end of days – the destruction of the planet. For others it is the dawning of a new age and the opportunity to set things right.

> *The truth about the Mayan calendar is really not difficult to understand. The problem is only that we have all been conditioned by a materialist mind that makes us look for the ultimate explanations in the material reality rather than in the divine plan. Needless to say, many, especially in the West, have egos that find it difficult to accept that they are subordinated to a divine plan that cannot even potentially be manipulated by physical means.*
>
> Carl Johan Calleman.

> *… And God said … let there be lights in the heavens to divide the day from night, and let them be for signs and for seasons and for days and for years …*
>
> Genesis 1.14. The creation of the Earth.

Although I accept that nothing is proven here, there are points worth considering; the Zodiac is divided into 12 houses, each of these houses or ages, is ascribed a sign, Pisces, Aquarius and so on.

Each of these ages clearly demonstrates influences and lasts for 2160 years, multiply 12 by 2160 and we get 25920 or one precession. This was the massive time scale the ancients measured with accuracy; it is recorded and proven they could do this (there are even greater and more vast scales of time measured in pre-history).

In the middle of the Zodiac sits the Sun, which is sometimes symbolised as a spider. The Zodiac is a complex symbol that can be interpreted many ways, for example, a cross dissects it, you have probably seen such examples, each section of the cross contains three houses, and these quarters are the four seasons of the year.

The cross also represents the winter and summer solstice, the time when the sun is at its highest and at its lowest in the sky.

The Holy Roman Empire worshiped the Sun until Constantine who was a sun worshiper, legalised Christianity for political reasons.

Constantine famously had a vision of the cross, it was revealed to him by the Sun. Thus another pretty dress was put on Sun worship to make it appear like Christianity.

We are inextricably linked to Summeria, Babylon, Egypt, Greece and Rome, and Sun worship was common to them all, they had all been progressively absorbed as each civilization took over the next.

Just as we appeared to take over America to subsequently appear to fail, and as Rome took over England and then it appeared to fail. We are blended and melded with these cultures and the same genetic bloodline of people throughout history has manipulated all these cultures and they use esoteric magic to do so.

Those people are the controllers of the god or deity on Earth those who are named Pope, King, Queen, Emperor and so on.

Those who manipulate the energy of the Sun against us, manipulate these 'gods.' Look … there … I just said it – now that's the proverbial jar of worms opened – religion is a Zodiacal Sun based belief system!

We are not solid we are sensitive and we are massively influenced. The Sun is the biggest influence upon us and we are bathed in its energy, there can be no greater power over us than the power of the Sun.

And this energy is manipulated against us.

The Sun has been and still is worshiped as a deity … as a God and this fact is hidden from us in plain sight. I want to demonstrate how we, as energy are influenced. Below, as in all symbology and sacred geometry, but also above and as a whole, we will discuss this more in the magic section.

Humour

The humour I most admire is wielded by those that make us think and view the world differently. The people who push the boundaries of convention are heavily censored and there are many mechanisms in place to ensure their messages are suppressed. The mediums that question our systems structure and challenge our mindset are very few, humour, writing and art remain precious and powerful tools to help us expose so much that is wrong in our lives.

When we begin to realise our programming; that we are relentlessly bombarded with concepts such as, you must win, be the prettiest, segregation, misinformation, belief systems, ego building. I love the X-Factor, just can't wait for the losers bit. How's Big Bro going to fuck with the wannabe's heads today and watch as they make utter twat's out of themselves in today's task … then let's judge and condemn them because we are all so fucking superior. Jeremy Clarkson for Prime Minister … he's such a lad isn't he? Make Al Gore the governor of the soon to be formed 'World Bank,' roll up roll up buy your carbon tax credits … or the worlds about to end. *Sorry about that last tirade … lost my sense of humour.* Furthermore the methods we deploy to police each other, and allow ourselves to be policed, once we begin to question and look into the agenda, the process invites us to see the world more clearly and therefore differently. The power of the magicians who make us laugh and move us emotionally is undeniable, but to describe what makes us laugh would be both tedious and beyond explanation because it is subjective; what amuses one leaves another unmoved.

> *Over the past 50 years Bob Hope employed 88 joke writers who supplied him with more than a million gags, and he still couldn't make me laugh.*
>
> Eddie Murphy.

As appealing as slapstick humour is, it has its limitations. Intrinsically to be humoured is to be entertained by an instrument that breaks down social barriers, creates interaction and lifts us into laughter, it is difficult to see the harm in that. In life there is something that will carry you even if your legs should fail, and that's a sense of humour. However we should be careful how we use this hefty instrument, because when we laugh at the guy who slips on the banana skin or gets the custard pie in his face, we laugh because it isn't happening to us.

Everything is funny as long as it is happening to somebody else.

Will Rodgers.

The role of the comedian falls into two parts; there are wits and there are clowns. There are those who are a mix of the two but I feel anyone who is prepared to amuse others by their own vulnerability and be judged on that account is someone to be admired. The truth remains however that behind the masks that the great clowns wear there lies a troubled person. Name your favourites and get some insight into their stormy personal lives, their difficult pasts. Billy Connelly, Freddie Starr, John Cleese, Frankie Howard, Tony Hancock, Spike Milligan, Peter Sellars, Richard Prior, Michael Barrimore, Benny Hill … or the many others who make us laugh … show me a funny man and I will show you a pained and tortured soul.

Those named are predominately clowns and depending on your view, they deploy wit and guile to varying degrees. There is another class of comedian who is much more rare; these are the people who deliver their message using comedy as a means of saying what would otherwise be too dangerous to say.

The man I most admire with this talent is the American comedian Bill Hicks. Bill died in 1994, he was just thirty-two, although his passing was before his time history has shown his words were beyond time. If you listen to his comments made twenty years ago on the first invasion of Iraq, they hold true to our present occupation. I guess he wasn't much of a fan of either Bush senior or junior, the puppets who sold the same concept to us twice on behalf of the men behind the curtains.

Bill Hicks was considered controversial and was undoubtedly an angry man. He didn't seem to care what others thought of him and released from this normal constraint he spoke his mind and many found this offensive. I was privileged to see him live in Yorkshire in 1992 in one of his last gigs, he was simply awesome and the world is a poorer place for his loss. I knew at the time I was witness to genius and although I didn't know he was a prophet then, time has proven that he most certainly was.

Other Americans with the talent to make us think differently include Lenny

Bruce and George Carlin, there are many others who deploy humour and the courage to speak their minds. Other 'mind-speakers' include Michael Moore (although I think he's sold out recently, which often happens) and Alex Jones admirably continues to bang the gong.

In the UK we have a handful of people brave and capable enough of giving of their truth, they include Rory Bremner. His style is clever and his mimicry powerful but he stays just within the parameters without stirring up controversy. (This is not a criticism of him, as he will only be allowed to go so far because of media restrictions). Another mind-speaker is David Icke, (who might have had an easier time of it had he used more humour). Icke was ridiculed and pilloried in a Terry Wogan TV interview in 1991. Icke recognised later that he was going through a spiritual transition. It takes a bit of courage to admit what most would regard as a frailty (such is the power of the programmers). However recently, once again on mainstream television, a programme was screened entitled, 'David Icke, was he right?' As the title suggests criticism towards him was much less scathing, time had passed and with hindsight many of the issues he had talked about had become true. Icke qualifies his treatment by acknowledging that anyone who stands up and questions the norm or the status quo will in the process be ridiculed, judged and condemned. I tip my hat to you Mr Icke; I respect you for the path you have taken. I suspect you have earned less, suffered more, and risked your heath, family and reputation in the process. You have been pilloried and have sacrificed much in the drive to speak your truth. In fairness to Wogan, I read that he admitted that he regretted the way the earlier interview had been conducted. Recently he interviewed Icke again and he enjoyed a better reception which is perhaps an indication that more and more people understand Icke, and as more of us awaken consciousness expands, in turn all of our vibrational levels are raised.

The world needs the genius that these people channel and demonstrate they serve as examples to us all because they show us what is available should we so choose. With open minds we need fear nothing from these people. The programmers need not censor us from laughter and another man's truth, we have the power to disagree or reject the claims of these modern day prophets, but there is an immense amount of energy expended in preventing them. Why should a so-called free society tolerate the truth being withheld from us?

Infinite love is the only truth everything else is an illusion.

David Icke.

The truth masked by humour is how a message can be delivered and get under the radar. Bill Hicks had visited and witnessed the events of the Waco Siege; it was here that US. Government agencies murdered men, women and children on American soil. The following is extracted from the book, Love all the People by Bill Hicks. He was on stage at Igby's Comedy Club, California.

And they said, you know, they had to break down the compound because child abuse was stepping up. Well if that's true, how come we don't see Bradley tanks knocking down Catholic Churches, you know? If in fact child abuse is your concern. Actually folks, I don't know if any of y'all have seen this, it's a tape, kind of bootleg going around, showing film of the Bradley tanks not knocking, as the official story was; small holes to insert tear gas, but crashing the building off its fucking foundations and fire shooting out of the tanks.

He makes more than one point as you squirm in your seat, one of the points establishes that a crime is only a crime by definition.

A lot of Christians wear crosses around their necks, You think when Jesus comes back he ever wants to see a fucking cross? It's like going up to Jackie Onassis wearing a rifle pendant.

Bill Hicks.

Dependant on your childhood programming this will either offend you, make you laugh or somewhere in between. You will feel laughter or a bedfellow of fear such as upset or annoyance. You may remain unmoved although this is both sad and unlikely.

To a Christian the cross symbolises many meanings, it confers a blessing and it consecrates. It is the most simple of symbols given power by childhood programming, all imbedded because of an association placed in our minds as we were growing up. Had we not been programmed, all the cross would represent would be two sticks; one over the other.

We therefore go on to feel comfort and inspiration from some symbols; we are also groomed to feel scorn and hatred at others.

The Christian Cross and the Islamic Crescent are two examples of how emotionally moved we are by symbols. Later the power of symbols is discussed more fully, it is important to understand what a vital communicative tool they are and as a result they are a massive influence on how we feel emotionally, how we are vibrating. Dependent on how we are vibrating will govern what we are asking for and what will form our reality.

Symbols are buried in our minds on a subconscious level as we are growing up. If a picture paints a thousand words a symbol speaks many volumes to our unconscious mind. Letters, words, logos, colours, crosses and crescents, flags and uniforms represent symbols. In less obvious and more subtle ways they affect us more than we presently understand, through architecture, advertising and art. We are surrounded by symbols communicating information to us as we try and make sense of our environment. They serve to guide and influence us and this is most often to our detriment and to our cost as previous childhood programming is activated. We live and we die by symbols.

Whatever the power of the message that they carry, it is vital we understand that they shift us emotionally and emotions are the governing force in both how we operate in our lives and what we manifest into those lives. Our emotions dictate how we vibrate and our vibration is either in tune with the Universe or it is not. We either resist or we allow. If we want to take back mastery of our own lives we must understand what the people who control us know, and the first step on that journey is to become acutely aware of our emotions.

If ...

If you can keep your head when all about you are losing theirs and blaming it on you;
If you can trust yourself when all men doubt you.
But make allowances for their doubting too;
If you can wait and not be tired by waiting.
Or being lied about, don't deal in lies.
Or being hated, don't give way to hating.
And don't look to good, nor talk too wise.
If you can dream- and not make dreams your master.
If you can think – and not make thoughts your aim.
If you can meet with triumph and disaster
And treat those two impostors just the same
If you can talk with crowds and keep your virtue
Or walk with Kings – nor loose the common touch.
If neither foes nor loving friends can hurt you.
If all men count with you but none too much.
If you can fill the unforgiving minute
With sixty seconds worth of distance run.
Yours is the Earth and everything that's in it.
And – which is more – you'll be a man my son!
From Rewards and Fairies.

Written in 1910 by Rudyard Kipling.

... a traffic accident in the summer of 1930, over two years before Hitler's seizure of power in Germany, when a car in which he was riding in the 'death-seat' (right from the passenger seat) collided with a heavy trailer truck. The truck braked just in time to avoid running over Hitler's car and crushing him. Because of the degree to which Hitler's psychopathology determined Nazi policy and success, the form of an eventual World War II would probably have been quite different if the truck driver had braked one second later.

Jared Diamond. Guns, Germs and Steel.
(Time Magazine listed Adolph as 'Man of the Year' in 1938.)

It is interesting to ponder that if a battle had reached a different result our history would be very different. On the 11th of October 732, the warriors of Islam reached the northernmost point of their invasion of Europe. They stood on the road between Poiters and Tours, which put them about 200 miles south of Paris. They had conquered vast amounts of land in the name of Islam; those lands included the Middle East, much of Central Asia, North Africa and the Spanish and Portuguese Iberian peninsular. Charles (the Hammer) Martel however had other ideas; in a battle which the Frankish leader won he reversed the tide of Islam. We can only guess what it might have been like to be now, reading the Koran in our schools, rather than the Bible. Then again, if we were taught both, we would realise just how similar they are.

Our lives and indeed our history is littered with the 'what if's.'

Image

I wish I could get one penny in every pound spent tomorrow in any City anywhere, (*well preferably London – if I'm pushed*) in the name of image.

We embrace image but it comes at a hefty price. The mercerised cotton T-shirt that comes in beautiful wrapping with a crocodile or a tick, or whatever logo placed upon it was possibly made in the Far East by labour entrenched in poverty. There are now in this 'civilised' world, more slaves than there have ever been, these are the people who make most of our 'designer' ware.

It is to our shame and it us who should feel poor, to know that another human being has to live in these conditions in order that we can aspire to an image. We hand over big money for the privilege of wearing these clothes and we act as an individual free advertising hoarding as we sport the manufacturers label over our proud hearts.

We are asked to eat the cereal that is best for those proud hearts, even if eating the box it came in might provide us with more nutrition than the content. We are urged to aspire to drive the latest model car, and it has to have that certain badge. And if your little Billy sees next door's little Mickey's playstation mark 40, thousand gigabyte … whatever … well he's going to seriously dement you or turn to crime to obtain one.

Virtually everything we buy and consume has image attached to it.

And of course everything we buy we do not necessarily consume. The West throws away enough food and wastes enough water to feed the rest of the world and in doing wipeout poverty and starvation overnight. Please take a moment to consider the following; there are 854 million people across the world that are hungry. This figure becomes greater as we become '*more*' civilised.

The figure for example a year ago was two million less.

Hunger is the most extreme form of poverty and its victims suffer illness, stunted growth and constant weakness. I am not suggesting that there are not deprived people in the West, but in poor counties there are no safety nets. In the West there are soup kitchens, food stamps and training available. Our infrastructure may be woefully inadequate and there are many casualties but with respect, I doubt if your reading this you are one of those unfortunates, and if your living in a region of West Africa and the crops have failed because of the fact the rains did not come this year then you have a famine and a drought on your hands … and you will not be reading this.

Our world is home to 6.6 billion people and counting. In 2005 over ten million children did not see their fifth birthday. Almost all of these deaths occurred in developing countries, three quarters of them lived in sub-Sahara Africa and South Asia.

> 'Human history is the history of slavery. No great civilisation or empire has ever existed which was not built on the sweat of slaves.'
>
> A.C. Grayling. The Reason of Things.

If we peer behind the façade of all the great cities we discover massive contrasts in lifestyle, sometimes the poor are separated from the wealthy by one or two streets, they are certainly separated by mindset. The many less well off constructed the city and their industry certainly supports it.

Grayling points out that there are more slaves in the world now than ever before. He estimates that around 27 million people endure forced labour camps, debt bondage, the sex industry, professional beggary, domestic servitude and, as he puts it, work without pay and under the threat of violence, which defines slavery. He speaks of the many children who are commercially trafficked and whose fate will be exploitation into prostitution or servitude.

> Those who are enslaved by history – who dwell on past wrongs, who keep ancient conflicts and quarrels alive, who even seek reparations for the wrongs suffered by their ancestors – would do the world a greater service by turning their attention to present day slavery instead. A concerted effort might open the gates of China's forced labour camps, free the Haitian sugar-plantation slaves, rescue the child prostitutes of Southeast Asia, and end the chattel slavery in Mauritania and the Sudan where slave markets still exist and where you can buy six children for one Kalashnikov.
>
> A C Grayling. The Reason of Things.

Half the world; that's over three billion people, are trying to survive on less than two dollars a day.

If you were to combine the wealth of the three richest people in the world it would exceed the gross national product of 48 poorest countries; that's a quarter of all the countries in the world.

The programming that guides and governs us in the West, which is to own and present our image with the process of individuality, and we sport our designer labels to express that individuality.

Why can we not just make everything *real* quality?

In the West we don't mend things anymore, instead we throw them away and buy another. In the emerging nations like India they build and repair and their resources are much less than ours.

Our cars are built to sell at a price, I don't pretend to understand how much more it would cost to put more rubber on a tyre or increase the gauge of steel on an exhaust to make it last twice as long as it already does, but the point is; it would not cost *twice* as much. Because the majority of the cost goes into making something, a deeper mould would use more material but in relative terms it would only cost a fraction more.

You can by a printer for your computer for less than £50 but when you come to buy the cartridge to replace the ink it will cost you over half of the price of the printer. It's a fantastic con repeated over and over again virtually in everything that we purchase.

Take a fairly crap song, 'Show Me The Way To Amarillo (Yes, I appreciate that music is a personal thing and what you like and I like, will differ). And so, as I prepare myself for the wrath of Tony Christie and his legion of fans, a fairly crap song, which made number 18 in the British charts over 35 years ago and was sung by the aforementioned Tony Christie.

As most of Europe will remember, Peter Kay who mimed it in order to raise money for the Comic Relief charity resurrected the song.

So we have the same song, sung by the same guy, another guy miming it only this time it is not sung by Mr Christie wearing a dinner suit, it is mimed by a comedian surrounded by various celebrities (including Mr Christie).

The song reached number one in the UK charts and remained there for seven weeks, becoming the UK's best selling single of 2005.

Did all those that bought the single do so because some of the proceeds were going to charity or perhaps a new generation had arrived that finally really appreciated the song at last?

Certainly everyone involved benefited commercially.

Comic Relief raised money to help children in poverty.

Tony Christie had his career resurrected with appearances in Middlesbrough and the Albert Hall and he has appearances booked for his UK tour and has re-recorded the tune.

It didn't do any harm to Peter Kay, a talented comedian from Bolton.

The Royal Dragoon Guards spoofed the spoof and such was the demand for people to watch their version, the Ministry of Defence computers crashed, and they had to be repaired … so lots of revenue there.

Plus it was very good for the lads in Iraq to have their moral lifted and the effects of post-traumatic stress disorder might therefore be further delayed.

Amir Khan, a handy British boxer, uses it in his entrance build-up to a fight.

A darts player or two have used it similarly.

A load of celebrities crept up the alphabet as their respective magnificence grew. Names like Keith Harris and Orville, Mr Blobby, Bernie Clifton and Oswald, Sooty and Sweep, Shakin' Stevens and even Sir Jimmy Saville, were given the chance to shake their stuff. And who can be critical of this? No one because it is all in the name of charity.

And for sure, it gets your foot tapping.

So everyone wins and all because of a change of image.

But sometimes the image branders get it badly wrong.

In the early 1980's, the Coca-Cola Company realised that their competitor Pepsi was eroding its best selling soft drink.

The Pepsi Corporation ran an advertising campaign called the Pepsi Challenge, the majority of tasters, (57%), found they preferred Pepsi.

Sales were becoming similar and this concerned Coca-Cola because they had always been the market leaders.

The Coca-Cola Corporation was spending an estimated $100 million dollars more on advertising and their drink was far more available to consumers.

Clearly Coca-cola had a problem.

Fortunes were spent by Coca-Cola to discover what was going wrong and in an attempt to recover their losses the unthinkable happened, Coca-Cola changed its secret formula and in further blind tastes, Coke was seen to draw level with Pepsi in the sip tests.

As a result New Coke was launched and then failed in spectacular fashion, the original formula Classic Coke reappeared and Coke re-established itself as the number one world best seller.

It is intriguing therefore to consider that in sip tests by thousands of consumers, a drink that was shown to taste worse, should now again be market leader.

One of the conclusions was that in the sip test, Pepsi tasted sweeter, in this small window of choice, this was the preferred drink.

So if you only test by taking a sip, consumers will prefer the sweetness, however when drinking the entire contents of the can or bottle the results are altered, or in other words the sweetness devalues.

Coca Cola Corporation might have saved themselves a fortune had they reacted immediately to Pepsi's sip Challenge and simply asked that people drink all of the drink, before passing judgment.

A man goes to a tailor to try on a new custom-made suit. The first thing he notices is that the arms are too long.

'No problem,' says the tailor. 'Just bend your arms at the elbow and hold them out in front of you ... you see ... now it's fine.'

'But the collar is up around my ears!' the man says.

'It's nothing. Just hunch your back up a little ... no, a little more ... there that's it.' says the tailor.

'But I'm stepping on my cuffs!' the man cries in desperation.

'No, bend your knees a little to take up the slack. There you go. Look in the mirror ... the suit fits perfectly.'

So, twisted like a pretzel, the man lurches out onto the street.

Reba and Florence see him go by.

'Oh, look,' says Reba, 'that poor man!'

'Yes,' says Florence ... 'but what a beautiful suit.'

Arthur Naiman. Every Boy's Guide to Yiddish.

Journey

Come take my hand and let's just go on a small diversion. A mental stroll if you would care to join me.

Whomsoever you are and regardless of how you see yourself by way of your own volition or what society has placed upon you, (the latter being the far greater burden). And yes, like me, if you're a man you might have a slight reluctance, because, sure it's kind of uncomfortable, unless you are openly gay – to take another man's hand, but please trust me if I can overcome yet another one of those foolish prejudices that we place upon one another, then my friend … so can you.

Relax, open your mind because brains are like parachutes … they really only work effectively when they are open; chill, breathe, perhaps think of a time when you were truly happy, because if you vibrate well … this will touch you more readily.

Love is a vibration … it's a long wave with little or no ripple, (conversely hate is a short wave).

We can *feel* love because we are love, but we can also feel how others are feeling, we can be on one another's wavelength. This can be demonstrated in a similar way, when a chord is struck on the strings of a violin, then the strings on a nearby violin … untouched by anyone … will start to vibrate to the same frequency and emit the same sound. A wavelength can be described as a sound and sound can affect our mood. A piece of music can inspire us to joy or reduce us to tears. Oh yes it can macho-man.

In 1999 some friends invited me to go to New York. They were boxing fans, and Lennox Lewis was fighting Evander Holyfield in Madison Square Gardens for the undisputed heavyweight championship of the World.

Even though I had lost my love of the sport that I had loved as a teenager, I thought it was an opportunity to see a place I had never been before, undoubtedly New York is something special to see and what better opportunity was I going to get?

There was worldwide interest in the fight; I think it remains the highest grossing event in Madison Square Garden and New York States history. The place was packed. The fight went the full 12 rounds and in my eyes and most others, Lewis was the clear winner. Whilst Lewis held his arms aloft in triumph and a beaten Holyfield slumped on his chair, the verdict of the three judges was announced – the match was a draw.

It was announced in the New York papers the following day that it took until four 'o' clock in the morning to find anyone who thought the draw was the right decision.

Later the statistics showed that Lewis threw 348 punches that connected to Holyfield's 130, and the British boxer landed 137 jabs to the Americans 52. This fight was a massive sporting event with world media attention and yet it didn't stop it being the biggest example of sporting corruption you are ever likely to witness. I was privileged to be there but it finally extinguished any interest in a sport I had once loved. Anyway, in the remainder of the break we still had a few days left so we did the usual and played on as many of the rides as possible; Statue of diabolical liberties, the Empires in a State Building, Flump Tower, etc.

One of the party then suggested we should go to a Broadway musical, so on successive nights we went to see 'Les Miserables' and the 'Phantom of the Opera.' Fantastic stuff. Sitting between two of the men on the trip, as the lights dimmed at the start of the show, I prepared myself for the start of 'Les Mis,' one of the guys nudged me and whispered 'do you think it's ok to sing along?' Funny was the tone of the break. At the end of both moving shows on two separate nights, all of us were at pains to wipe away the evidence of upset; the tears from our cheeks before the lights came on, fearful that we would be spotted by each other because we had dropped our masks for an instant and our weakness were revealed – shamed to be seen to have been genuinely moved by the show we had just watched.

It was a moment I savour – three supposed macho-men all with tears streaming down our cheeks. We are moved by more than just sight and sound, any sort of wavelength emanated can mould us, move us, change us and therefore alter us. Sand, salt or sugar on a dark piece of cardboard resonates and changes shape as scales of notes are played. Patterns emerge and structures are formed. Sound is everywhere in the Universe and plays an important role and is a tremendous influence in our lives.

Sound is another form of the myriad of vibrations that affect us, Sound touches and influences us, but most importantly it changes us. As we learn more about sound and realise its power we will harness it for many uses, we will use it to heal and to move heavy and bulky objects. At the moment most research goes into its negative uses and presently it is used in the hands of the military and the police as a weapon.

A calming voice can soothe, our speech is produced with chords. Sound can alter molecular structure and since all matter … including ourselves is made of energy … then so we are affected. This is what we infer when we say that we are moved by music.

Our lives are journeys and much of what we do now is given over in great swathes of our time to fulfilling our basic needs. Our desire to be fed and watered, find shelter and warmth are most important, the desire to procreate and nurture our children also runs strongly through our wants and needs.

When we find we don't have to expend so much time and energy to meeting these needs, there lies the promise of a fantastic future, (that includes our fears, our worries and the resultant stress that for many of us goes with this procedure) a future where our desire could be focused on who … or what … we want to become, whether that is simply to become a better human being and the development of the god that lies within us all.

In the near future lies the ability to develop biotechnology, which would stop the animal holocaust. Genetic engineering will enable us to produce edible cellular protein; all types of food will become tastier, more beneficial, more digestible and indistinguishable from the animal products that we presently consume. The morality issues will become more compelling when it becomes more economical to do this. The benefits of a cruelty free diet will be overwhelming and as romantic a view as this might seem, the sentient fellow creatures that we share this earth with and we currently abuse will be given status similar to children.

Look at every path closely and deliberately. Try it as many times as you think necessary. Then ask yourself and yourself alone one question. This question is one that only a very old man asks. My benefactor told me about it once when I was young and my blood was too vigorous for me to understand it. I will tell you what it is: Does this path have a heart? If it does, the path is good, if it doesn't, it is of no use.

Jack Kornfield. A Path with Heart.

We are not humans on a spiritual journey. We are spiritual beings on a human journey.

Stephen Covey.

Judgment

Judgment is something we automatically do. The concept of 'an eye for an eye and a tooth for a tooth,' with it brings the prospect of a blind population … but the upside is … the denture manufacturers are going to get seriously wealthy.

> *Follow your heart, your dreams, your desires. Do what your soul calls you to do; whatever it is, and allow it to be finished; then you will go on to another adventure. You will never be judged – unless you accept the judgment of those around you. And if you accept their judgment, it is only your will to do so – for the experience.*
>
> Ramtha.

This wonderful message tells us that one can tune into what the soul is calling you do. In order to enable this we can meditate or consume drugs, mindful that technically drugs are the 'cheap' ticket to the objective however and as in most things, there is the 'good' use of something and the abuse that negatively harms us.

We must empty out the vessel we call our mind otherwise there is no room to receive. The stressful lives we lead are not conjusive to this and that's why people walk dogs, dig allotments, walk hills, fish, listen to music, go on holiday, (which can be even more stressful … but the intent was there).

We might think we are just off to watch Melchester United because of our love of football … but there are many more powerful forces at work.

(Sorry if I'm going off track a bit here but I'm on a roll and as I mentioned at the start of this, the seven or so friends I would normally delivering all this to … will have by now … broken off into two groups and be talking about something else).

Ok, yes, judgment and football … right let's get into that.

Your Dad takes you when you're a little Master aged 8 (plus or minus say 2 years) and you don't know it then … but your hooked … the chip is in place.

You may get healthy one day and lapse … once you discover girls and beer and other distractions but you will soon be back. Once your Master … becomes a mister.

So that's the programming dealt with.

Other forces include the realisation that football is tribal and that's great because it allows us to act in a way we wouldn't dream of as an individual. We can release our frustrations or as they say in my native North East, 'have a good shout and ball.' It's one of the few places where it's ok to see a grown man cry, cuddle a relative stranger and kiss other men in a similar way they do on the pitch. The players are the new gladiators and it's totally acceptable to spit.

Bonding, affirmation, common interest and a sense of belonging … it's all happening on the terraces.

As an individual we are often frustrated by our lack of power … but as a member of a thirty-thousand-strong choir you become unstoppable … awesome.

Everyone involved in profiting from our implanted addiction knows this simple truth; it is shown by the way the players, the manager, directors and chairmen of all football clubs, treat the fans with appropriate reverence. Read the quotes made with deference to the fans; 'the fans were great,' – 'without the fans support we wouldn't have achieved what we've achieved this season,' – 'it's like having 12 men on the pitch when the fans get behind us,' and so on … they all touch their forelocks to us the masses … it's called football speak, read any football programme if I haven't convinced you.

So football … just like many meme's … including politics sucks up big-time to the masses. That exchange of energy has a finite balance but it suits both parties; the mass of fans on the one hand funding the machine and those that profit from them on the other. Until of course this uneasy balance tips, for example; you can only put the price of a season ticket up by so much pre-season, and this must be measured against the romance of the coming season and price of passion that the fans are willing to pay. Judge the balance wrong or try loosing a few of the opening matches and heads roll in this high stakes business.

Another form of judgment (lest we judge and therefore condemn). When we gossip about someone we are judging and we are not equipped to do this. We are not in a position to judge because we do not have all the facts. All the facts are unavailable to us. We cannot know another persons story, we don't know their motivation and we cannot walk in their shoes.

Gossip is a poison and the same dynamic that gossip uses, which is one of alienation, is used against one other, individually and collectively. When we talk negatively about another individual we are building a case with the hope of the compliance of another, all in an effort to dislike them. We are in effect sowing the seeds of hate. We do this as individuals and we do this together. We have no right to do this, (apart from the fact it is low vibrational stuff and a total waste of energy) because we do not know the full story, we might know facets of it, but we do not know the absolute truth, to know that we would have to be them. And we cannot be them while the ego has been served to separate us in judgment.

When we ridicule, judge and condemn another person, what we do and say is not a reflection of those we gossip about, it is a reflection of ourselves. As difficult as it is to stop the habit the upside is the great feeling that it gives us. If we do not judge and condemn we go into instant forgiveness default mode. If we are able to do this often enough it we break the old habit. As a result our minds are not poisoned and the energy we conserve is considerable.

The other advantage of not judging would be that collectively – we would change the world.

The seat of knowledge is in the head.
Of wisdom, in the heart.
We are sure to judge wrong, if we do not feel right.

William. Hazlitt.

Be wiser than other people if you can, but do not tell them so.

Lord Chesterfield.

You must look into people, as well as at them.

Ibid.

Every saint has a past and every sinner a future.

Oscar Wilde.

Never judge and never condemn and there are no exceptions to this.

Knowledge

Knowledge speaks but wisdom listens.

Jimi Hendrix.

The true seeker of knowledge naturally strives for truth and is not content with common opinions but soars with undimmed and unwearied passion until he grasps the essential nature of things.

Plato' s Republic.

If we knew what we were doing they wouldn't call it research.

Albert Einstein.

Our scientific power has out-run our spiritual power. We have guided missiles and misguided men.

Martin Luther King. Jnr.

Knowledge will forever govern ignorance, and a people who mean to be their own governors, must arm themselves with the power knowledge gives. A popular government without popular information or the means of acquiring it is but a prologue to a farce or a tragedy or perhaps both.

James Madison.
(Fourth President of the United States).

I've been making a list of all the things they don't teach you at school. They don't teach you how to love somebody. They don't teach you how to be famous. They don't teach you how to be rich or how to be poor. They don't teach you how to walk away from someone you don't love any longer. They don't teach you how to know what's going on in someone else's mind. They don't teach you what to say to someone who's dying. They don't teach you anything worth knowing.

Neil Gaimen.

Today there is a wide measurement of agreement, which, on the physical side of science approaches almost to unanimity, that the stream of knowledge is heading towards a non-mechanical reality. The Universe is beginning to look more like a great thought than a great machine.

Werner Heisenburg. Physics and Beyond.

You only need two things of quality in your life; a good bed and a good pair of shoes.

Because when you're not in one – you're in the other.

K Graham

Life

As long as you know who is kidding who.

Gerald Robson.

Develop an interest in life as you see it, the people, things, literature, music – the world is so rich, simply throbbing with rich treasures, beautiful souls and interesting people. Forget yourself.

Henry Miller

Don't ask what the world needs – ask what makes you come alive and then go and do that. Because what the world needs is people who have come alive.

Howard Martin.

The purpose of life is a life of purpose.

Robert Byrne.

Life is not about what you want. It's about wanting what you've got.

Give what you can, take what you need.

If nothingness awaits us, let us live as if that is an unjust fate.

We appreciate and are moved by so many of the spiritual things in life, those indefinable moments where we feel; joy, synchronicity, love, the embrace of awe and yet we still deny.

Until you understand that nothing can happen to you, nothing can ever come to you or be kept from you, except in accord with your state of consciousness, you do not have the key to life.

Paul Twitchell. The Flute of God.

The most unfair thing about life is the way it ends. I mean, life is tough. It takes up a lot of your time. What do you get at the end of it? A death! What's that, a bonus? I think the life cycle is all backwards. You should die first, get it out of the way. Then you live in an old age home. You get kicked out when your too young, you get a gold watch, you go to work. You work forty years until your young enough to enjoy your retirement. You do drugs, alcohol, you party, and you get ready for high school. You go to grade school, you become a kid, you play, you have no responsibilities, you become a little baby, you go back into the womb, you spend your last nine months floating.

… And you finish off as an orgasm.

George Carlin.

Often people attempt to live their lives backwards; they try to have more things, or more money, in order to do more of what they think they want, so they will be happier.

The way it actually works is the reverse. You must first be who you really are, then do what you need to do, in order to have what you want.

Margaret Young.

Life is like a blanket too short. You pull it up and your toes rebel, you yank it down and shivers meander about your shoulder; but cheerful folks manage to draw their knees up and pass a very comfortable night.

Marion Howard.

Life is a comedy for those that think and a tragedy for those that feel.

Horace Walpole.

It is no good to say at the end of your life. 'I have made a living, but I have never lived.'

And to live means to follow your own path, not someone else's in exchange for love. Your own path means to get in touch with your own spirituality.

Elisabeth Kubler-Ross.

When I am working with a private client on their goals, I will often ask, 'If you carry on as you are, will you achieve it?'

To my amazement, they always know the answer, and more often than not that answer is 'no.'

One of the most significant differences I've noticed between the people who succeed and the ones who struggle is whether they look into the past or the present to create their future. If you continually look to the past, you will always feel that history is doomed to repeat itself; if you look to the present, you will always find there is some new choice you can make to enhance your possibilities.

No matter how much you've struggled in the past, every moment of every day provides you with an opportunity to make new choices and create new results.

Paul McKenna. Change Your Life in 7 Days.

Life is just too short to carry problems around with you. The problem is that most of us do.

We spend lifetimes worrying about events in the past and things that will probably never happen in the future. Whenever we have a problem it is about the past or the future and dwelling upon these problems provides them with the energy they require to stay alive. We fan them to light by visiting them often and become habitualised in exposing ourselves to them.

Like every habit the viewing of a problem can be broken by mindfulness … that is the knowledge that we are revisiting and then stopping ourselves by recognising that we are doing it.

You can be obsessed by remorse all your life, not because you chose the wrong thing – - you can always repent, atone: but because you never had the chance to prove to yourself that you would have chosen the right thing.

Umberto Eco. Foucault's Pendulum.

The battles that count aren't the ones for gold medals. The struggles within yourself – the invisible, inevitable battles inside all of us – that's where it's at,

Jesse Owens.

When we are so ignorant of life, can we know death?

Confucius.

Maybe all one can do is hope to end up with the right regrets.

Arthur Miller.

In life we do what we must.
In truth we get by the best way we can.
We are all on the wheel of fortune.

Moll Flanders. Daniel Defoe.

Life is just a chance to grow a soul.

Powell Davies.

Zigong asked: 'Is there any single word that could guide one's entire life?'

The master said: 'should it not be reciprocity? – What you do not wish for yourself, do not wish for others.

Confucius.

Love

You don't own love, it owns you.

Have you ever been in love? Horrible isn't it? It makes you so vulnerable. It opens your chest and it opens up your heart and it means that someone can get inside you and mess you up. You build up all these defences, you build up a whole suit of armour, so nothing can hurt you, then one stupid person, no different from any other stupid person, wanders into your stupid life ... you give them a piece of you. They didn't ask for it. They did something dumb one day, like kiss you or smile at you, and then your life isn't your own anymore. Love takes hostages it gets inside you. It eats you out and leaves you crying in the darkness, so simple a phrase like ' maybe we should just be friends' turns into a glass splinter working its way into your heart. It hurts. Not just in the imagination. Not just in the mind. It's a soul-hurt, a real gets-inside-you-and-rips-you-apart pain. I hate love.

Neil Gaimen.

Love is a space in which all other emotions can be experienced.

Robert Prinable.

Love is just a word until someone comes along and gives it meaning.
  The most important thing in life is to learn how to give out love, and to let it come in.

Morrie Schwartz.

For it was not into my ear you whispered, but into my heart. It was not my lips you kissed, but my soul.

Judy Garland.

Just because someone doesn't love you the way you want them to, doesn't mean they don't love you with all they have.
  Ever has it been that love knows not its own depth until the hour of separation.

Kahlil Gibran.

Love takes off masks that we fear we cannot live without and know we cannot live within.

James Arthur Baldwin. (American Essayist, 1924-1987).

Love is energy of life.

Robert Browning.

Never date someone who is more beautiful or more insane than you.

If you love something let it go, if it comes back it is yours, if it does not – it never was.

You can shed tears that she is gone,
Or you can smile because she has lived.
You can close your eyes and pray that she'll come back,
Or you can open your eyes and see all she's left.
Your heart can be empty because you can't see her,
Or you can be full of the love you shared.
You can turn your back on tomorrow and live yesterday,
Or you can be happy for tomorrow because of yesterday.
You can remember her only that she is gone, or you can cherish her memory and let it live on.
You can cry and close your mind,
Be empty and turn your back.
Or you can do what she'd want:
Smile. Open your eyes love and go on.

David Harkins.

Love recognises no barriers. It jumps hurdles, leaps fences, penetrates walls to arrive at its destination full of hope.

Maya Angelou.

Love your enemies, for they tell you your faults.

Benjamin Franklin.

Thou hast been …
A man that Fortune's buffets and rewards
Has taken with equal thanks…Give me that man
That is not passion's slave, and I will wear him

In my heart's core, aye, in my heart of hearts
As I do thee …

William Shakespeare. Hamlet.

We like people for their qualities but we love them for their faults.

Hellboy.

The soul is made of love and must ever strive to return to love. Therefore, it can never find rest or happiness in other things. It must lose itself in love. By its very nature it must seek God, who is love.

Mechthid of Magdenburg.

Love is an abstract concept and we flatter ourselves that we can distinguish what it is and what it is not, but as long as we are engaged with our ego we are prohibited from finding love in its pure form.

So many of us search for love but we get confused as to what it is we are actually looking for, very often our search is for companionship, passion, intimacy, validation and support, we want acknowledgement, we are predisposed to procreate, we want to escape from our present environment, we seek help and look for admiration, we need understanding, approval and esteem, and so we go searching for these prizes under the one umbrella we call 'love' and this is clearly delusional because none of these things – along with the many more that are encapsulated under our adaptable brolly – has much to do with love.

Love is easier to experience than to explain but to define love properly is to go against our childhood programming. We are taught that love means exposing yourself to the pain of being deeply hurt by someone you have allowed yourself to trust, we are taught that to love we have to sacrifice and we are very often witness first hand when love turns to hate which it very often does and so this is what many of us grow up to believe.

We are told that love is blind but it is not – romance and false expectation is blind, love is a boundless, all encompassing, infinite feeling that we corrupt by selecting what we want from it and so we go in search for something we imagine we know and because we don't understand it fully – we cannot recognise it properly – and if we don't know what it is we cannot possibly find it.

Not that this has prevented writers of poetry and music from trying to express and define love. Love comes out easily top of the list of the most used emotional word throughout literature and music. Unfortunately what is most often referred to is romantic love and this should not be confused with unconditional love. Romantic love is rarely if ever a pure form. Generally with the notion of romantic love there comes a want, a need, a yearning, a desire, a requirement.

Someone can only break your heart because they did not measure up to your expectations. If you are that most rare of animals; a rounded and complete person, then you cannot have your heart broken *(me and all the others in the world meet in a phone box once a month – there is plenty of room for new members).*

So for most of us ultimately, romantic love will always come up short of our expectations. But it doesn't stop us returning to the well.

Pure unconditional love however is a different matter, this is the love that we came from and to which we are compounded to return, and this is the love that we yearn for. Love is encrypted into our very being, love is ego-less and love touches us, we can feel it in our hearts and it reaches to our inner-core, we resonate with love because it is simply what we are, if you doubt me it is only because you have forgotten what you knew when you started your separate individual journey at birth. *(That's just before they whack you on your arse as an introduction to what will be forthcoming).*

Love is the highest possible state we can attain, it is an extension of what we are and to know love we must give it. You cannot find love because you are love and to remind ourselves of what we knew before we first started to build our egoic, separate boxes we need to perform mastery – we need to practice mindful self-recognition – not the delusion that we are programmed into which is special, selective love.

Love is not to be special, seeking constant approval, attention and recognition because these are the results of the ego, love is not about me, me, me – it's about Oneness, and when we are growing up we are unlikely to hear this in the home, we will never hear this in the media and no-one will ever whisper it in our ear.

We can glimpse love but we cannot fully embrace it whilst locked into the ego. When we allow ourselves elevation into the condition of love, everything around us looks better, love enables us to bloom, in other words in love we are ourselves.

Our reality is radically affected by our thoughts and in any given moment we are making decisions based on the scale between the best possible alignment to our source, (the same as god – the same as love) or the worst form of non-alignment – which is fear. Choose pure love and you will follow your intuition and flow – choose fear and you're trapped with your intellect and your ego and severed from our Conscious Source.

Love and do what you will.

St Augustine.

Madness

It is a fool's prerogative to utter truths that no one else will speak.

Neil Gaiman.

We are all mad.

There are simply degrees of madness whereby some of us are saner than others. In your assessment of madness don't do what most people are programmed to do, that is measure how much an individual is not prepared to conform. The less he conforms the madder he is just might not be the case.

At school we used to walk past an asylum to get to the playing fields. Amongst my fellow pupils rumour abounded with stories of the monstrous inmates that were held in padded cells in the bowels of this wicked, dark place. The rest of the inmates were allowed to wander the grounds and through my eyes as we passed by, it just looked like a school playground only full of grownups, the dynamics of the many men in the vast quadrangle was similar to the playground, but the pace was slower – sadder.

I would often stop and sit on the wall and talk to a couple of the inmates. This simple action always had the same result; the majority of the inmates, from all corners of the square, slowly but surely would shuffle their way towards whoever I was engaging. I suppose they were bored and curious to see what was going on.

Early on I used to get a fair amount of stick from some my fellow pupils, nothing other than one would expect, my behaviour was never normal and as this became a fairly regular occurrence I suppose people just got used to it. There were many of the inmates of the asylum who would just stand around and listen to the crack, pretending they were not really interested and were certainly loath to join in, but there were also quite a few, who would talk as we engaged in conversation for as long as I chose to sit on the wall that divided 'us' from 'them.'

I can still see many of their faces and remember some of their names; Barratt, a painfully thin little guy with a hearing aid in one ear and a radio with an earphone plugged into his other (spare) ear. I got to learn he was constantly tuned into stations that talked about football.

He supported Leeds United, I support Newcastle United, *(I know a life of pain)* and because we had found common ground we always talked exclusively on the subject of football. If you asked Barrett what colour the sky was or what he had had for his breakfast, you could not get a word of sense out of him. But if you asked him about football and I mean *anything* about football, he would light up and to this day I have never met anyone who knew so much about the game, (even more than Newcastle's most famous expert; Melly Mel from Pelton Fell, who no longer drives a Cortina GXL) yes, Barrett was a walking encyclopaedia, a world expert when it came to football.

As time passed by I engaged more of the inmates and as we shared our perceived 'madness,' I learned much from these people who society had judged outsiders. By the time I had left the school I knew the wall I used to sit on that served to separate us was much thinner than I had previously imagined and that was another thing they didn't tell me as I was growing up.

The greatest blessings come by way of madness, indeed madness that is heaven-sent. It is when they were mad that the prophetess at Delphi and the priestess at Dodona achieved so much for which the states and individuals in Greece are thankful; when sane, they did little or nothing … madness is a divine gift.

Plato.

Many people who are considered out of sync with what we consider normal behaviour will behave in many different ways. Much is assumed when the labels are dished out; the quiet man, the hero, the clown, the recluse, the self-destructive, etc.

Many people have to find their own way back from what we deem to be madness. Call any so called imbalance what you will – the truth is that very often there comes a breakthrough, a catharsis, which will take the person forward.

As difficult as these times are when we reflect back upon them, we are able to see how they helped us in our spiritual growth.

History is littered with famous people, who having spent time lost in the abyss found their way out, for some it is gradual for others it happens in one revelatory moment.

Never be surprised where and when we receive an education ... but always try and be ready.

I genuinely would never worry about madness; I might worry more about a lack of it. I am not talking about a guy in a dark street running towards you wielding a meat-cleaver madness; I am talking about people who just aren't '*having it*' completely. My theory is the more normal you are; the more programmed and conformed you have become. I think that a much nicer word for madness is eccentricity. I am as eccentric as hell and what makes me unhappy is when I am called upon to mask that from the World.

I was going away to Manchester for a year on a training course (*great City – rains a lot*) but needed to earn some money while I waited to go, so I started working for a tarmacing company. I was nineteen and being the youngest of the six-man gang in the style of the great British tradition – you get all the shite jobs.

We were working at St Nicholas's, an institution for people that society had no other answers for. St Nick's was known as a famous 'nuthouse' in Newcastle and there we were laying tarmac on the car park. On this particular occasion the wagon came and dumped twenty tons of tarmac, the heavens opened immediately right on cue, but the tarmac had to be laid otherwise the rain will cool it and you have a substantial and solid fifteen foot hill on the drive.

So we set to our task and all the while one of the inmates was watching us from a big ground floor window. We laid the tarmac in record time and the five other guys in the gang threw their tools down and ran for the van, where there was warmth and shelter, hot drink and food, most of the things that prevent you from falling very ill with flu or hypothermia or whatever.

But my work was not complete as my colleges and their sudden disappearance reminded me. Because now the tarmac needed to be rolled and that took about another long hour, with me walking up and down the freshly laid tarmac with a three ton roller, (the same three ton roller that put me through a farmers picture window three weeks later, but that as they say is another story) so now I was totally piss-wet through to my skin, freezing and was at this juncture feeling a little sorry for myself.

And the guy is still at the window, staring and watching my every move and forgive me but – *yes* – I thought his face was a little vacant, but then again it might just have been me because I was beginning to *hate* him.

For the next hour he watched me totally vacant of expression; like a game of very slow-motion tennis, with his mouth wide open and only his head moving from side to side.

Finally finished I began my run to the comfort of the van, but the watcher-at-the-window distracted me by knocking really loudly on the glass, I just had to know what he wanted and I can't explain why but I could not help myself as I diverted towards him; like a drowned rat as I mouthed, *'what?'* abruptly at him through the window.

As he stood up, I noticed a most presentable quilted dressing gown over evidence of some very smart pyjamas and as he lifted the sash window with ease, I saw through a fog of raindrops and rage that behind him there was a TV on and various folk chilling out. The window was now raised and the warmth hit me and my misery was complete and I repeated to him, *'what is it you want?'*

The watchers reply was clear and haunts me to this day.

'I just wanted to tell you something son,' he said looking down at me – 'and *you' (he points at me)* 'think that *we' (he points at himself)* – 'are fucking daft?' and he tilted his head and winked before dismissing me from his gaze, shutting the window, turning his back and walking away – back toward the comfort of his circumstances.

When we remember we are all mad, the mysteries disappear and life stands explained.

Mark Twain

Children waiting for the day they feel good
Happy birthday, Happy Birthday
Made to feel the way that every child should
Sit and listen, sit and listen
Went to school and I was very nervous
No one knew me, no one knew me
Hello teacher, tell me what's my lesson
Look right through me, look right through me.

Mad World. Tears for Fears.

I am interested in madness. I believe it is the biggest thing in the human race, and the most consistent. How do you take away from a man his madness without also taking away his identity? Are we sure it is desirable for a man's spirit not to be at war with itself, or that it is better to be serene and ready to go to dinner than to be excited and unwilling to stop for a cup of coffee, even?

William Saroyan. Sweet Drive, Sweet Chariot.

You know the world is going crazy when the best rapper is a white guy, the best golfer is a black guy, the tallest guy in the NBA is Chinese, the Swiss hold the America's Cup, France is accusing the U.S of arrogance, Germany doesn't want to go to war, and the three most powerful men in America are named 'Bush', 'Dick' and 'Colon.'

Chris Rock.

No great genius has ever existed without some touch of madness.

Aristotle.

The human race has one really effective weapon, and that is laughter.

Mark Twain.

If you look back in history the condition of madness is almost commonplace, it is to be found everywhere and at all levels of society.

To recognise one's own insanity is, of course, the arising of sanity, the beginning of healing and transcendence.

Eckhart Tolle. A New Earth.

Madness is the way we live and many of the things we believe to be true – the ideals we will fight for and die for in the belief it will make us free, madness is believing in the politician and that your vote really does count, madness is the worship of celebrity, madness is the lie that we are free, madness is accepting this is all we could be.

Madness is all around us in the way we treat one another.

Madness is watching a Hollywood blockbuster or the News and allowing it to influence us to thinking that's its right to die for a flag or those those who control us by falsehood care for our well-being, after all they are the ones who programmed and coerced us into the belief that the cause we will die for is just.

Madness is the masks we observe in others and the ones we don ourselves.

Madness is a world where we waste 30 per cent of the food we buy while there are people in the world who are starving.

Madness is in the acceptance of the chemicals, through diet and vaccination, which allow us to accept toxins like mercury and fluoride into our bodies, which makes us dumb.

Madness is sitting in an office for forty years and for the last five of them looking forward to our retirement.

Madness is thinking that things will change when they cannot as long as we think and therefore act the way we do, and madness is feeling fear because it is fear that allows us to be controlled and thus – and ironically – condemns us to the madness of fear.

But madness can be constructive as it enables the viewer to see things more as they really are and yet we alienate madness and say those who appear to be mad are out of touch with reality, of course they are, they have in part escaped while others perceive momentarily through dream, deep thought, dance, drug or drink, the Oneness of it all.

Perhaps madness is the knowledge that only *you* can change your individual self and change this madness that we have created.

It's almost crazy isn't it?

The question is: what is a sane man to do in an insane society?

Catch-22. Joseph Heller.

Manners

Manners are part of programming but they are a necessary part of functioning within a society. Manners are standards of conduct, which we show when dealing with others. If you forget your manners your unlikely to be punished but they do show much about us as individuals.

In our dealing and interactions with others I have found the biggest truths or deceptions can be masked. It is very often that it is the little things that show us the bigger things about a person's makeup or character.

The old expression says 'manners maketh man,' there is great truth in this adage. Manners may differ from place to place but they make a statement about us and open doors that rudeness would keep closed.

Perhaps the door in the following is a decent example of where we are able to deploy manners.

The film 'Goodfellas' shows young Henry Hill, growing up in his neighbourhood, New York's Little Italy; he observes the way the many gangsters seem to get everything they want. They have the cars, money and lifestyle that young Henry aspires to.

Early in the film, as Henry's power grows, he sees a girl he likes and asks her out on a date. Henry is of Irish–Italian stock and the object of his attention is a girl called Karen, who is Jewish. Because of her strict upbringing and her parent's views, Henry tells Karen's mother at the front door of their house he is half-Jewish. The parents accept this lie and Henry and Karen go out on their first date.

As Henry is getting ready to take Karen out he receives some advance advice from the guys he is now forming alliances with. They suggest that Henry put Karen through a small test. When he pulls up in his car outside her house, he should park so that the passenger (her) door is next to the pavement. He should then get out of his door onto the road and lock the car. When she walks to her door he should open it for her and let her in. When she is settled in her seat shut her door and then walk around his car to the drivers side. When he gets to his door if she hasn't reached over and pulled his lock open so he can get into the car, the advice follows, don't bother taking her out again, she isn't the one for him. Karen, had she reached over, was displaying thoughtfulness, empathy, decency, consideration, kindness and manners … not a bad little test.

I was taken with this story and a few weeks later nine friends were sitting in a restaurant when I recounted it. Having told the story, I closed by saying what had become a favourite adage of mine, 'you see it's the little things that give us away.' Put another way – the little things in a person's behaviour say much about the bigger things.

Perfectly and as if on cue the guy sitting opposite me (not known for the generosity of his spirit) proceeded to pick up a full bottle of wine from the middle of the table and fill his glass – just his glass – no one else's – and said, 'Aye it's a good one that.'

I nodded, indicating the glass he had filled and said, 'I rest my case.'

He told me to go forth and multiply.

As Mark Twain said, 'It is difficult to be direct and affable.'

Magic, symbolism and sacred geometry

Manifestation is not magic. It is a process of working with the natural principles and laws in order to translate energy from one level of reality to another.

David Spangler.

There are broadly two forms of magic. The first form (that I don't want to talk about here) is trick magic. That is slight of hand magic – saw the lady in half – get hung in a box off a crane for a month – make a tiger disappear and reappear on the other side of the stage … because this is trickery magic. And whilst it is clever, it is only clever because we are deceived, once you know the way the trick is performed it loses its magic and therefore it loses its power.

Remember the wonder we had as children when the world seemed full of natural magic, *well it is*, we just went and got a programmed education and forgot. True the education made us realise how it some of it worked and while we still might not know how they do the 'saw the lady in half' trick, we kind of know that mirrors or a contortionist or a double is used.

Now I am sorry if I am bursting any bubbles here, I mean I still haven't fully forgiven the guy that told me Santa Claus wasn't real, but I am certain my father did it – so he could save money.

So no, not trickery magic because as clever as it might be, it is not what we are talking about here.

Those that now talk about the Law of Attraction, which is a Universal Law, do so perhaps because it could be interpreted as magic and the word magic for many conjures up prejudice in us. Aleister Crowley defined magic as, 'the science and art of causing change to occur in conformity with the will.' Crowley spelt magic 'magick' so as to define and distinguish it from stage or slight of hand magic.

The second form of magic is the manipulation of energy; it is the power of mind over matter, extraordinarily powerful and used all over the world for as long as man has been around. All esoteric magic is concerned with is methods for developing the faculties of the mind so that natural laws or Consciousness can be manipulated. Practised by shaman, wizards and witches, practitioners of both black and white magic. Oh, yes and practiced by each of us on each other as well.

Looking at human interactions between each other we can observe how we practice magic constantly – we call it gossip. This is black magic and powerful stuff, we gossip about those we know and those we don't know.

We think it draws us closer to one another when in truth it drives us further apart. The gossiping programme again takes place in childhood, we listen to those around us giving their opinions and it becomes part of our behaviour.

Gossip spreads like a virus and influences our views on people. It might be difficult to 'speak as we find,' because of the reputations that very often precede us but it is far healthier in the long run. Just one snippet of information can jaundice us towards someone, and that's how the virus starts, infecting everyone who comes into contact with it.

Gossip ruins people and is very often unjustified, the person who delivers the virus and infects you will always have their own agenda, they want you to feel as they do and it increases their power. We then are invited to do what they are doing to us, which is judging and condemning.

When friends become enemies or countries go to war the dynamics are the same; the alienation of an individual is the same as alienation of the people of another country. It starts with badmouthing, building the case against them, finding support, dislike the principles they may or may not stand for, finally we have justified through a series of pantomimes, just why it is we have come to hate them, and these are the bricks we build in the wall that will finally separate us – and then we can go on to serve our agenda.

We need to redefine our own thoughts and we will then find we are automatically enabled to see others differently.

Occultists the world over know that once a symbol is created, it acquires a power of its own, and more power is created when such symbols are created without the uninitiated knowing about it. And the greatest power of all is created if the uninitiated never find out about it.

When the architect, Pierre Charles L'Enfant, who was a freemason, laid out the Government Centre of Washington, D.C, in 1791, he planned more than just the streets, roads and buildings. He planned to use the layout of Government Centre to hide certain occultist magical symbols, which, when they were instituted, became one large Luciferic, or occultist symbol.

An occultist magical symbol is defined as ' … an image, which hides an inner meaning. This meaning is usually cunningly hidden behind a form …'

(Fredrick Goodman, Magic Symbols).

On the afternoon of October 13th 1792 a group of Freemasons marched from Georgetown and laid the corner stone of the White House. There is only one known written account of this, 'The President's House,' as it was first called was the first public building to be built in Washington. James Hoban, a young Irish immigrant's blueprint was chosen. On May 25th 1795, Hoban had placed an advertisement in the Pennsylvania Evening Herald offering his services as an architect. Business was a little slow so following advice from friends he joined a Masonic Lodge and thereafter his career took off. Following several projects he was chosen to oversee and implement the construction of the White House.

Hoban based his design on the Leinster House in Dublin, a building just south of Temple Bar and Trinity Collage. The area had many celebrities including George Bernard Shaw, a founder member of the Fabian Society. Bram Stoker the author of Dracula. The wine waiter at their favourite restaurant was Alois Hitler Jnr, the older half-brother of Adolph. (Who was arrested and charged with bigamy).

The man who built Leinster House was James Fitzgerald, the 20th Earl of Kildare. Construction began in 1745; the year 'Bonnie Prince Charlie' was defeated at Culloden. Two years later Fitzgerald married Emily Lennox; whose father Charles was the Duke of Richmond and godfather to King George II. Through this favourable marriage James was made Viscount Leinster in 1749 by George II and later Duke of Leinster by George III.

(The Duke's nephew was Lord Edward Fitzgerald, who founded the United Irishmen and led the failed Illuminati uprising of 1798).

The Duke was a key figure in Irish Freemasonry, in 1779 he and Dr.G.A.Cunningham of Dublin wrote to Thomas Arthur of Irvine in Scotland requesting permission to form a lodge of the same name in Dublin. This was the Kilwinning Lodge No. 75, also known as the High Knights Templar of Ireland.

Incidentally James Fitzgerald was related to one of the original Knights Templar, his ancestor was Maurice Fitzgerald, who invited the Templars to organise banking houses in Dublin. So James Hoban, a Mason, chose the Leinster house, which was the birthplace of Irish Freemasonry, as a model for the USA's executive mansion.

Friday October 13th 1307, was the day the French King Philippe IV had the Grand Master of the Templars, Jacques de Molay arrested and subsequently burned at the stake.

Philippe IV (who conveniently had his substantial debts wiped out by his actions) persuaded Pope Clement V and they conspired together to arrest, dissolve and destroy the Order of Knights Templar. This was the time of inquisitions and those Knights that were arrested were coerced and tortured to confess to scandalous and perverse actions. Jacques de Molay confessed to denying Christ and trampling on the Cross, which resulted in the Pope ordering the arrest of all Knights Templar.

The many Knights that escaped formed again secretly into such clubs as the Knights of Malta and the Hospitilars. At the time the Templars owned the largest fleet of sailing ships in the World, they scattered to Malta, Scotland and elsewhere, taking their wealth with them. In Scotland they fought under the leadership of Robert the Bruce at the Battle of Bannockburn, for the independence of Scotland.

They were the early influence of Freemasonry and by merging their knighthood with the early freemasons they were able to control their power hidden from view and preserve their rites throughout time to the present.

A small island off the fog-shrouded coast of Nova Scotia may contain the World's greatest treasure, the booty of the Knights Templar, missing since the 14th century.

The debate remains unresolved but the truth remains someone with incredible knowledge and resources went to an unbelievable amount of trouble to conceal something. It is a fascinating story and there is a wealth of information out there, it is known as the Oak Island mystery.

The magic of symbology is and always has been known to the powerful hierarchy. Symbology goes back as far as history allows us to view, to the Ancient Egyptian priests and God-Kings or Pharos, these illuminated brothers worshipped the Sun – just as we unknowingly do today.

We can call magic by many different titles; the law of attraction, spell casting, gossip, praying or cursing, but we struggle to understand how it works.

What scientists call the Planck Scale is the smallest subatomic levels of measurement. It indicates that particles of (subatomic) matter can be in several places at the same time – bizarre but true.

What is even more bizarre is that they don't seem to decide on which of those places to be – until they are observed then they snap into place, scientists refer to this phenomena as the collapse of the wave field.

Logic therefore dictates that the mind can as a result, control matter – all thought produces form,

When more of us realise this we will regain our power and live the lives we were designed to live.

Sacred Geometry and the resultant architecture of buildings has a profound effect upon us. We can identify immediately when a sound is pleasing to us, however subconsciously we find it difficult to know what influences are at work upon us when we entering a cathedral or a mosque. We will discuss sacred geometry later but I cannot stress enough the importance of how form radically and deeply affects us.

I don't pretend to understand what fundamental change happens to us as we walk the maze at Chartres Cathedral, enter the Great Pyramid at Giza or enter the portals of any municipal building, but I would bet anything that we are being altered, manipulated and changed. And having won that bet I would double up and place all my winnings on the fact that we would be far better off without the corruptive power of man-made geometry and logo and far better off in the natural agenda-less sacred geometry of nature.

Are we really supposed to accept the consideration that magic manipulation by illicit means is good for our well-being? From the floor-plans to the roofs of our Man-made structures to the street plans of our cities, our monuments and obelisks are all built to a plan and those plans are guided and are drawn by people who knowingly or unknowingly guide us in turn.

Nature has the same blueprint but it has no agenda, its intentions are benign.

The foundation stone for the Pentagon was laid in a Masonic ceremony on September 11th 1941. The people who reside at the hierarchy of our society; those that hold the real power are with us now and have always been.

For want of a better description they are magicians. The secrets these people hold have been passed like a baton, handed down through bloodline from one generation to the next, their secrets are held in the rituals that they practice. These rituals change and alter our very core, they change our vibration, they influence us at a sub atomic level and they corrupt our DNA which is the blueprint of our structure; they affect how we act and how we think.

The truth is that magic is practised upon us every moment of every day. Whether it is good or bad in the conventional sense is up to us to define, only each of us as individuals can define good or bad. However as long as we give away our power to feel and therefore to act in any negative way then we allow magic to be practised upon us.

I cannot prove to you that walking the maze at Chartres Cathedral makes us think or act differently in a bad or negative way and I accept this is not good enough to present as a fact, because I simply *feel* as if it does, but that's good enough for me personally so with respect, you can only decide for yourself. So some people are going to say they haven't got a clue what the hell I am on about and others might concur.

It is a vibrational thing.

Yes I am probably oversensitive but it is highly likely if your not then you could be, in fact the only reason your not is because you are blocking.

You are a mass of energy that has made an agreement to process other energy thus we get drawn, repelled and influenced as a result and if the energy that is You goes through a ritual such as encountering a logo, passed between two pillars, walks on black and white tiles, receives initiation through ceremony, groomed to be a groom, stands in natural or manipulated energy or to put it another way; gets washed in music, witnesses horror, feels love, climbs a mountain, watches a film then we are influenced and if we are influenced it follows that we are altered.

But my question is; are we altered for our benefit or to our cost?

Will the results of our encounter enable us to grow, to aspire to become better or are we being urged to buy a hamburger, seek power over others, follow some agenda, agree to something we would normally inherently despise and we are therefore complying with a malevolent force?

When we enter the doorway of a church or a mosque and stand in awe under their domes, we are in a manufactured environment.

Conversely, when we stand in awe of nature as we witness and wonder we are undergoing feelings and vibrations naturally produced. All the important buildings on this earth are built upon energy sites because this allows the manipulation of energy.

The pillars of Joachim and Boaz are represented everywhere; the height of the sun and the depth of the sun, the winter and summer solstice, and exposure to these pillars especially through ritual or in other words a conscious, manufactured effort and the result is change.

A child at his first foxhunt (or bullfight or whatever trauma he is exposed to) when his face is smeared with the animal's blood, he is altered and he is changed. Every gathering of people involves ritual based on belief and tradition. Baptism and the marriage ceremony for example, both alter and change the initiate. Just as when the Queen knights a subject. Watch the rituals of monarchy and realise how ancient these practices of magic are and furthermore what these rituals really achieve.

When people collect themselves together more power is produced, just as coupling batteries together increases power. If the work that is done in these gatherings is for the common good then we should have no problem, but when we don't know the real reason because we are 'uninitiated,' then we are being deceived and tricked.

Magic and religion are so conjoined it is difficult to separate them and we should realise that religion consists of an appeal to the gods whereas magic is an attempt to force their compliance.

Architecture incorporates symbols and the power within these symbols is vibrational, when we pass through the portals of the grand buildings we visit, we are influenced in a similar way as we would be by music but without hearing a sound, the way these buildings should be constructed should be compatible with the visitor or inhabitant.

Symbols have the power to influence us, we live by them and we die by them. Symbols are used in ways we do not understand by those that seek to control us. Symbols indoctrinate us on an unconscious level and give power to those that understand them. The few people who understand them are the peak of the pyramid; they are *not* the millions of churchgoers or freemasons who unknowingly for the most part, 'do their thing' in a ritualised environment.

The floor of every Masonic temple is the same, as is every church and cathedral; black and white squares the same pattern to be found on every policeman's uniform and hat. Furthermore, meetings held in secret that benefit the few to the cost of the many cannot be justified.

I have a question for the men behind the curtains – is it our god we are worshipping or yours?

When it comes down to our inherent wish to understand the Universe we live in we are compounded to put everything into human terms.

We have no other option – after all we are human.

For some mathematics is the key to understanding, for others it is letters or the words they form that enable us to make better sense of everything. We radically underestimate how numbers, letters, symbols and codes affect us in fact that they define our very existence.

But these tools only allow us to see tiny facets and aspects of the Universe because we made these models up and they serve to enable us to understand and communicate with one another.

Magic exists, not slight of hand magic because as clever as it seems when you know how the trick works, you realise how simple it was to perform. A trick is great because it enables us to be childlike and suspend our belief in 'reality' – a great diversion – but magic it isn't.

The obvious is that which is never seen until someone expresses it simply.
Kahlil Gibran.

Everything in the Universe is trying to be something else because it is drawn toward being stable. Of the elements that make up our Universe, it is only iron that is relatively stable therefore unless it's made of iron; it wants to change into it.

Everything is in flux and demonstrates a will to change, this 'will' could be described as Consciousness, magic is performed by man to engineer a desired outcome therefore magic is the manipulation of energy.

Consider what would happen if you took away the space from between matter. Everything in the universe would scrunch together into a volume no larger than a dust speck. We notice that hasn't happened. Why not? Something prevents it. That something is space itself … Space resists being pushed about. Space is what keeps everything from happening in the same place.

Konrad Finagle. Theory of the Void.

Which is interesting because this virtually unheard of physicist who died in 1963, was inviting us to finally admit to the certainty that even empty space is every bit as 'real' as anything else talked about in physics. Space it is not empty nothingness, a fabric connects every particle; there is no void it is simply matter with zero density. He was also tempting us to visualise conditions before the Big Bang; take all the space away in the Universe and we are left with how it began – a speck of dust.

If the theory of the Big Bang is correct it would make sense of the fact that everything in existence is One in that everything emanated from One and that is one of the points I am trying to make on these pages.

Vladimir Poponin and Peter Gariaev carried out research at the Russian Academy of Science; they detected the electromagnetic fields of DNA within a vacuum in what they called the DNA Phantom Effect. They tested the behaviour of DNA on photons within the vacuum and found that these photons, (that are the light particles that make up everything in the Universe) behaved differently when introduced to DNA; in other words living material made the particles position themselves differently. Furthermore when the DNA was removed from the vacuum the photon particles did not revert back to their previous random state, they remained ordered.

Scientists being scientists are urged to find conclusions and they concluded there was either a force at work that remained after the DNA was removed or a form of energy we are unable to detect linked the DNA and the photons.

This then is Consciousness in evidence, it is the intelligence that is responsible for our physical reality, and DNA changes the behaviour of photons.

In a recent televised experiment on ITV1, three male identical triplets aged 21, were asked if they had any thoughts or feelings whereby they felt connected when as individuals they were apart from each other. They were sceptical and refused to accept that they were linked in any other way than convention dictates. One of the boys was wired to a machine that delivered random mild electric shocks. The other two boys were connected to monitoring equipment in complete isolation. The two boys on the monitors in detached rooms had no conscious thought of anything happening during the experiment, but the monitors told a very different story as they rose and fell in perfect harmony to the shocks administered to their brother.

According to Gregg Braden in his book, The Divine Matrix, he goes into depth on the subject of our connection and place in the Matrix, which I prefer to call Consciousness. He writes about the Phantom Effect and a study reported in Advances Journal in 1993 which said the Army performed experiments to determine precisely whether the emotion and DNA connection continues following being separated and if so at what distances?

The researchers started by collecting a swab of tissue and DNA from a volunteer's mouth. The sample was isolated and taken to another room in the building, where they began to investigate a phenomenon that modern science says shouldn't exist.

In a specially designed chamber the DNA was measured electrically to see if it responded to the emotions of the person it came from, the donor was in a room several hundred feet away. In this room, the subject was shown a series of video images designed to induce emotional responses. During the experiment his DNA was measured for its response. Although the donor was hundreds of feet from the DNA sample the DNA responded and acted as if it was still physically connected to his body.

Dr Cleve Backster, who designed the project, said the Army continued this experiment moving the subject further and further away from the DNA. At one point 350 miles separated the donor and his cells but and the results remained the same, their DNA and the subject were still connected. They even measured response time with an atomic clock in order to prove that there was no time lapse and that the emotions given out and the DNA responded simultaneously.

The book that has had the most impact on me is called 'A Course in Miracles,' or 'ACIM,' as many people know it, it was first published in 1975. I was drawn to this book and it was always around me but I only opened it a few times and tried to understand it. Looking back I feel I just wasn't ready to understand and appreciate it, it might have had something to do with the fact that I was consumed by my ego and in various stages of dysfunctionality which included the use of various narcotics and analgesics.

In 2004 I was given a book called The Disappearance of the Universe, written by Gary. R. Renard, this book is similarly deep and spiritually rich in content, but I persevered and on gaining great insight from this book it transpired that it became the key to my better understanding of ACIM. A book published in 2007 titled 'Take Me to the Truth - the undoing of the ego,' by Nouk Sanchez and Tomas Viera provides the reader with similar insights.

These books invite self-study and present us with profound insight about our thoughts, beliefs, and feelings. In ACIM the miracle is the healing that comes from Spirit and results in a shift of perception. What once caused negative states such as fear, guilt or anger can then be seen with love and understanding.

The Course teaches that our reality is an infinite, eternal, formless, loving being that is an expression of God and that God is the Source of all that there is. The Course states that we are an extension of this Source, however the reason that we do not fully realise this is because of our belief in separation from our Source. The Course says, 'Into eternity, where all is one, they're crept a tiny, mad idea, at which the Son of God remembered not to laugh.'

In believing we could separate, we imagined a world of separation on a Universal scale. Into this illusory world, we are born as individual bodies and we experience birth and death. Instead of the joy of absolute Oneness with God and love, we find ourselves in a world of duality. This is obviously at odds with Oneness or the infinite perfection that God created.

A world of duality, of light and dark, black and white, good and evil and time and space. Instead of knowing our infinite spiritual selves we form limiting concepts of ourselves and suffer loss and deprivation as a result. We are afraid and as a result we attack one another and ourselves. We struggle through life, feeling inadequate and never finding the satisfaction we seek. But the Course teaches that, ultimately, all of this is but a dream and we are merely sleeping. The Course serves as a vehicle to awaken from this dream or as many would put it this nightmare.

The Course explains how our function in the world is to heal from our separation and realise the truth about who and what we are. This healing is accomplished through the healing of our relationships with others, this always involves some form of forgiveness; however, the Course in defining forgiveness makes clear that forgiveness is about releasing false perceptions that are based on false beliefs about who and what we are. It explains that we always encounter ourselves in others. When we are upset with others, it is because we are distressed by our buried, hidden concepts of ourselves and we are projecting those images onto them. The powerful realisation comes when we are finally willing to search our own minds instead of blaming others for our own unhappiness. We then forgive the others for what we saw mirrored in them. This heals the separation thoughts in our own minds; we experience miracles in our relationships and discover the love that unites us all.

Miracles take many different forms and in any situation where we feel any form of fear rather than love, we can seek a miracle. With fear seeming to predominate our world's thinking our task is to recognise the need for love and seek inner healing. Through miracles, we can heal our minds and see a very different world and embrace and live a happy dream.

For reasons we cannot understand, a thought of separation from God, which the ACIM calls the ego, entered the collective mind of the energy that went on to construct the Universe. We flatter ourselves because of our egos and the separateness and beliefs that the ego creates gives us the idea that we could take the place of God and become the Creator. God's answer to this was the creation of the Holy Spirit in our mind to correct this 'tiny mad idea' of separation.

Choosing not to listen to the Voice of God, we experienced an overwhelming sense of sin at what we thought we had accomplished. From this act of sin came guilt and we were thereafter easily programmed into the fear of God's punishment. Our minds became split into the wrong mind of the ego, and the right mind of the Holy Spirit.

As the Course puts it, a veil of forgetfulness falls over our decision and this illusory world appears very real to us. However we are still safe in heaven although lost in our dream of exile. So powerful is this illusion that we cannot awaken without the help of the Holy Spirit, we therefore need to allow or ask and to do this most effectively we need to undo the programming that was communicated to us as we were growing up. Presently we perceive our bodies as real and not spirit, solid non-vibrational forms. The ego trains us to deny our guilt and to project it onto others; this dynamic is really very interesting. From a personal view it is difficult to make an accurate assessment of ourselves which is why self-analysis is so tough, we all know people who are prepared to present us with all that is wrong with our lives but seem unable to deploy that advice to their own lives. We project outwards and inwards and both of these are dubious abilities because they both cause harm.

If you listen to what people fear you will gain incite; those that blame others for dishonesty are very often dishonest themselves, heavy drinkers of alcohol are often 'very concerned about a friend who is drinking too much,' many macho men rant a little to strongly against gay people perhaps fearing their own deep-seated desires and so on.

The bottom line is the fact that we project in order to ease our guilt.

That guilt, which is our own self-hatred, now appears to be created by people and circumstances that are outside of ourselves. We now feel justified in feeling anger towards others and attack in self-defence becomes a necessity, with this thought process activated we then go on to form special hate relationships and we do this as individuals and we do this collectively.

Conversely because we feel lack within us, the ego counsels us to find people who can fulfil our imagined needs such as security, sex, money, status, career etc, and from this feeling we build and form our special love relationships. To awaken from the dream and regain the vision we have lost we need to undo our belief in separation from God. According to ACIM, The Holy Spirit's plan is to enable our awakening which is called the 'Atonement,' which is a different way of looking, a correction of our programmed perception.

We begin to learn that the world is both a neutral and benign mirror of the beliefs in our mind. No person or event has the power to give or take away our peace from us. When we get disturbed about someone or something that is 'out there' in the world we are only seeing a projection of some part of our mind that has not forgiven, we are therefore self-testing. When a negative emotion is manifested within us, we fail the test but if we allow the Holy Spirit's counsel of forgiveness to enter our mind we can begin the journey of undoing separation by joining together with others. We forgive by first removing our projections from the world and then bringing them back to our mind from where they first began, after all we emanated these projections and only we can deal with them by they're dismissal. As a result we have the opportunity to heal our mind by ceasing to judge from its ego content. It is our self-judgment that prevents our mind from being healed by the Holy Spirit and it is through guilt that we are programmed to think we deserve punishment and not healing. We are programmed to default to fear rather than love.

As we grow and learn to stop judging ourselves we allow the ever-present love of the Holy Spirit to remove guilt in our mind. This shift of perception from the ego's world of separation and attack, to the knowledge of Holy Spirit's voice of joining and forgiveness is what ACIM calls a miracle. As we practice forgiveness in our relationships, we start to undo the guilt that covers and blocks the memory of God's love in our mind; this was the guilt that the ego urged us to feel regarding our separation. We begin to see that we have not been running away from God's anger because that is programming. God does not have anger because God is love therefore what we are actually running away from is God's love. With that realisation we allow the consciousness of God's love back into our mind, this enables our ego to disappear and as ACIM tells us, this is our greatest fear.

Relationships then become opportunities in which we learn to forgive ourselves by forgiving others and anything that disturbs our peace remains an unresolved issue within ourselves. The Buddha and The Christ Mind provide us with the best examples in teaching this lesson of forgiveness and this thought process is the cornerstone of every religion. We come to realise that when people attack us through fear what they are really asking for is love. As a result we begin to allow the Holy Spirit to transform our world from the prison of the ego and into a teaching device that will awaken us from this dream of separation.

When we open our mind to the knowledge of who we really are then we can live in this world in complete peace with joy and nothing can disturb or remove this. We have evolved to perceive everyone as our brothers and sisters whose reality is eternal spirit and to whom we extend the love of the Holy Spirit.

If we are urged to guide our children then this is the magic that they should be taught – this then is the sort of wizardry that they should encounter – this would change our world for the better in a heartbeat.

ACIM refers to the Big Bang as taking place because of 'a tiny mad idea,' - an idea of separation – this was the 'Bang' in the Big-Bang that kick started the whole thing, originally there was just God or perfection or Oneness and then Consciousness decided to form and then there was dualism or 'twoness' and Consciousness thereafter went onto create the Universe and although I keep mentioning that Universal Consciousness Energy or Source is where we all came from, strictly speaking Consciousness is the first separation from perfection – from love - from God. It is therefore important for us to realise two points. Firstly, Consciousness is not a pure form because it contains ego and the idea of separateness. Consciousness can be benign as it is in the process of forming energy into matter but it can also be manipulated as it has been from the mystery schools of the ancients to the modern day. Secret affiliations that permeate throughout all society and always manipulated by the very few to control us. And the second point we need to remember is that Consciousness or the other multitude of words we search for to describe the ether, the matrix, that funny feeling, god or love, therefore Consciousness is just a word. The word Consciousness is just a symbol to help us understand that everything is One and all is well.

Accessing Consciousness is the nearest we can get to God whilst we are in our matter-based spacesuits and the bridge we cross to Oneness – perfectness - to love and to god - is called The Holy Spirit. So the question is raised, how do we get to God? We do so by waking up from our dream, we wake up by reducing the ego; by no longer judging and condemning - that means instantaneous forgiveness of every single-thing. This is called quantum forgiveness and it washes our impurities away in a painless act of love should we have the courage to embrace it.

The 'Bang' in the Big Bang was Consciousness causing the first separation from God, and what caused Consciousness to separate was ego, in other words the desire of separation. Therefore ego is a manifestation of Consciousness and it is our ego that blinds us to the perfection that is God.

William Blake painted 'The Red Dragon,' a picture that was featured in the books of Thomas Harris and made into the films 'Manhunter' and 'The Silence of the Lambs.' I guess both Blake and Harris must have been absorbed by the miracle metamorphism of the ugly bug that spins its cocoon goes to sleep to later emerge as a beautiful butterfly or moth. These three transitions represent enormous, irrerrecognisable changes and they are also representative of rebirth or reincarnation.

Where I am trying to go with this is to suggest a comparison with ourselves – as long as we are trapped with our ego we cannot emerge from our cocoons, we are unable to transform and carnate and we remain more solid, more matter based, grounded, restricted and as a result more blinkered. With the quelling of ego comes the emergence that we, the same as the butterfly, take on a bright new view of the Universe and enjoy a transition to enlightenment.

And no, I am not suggesting that you or me are like chrysalises or caterpillars, I am trying to suggest that was perhaps what Blake and Harris were in part trying to symbolise.

I mean – would never dream of dropping silently out of a pine tree and killing a dog.

When all our impurities are burned away through pain or incite and we carry no further baggage, we have no fear, we become enlightened, we don't have to come back to psycho-planet, we have broken the cycle, we return to Oneness – to perfection – to God and we get there via what many call the Holy Spirit and we get there through love because love is god.

All matter is energy reduced to a lower vibration.

And if you can manipulate energy you must also be able to manipulate matter, because the nature of matter is that it is more dense than if it were high vibrational energy, as is in the case of light, (energy) is less dense than your dog or your dining room table (matter). However the same atoms have simply made a quantum decision through Consciousness to become more 'solid' matter and they are simply vibrating more slowly.

When your dog or the dining room table finishes with its life's purpose its energy will revert to something else … which will still be energy and therefore resume the potential to become matter again.

'We are the dust of the stars,' I don't know who originally penned this and when I first heard this I didn't get it straight away, but it stuck with me as I liked the romantic view it enabled me to have. As time has gone by now I understand, we really are the dust of the stars; I mean how awesome is that. Every atom in your body that makes you - YOU - was forged in a star.

Another sobering thought; there are more atoms in *one* glass of water – than there are glasses of water – in all the oceans in all the seas.

Virtually everything that is 'out there' all the time is in a state of transition, a condition of flux; that's a stone, a tree, a star and ourselves – everything. Nothing stays the same (which is one of the major sources of our problems in that we try to avoid change).

If we are fortunate we find time in our busy lives to look upward to gaze upon the same firmament that every human being for thousands of years has gazed up at. We can only look in awe and wonder at how insignificant we are in this scheme of things, (and we've usurped our ego, albeit temporarily).

And then, think again and know with certainty that you and me are a facet, a part of all of this and *(because we are energy and energy cannot be manufactured or destroyed)* we go on and it does not finish here. Everything is constant, everything is cyclic and we should not resist our demise because this is the natural part of this order, we should not fear death the way we are programmed to do; it is simply a return from whence we came.

Anyway back to magic.

In a nutshell – magic is the manipulation of energy – which includes matter.

Now this is where there is a potential problem because it is said that there are two types of magic; black magic and white magic. But I think that's another programming trick and it is therefore something else we are supposed to believe. It is suggested that black magic is to do 'bad' and white magic conversely is to do 'good' – but it is you and only you – that defines what is good and bad.

Because of childhood programming one of the equations in life that we are constantly invited to consider is whether we are – good or bad. This has a massive impact and to a large extent shapes our perception of reality.

Your *good* can be someone else's *bad,* in any event I suspect those that are practising magic – certainly the real powerful stuff – don't care how it is perceived, the fact is that they are practising magic in order to influence us and in turn benefit themselves. It is not the wizards concern for the welfare of the subject; his object is to alter something or someone for his own requirements. And this is occurring all the time all around us and for the most part understandably, we are totally oblivious.

> *The oldest and most respected scientific society in the world is called the Royal Society. The early members of this society read like a who's-who of scientists – Hooke's Law, Boyle's Law, Huygen's construction, Newton's Laws, Leibniz's theorem, Brownian construction. These 'Fellows of the Royal Society,' also included Christopher Wren, John Evelyn, John Wilkins, Elias Ashmole, John Flamsteed and Edmund Halley.*
>
> *But the men who founder this society were not just the first scientists – they were also the last sorcerers.*

Extracted from, Robert Lomas. The Invisible College.

King Charles II restored the Stuart line of kings to the throne subsequent to the Civil War in which Oliver Cromwell had overthrown the monarchy. According to Freemasonry and the Birth of Modern Science, by Robert Lomas, Charles was not only the Royal Societies patron but he was a Freemason, The Royal Society was in fact the intellectual offspring of Freemasonry and this served as a blueprint and the organised network that the group were committed to. These men changed the world forever.

The view of a Freemason

> *I call Freemasonry a religion, as that's exactly what it is. There are only two religions in the world. Firstly, the invisible church, the body of Christ, where God calls his people from every nation, tribe and tongue into eternal salvation through the precious blood of his son Jesus Christ at the cross of Calgary. God's grace and plan of redemption justification and sanctification, before the foundation of the world: this religion or relationship with God is called Christianity.*
>
> *The illuminated of elite initiated priests of the thirty third degree, Knights Templars and Freemasonry brotherhood, called and chosen out of nations, tribes and tongues by Satan to serve him and carry out his evil plan throughout history. It is syncretism or the uniting of all religions on earth. Buddhists, Moslem, Hindu, so called Christians and wherever else you may happen to be. It doesn't matter as they all recognise the one god Lucifer (light bearer) or better known as Satan.*

Martyrs of Revelation in the New World Order.

As concerning as this last piece may be, it does lift the veil on the views of the mechanics of the hierarchy of Freemasonry and it also alludes to the fact that it is Satan who is being deified and the Sun that is being worshipped.

The following is from the website 'Masonic Traveller.' It shows both the naivety and the truth of the average Freemason, a superb trick played out for thousands of years, keeping us the masses in ignorance, controlling us to serve the few people in the world that have all the power, all the money and most importantly all the knowledge, knowledge that is our birthright.

My wife records Oprah, and on occasions I watch it with her at night when we get home from work. It just so happened that on February 8th, she had a panel of speakers who were there to do their best to plug the profundity of 'The Secret', a new on-line film/DVD that proclaims to reveal centuries hidden knowledge in the span of a 90-minute motivational speech.

After watching the original episode of Oprah on the 8th and her follow-up on the 17th (where the 'O' did some fancy dancing to the 'no this isn't an anti Christian message' song), I had to admit that I felt compelled to see exactly what 'The Secret' was all about.

After watching it tonight, I'll be damned; the message it presents is pretty spot on.

I wasn't really sure what to expect. Probably some new age hocus-pocus or some motivational speakers saying you have the power to do what you want (which it was in many ways), but this video took it a step further. It said something I have been saying (and doing) for a while now through my own sort of personal discovery of all things Masonic. The message was that we (people) are a part of the God conscious Universe, and that our energy resonates with the rest of the Universe, and that this energy, when harmonised, has the potential of ANYTHING, good or bad. This harmonic energy is what we put out into the Universe also attracts back to us, depending on what we think, feel desire, wish or pray for. And our attitudes contribute to what we get in return.

From the Masonic perspective, the degrees of masonry illustrate our ascension into this thought. That, as we are initiated into this ideation and taught how to interpret from which we learn our ultimate step, the placement at the doorway of God, the inner chamber of K.S.T. our thoughts attenuated into this celestial divine, not without as some external force, but within, as our own manifestation of that Creative Force. We, widow's sons, are the creators of our Universe.

The philosophy in 'The Secret' should be simple to understand by any Freemason who watches it. Even simpler now that it has been broken down to its barest components, which are: 'Know Thy Self' and 'Follow Your Bliss.' With these two axioms, you can control your Universe.

For those wondering though, where the producers came up with this Secret Teaching, they give you glimpses at the beginning alluding to their origins, The

Knights Templar, Rosicrucian's, The Romans, The Egyptians, and so on… But there may be some true point of origin here. Out of Hermetica, there comes a myth, the myth of the Emerald Tablet of Hermes Trismegistus. On this tablet were written 13 point of wisdom and these points create the foundation of this transformative thought.

The 13 points on the tablet are;

The truth, certainty, truest, without untruth.

What is above is like what is below. What is below is like what is above. The miracle of unity is to be attained.

Everything is formed from the contemplation of unity, and all things come about from unity, by means of adaptation.

Its parents are the Sun and Moon.

It was borne by the wind and nurtured by the Earth.

Every wonder is from it and its power is complete.

Throw it upon earth, and earth will separate from fire. The impalpable separated from the palpable.

Through wisdom it rises slowly from the world to heaven. Then it descends to the world combining the power of the upper and the lower.

Thus you will have the illumination of all of the world, and darkness will disappear.

This is the power of all strength – it overcomes that which is delicate and penetrates through solids. This was the means of the creation of the world.

And in the future wonderful developments will be made, and this is the way.

I am Hermes the Threefold Sage, so named because I hold the three elements of all wisdom.

And thus ends the revelation of the work of the Sun.

From these points you can learn the secret.

The only thing I don't agree with is that the 'The Secret' is wisdom for those who care to know about it. The owners of 'The Secret' didn't hide it. It has been alive and vital in the mystery schools of antiquity for aeons; all anyone has to do to gain the secret is just ask …

Maybe, as in ages past, this is the new mode of transference. This is how the secret teachings of the ages are to be communicated to the masses, to merge with our subconscious and manifest into daily life, so it is never forgotten again.

There is great truth in these words and in reading them I suspect we would view the author as a perfectly decent human being. The secret teachings he referred to will never be revealed to him or to us, because it would finally prove that manipulation on a grand and devious scale has been practised upon us.

The people that control the world do so through manipulation and this magic is practised at its most powerful through ritual. In the ritualised rite of passage that must be taken to become a Freemason the initiated is blindfolded (this is where the term 'hoodwink' originates). To be initiated is to symbolically die and be reborn, ending a life to start a new one. The process is a frightening experience linking emotional fear and manipulating Consciousness in an act that transforms the individual. This is the goal of the Masonic quest and of all initiation.

Every ceremony involves initiation; every initiation alters and changes us. Every person on the planet has been initiated; every one of us has been hoodwinked.

The word Mason comes from the Old English 'magician,' which is the verb to make, in turn the word magician is from the Greek 'magike,' or the art of the Magi, the word used to describe The Three Wise Men of biblical fame. Magic originally consisted in the study of wisdom, and those that practised it were adept in astrology, divination and sorcery.

Symbolism is the language of the Illuminati because it is the language of the subconscious and this is another major subliminal technique, as with the use of phallic symbols of many kinds. The bloodlines and their Illuminati network are obsessed with symbolism and their symbols and codes going back thousands of years can clearly be found throughout American society and the rest of the world, especially the British Empire. The ancient Illuminati symbol of the pyramid with the capstone missing (the pyramid with the all-seeing eye) was placed on the dollar bill in 1933 by President Franklin Delano Roosevelt, one of the highly significant front men for the Illumianati in the United States during the 20th century. The most obvious Illuminati symbol is the eternal flame or the lighted torch and this represents the 'Illuminated Ones,' the initiates illuminated into knowledge that the rest of the population is denied. The Statue of Liberty most famously holds the Illuminati lighted torch. This was given to New York by French Freemasons in Paris who knew what she and the torch really symbolised. There is virtually a mirror image of the Statue of Liberty on an island in the River Seine in Paris. As the bloodlines came up into Europe and across the world they naturally brought their symbols with them. The Statue of Liberty is the symbolic image of the goddess worshipped by the Illuminati bloodlines since they were based in Babylon (and before). She goes under many names, including Queen Semiramis, the 'branch bearer,' who was symbolised as a dove.

David Icke. Tales from the Time Loop.

A word is a symbol, as is a letter that makes up a word. Imagine for one moment and step away from your teaching.

What do the following represent to you? A, F, H, I, K, N, Y, Z. Of course we would answer – letters – that's a programmed education.

But if you knew no better – if you had just looked at them for the very first time with no preconceived notions, you might say that each of those letters represents nothing more than three sticks joined together. But from the arrangement of the 26 'sticks' or symbols that make up our alphabet man has managed to convey every emotion possible.

I cdnuolt blveiee that I cluod aulaclty uesdnatnrd what I was rdanieg.

The phaonmneal pweor of the hmuan mnid Aoccdrnig to rscheearch at Cmabrigde Uinervtisy, it deosn't mttaer in what oredr the ltteers in a word are, the olny iprmoatnt tihng is that the first and last ltteer be in the rghit pclae. The rset can be a taotl mses and you can still raed it wouthit a porbelm. This is bcuseae the huamn mnid deos not raed ervey lteter by istlef, but the word as a wlohe.

If we accept that everything we learn and understand, is carried to us in the form of symbology, which we then go on to try and make sense from. It follows the assembly of 'sticks' form letters and the making up of words is simply a tool to enable us to understand something or communicate in order someone else can understand. The same is true of mathematics, the language of Chinese, of music, it's true of a model of an atom or a DNA molecule, (it doesn't really look like that it is just a way of getting us to understand physics).

Hearing sound or seeing the most basic of data can influence us, it can even save life.

The coastguard upon hearing the International Morse code distress signal (... --- ...) will dispatch a rescue mission, this then is not a bad example of what is being suggested here, but whatever we are being invited to understand originated in earlier programming.

It's our emotions that are being called upon and we are presented by a huge cartel of emotional shifts by how we react for example; if your cherished daughter is going to her first official engagement this evening, your feelings about the event will be affected by what is printed on the tickets – is it a 'ball' or a 'rave?' Even though in essence there is no great difference, at both events there will be drink, drugs and boys but those little words communicate two very different meanings, it is therefore our view on how this will affect us, our views that were placed in childhood and reinforced as were growing up.

Everything we process is a vehicle to assist us to understand and communicate. This is why symbology exists, to prompt a thought or manipulate us to understand, knowingly or unknowingly. Assemble those symbols in the right form and we can be moved to tears, overtaken by anger, subjected to fear, taken to joy or feel the warm embrace of love. Everything exists though our interpretation of it and we interpret much using our five-senses through language and through ideas, or as a wizard might say, energy is power when you know how to harness it.

> *The main land of Europe never produced an alphabet of its own. Our own alphabet has its roots in pictographs. Our letter 'A' comes from the Semitic aleph, meaning 'ox', and originally was a rough depiction of an ox's head.*
>
> Bill Bryson. Mother Tongue.

So we began to use pictures or symbols to form sounds to make ourselves better understood in order to communicate.

Bill Bryson suggests that there are two ways of rendering speech from writing. One is with an alphabet (a series of symbols) such as we have and the other is with a pictographic-ideographic system, such as the Chinese use, (still a series of symbols).

The Swiss psychologist, Dr Carl Jung wrote that our unconscious carries the keys to the highest wisdom of our kind, in the form of inborn images (archetypes) of human potential and relationship that reveal the pattern and meaning of our human experience and guide us in making major life decisions. He called the unconscious the friend of the soul.

One of the oldest arguments appertains to nature (inheritance) or nurture (environment). In essence nature says we are born predisposed to certain behaviour, nurture says we are born as blank slates and our environment thereafter will educate us. No one seems to be able to fully agree on either argument.

What Jung and others were in essence trying to show was that you come into this world with say; a predisposed fear of snakes, rather than you are taught to be afraid of them. However most psychologists seem to agree that our disgust toward something is learned. It is a daunting subject and remains unproven.

Parents of a newborn baby will inform us that the infant very quickly displays individuality and unique personality traits. But as interesting as such debates may be Jung himself was not a materialist, but a mystic. He dabbled in astrology, the Kabbalah and in alchemy and was therefore clearly open to aspects of a metaphysical nature; he saw clues to some greater spirit based reality. He used the theory of the collective unconscious not only to explain similarities across cultures in mythology and psychological functioning to explain phenomenon like precognition, telepathy, and synchronicity. Jung considered these all manifestations of the collective unconscious that is, our unseen connection of one soul to another, and of our connection to a higher order of intelligence. According to those with materialist leanings, but who are still willing to incorporate Jung, these archetypes are something inherited at birth genetically, like blue eyes and curly hair. Or they point to the fact that all human beings share a common physiology, a fairly common way of perceiving the world through our basic biological faculties, our five senses. We also have a common nervous system and common basic needs for food, warmth, and touch. So it makes sense that there is a basic shared quality to our longings and perceptions. However whether we are drawn to a person because we entered the world predisposed to like something about them, or because we learned something in our formative years that draws us to them is not important because there exists another possibility as we are growing up and that communicative shared phenomena is Consciousness, and that is how we are falsely manipulated.

We give energy and a life to a symbol whether it is hidden or not.

This is the power of symbols, they guide us and enable us to make communication with each other; each symbol whether it be spoken, written or is encoded in a building, given to us in an advertisement or produced within a ritual has power.

The power to alter us, and whilst most of us are comfortable with change through learning, I firmly believe we are influenced to a massive extent without our conscious knowledge and therefore by default, solely without our permission.

Symbols are everywhere in our lives, they have a powerful effect upon us, we glance at a road sign and learn which way to go, how far we need to go, of the obstacles ahead, and what speed we are all supposed to stay under during our journey.

We learn vast amounts of data from symbols and their power cannot be underestimated. Children are in the same position as they learn and absorb data, children's stories are packed full of symbolism, look into any of the stories they are taught, stories such as Pixar's, 'Monsters' Inc' and the Dementors in the Harry Potter novels, they use the notion that the use of our emotions is something to be fed from.

Within all fables, nursery rhymes and fairy stories the occult exists, the esoteric meanings contained in these stories that we innocently encourage our children to watch is contained everywhere. The wicked witch is all pervading and her magic extends beyond the story.

The Disney Corporation took the story of the seven dwarfs, the cosily named Dopey, Happy, Bashful, Sleepy, Grumpy, Sneezy and Doc from the Grimm brothers who were cabalists. The idea of the dwarfs were taken from Scandinavian folk-law but in the original story they were seven earth demons called Toli, Skavaerr, Varr, Dun, Orinn, Grerr and Radsvid. Sleeping Beauty is put to sleep and triggered by a kiss to awaken her; these stories are full of spells, altered states and drugs. Practically every story contains the magic of the occult. Americas greatest fairy tale is the Wizard of Oz, the stories of C. S. Lewis, the tales of Jules Verne, most poetry, all advertising, the list is endless, look into virtually any story and find spell weaving.

It is unbelievable what we think we are teaching children and what they are actually taking in subliminally. The occult did not stop programming people with dissociative states and triggers because when the ancient mystery schools faded they were carried into the present through the secret societies – as a result casting a spell became hypnotism.

'Spell' has two different meanings, which are connected: A spell means enchantment or a spell means a period of time. Through childhood programming we have become enchanted for a period of time. Another definition once again alludes to the power that spell making has over us. In the past words were considered so powerful and such a massive influence upon us, that even in the present day we are invited to 'spell' correctly.

We are enchanted into many thought systems including celebrity worship, obeying the lies of those we imagine are better and know more than we do, by doing guilt. We are manipulated by esoteric symbols implanted in our subconscious minds, individual and mass hypnotism is rampant, as a result we are moved by unseen forces in this materialistic construction we have built where virtually nothing is the way it seems and most of it hidden in plain sight.

Symbols exist everywhere, in writing, myth, logo, in fairy tales, art and arts modern day manipulator the television and throughout every building of importance.

I have problem with a symbol placed in a child's subconscious mind by those that seek to manipulate, control and use us - to behave, think and act in a certain way. These symbols are both hidden and in plain sight and they alter and change us on a subliminal level.

They are the manipulation of sacred geometry and this is going on at a far greater level than we appreciate. But the solution lies in the hope that to recognise something is to become aware of it, and being aware of something at least gives us back some power, to be mindful and therefore enable us to do something about it.

2012

The New World Order's agenda is accelerating because the men behind the curtains know we are nearing this date, the danger for them is paramount because should enough of us awaken and shift our consciousness, we would rebel against our treatment and this would empower us and at the same time leave them redundant, our incite will enable us to see more clearly that we are all connected … all part of life, all One.

We will then realise the magnitude of the crime perpetrated against us is a crime which we are all in some way, both a part of and responsible for. This is why our society is so sick and out of balance.

Those that stand in the shadows behind the superpowers, their allies and the leaders that they have groomed and appointed; the people who are blinded through their egoic, seductive positions of power continue to prepare themselves through control, propaganda and lies, to subjugate us. When the inevitable happens, and enough of us realise the extent of the deceit that these magicians have performed upon us and tricked us with, their hold over us will disappear.

We have become the outsiders with our lives cut off from Source, the people we should most admire, whoever they might be, serve to demonstrate access to Consciousness, they are in effect channelling … and we call them mad. In comparison, billions of people follow religions where angels are said to reveal insights to various prophets – let's be clear here we are talking of people who hear voices in their heads and if you took all those people out of religious texts and bibles, they would become substantially thinner books.

It would appear that we accept madness when it is convenient. I remain convinced that it is not just prophets or 'special people' that possess these gifts because we can all of us access Consciousness – no matter how crazy this sounds.

It doesn't matter who you are, what you think of yourself or what you are bound to - we are all One, all the same, just passing through. But one of the lies that we have bought into is that we cannot be or become the source of our admiration and we therefore project onto our celebrity or our hero, the attributes we most admire - that which we would be. And if you agree with me here we are therefore moved to concede that the reverse applies and that which we dislike most in others, is because of what we most fear and is rising in ourselves.

This realisation is very powerful medicine but like all decent medication, it is a tonic.

The magic that we practice upon each other and is practised upon us - if the spells were broken and the poisons removed, we would realise the simple truth; we are all the sons and daughters of god. We would then be free of our prisons and plugged directly into our Universal Creative Consciousness from where we came and to which we return. Is it any wonder that those who profit from us do not want us to come to this realisation?

Once we realise this, 'they' would become redundant and would remain redundant until 'they' allowed the principles that the rest of us were enabling – and because we were now living open lives of less ego and more love – we would naturally help them.

I just love it when everyOne wins.

Look around you and witness the growth of control as we accelerate to what could be the most constructive and wonderful time for us human-beings as we grow and awaken, and watch for how the ego driven agenda will continue to gain in its momentum in an attempt to survive and keep us down.

And we might be well served to remember that we only give fear power if we react to it. We develop from our experiences but we should learn to trust our instincts more than we do and we should remember and recognise our ability to access Universal Creative Consciousness and its benign intelligence instead of living in our minds, in our own heads, disconnected. The Consciousness that vibrates through everything is ours to process and if we did we could escape this prison we call reality, we would then know with clear and certain clarity, that we are all One.

As we navigate through our complicated lives, I think we deserve to know what truth is and not to be manipulated into thinking and acting against our instincts. I don't trust the people who have consistently lain down the same manipulative symbols for thousands of years. These symbols have been carried from the mystical secret hierarchies of ancient esoteric magicians and propelled into our modern day lives.

Am I being too cynical; how can a visit to such an awe inspiring place like a cathedral, a museum, a public building, a place like the Great Pyramid at Giza, or any of the many energy sites throughout the world – how can this become an opportunity to slip something into the back door of our subconscious?

Why then, is the same symbology and ritual repeated over and over again, everywhere and why are these buildings placed upon all the major energy sites throughout the World?

Our government leaders use the technique of deceptive and psychological manipulation during speeches, hand gestures, pauses, repetition, body language and covert hypnosis. These subliminal messages serve to trigger our unconscious and shift us emotionally; this diminishes our rational judgment and alters our behaviour. They say one thing we are aware of while implanting something completely at odds and against what our rational mind would accept. This method of covert hypnosis has been practised for years, it is unnecessary to name names, they all do it and we must forgive them because they themselves are acting under the same duress, they have been programmed, they believe their cause is just and they cry for love. An examination of Dr. Milton H. Erickson and his Erickson trance induction is one of the many techniques. This is a language that literally changes how you consciously think while you remain unaware. This is mind control on a grand and dangerous scale; this is what is evident in the passion and fervour of the crowd, from a political rally to a rock concert. What is being communicated is fraud as the unconscious mind responds to symbols, metaphors, logos, repetition, contradictions, triggers, leads and openings which were implanted when we were growing up. As young masters we encounter powerful hypnotists; our parents, guardians, teachers, religious leaders and the media, as one leading hypnotherapist has stated; I believe that people live most of their lives in one trance or another and my job is generally not to hypnotise them, but to de-hypnotise them.

We are processing and receiving masses amounts of information and so much is beyond our five-sense comprehension.

One day soon we will look back and realise, or to be more accurate we will remember just how much we have been influenced and we will be both amazed and disgusted because every nuance within every ritual, in every sign and everywhere we turn others seek to manipulate us. Children watch a cartoon and are exposed to the same conditioning and this conditioning has an ulterior motive, even if it is only to buy chocolate or hamburgers.

We can watch a film that makes us laugh and makes us cry, that entertains us, whilst some part of us is programmed though the back door of our subconscious.

Occultists the world over believe that, once a symbol is created, it acquires power of its own, and more power is generated when such symbols are created without the profane (the uninitiated) knowing about it.

http://cuttingedge.org/n1040.html

Why is it, without exception, that wherever we see an obelisk (male energy equals the representation of the penis or phallus) we find a dome (female energy equals the womb)? (Canary Wharfs phallus equals Millenniums Dome).

Why are our buildings massively influenced by architecture going back more than 5500 years, buildings represented by the same pillars that were present in Solomon's Temple, and why are the street plans of places like Washington DC, airports and buildings laid out in occultist patterns or grids?

A restrictive, magical, transformative, programming, training tool – the tie.

The tie is a symbol that makes statements on a few different levels.

It has been described as phallic in that it is a pointer to our sexual organs. It makes a statement about the wearer stating conformity and placed on it can be further symbols such as which club the wearer belongs to, what school he attended, a tie says much about the person who wears one. A glance at some can even declare what the wearer had for lunch.

What sort of message is this symbol sending out to others? Are we transmitting messages knowingly or are we unconsciously transmitting something else along with what we intend?

The wearing of a tie symbolises the rope around the slave's neck.

In Freemasonry there is more symbology to be found than anywhere else, when a Freemason is converted and initiated in a plethora of symbology, one of the symbols he will wear prior to passage into 'The Craft' of Freemasonry is a noose of rope around his neck, the noose is worn as one would wear a tie.

There are more ties in the world than ever before and there are more people in slavery than ever before. The tie symbolises conformity, constriction, control and servitude, it is a uniform and it serves no other useful function.

And yet we put ties round our necks and collars on our dogs. The constrictions of conformity and the symbols of control.

What we consider is an expression of our individuality is the direct reverse.

Since so much in our society is precisely the reverse of everything it seems to be and the tie is yet another example.

'You say they create their own reality said Veronika, 'but what is reality?'

'It's what the majority deems it to be. It's not necessarily the best or the most logical, but it's the one that has become adapted to the desires of society as a whole. You see this thing I've got around my neck?'

'You mean your tie?'

'Exactly. Your answer is the logical, coherent answer an absolutely normal person would give: it's a tie! A madman, however, would say that what I have around my

neck is a ridiculous, useless bit of coloured cloth tied in a very complicated way, and which makes it harder to get air into your lungs and difficult to turn your neck… If a mad person were to ask me what this tie is for, I would have to say, absolutely nothing. It's not even purely decorative, since nowadays it's become a symbol of slavery, power, and aloofness. The only really useful function a tie serves is the sense of relief when you get home and take it off, you feel as if you've freed yourself from something, though quite what you don't know.'

Veronika Decides to Die. Paulo Coelho.

A symbol is something that stands for an idea or ideas. The information locked up in one small sign or drawing would often require a volume to explain its meaning.

Great teachers and storytellers use parables and fables to tell stories that enable us learn deep truths and understanding. We find it easier to make sense of the world through an allegoric story. The use of allegory, fable and parable is a major tool in the teaching of children. Fables tend to personify animal characters such as in cartoons; the typical parable uses human agents to tell earthy stories, with heavenly meanings.

A joke, a story, parables, fables, anecdotes, illustrations and symbols help us to see the bigger picture in life however they are also a means of manipulating us.

Words are our servants, not our masters. For different purposes, we find it convenient to use words in different senses.

Richard Dawkins. The Blind Watchmaker.

But are words, patterns, and images our servants? If words can wound then clearly they are our masters, when used to express love then perhaps they become our servants. Patterns influence us, we associate a company logo and often we don't need to see the word; McDonalds, Adidas, Coke, Lacoste, BMW, etc. Almost any ten year-old boy in this country could look at a photo only showing Wayne Rooney's foot and be able to identify him from his footwear. We see a pattern and know its meaning and therefore its power.

Images *stick* with us.

'Kill them all.'

In 1209 the forces of the church numbering 30,000 men, massacred many of the population in the Languedoc region of France. During what became known as the Albigensian Crusade.

'Albigensians' were the name for the Cathars who were Christians. Pope Innocent aimed to drive the Cathars from the region and restore the authority of the Catholic Church. The northern French barons who joined the holy father's crusade saw an opportunity to acquire land, wealth and power by subjugating the fiercely independent southern nobility.

Crusading had become important in medieval times since the late eleventh century. During the fourth crusade at the siege of Zara in 1204, Crusaders had turned upon fellow Christians on European soil.

The leader of the Christian forces (Orthodox Catholicism) asked the Prelate sent by Pope Innocent III, just how he would know who the heretics were when they stormed the city.

The Holy Father's reply was, 'kill them all – God will know his own.'

On this instruction they proceeded to murder Cathar and Christian alike in the surrounding communities, in an act of genocide that depopulated much of the population of Southwest France. This crusade changed the history of France and signified the end of the independence of the south and with it the ideals, traditions and way of life of its people.

In the town of Beziers where at least 15,000 people were slaughtered, some of them were seeking sanctuary in the church.

The Pope's Prelate wrote to his Pope Innocent III, 'neither age nor sex nor status was spared.' This war, declared by a pope, lasted 40 years and was responsible for killing the Cathars to the point of extinction. Their sin was heresy and they were considered a danger to the Catholic Church. They died to further the agenda and they died because they did not share a belief with Catholicism.

The Albigensian Crusade was semi-secular and political and as the Encyclopaedia Britannica states; this crusade 'threw the whole nobility of the north of France against that of the south and destroyed the brilliant Provencal civilisation.'

The French nobles had returned back home after the Fourth Crusade (1202-04), and were still hanging around and available in 1209. They tended to be hostile to the nobles and population of Provence because it was not part of the Kingdom of France and they differed from the French culturally and mostly spoke a different language called Provençal. The Pope had promised the nobles indulgence and favour and they didn't have to go far to find them or to fight for long … just some 40 days. Simon de Monfort saw a possible gain in territory and eventually won Toulouse. That territory then changed hands a few times, Monfort was killed and the French king, Louis IX eventually stepped in and in 1229 claimed Toulouse and other territories for the Kingdom of France. The papal legate's comment at Béziers could almost define the entire religious fight against heretics. A young Spanish priest named Domingo was sent on a mission to Provence and he saw the Cathar heresy being openly practiced. He resolved to devote himself to the eradication of this heresy and soon found his way to Rome where the idea was hatched to form an order of friars to combat this heresy. He got his instructions and by 1215 had put his Order of Preachers or Dominicans straight onto the job.

The Office of the Inquisition was officially established in 1231, and the Dominicans have been charged with its execution ever since. (It became the Holy Office in 1908, and in 1965 became the Congregation for the Doctrine of the Faith.) The Inquisition was authorised to use torture, confiscate property and imprison. (This was a tadge more severe than taxation but deployed the same principles). Death was meted out by the secular arm on the suggestion of the Inquisition.

In Provence another weapon was used as citizens who pointed out heretics were rewarded by being given the alleged heretic's land. (A similar thing happened in 1942 to the Nisei who were American citizens of Japanese descent living in California).

The French nobility moved on when the indulgences were cut off which suited the Pope who needed the indulgences as rewards for another Crusade – the Fifth.

Because of the tenacity and ferocity of the Dominican Inquisitors, the heresy was ruthlessly crushed along with much of the population of both heretic and correct Catholic alike. The independence and culture of Provence was destroyed but the Church was saved.

In 1145, half a century before the Albjgensian Crusade, Saint Bernard himself had journeyed to the Languedoc, intending to preach against the heretics. When he arrived, he was less appalled by the heretics than by the corruption of his own Church. So far as the heretics were concerned, Bernard was clearly impressed by them. 'No sermons are more Christian than theirs,' he declared, 'and their morals are pure.'

De Rougement, Love in the Western World.

Since Saint Bernard was instrumental in the Templars founding, financing and growth it transpired that he took little time to change his mind.

King Philip IV of France sought to destroy the Knights Templars mainly because he owed them substantial amounts of money, in destroying them he was rid of the debt and able to seize other assets. To disgrace and discredit them first he needed to prove that they were heretics. Heresy was a useful tool that lasted from the destruction of the Cathar's at Albi through to the Salem witch-hunts of the American Colonies.

Those that the controllers – control.

The Knights Templar quickly gained fame and power largely due to the backing of Bernard of Clairvaux, he was referred to as the second pope in the command chain and had become the chief spokesman of Christendom; he also was responsible for helping to draw up the order's rules of conduct.

The Pope, Bernard de Clairvaux and the Knight Templar, directed through the Count of Champagne, used accumulated wealth to build Chartres Cathedral. The building established several new architectural features never seen before, its construction conceals ancient cubits of measure and an esoteric device known as the Chatres Maze it is forty feet in diameter. If you follow the maze you find yourself moving back and forth in a spiral, its object is to influence the initiate into an altered state. Other visual tools such as the great Rose Window displays the signs of the zodiac. A mass of sacred geometry and the measurement of the Suns movement is evident throughout the building.

These are tools for personal transformation; a sort of personal alchemy to induce changes in our DNA.

The Master Stonemasons and the Knights Templar became inextricably linked. The list of secret societies is long but they share the same traits; the few control and manipulate the many and the same few sit atop them all.

When we pray, encounter a symbol, gossip, make a plan or cast a spell we are using the Law of Attraction, what we are doing is stating an intention. We are sending out a magnetic rocket of intent into the Universe – we are performing magic.

Our subconscious mind will take our intent, our asking, and marry us to that desire. Just like the onboard computer on an aeroplane or the satellite navigation in your car.

Magic is the earliest and most effective form of applied psychology. Shaman, witches, druids and all the secrets held in occult (hidden) and esoteric (understood by a few) societies and throughout their ceremonies and their instruments, all those involved in the hierarchies of religion, those that control us, all perform magic to influence us.

It is time to remember, because deep down instinctively all of us know this simple truth; we can be anything we want and do anything we want, we just need to believe we can. We need to allow ourselves by granting ourselves permission.

Society has brainwashed us from birth to believe we can't – it's difficult – it's impossible – don't – I wouldn't if I was you – her at number 24 will tell the neighbours – it's embarrassing – it's not nice – it might be against the law – people won't like you – you won't like yourself – etceteras – as a counterbalance; if were we left to realise our own individual power and break from those who control us – it follows we could not be controlled.

We are therefore less than we could be.

We know deep down of our energy, power and potential but by our way of life we are largely robbed of this power. We are programmed to default to the lower emotional states. It's never – all is well – it's great to be alive – and what a lovely day it is, instead it's always – my head hurts – ain't life a bitch – and it's too hot or it's too cold. That is to say we flick to fear far more readily and more often than we flick to joy and love. It has been made hard for us to be happy and full of love and easy for us to be miserable and full of fear. This then is the magic of programming and it is practiced upon us and we play it out upon one another constantly. We are invited to change our emotional state many times a day. The two-minute segment about the bunny finding his way home to cheer us all up at the end of every depressing news bulletin is representative, proportionally – because for many people their entire lives are about twenty-eight minutes of felling sad and two minutes of a bit of joy and love.

At the very least it should be the other way around.

We get a couple of minutes of joy and we start and think – *this is great* and we then start worrying that we don't deserve this – it's bound to end soon or someone comes along and upsets us; 'I wouldn't, do, wear, say, think or be that if I were you.'

Think about those around you if you find it tough to look into the mirror of your own emotions, and watch how others invite us to default to negativity, we practice this magic on each other because we are programmed to do it, it is a habit and a habit is the opposite of mindfulness.

We have to remember – to remember.

To be mindful of this structure is to see that those that benefit from us, to our undoubted cost would simply loose their power.

All we need to do is believe once again, it is the song you have been singing since the moment of your birth.

'THE UNIVERSE IS CONSCIOUSNESS,'

It is minded and it contains ego.

Sacred Geometry

At school I had a hard time with maths, I found the subject boring and uninteresting. I held the view that some people just seem to have a natural propensity to understand maths, and as I was not one of them when the subject came up, my blinds came down.

I wonder now that had those same teachers invited us to understand sacred geometry and its relation to 'how things work throughout the Universe,' how many of me and my fellow classmates would have been stimulated to shiny awe, rather than crushed to desperate bore. An introduction to sacred geometry at the very least should be part of every child's education however it would seem that the vast majority of people come to the subject of their own volition and by instinct. Which, when I think about it, is how you ended up here reading this – *nice one.*

Sacred geometry is described as the language of God. It is the blueprint of creation, the beginning or genesis of all form. It is both a vast and fascinating subject. It is present everywhere and people have recognised it and tried to understand it for ages, past and present. Sacred Geometry can be converted to a set of mathematical values, which allow us to understand the nature of each form in nature and its vibrational resonance. It assists the interpretation metaphysical principle of the inseparable relationship of the part to the whole of the cosmos. It demonstrates both the Oneness of the Universe and the diversity of it.

In nature it is shown in our DNA (indeed all DNA), in seashells and sunflowers, all crystals and honeycombs. The evidence and repetitiveness of sacred geometry is found in man-made objects such as the Great Pyramid and in all religious buildings. Scholars and artists including Leonardo da Vinci, Plato and Pythagoras, all used sacred geometry as a manipulative tool.

It is demonstrated in the rhythm and harmony of music. In the natural Universe it is evident in galaxies and all life forms and in man-made objects such as art and in architecture.

We previously talked of 'as above so below,' the use of sacred geometry enables us to make sense of this proposal and to understand and witness how this works, from the humble pea to the pyramids, the arrangements of leaves on a tree, from a pine cone to the Parthenon, and from sub-atomics to spiral nebulae, sacred geometry is evident.

Sacred Geometry is the results of the Universal Conscious Mind at work.

The most incomprehensible thing about the Universe is that it is comprehensible.
Albert Einstein.

Masks

We wear masks from the moment we step from our beds, (which is possibly why many of us don't like getting out of them in the morning). The real 'you' is highly unlikely the '*you*' that you present to the world.

We wear masks because of a number of reasons; the person we wish to be perceived as, to cover our weaknesses and conversely to present our strengths. Without them we feel that we might not achieve our objective.

We are masking when we smile at someone we don't like or when we laugh at a joke that we do not find funny – or we simply don't get. When we are overwhelmed by a situation we are inclined to drop our masks and reveal more of our true feelings.

When we wear a mask we are role-playing, when we role-play we are acting and have become unconscious. If you find yourself acting this realisation creates a gap between you and the role you are playing. Wearing a mask devalues us; the flow between mask wearers is not authentic.

In the many pyramidal organisations that we become involved in, such as the church, business, the legal system, the military, banking and government. Genuine interactions are impossible because everyone is wearing a mask – playing a role – acting.

Our social mask is described as our alter ego or persona. Dr Jeckle and Mr Hyde in literature were the same person, but the two personalities were unaware of each other and both were very different.

A modern reworking of this story can be seen in the film American Physco; only here the duality of the character is more aware of the two main parts of his persona. The film shows Bateman, the lead character, who is a mix of introspecting, self-hatred, outer-loathing, lust, conformity and schizophrenia.

On the one hand Bateman, a 27-year-old Harvard Graduate, Wall Street broker has all the material trappings of success and on the other he is a monster with an insatiable blood lust and a complete lack of empathy for his fellow human beings.

This film shows the decline of our society in vivid fashion, it graphically portrays all that is repugnant, despicable and hideous in our culture today.

Makeup is used to profound effect, when Bateman is under stress his face looks plastic, glossy and sweaty and it appears he is literally wearing a mask, and the mask is beginning to run. (Mascara is the Spanish name for mask).

Masks are manifestation of the ego and we wear different ones for different occasions and when around different people.

Watch how peoples' accents change in accordance with the people they are talking to. Our behaviour alters as well, we are adaptable and want to find common ground with others and the chameleon-like performances or dramas we enter into and observe in others is both enjoyable and highly enlightening, it allows us incite into a persons character but only when we glimpse behind the mask.

Everyone wears masks because we are programmed to do so and as the name suggests, a mask says we are covering something up, ultimately one has to say that we are projecting a false image in order to acquire something for ourselves. Masks are simply shields that we hide behind as they protect whatever it is we think needs guarding. The mask is both the construction and the shield of the ego.

I wonder what better use we could put the energy to that we waste in holding up our masks.

I am totally convinced that the person speaking is my real self. This is not true. I am 'glued.' Glued to the part I am playing at this moment.

Peter Brook. Playing a Role in Life.

Between the person we really are and the person the world has turned us into we wear masks.

The programming we endure from parents, teachers and friends is fairly direct but other influences such as; television, politics and culture in general will lead us along similar paths that all of us have endured for generations.

Our ideas and beliefs are borrowed from others and have little to do with who we really are deep down inside.

I suppose an adage becomes an old adage because it has survived the scrutiny of time there is therefore much truth in old adages; 'appearances can be deceptive,' is one of those survivors, and a mask is a deceptive appearance.

We are raised on comparison;

Our education is based upon it;
So is our culture.
So we struggle to be someone
Other than who we are.

J Krishnamurti.

It would be impossible to calculate what a waste of potential has been enforced upon us by denying the child we all once were. It is every child's birthright to be given the tools to fully express themselves.

Natural talent is everywhere, especially in the young before it is stifled and sacrificed for what we call a conventional life, prior to the donning of the many masks we feel compounded to wear.

The people we most admire might have overcome great difficulties and made huge sacrifices to achieve wonderful things. But they all share one thing in common, they were given or were provided with; the instruments, the vehicles, the materials, which allowed them to produce and demonstrate their talents.

Without consideration of their motivation or their egos, know that Beethoven had access to a piano, Leonardo da Vinci was encouraged and helped to draw, Michael Jordan was allowed to play basketball, Muhammad Ali was given the chance to box, Lewis Hamilton was given the confidence to drive.

You name them – any of them because they all – any of our heroes – anyone you regard as talented or gifted without any exception, was given a chance, the opportunity, to shine and a chance to demonstrate their grace. Their talent was discovered and they were allowed to run with it.

(I am not suggesting that after the spark is lit en-route to stardom, people do not have to mask themselves to progress, however the lifestyle that usually comes with the fulfilment of talent does enable the person to behave nearer to their natural self).

Who knows what potential lies in the billions of children who will never encounter the chance, the spark and as a result be given the opportunity that would give them the vehicle to express their own individual greatness. This lack should be regarded as one of humanities greatest failings. Talent is out there in abundance in the bright and shining stars of the future but how many of them will realise their enormity?

Very, very few, is the answer.

And those that control us should hang their heads in abject shame.

Meditation

The key to knowing.

Meditation allows one to look inwards and know that all the answers to all our questions are inside us. But to access the answers one must penetrate into the unconscious part of our mind. And life under the surface of the iceberg is a very different place than the realm we know as the conscious or what we have come to understand as 'real' or 'reality.'

Meditation is a personal and subjective experience and as a result it is difficult to describe, but it is an attempt to see things in the raw, I cannot stress how important meditation could become to you, but it does take perseverance.

There are many sources that attempt to teach us to meditate and if you want to go down this route, one of meditations cornerstone principles is to attend to your breathing. Being aware of our breathing distracts us from thinking and allows us to be in the present, and it is only in the present we can banish the voice of the ego who chatters to us all the time, this then allows us to find the room within us to attune ourselves to Source.

Busy the lower brain with some routine task and the higher brain is freed.
                                                                Aleister Crowley.

I have learned through the spiritual people I have been fortunate enough to encounter and from the more constructive books I have read, there is a common conclusion; all of the answers lie within us.

The question that remains is how do we access this knowledge and gain this information? An efficient way is by meditation however this is really tough; after all we are not in the same circumstances as those bald, saffron-coloured robe-wearing monks, who sit cross-legged on beautiful mountainsides contemplating with clear and open minds.

Instead we have become the direct opposite with cluttered lives that force us to be constantly on the move and stress levels that leave many of us wound up to breaking point and take some of us beyond. Lives where many of us use drugs to quell the pain as a means of temporary escape.

So where do we get the opportunity to find the peace, solitude and calm that is required to access our inner selves, to look within and past the programming, to find clarity and clear the way to access the higher force of Universal Creative Source Energy, to open ourselves up to channel the good stuff as it were?

The Universe is Conscious.

We are receivers and transmitters.

Our dials are out of sync and as a result we are tuned to the wrong station.

Our bodies are the spacesuits that allow us to live in this matter based dimension or realm; our bodies require us to perform a series of functions in order they might survive.

We need to breathe to oxyinagate our blood, we need to eat in order to provide fuel for our bodies to operate, and these and many other functions are done automatically at a subliminal level.

Our bodies are simply vessels that carry us around as we live and learn.

For many of us in the West we might not realise it, but we are meditating when we walk our dog on the beach or when we tend to our gardens; there are many ways we try and switch off.

I realised this one day after a phone call to one of my closest friends who was living in London, his wife would often answer the phone when I rang him and we would have a quick chat before she handed me over.

She would often say during our exchange of pleasantries – 'did you enjoy yourself fishing?' The first couple of times I never questioned, I just replied that I did, but then one day I said – 'how did you know that I've been fishing?'

'I can always tell from just talking to you, you seem calmer, more peaceful.'

I was amazed that she had this incite into me. (Or hell, I must have been very crazy). I knew it wasn't the actual fishing that relaxed me; it was rare that I even caught a fish. But friends had taken me fly-fishing a few times and it was therapeutic. I would wander miles up and down beautiful stretches of riverbank immersed in nature, pausing only to place a fly on the water and marvel as a fish jumped and completely ignore my lure. I was oblivious to the fact that by being at One with the setting I was emptying my stress into the beauty of my surroundings.

I was not aware but I was meditating and as a result emptying out the stress and making room for the good stuff to flow and influence me.

Many of us in pursuing a task; sometimes the most natural and mundane of pleasures, we find we get absorbed to the point where, whether we realise it or not we are meditating.

There is a pleasure in the pathless woods.
There is rapture on the lonely shore.
There is a society where none intrudes.
By the deep sea, and music in it's roar.
I love not the man the less but nature more.

Byron.

We have our bodies; they carry us around, but what of our minds? I have likened the body to a vessel; when it's full we have no room to get anything else in and this is when the trouble starts.

All the fibres of our bodies, our organs, veins and arteries, our muscles they all function much more effectively when we are relaxed. We need to warm up and loosen our bodies before any physical exercise can be undertaken, but when do we actually ever loosen up, relax and attend to our minds?

There are many examples of how our minds manifest change in our physical selves – our minds move us in the following examples –

When we see someone who is prone to loosing his temper we refer to them as hot-blooded. Having ranted and exhausted his rage, we suggest he has vented his spleen. We talk to a friend who has just finished a relationship and they speak to us of their sorrow, time will ease their broken heart we tell them. We spill our guts in confession. When nervous we get butterflies in our stomach, when we get scared we remark, 'I was shitting myself,' and we refer to the hairs on the back of our necks standing up. Someone who robs us of energy can be called a pain in the neck. It is with a heavy heart we deliver bad news. We become flushed with rage or passion. We get bad news and feel sick to our stomachs. We get goose-pimples when frightened or moved by awe. We go red with embarrassment or we are flushed with success. Our bodies react to our emotional state, as a result our emotions have great power over us. (And if you don't believe me I am going to start taking about erections).

We say that we're looking forward to our holidays, we really need a break and we can't wait 'to get away from it all,' but for many of us, we go away and cannot escape the stress of an unhealthy relationship and in fact it might become even worse when we are subjected to close proximity. We may be sitting on a plane bringing us back from some sunny-climb, thinking we still *need* a holiday.

We are so addicted to looking outside ourselves that we have lost access to our inner being almost completely. We are terrified to look inward, because our culture has given us no idea of what we will find. We may even think that if we do, we will be in danger of madness. This is one of the last and most resourceful ploys of ego to prevent us from discovering our true nature.

So we make our lives so hectic that we eliminate the slightest risk of looking into ourselves. Even the idea of meditation can scare people. When they hear the words ego less or emptiness, they think that experiencing those states will be like being thrown out of the door of a spaceship to float forever in a dark, chilling void. Nothing could be further from the truth. But in a world dedicated to distraction, silence and stillness terrify us; we protect ourselves from them with noise and frantic busyness. Looking into the nature of our mind is the last thing we would dare to do.

Sogyal Rinpoche.

Everything you have ever seen, heard, done or experienced is in the mind.

Mind does not occupy a special place in our bodies, unless we succumb to living within our own heads. Left to its natural course and its own devices mind is simply within us and flowing through us, it is Universal Source Energy – Consciousness, this is the Creative Force, the religious amongst us call this energy by the names of god – well that is unless you're a priest and then in your role as a priest you're manipulating it – yes – okay – probably unknowingly – and your manipulating it because you need to feed your ego – yes – okay – unknowingly.

And because of your own programming you are leading, influencing and programming others to think your correct and important because you can get them to your version of god; the belief system you have been programmed into.

– As if You wouldn't have found your way there anyway.

– You came from Him.

– You are a part of god.

You fully know the unabridged, unbiased, untainted, clarity of truth and love – it is what You seek – it is a return to what You are.

We can block this but we cannot avoid it because it is part of us.

The right way to access this is by being still, centred and in the moment, only by being quiet and allowing can we properly tap the Source.

We are all intuitive and when we marry ourselves to our Creative Consciousness Source we allow feelings beyond our five-sense reality.

Our intuitive self has enormous power when we are prepared to listen.

We can only really listen when we are still and present.

Our minds are like a glass of muddy water, when shaken and stirred the water becomes dirty and unclear. Once we rest the glass and leave it to settle, then the water becomes clear.

Once you listen to your inner self you will wonder why you came to neglect it for so long.

Instead of the occasional incite when, for example, you just knew what was around the next corner or that a person was lying to you or you just had this funny feeling – maybe I should buy *this* book! (thank you x) – these moments will last and will grow in power once you practice inward looking (meditation).

Finding the time to do this is another matter, we are programmed into noisy busy lives and we feel guilty because we are led to think idleness is bad and we are therefore afraid of stillness.

Being comfortable in our own skin is not easy.

For many of us this is the life we have created for ourselves.

We need to stop the rackets in our heads; the fear instilled in us at every turn – there is nothing to fear not even fear itself.

We need to stop observing ourselves from the outside and experience ourselves from the inside.

Stillness can cause us concern; many people cannot go for one day without human contact, energy and communication.

Living for just one day with no outside interference can be very revealing.

Stand in nature and you will blend, you can communicate with everything around you and as bizarre as that might sound just try and instead of walking through a wood, (not a park which is ok – but it is a construction of mans' hand) sit down and contemplate and feel the magic.

You are part of all of this life around you, everything you are is connected to everything else and the boxes you have been placed in cannot separate you unless you give them the power to do so.

You are not separate; everything within and without is One.

There are no boxes, there are no boarders, there are no flags and only in our minds do these preposterous, stupid, ideas flourish.

Separation exists only in the mind.

Separation is a product of the ego.

Meditation destroys ego.

All is One. All is well.

Memes

Richard Dawkins, a famous and well-respected biologist coined this word in 1976, he refers to a unit of cultural information, which can propagate from one mind to another in a manner likened to genes. Dawkins gave as examples of memes; tunes, catch phrases, beliefs, clothes, fashions, ways of making pots, or methods of building arches.

In other words the transferring of an idea to a target or targets and how they are spread. Every body of people, regardless of race, colour, creed or ideology, carry the promotion of the meme.

A fashion is nothing but an induced epidemic.

George Bernard Shaw.

Dawkins defines the meme as a unit of cultural transmission or a unit of imitation. I don't suppose for one second Dawkins was altering the word 'mimic' to create his own meme. I don't want to be flippant, I consider Dawkins hit the button with this way of seeing how we operate in the World and surely even the most blinkered of us must admit how easily we are seduced by memes. Just look again at the money poured into advertising and the effort to get you to remember that jingle, that catchphrase or just the cleverness behind that thirty-second attempt at brainwashing.

- If it didn't work they wouldn't do it.

According to ancient traditions the way to gain experience of spiritual knowledge is for a master to initiate a pupil in a chain of transmission.

The East refers to this form of 'memeing' as a *satsong*, this process is not only about the transfer of information but a flow of mind manipulation, a sort of alchemy to bring about change.

Plato wrote the Allegory of the Cave in which he seeks to alter our perceptions on reality, he is asking us to perceive an imaginative image which casts an hypnotic spell that alters the initiate into belief.

Plato calls this process mimesis.
This process is all around us.

Mind

When we are asleep and our eyes are closed we can still visualise, we can still see.

It is your mind that sees.

Heaven and hell are the places we create, both can be found anywhere in the world and we create them by how we think and therefore act but they are nothing more than the manifestation of mind and we therefore choose where we want to visit and indeed how long we wish to remain.

If it were possible to become free of negative emotions by a risk-less implementation of an electrode – without impairing intelligence and the critical mind – I would be the first patient

Dalai Lama. Society for Neuroscience Congress 2005.

The mind is its own place, and in itself can make a Heav'n of Hell, a Hell of Heaven.

Satan, in Milton's Paradise Lost.

The third-rate mind is only happy when it is thinking with the majority. The second-rate mind is only happy when it is thinking with the minority. The first-rate mind is only happy when it is thinking.

A A Milne.

The most expensive piece of real estate is the six inches between your right and left ear, it's what you create in that area that determines your wealth. We are only limited by our mind.

Dr. Dolf de Roos.

The subconscious mind makes no distinction between constructive and destructive thought impulses. It works with the material we feed it, thought driven by fear, just as readily as it will translate into reality, a thought driven by courage or faith.

Napoleon Hill.

To think bad thoughts is really the easiest thing in the world. If you leave your mind to itself it will spiral down into ever increasing unhappiness. To think good thoughts, however, requires effort.

James Clavell.

As you think, so shall you become.

Bruce Lee.

To grasp how we function we would be better off realising that the brain and the mind are not the same thing. The brain is an organ, which is an organically programmed machine and our brains are programmed by our worldly experiences therefore our mind is run by the ego, however mind is a part of Collective Consciousness and we have the ability to tune into this vibrational flow.

Our mistake is to internalise mind, this is the ego at work fighting silently for its sense of self and this is the major reason for our dysfunctionality.

All mind is joined through Collective Conscious, when we cut off from Source and as a result we internalise problems within our mind we can offer ourselves no real or lasting solutions whilst we are trapped in this way. Our minds need to be open and accessing, not blocked and withheld inside us.

The mind of the ego and the mind that is the Universe; two very separate roles and two very different outcomes.

Man's power of choice enables him to think like an angel or a devil, a king or a slave. Whatever he chooses, mind will create and manifest.

Fredrick Bailes.

The greatest discovery of this generation is that human beings can alter their lives by altering the attitude of mind.

Albert Schweitzer.

Mindfulness

Buddhist teaching tells us that to develop spiritually one must be mindful, however we are programmed into habitual behaviour so most of the time we find ourselves living lives that are far from mindful.

A good example of lack of mindfulness is in the way we eat. Obesity is rife throughout the Western World. There are several reasons given for this: affluence, overeating, a sedentary lifestyle, poor parenting, bad diet, etc.

We are never hungry, I ask you to consider when the last time you were hungry, truly hungry? And I would lay odds you cannot remember. For those of you starving and reading this, I apologise, however again I would lay odds that if your starving you will not be reading this as you have no time, your quest lies elsewhere, in any event if the rest of us who were overeating were truly mindful then it follows that you would not be starving.

In order to consume food or drink we need to be mindful, consider what we are doing, shut out as many of the distractions around us as possible, this must also include the constant racket of the ego formed in our own minds. You know the voice that nags away internally; do I have the money to pay my way in the World? The car is playing up, the kids are playing up, the husband/the wife is playing up, the boss is on my case.

We should be mindful of what is on our plate. Dependent on your taste and appetite this could be a prime rump-steak, a breast of chicken, or a handful of organic sunflower seeds.

The steak – as your knife cuts through it remember this is a piece of muscle and fat given up reluctantly by a large mammal. This beast possibly suckled (as you possibly suckled), from their mother. Remember, as the blood on your plate runs from the steak, it once ran warm through this animal's veins, just as yours does. Give thought for her life and know she had to give it up for you.

The chicken – probably never saw the light of day in his short forty-day life span, at the end he was grabbed by the leg, taken to a slaughterhouse, passed through an electrified water bath (which is supposed to stun him into unconsciousness, but often fails), his neck was cut (he often survives this) and he is plunged into scalding water to loosen his feathers. As he dies his eyes are still pale blue because he has not reached maturity. His short life has seen him pumped with antibiotics and he and his fellow unfortunates lived cramped in their own faeces, in abject boredom and some resorted to cannibalism.

The sunflower seeds – what would they have achieved were you not eating them? The title on the box might say ' full of sunshine.' Be mindful of the sun in which they basked. Picture the flower and the elegance of a field full of them as they turn their heads to follow the sun as if under instructions in some silent orchestra. Wonder at the seeds potential, the enormity of what would happen should you spare just one, plant it and watch it grow. The miracle of the knowledge locked inside this tiny seed which if unlocked would not only grow in replication of its parent but also would go onto produce its own seeds and therefore perpetrate the circle of life.

> *Every time you consume factory-farmed chicken, beef, veal, pork, eggs, or dairy you are eating antibiotics, pesticides, steroids and hormones.*
> Rory Freedman and Kim Barnouin. Skinny Bitch.

When the sign over the butcher proudly boasts 'Fresh Meat,' he is not telling the truth; we cannot eat fresh meat because it would be stiff with rigor mortis. We can only consume meat when it has become soft or in other words when it has started to rot. The process that allows the meat to go soft is bacteria.

(The growth hormones, vaccines, and antibiotics that were pumped into the animal hardly hinder the bacteria's work but they surely can't be good for us).

Without microbes doing their work there could be no tenderness in our chops or juiciness in our steak. We have a lot to thank bacteria for and it also has to be admired, in ten hours 100 microbes can become 100 million, but we should hesitate to appreciate one of its aspects; when meat or game smells a little high that is just nature at work. What goes in must come out, everything that eats needs to defecate and that cheesy smell is microbe shit.

Unseen to the naked eye there is a universe of bacteria right under our noses. It is in the air, on the ground, in our food, in our beds, on our bodies, pretty much everywhere. Without bacteria life on Earth would fail.

I no longer eat red meat and avoid battery chicken, so if I was a bit strong on the mammals and the birds once again I apologise. On the other hand, if you were mindful the next time you are presented with food and it does not seem to hold the same appeal, then I have proven my point – *your mindfulness would have increased.*

Another example of a lack of mindfulness is the advent of the plastic bag; in Britain we get through 13 billion bags a year. Our convenience in carrying our goods away from the convenience store is unfortunately more than inconvenient to the animal that comes into contact with one of these bags. Plastic bags kill the magnificent green turtle because they mistake them for jellyfish; they eat them and suffer a slow agonised death by starvation as they wrap around the animals intestines. Similarly these bags kill seals, dolphins and birds by strangulation. They kill whales such as the Minke whale.

Plastic bags decimate wildlife. The average British family is issued with 800 of these bags every year. Something we use for a few minutes takes up to a thousand years to decay.

Mindfulness gives a respectful nod to the bumblebee because someone has calculated that it takes two million flowers for one bee to make one pound of honey. Furthermore and in a good example of a lack of mindfulness, we have so seriously decimated the bee through pesticides and the sterility of lawns that we are beginning to realise just how important these little creatures are, it is estimated that one third of all the food we eat relies on the participation of the bee. Bees' communication sees them responsible for vegetables, fruit and flowers, which cannot survive and multiply without pollination. In large areas of the US reports indicate a decline of up to 70%.

Should the bee become permanently irradicated there would be no more pollination, no plants, no animals and within a very short time, there would be no more man.

Two Buddhist monks were walking for several miles through woodland and grass. The surrounding scenery was beautiful and they had been walking for some hours in silence as they were part of an order that, from time to time, vowed silence until after their evening meal.

They found themselves by the side of a rushing river in flood and they noticed a young girl looking at the river with trepidation. The girl asked the monk who was nearest to her, who was the younger of the two and the larger framed man, if he would be so kind as to carry her over the river as she was scared of the torrent she faced.

The monk was a powerful man and picked her up easily in his arms and duly obliged, placing her gently on the other side of the river. The girl thanked both monks profusely and they in turn nodded and smiled at her, still not speaking as they went one way and the girl the other.

Several hours later, the monks sat down to their evening meal. As they finished the clock on the wall chimed six-o-clock, this signalled the end of their silence. The smaller monk was bursting to speak and the first thing he said to his travelling companion was. 'Why did you carry that girl over the river today?'

'Well, why not?' replied the bigger monk.

'Because I am not sure you should have carried her.' he pressed.

'I put her down on the far side of the river,' said the big monk, 'but you my friend – you have carried her all day.'

On life's journey faith is nourishment, virtuous deeds are a shelter, wisdom is the light by day and right mindfulness is the protection by night. If a man lives a pure life, nothing can destroy him.

Buddha.

If you are doing mindfulness meditation, you are doing it with the ability to attend to the moment.

Daniel Goleman.

Try this experiment. Find somewhere quiet, find a seat and take a few breaths. Relax as best your able. For a short while, even if it's only a minute, allow your mind to go blank. Visualise an imaginary board in front of you, the board is blank, there is nothing written on it. With your eyes closed focus your attention on your breathing. Normal breathing – in – and – out. Keep your attention on your breath and every time your mind wanders bring it back to your breath.

If you have never done this before it is the first steps to meditation. It is difficult to stop your mind from wandering and this only improves with practice, after all you are trying to break a habit. Breaking habits are one of the most difficult things we will ever attempt.

But even after a minute you will feel calm.

This feeling of being relaxed is the start of mindfulness.

It is the beginning of contemplation, all religions; all spiritual practices have adopted this method. There may be many variations, but this is meditation and it is the key to knowing and the way to becoming. If mindfulness is being aware of the right here and the right-now then habituation is the direct opposite. Habituation is unmindfulness.

Habituation means we are not in the moment, we are on autopilot and unaware of our actions. We are thinking our usual thoughts and living our usual dreams, responding to rather than embracing our surroundings. In this state we are largely reactive as opposed to proactive.

Habit is necessary – but it is not mindful. Some habits are necessary and if you were to diagnose your habits you might find you have more good than bad, but with respect you would be in a minority. If you have a habit of turning right to the gym rather than left to the pub, that is arguably a good habit.

Mindfulness can overcome bad habits or convert bad habits into good ones.

In Britain and America many of us are inclined to overeat. We are reminded of the consequences of shovelling enormous quantities of high fat and high carbohydrate foods with the resultant epidemic of obesity and its associated health problems. This is an example of not being mindful.

In Britain and America many people eat almost on the run, at their desks in the workplace, at home in front of television, often providing ourselves with the wrong fuel at the wrong time and under the wrong circumstances.

There is a different collective way of eating in France; indeed their mindset is different in many ways. The people seem to remember that by the force of their will, they brought down a monarchy in The French Revolution, (1789). and similarly French students were responsible for the fall of President De Gaulle.

At 5 minutes to noon midday, you will be virtually thrown out of any shop because the French insist on taking a two and a half hour lunch break. They embrace with fervour a 35-hour working week and when they wake after a rested weekend on Monday they seem to have re-christened it *S'monday* with many banks, shops and restaurants (if they open at all) working limited hours.

But the French have different eating habits that illustrate a degree of mindfulness. They eat many fatty foods and yet are predominantly thinner and healthier. They savour by eating more slowly and by having less food over more courses; they extend the ritual and enjoy the process.

Money

The real value of money is knowing what you would be worth if you did not have any.

If someone hands you a million dollars, best you become a millionaire or you won't get to keep the money.

Jim Rohn.

The average salary in the UK is about £25,000. If you earn this, you are richer than 97% of the rest of the world.

Karl Moore.

It is said that money is the root of all evil. Money is not evil (a noun cannot be evil); it is what we do with it upon its acquisition that defines its use. Money is energy and therefore it wants to flow. Put simply, money is the nearest form of valuing energy that we have. Money is energy and has power because we place value upon it.

As in everything that enables function and communication; letters, words, figures, symbols, space, time – we made up these ideas – these meme's. They serve as agreements between us and nothing more. We therefore set their value.

As a result of earlier conditioning, we judge and consider categorising everything into either 'good' or 'evil,' this is worthy of some thought. There really isn't anything on the face of the earth that is good or evil, because we ourselves, define what is good or what is evil.

A stone is not evil, but if we pick it up and throw it through someone's window we are using the stone to perform an act that could be seen as evil. If that same act meant that air was allowed into the room and there was someone suffocating on the floor and the air revived them and they were saved, the act would be seen subjectively as good.

It is the same with everything; guns, money, drugs, cars, the usage of words. Everything depends upon our interpretation and usage.

A gun cannot shoot someone until the trigger is pulled, we hear the statement that 'guns don't kill people, people kill people.' In the same way money can be used to advance a good cause, such as helping people who have none, and can be used for evil such as financing a war.

There are no good or evil drugs, although we are programmed to believe otherwise, it is what we do with those drugs that is important and defines them.

Good and evil are open to interpretation by us and what you might consider an act of evil another might regard as an act of good.

Music

After silence, that which comes nearest to expressing the inexpressible is music.

Aldous Huxley.

And the dormouse said – 'feed your head.'

Jefferson Airplane

Change your heart look around you, it will astound you.

J. Warren.

When you've seen beyond yourself – then may you find peace of mind is waiting there – and the time will come when you see we're all one, and life flows on and on, within you, without you.

George Harrison.

You don't need eyes to see. You need vision.

Faithless.

Music influences us on many levels. We can feel and hear music, on TV or a concert we can visualise and when you have a medium that dramatically affects two senses and arguably affects them all, then you have a very powerful instrument.

Music is a vibration that we feel throughout our entire body. It can stir our emotions and lift our spirits and it has the power to move us. It has the ability to make us feel and act differently. This is why we have had to endure the blandness of elevator music in shopping centres, supermarkets, department stores and even public toilets – and of course lifts. Elevator music has become the generic term for piped or canned music. We are subjected to it when we hold on the telephone, walk through an airport or visit the doctor in his surgery.

Apparently the number one contender is 'The Girl from Ipanema,' but there is one thing for sure the music will not be chosen to make you want to dance or tap your foot, it is unlikely to make you feel happy, it exists to sedate and subliminally relax you – and if you find yourself singing along have a word with yourself!

It has come into existence because it works but it is yet another example of how corporations and companies manipulate us. Why should the beauty of music be robbed of its soul and reduced to play tinny, hollow love songs in the jungle that is consumerism? Does it keep us in the store a little longer to squeeze more profit from us? You bet it does, we are expected to feed the heartless economic ambition of a retail chain.

The company wants you in the store, wants you to stay in the store and wants you to spend, it doesn't care why your there. This is hardly a genuine experience. It is another step toward the removal of what it is to be human and we should not be used as puppets to further their selfish aims.

Living is easy with eyes closed, misunderstanding all you see …

John Lennon.

'Take a music bath once or twice a week for a few seasons, and you will find that it is to the soul what the water-bath is to the body.'

Oliver Wendell Holmes.

Ringtone's now account for 10% of the worlds music market. They generate three billion dollars a year.

So tell me just how come the Taliban
Sat burning incense in Texas
Roaming round in a Lexus
Sittin' on six-billion oil drums
Down with the Dow Jones, up on the NASDAQ
Pushed into the war zones.
It's a commercial crusade
'Cause all the oil men get paid
And only so many soldiers come home
It's a commando crusade
A military charade
And only so many soldiers come home

Part of 'Illegal Attacks.'
Ian Brown backed by Sinead O'Connor.

In many traditions, it is believed that sound was before everything. For the Aborigines, the creator-ancestor of the dreamtime sang the world into existence. For Christians, in the beginning was the Word. The Egyptians, Vedic Indians, Plato, Sumerians, Chinese and Babylonians considered that music was the master metaphor for creativity and life. Pythagoras discovered that harmonics and their mathematical relationships underlie the structure of all creation.

Dr Hans Jenny has demonstrated how different sound frequencies beamed onto liquids and powders will each form a particular geometric design. This gives support to the Druidic and Native American beliefs that all objects in our world have a sound and that if the body and mind are sufficiently stilled, we can hear the sounds of rocks and trees and objects around us.

Yogis believe that 'Om' is the combined sound of everything in the Universe singing to God.

Sound is composed of vibrating particles of energy. When the open vowels are elongated in tone or chant, magical vibrations are produced and these are the harmonic overtones, which spiral higher and higher. These magical forms of resonance have been held as sacred by many cultures and those of the present day that have been less tainted by modern 'civilisation.'

The overtones are powerful healers. Dr. Billie Thompson says that 80% of the sounds that stimulate the brain and charge the nervous system are above 3000 hertz and these are the higher overtones. Like everything in the Universe, us, our organs and energy centres (chakras) are resonating at particular frequencies.

Disease is a vibration and when disease manifests, the frequencies alter and change. The resonance of the correct frequency can encourage healing. This can occur in accordance with the principle of entrainment by which vibrations that are more powerful and more harmonious will affect less powerful and less harmonious vibrations of a nearby person or object.

Sound healing has been used with success to treat many disorders ranging from autistic children to older stroke victims and those with Alzheimer's disease.

Don Campbell claims that harmonious music can:

Slow and equalise brain waves.

Affect heartbeat, pulse rate, respiration and blood pressure.

Reduce tension and improve body movements and co-ordination.

Increase endorphin levels.

Boost immune function.

Regulate stress-related hormones.

Change our perception of time.

Strengthen memory and learning.

Stimulate digestion.

Much success is presently being achieved through 'sonic births' at the 'Muse in the Schools' project based in New York. Every cell in our bodies carries the awareness of perfect rhythm, since we are nourished by the life-sustaining rhythms of breath and heartbeat. These rhythms are audible to us from our mothers when in the womb. It is believed that the music from virtually every culture has been created with the heartbeat rhythm as its source. This no doubt accounts for the beneficial effect that most music has on us. Our brains pulse electricity with rhythms that carry us from the depths of sleep to peaks of excitement.

We are also influenced by external rhythms. The diurnal rhythm affects us at a cellular level and fluid and salt levels respond to this. If we sit by the seashore, we can connect with the ebb and flow of the waves and the rhythm of the tides. Since up to 70% of our bodies are water, we are open to influence by the moon; the moon affects women's menstrual cycles. Our lives can also be open to influence by longer-term rhythms such as seasonal, solar, astrological cycles and life and death. It is harder for people who live in cities to maintain that connection to the diurnal and seasonal rhythms.

We need rhythm to nourish our souls. Babies are calmed into sleep with the rhythm of rocking. Young children have natural rhythm and this can be seen as they play chanting and skipping games.

Sadly in our culture, music has generally become trivialised into short-term entertainment or distraction that is controlled by a big industry. This is a far cry from the universal, ancient view of sound as magic and music as the creator energy of the cosmos.

The Power of Sound and Rhythm.
Primrose Organic and Sacred Earth Centre.

Music and rhythm find their way into the secret places of the soul.
Plato. (428–348BC)

There is no place like Om

'Om' (pronounced ohm or aum) is said to be the vibrational sound (or superstring) of creation. It is the sound of the Earth and the heart of existence. It is the sound that makes us feel at one with the Universe.

It is the ultimate mantra and this sacred sound when hummed is used with huge significance in both Hindu and Buddhist traditions. Om contains all sound, just as light contains all colour. It is also used extensively as a symbol and the thought emanation and realisation of 'om' has been used for thousands of years extensively throughout the world. Om is a vibration; it is audible in all of nature, alive in the wind and ever present in both the animal kingdom and ourselves and we feel joy when we are attuned.

In the beginning was … the word.

Genesis.

The sound of god's Voice said, 'Let there be …'

For in the beginning of the times so did we all share in the Holy Stream of Sound that gave birth to all creation.

Essene Gospel of Peace, vol 4.

…The Creator… knew that he was alone. This solitude became unbearable and he longed for other beings to share the new world with Him. The thoughts of the Creator became the gods and everything else, which exists. When his thoughts had shaped them, his tongue gave them life by naming them. Thoughts and words were the power behind creation.

The Waters of Chaos. Ancient Society.

Music is the language of the spirit, it opens the secret of life bringing peace, abolishing strife.

Kahil Gibran. (1883-1931)

Mystical happenings

In the late 1960's a sociologist Stanley Milagram started the theory that there were six degrees of separation between everyone on the planet. Milaram's theory said you could link for example; a native in the jungles of the Amazon and the Pope; the native would know a guy who he bought supplies from ... who would know a musician from London who had a cousin ... you get the idea.

I was talking about this today when I got a phone call from Annie this evening. Last night she and her close friend Jenny were meeting up with Annie's cousin who was over from Ireland. Annie and her cousin Gavin had never met before, and the idea was to meet in a pub. Within a few minutes of conversation, Jenny and Gavin, realised they knew each other through their work as they had sent and received many emails to each other over six years of communication – just two degrees of spooky separation.

A man stumbled up to the only other customer in a bar and offers him a drink. As they sit at the bar they engage in conversation.

'Cheers,' says the second man raising his glass 'where do you come from?'

'I'm from Ireland,' comes the response.

'No?' says the first man, 'I'm from Ireland now let me get you a drink.'

With that they drain their glasses while two fresh drinks are served.

'Where in Ireland?' asks the first man.

'A little place by the name of Limerick,' comes the reply.

'Really that's quite amazing, I was born in Limerick.'

'Well then we better have another drink to Limerick and to Ireland,' says the second man.

The barman replenishes their empty glasses.

'What school did you go to?' asks the first man after a while.

'St Agnes of the Cross and I left in 1975.' Came the reply.

'This really is quite remarkable,' said the first man, 'why I attended St Agnes and left in 1975 as well.'

Another customer enters the bar and orders a drink as the barman pours it the new customer asks him, 'much happening?'

'Not much – it's bit quiet,' says the barman. 'But the O'Reilly twins are pissed again.'

I am sure that there still exists a long forgotten law in England appertaining to fortune-tellers. It says that if the authorities wanted to they could prosecute those that portend the future as a means of taking money. With June 2007 being the wettest month on record since records began and August 2008 being the darkest I think this law should be resurrected and all weather-forecasters brought to account.

I mean that's all they are doing, being paid to tell the future and getting it badly wrong. Weather forecasters should simply tell the truth when it comes to their specialist subject, I mean did they not have to pass exams? 'Now here is Today's Truthful Weather Forecast' – it will very likely piss down with rain all day for you cloth hats who live north of Luton – and for those of you gentle lovely people – those of you who like me, live south of Luton – you can play golf – plan a picnic – actually get to take the top off your overpriced convertible car – but still remember to moan about oil prices, the stock market, the economy, the price of your house – oh – and the weather.'

In fact they would only need to make one programme – one programme repeated every single day. It wouldn't make much by way of entertainment – warm, pleasant and dry up to the north circular road – rainy, grey, dull and overcast for anyone living above it – boring, yes – repetitive, sure – but far more accurate.

Weather forecasters, when they get their mumbo-jumbo forecasts wrong, if they knew they were going on the ducking stool, or getting burnt at the stake as a sacrificial offering to the weather gods, then they might just be a little more accurate before they laid their truths upon us.

Never assume

My dear old Dad told me when I was about 14, *'never assume.'* As with the majority of things I did not agree or perhaps more importantly I didn't agree because I just didn't 'get it.'

So there I was walking the dog on the beach last winter and the place was deserted, it was cold but in a good way. Anyway I could see an island silhouetted almost on the far right of the horizon and I was admiring its beauty. The dog retrieved her ball so I turned away to throw it for her again. As I did I thought, I wonder if the island will look as beautiful when I turn back to look at it? … in fact will the island still even be there? And at the same time I realised that my Dad was right, I was assuming it would be. So finally I got it. Yes he was right; it was highly unlikely but nonetheless just about possible that the island might have slipped into the sea.

Not because of an earthquake or anything because then I would have felt the ground shudder and the last thing on my mind would have been the welfare of the island because, I would have been running away. Yes, I was assuming the island was still there. So my Dad was right and you should never assume.

However the fact that we do assume is a right result and saves us an enormous of time, I mean can you really imagine if we didn't?

When you are about 14 you disagree with everything your peers say anyway as a matter of course, whether you get the point or not. This is part of the resistance you have before what they call adulthood. Coincidently the precise time before Master becomes Mister, and whilst there is no agreement on the exact age of when this metamorphous happens, it's about the same time that you become embarrassed by your parents but try and enjoy the moment because it is your last rebellion before they break you.

Assuming, as a rule of thumb, should be kept at as bigger distance from us as possible. You are arguably better off assuming China has slipped into the sea rather than the assumption that your girlfriend loves you. Making assumptions within relationships is the root cause of many problems.

Most often an assumption is made because we do not have all the information and are prepared to fill in the gaps with romantic notions. We are unable or unwilling to do our homework and assumptions are the glue that very often binds our beliefs together. And here we have yet another anomaly; since close relationships with one another are just about the toughest thing we do in life and are the cause of so much pain, why are we made to feel inadequate by everyone who programmes us when we are not in one?

- 'Have you got a boyfriend yet?'
- 'Are you seeing anyone?'
- 'Are you bringing anyone to the party?'
- 'Every princess has to have her special day.'
- 'You better settle down soon or you'll end up lonely, sad and alone.'

It suits the system so much more to encourage making our relationships law through vehicles like the ritualised initiation of the marriage ceremony. We get tax breaks if we are married. You can borrow more money if you are married and 'stable.'

Just like the film we remember from childhood – it never changed but we did and we are supposed to change and grow in conjunction with one other and we wonder why sometimes we break the promises we made and then we beat ourselves up because we did – and we do guilt which takes us to a place that many people find tough to escape from.

I know too many people who 'are staying together for the sake of the kids,' and so few others that know it's OK to be by yourself, that there is nothing actually 'wrong' with you.

When you say 'yes, I will be bringing my partner to the staff dance,' then others, similarly betrothed will sigh with relief – you will all be in the same boat – even though the lads will end up with the lads in one room while the girls do their thing with the girls in another.

So we get all that programming and we embrace marriage and we get to follow a well-worn path, that doesn't always suit the people who have to walk it. One other consideration worthy of note; we humans share many a trait with our fellow animals and one of those traits both dictates and demonstrates that it is the female of the species that chooses her mate.

Now, it's at this point where I could really get into trouble for this, but like the coward I am, I am going to leave an exit door open behind me by adding; I am offering this up as a comfort to those of us who are beating themselves up with negative, fearful, draining emotions made manifest by beliefs programmed into us and doing the resultant guilt-trip because we cannot endure the vissitudes of a an intimate, sexual and close relationship.

Stop it now please.

So hopefully that gets me off the hook with everyone who loves each other in a intimate, sexual and close relationship – without agenda – unconditionally – forever.

It's just I never met you.

If anyone is inclined to agree with me on this one and then are silly enough to go onto voice your opinion; prepare yourself to be called cynical by the vast majority of people and be ready to get into a lot of loud arguments after your pudding at dinner parties.

News and Media

Another one that puzzles me is – why is it that all the news stations and all the newspapers carry exactly the same news.

There seems to be a lack of imagination. Sure if the big story today is bird flu I suppose we need to know about it. If it really is bird flu, which it normally isn't, I mean there is often a scare then a few days later it gets buried because 'experts' got it wrong then spin happens and makes it 'right.' In any event, I don't get too worried about a bit of bird-flu – and pig flu is probably no more harmful than bog standard flu but hey, let's go spend billions of pounds on pharmaceutical gear because the share price improves, we get something else to stress about, people get kept in jobs, it takes our eye off the shit job politicians are doing about the economy or stealing money by fraudulent means… but if ox-flu or whale-flu breaks out - now that's a different matter. The media obsesses with the strangest of subjects, while it often ignores what to many would seem important. Are dark forces at work here?

You dear reader may have guessed by now that I am a little bit of a conspiracy theorist (your supposed to shirk at the words – we are programmed to do so) so to that question I am going to answer, without question, for certain, affirmatively, absolutely – YES.

But then we live in a free country don't we? And we have freedom of speech don't we? The truth is we do not, everything is censored, filtered, spun and programmed to programme us, once you start to realise then the News (at 6 or 10 on BBC1, 2,3,4 etc, CNN, Fox, Sky, all the 'independent' channels), they all carry the 'news' and the news is all the same.

The real frightening part is two-fold, what else is *really* happening in the world and why are we being fed this rubbish?

The same structure holds the media together and we are fed the crap that those who control us want us to absorb because most of the news is a series of thinly disguised memes designed to further the agenda.

Headline news for much of the latter part of 2007, reports the unfolding tragic story of the little girl who disappeared in Portugal. For six month this story has made headline news as we witness various twists and turns. I do not want to offend anyone's feelings on this highly emotive subject. I am heartfelt sorry for the little girl, her parents and family and I pray that love finds a way to bring closure to this awful situation. The question being poised here is not about the unarguable wrongs of the situation. The question I am asking is, what about all the other children throughout the World that go missing every single hour of every single day?

Everyone has a voice of reason inside them born of Creative Consciousness Source Energy that we can all access. This voice of reason was there when we were children, in other words we brought it with us when our lives began, it is part of us. It is through sets of beliefs that were forced upon us and through the constant conditioning and programming we are subjected to that this voice is questioned, quieted, and buried.

In our search for the truth we need to find that voice and access Consciousness, it speaks to us within our minds and it knows the truth is not to be found within 'the news.'

We now have endless stories of ... war ... plague ... kidnapping ... virus ... famine ... cancer ... negative equity ... burglary ... drought ... flood ... rape ... torture ... prison ... murder ... injustice ... interest rates ... stock market dropping ... food shortages ... oil prices ... house prices falling ... fraud ... fire ... worthless pension funds ... unemployment ... recession ... abuse ... pensioners choose to eat or heat ... cruelty to animals ... terror ... identity theft ... hoodies ... poverty ... shootings ... stabbings ... it never ends ... it is unrelenting and it is shovelled at us from everywhere in a constant stream.

What is the common denominator here? – FEAR.

Fear is the 'Chairman of the Board' of the Emotion Corporation PLC.

Fear is the emotion that means we cannot function properly.

'The news' stimulates our fears, builds upon them and finally we look elsewhere for a solution with the cry 'what are *they* going to do about this?' Please believe me the solution to the problem will be found, it probably won't make the news (unless it serves the agenda) and no and for sure we will not profit from the outcome and we will be called upon to contribute to the 'solution.'

We will not be *asked* to contribute by our elected officials whose job was supposed to be that they would serve us – *we just will*.

The news is a never-ending stream of fear, manifested by a series of never-ending, supposedly unsolvable problems as we live our lives anxious, helpless and confused and therefore so easily to control.

So that's the news on the television sorted out – now for my views on the press and the newspapers – *all* exactly the same as above.

Plus – here's Tracy from Maidstone's tits. (Bless).

News is what somebody somewhere wants to suppress; all the rest is advertising.
Alfred Harmsworth.

News programmes gain viewers by satisfying people's need to believe that evil stalks the land.
The Happiness Hypothesis. Jonathan Haidt.

Be aware that the media is controlled by the few. Use your instinct to discern, there is very often an agenda that is hidden from us. Usually it is a case of problem-reaction-solution. A problem created forcing our reaction to ask for the solution, a solution that those who control us wanted in the first place.

Watching television is like taking black spray paint to your third eye.
Bill Hicks.

The price of flat-screen televisions has plummeted recently. The luxury of a 42' inch television, eighteen months ago was at least £1500, now they can be bought for a third of that price, now that's become a bargain but it's also one hell of an energy-field we have to suck our heads out of when we do decide to go to our beds.

In his book Children of Change, Emery shows how television affects children. Since children tend to absorb rather than analyse information, 'conscious functioning is impaired,' they become indifferent, 'more like sheep than people. He wrote, 'in other words, television can be seen partly as a technological analogue of the hypnotist.' Writing in Human Relations (August 1959), he said, 'the psychological after-effects of television are of considerable interest to the would-be social engineer.'

Many times in the past we were told that we are behind America when it comes to fashion, products or whatever. In this shrinking world with the growing elements of the Internet, television and cheap, quick and easy travel, that gap has been eroded to nothing.

The 'pond' we call the Atlantic was formerly a great divide, however it has shrunk in our collective mindset.

But look for a moment at the echo that bounces back from the melting pot we call the USofA. Well firstly and most importantly they've got Jerry Springer (the next Governor of the State of Ohio?) and we've got Jeremy Kyle (the next Mayor of London?). If you want to watch people judge and condemn one another, just click that remote onto either of these programmes. Whilst touching on the subject of these two wonderful men – examples to us all of everything that is right in our society, (who earn their livings by scornfully extracting 'entertainment' from the dysfunctional – after they've had a few liveners and been coached in the green room). It is Jerry and Jeremy that seem the leaders and peddlers of the quest to introduce us all to the 'benefits' of the lie detector test.

(They are not of course because they are just being manipulated as well and we should not judge and condemn them).

However surely these two golden and shining examples to us all, with their messianic preaching to us on how to live a pure and blameless life, cannot be paving the way for us to blindly accept the future of the commonplace usage of the lie detector in everyday life? – watch this space, it's happening as we sleep.

Future programming will likely include; the 'wear your ID card with pride' campaign, (its already law – it just isn't being enforced yet) followed by; the 'let's have one surveillance camera for everyone please' battle and then the 'I love my microchip implant and feel the government and in fact anyone who wears a uniform, is right all of the time' crusade.

- You just know it makes sense.

Pressure on ITV to investigate The Jeremy Kyle Show after a judge condemned it as 'human bear-baiting' grew last night when Europe's biggest psychotherapy organisation called for a review of the way the programme treats vulnerable members of the public.

The popular daytime talk show was described as 'trash' last week by district judge Alan Berg as he passed sentence on one of its guests for head butting another in front of the cameras.

After a week of allegations that interviewees are deliberately 'wound up' or plied with alcohol, UFI, the company which runs Learndirect, the government's adult education service, cancelled it's £500,00-a-year sponsorship deal.

The Observer UK. David Smith. Sunday September 30th 2007.

Odds

The odds against winning the national lottery jackpot with one ticket are 13,983,815 to 1.

Winning anything with one Lotto ticket is 53 to I
Being dealt a royal flush at poker is 649,739 to 1
Hitting a hole in one with any one shot 42,952 to 1
All four players drawing perfect hands of whist
2,235,197,406,895,366,368,301,559,999 to 1
Being murdered in the next year 80,000 to 1
Being struck by lightning 6000,000 to 1
Dying while playing in a football match 25,000 to 1
Dying in a railway accident 500,000 to 1
Dying under the wheels of a bus 1,000,000 to 1
Dying in a plane crash 10,000,000 to 1
Choking to death on food 250,000 to 1
The odds against two Welshmen having the same surname 15 to 1.

Beyond Coincidence. M Plimmer and B King.

In the land of the free, where all dreams are possible – once you dispose yourself of the nightmares, there lives about 302 million people.

In the democracy that they call America, I suppose the odds against a father and his son being elected to the Presidency must therefore be about 150 million to 1 – so that's never going to happen.

Odds of being murdered … 18,000 to 1

Of getting away with murder … 2 to 1

Killed by lightning … 576,000 to 1

Of being on a plane with a drunken pilot … 117 to 1

Of having your identity stolen … 200 to 1, however recent events continue to prove that the odds on this are massively shortening.

One man's meat is another man's poison

As mentioned, I'm writing this in France because I need solitude to concentrate plus I am easily distracted and have a rubbish concentration threshold, if I were into self-diagnose a low attention span deficiency would be in the long list of my abnormalities.

I had been alone for about three weeks and so just before a full bout of cabin fever hit me a friend came to stay to tie up the purchase of a property she had found in the Dordogne. She mentioned she had seen some wasps going into a vent in the roof of this house where we are staying and was worried that they might prove a nuisance. So I was made aware of a 'problem' that I previously did not know existed and started to worry, telling myself '*if the wasps are in the roof they will easily get into the house,*' and I began to vibrate badly.

Luckily that night I bumped into Chris who proved himself both a countryman and a philosopher because when I told him of my wasp worries and asked him what I should do, his reply in response was simple.

'Why not just pull a chair up outside and watch them, it will really chill you out. They are amazing and absorbing to watch. If they're not bothering you, why bother them?'

This is for me a classic example of how each of us views the same situation differently. And yet again I shake my head and realise I still have a way to go – it's like I know this stuff but keep forgetting all the time.

It's only practice and the 'want-to-do-it.' But I carry the hope that I might just get there one day and stay there, permanently. And I just thought I would mention this at this juncture so that you don't beat yourself up for too long when you forget. It wasn't that long ago when I was lost for years, then it was less and I have probably got it down to days recently.

It will be great when I can make it go away forever. Incidentally the wasps also went away with no involvement from anyone and due to my adjusted vibration – were not gassed.

Another example of how two people can view the same situation very differently, comes the following story. I don't know who wrote it. I tracked it down to a website called 'aspire now,' (and they don't know who wrote it either so I changed it a bit).

An American investment banker was holidaying in Mexico. He found himself standing at the end of a pier near a small coastal village watching a little boat dock. There was only one fisherman aboard and he stepped onto the pier holding several large yellow fin tuna. The American complimented the fisherman on the quality of the fish and asked him how long it took to catch them.

'Only a little while,' the fisherman replied.

'Why don't you stay out for longer and catch more fish?' asked the American.

'I have enough fish now to feed my family,' explained the fisherman.

'So what do you do with the rest of your time?' The American asked.

'Well I sleep late, fish a little, tend to my vegetable patch, play with my children, take a siesta with my wife Maria, take a stroll down the village in the evening where I sip some wine and play guitar and sing with my amigos. I have a good life,' said the fisherman.

The American scoffed, 'I am a Harvard MBA and I am very successful and I could help you. You should spend more time fishing and with the proceeds you could buy a bigger boat. That bigger boat would catch more fish and you could then buy more boats. You could end up with a whole fleet of boats. Then instead of selling your catch to a middleman you would sell directly to the processor, eventually you could open your own cannery. Then you would control the product, the processing and the distribution ... you would need to leave this small village and move to Mexico City, then to New York, where you would run your ever expanding business

The fisherman asked, 'How long will this take?'

'About fifteen, maybe twenty years,' came the response.

'But what then?' said the fisherman?

'Then,' said the American, 'this is the best part, when the time is right you would announce an IPO and sell your company stock to the public and become very rich, you would make millions.'

'Millions?' said the fisherman. 'And then what?'

'Well if you have all that money you can do anything you want,' came the American's reply.

'Sure,' the fisherman said as he rubbed his chin and considered before replying, 'I could retire, move to a small fishing village, sleep late, do a little fishing, tend my vegetables, play with my grandchildren, take a siesta with my wife Maria, take a stroll down to the village in the evening, sip some wine, play my guitar and sing with my amigos.'

The Taliban in Afghanistan destroyed two ancient statues of Buddha in 2001. The leaders of India and Pakistan both voiced their outrage on behalf of many millions of their countrymen.

The Taliban Foreign Minister, Wail Ahmad Mutawakil, said. 'We do admit all these statues were the cultural heritage of Afghanistan, but we will not leave the part which is contrary to our belief.

Having upset every Buddhist on the planet (*which is more or less OK – because they will be forgiven*), the Taliban then sacrificed cows to apologise to God for taking so long to blow the statues up – and in doing upset all the Hindus for whom the cow is sacred.

The chances are if your witness to someone in another part of the world drinking blood from a cow, you will be repulsed, (the Masai drink blood directly from their cattle). Clearly the person who is drinking the blood is not repulsed; the animal suffers only a small wound that will quickly heal and the person who took the blood was doing so because he needed sustenance, but we find the process disgusting.

I wonder how the same person would view the way we take and consume milk from a cow and wonder if they would approve of the way we keep the animal during its miserable life. In a similar way we baulk at seeing a man in Africa eat a locust, just as we are repulsed when we watch the contestants in a 'I'm a Celebrity Get Me Out of Here,' trial as they try to eat a maggot or a kangaroos testicle.

We are taught to accept what we can and cannot eat; we are programmed to be attracted or repulsed.

Our disgust is learned; our repulsion is programmed.

It follows that the hungrier you are and the more scarce nutrition is, the broader your spectrum of what you can and cannot eat will be. It is not too much of a stretch of imagination to like the taste of prawns and be comfortable to eat them or be repulsed by them, as they could be perceived as insects of the sea.

In 1657 a Japanese priest set a kimono on fire in Tokyo because it carried bad luck. The fire he started spread until over 10,000 buildings were destroyed and 100,000 people died.

Francesco Della Barche invented a catapult that could throw three thousand pound rocks into battle. He accidentally got caught in his machine and it hurled him into the centre of town. He fell on his wife and killed them both.

One man's meat is another man's poison and only you can define what is good and what is bad, the rest of the Universe and everything in it – does not have an opinion.

One Story

Pop music has been around for as long as most of us can remember. I find it amazing considering that in music there are only a limited number of chords a musician can use and yet the originality and imagination used to move us emotionally just keeps on coming.

However, the vast majority of music has only one theme and that is love; the absence of it, the finding of it, the identifying of it, the questioning of it, the losing of it and the regaining of it. As an example of One Story then 'love' must be the most common noun in the history of music.

This is a generalisation, but there is a reoccurring theme that runs through all story telling, however the story might be delivered through a book, a film or just verbally, the tendency is for they're to be a hero. As the story unfolds the hero proceeds to go on a journey and that journey is one of a learning curve. He starts his journey with a degree of innocence and falls into the abyss, he fights and struggles against evil and he is tested on many fronts. He falters and he falls but finally emerges a different, stronger and more enlightened human being.

On his journey he will encounter many trials; he may get betrayed by those he trusted – his intellect will have been tested – he might have lost the girl he loved – and then found her again. He will have encountered many dangers on his journey and fought with monsters and demons (himself) and we gripped our seats because at the time we really thought he wasn't going to make it.

It doesn't matter who plays the starring role it could be Jason with his Argonaughts, Uma Thurman, Arnold or Rocky, Clive Owen or Odysseus, Brad Pitt or Steven Segal. Every story is the same story – read it and weep.

Because the hero is you and the story is representative of the story of your life.

When we watch a film and become absorbed into the tale we show empathy for the hero; so much so we become 'the hero' at the same time projecting ourselves into the story.

Every story has a hero and you are supposed to relate so closely with his actions that you become him.

This knowledge is used to manipulate us, (for example it strengthens patriotism) you think your settling down to watch an action film with John Wayne or Bruce Willis in the central role as they; dodge the bullets, meet out instant justice, fight for the flag, gain respect from their fellow man, get the pretty girl – think again because you're watching carefully constructed propaganda.

Filmmaking contains powerful magic and those that control us know how influenced we are by the seductive messages they urge us to embrace.

This projection is wonderfully explained in the following passage and as it shows, projection can be performed inwards as well as outwards.

The body is the central figure in the dreaming of the world.

There is no dream without it, nor does it exist without the dream in which it acts as if it were a person to be seen and be believed.

It takes the central place in every dream, which tells the story of how it was made by other bodies, born into the world outside the body, lives a little while and dies, to be united in the dust with other bodies dying like itself. In the brief time allotted to it to live, it seeks other bodies as its friends and enemies. Its safety is its main concern. Its comfort is its guiding rule. It tries to look for pleasure, and avoid the things that would be hurtful. Above all, it tries to teach itself its pains and joys are different and can be told apart.

The dreaming of the world takes many forms, because the body seeks in many ways to prove it is autonomous and real. It puts things on itself that it has bought with little metal discs or paper strips the world proclaims as valuable and real. It works to get them, doing senseless things, and tosses them away for senseless things it does not need and does not even want. It hires other bodies, that they may protect it and collect more senseless things that it can call its own. It looks about for special bodies that can share its dream. Sometimes it dreams it is a conqueror of bodies weaker than itself. But in some phases of the dream, it is the slave of bodies that would hurt and torture it.

The bodies' serial adventures, from the time of birth to dying are the theme of every dream the world has ever had. The "hero" of this dream will never change, nor will its purpose.

Though the dream itself takes many forms and seems to show a great variety of places and events wherein its "hero" finds itself, the dream has but one purpose, taught in many ways. This single lesson does it try to teach again, and still again, and yet once more; that it is cause and not effect. And you are its effect, and cannot be its cause.

A Course in Miracles (Penguin) p585

Oneness

Oneness is a spiritual term referring to the 'experience' of the absence of egocentric, identity, boundaries and according to some traditions, the perception of an absolute interconnectedness of all matter and thought in space-time or one's ultimate identity with God.

In the collected wisdom of all the world's religions it is confirmed, when the inherent similarities are revealed, that our differences are superficial and that our similarities go deep.

I honour the place within you where the entire Universe resides I honour the place within you of love, light, truth and peace. I honour the place within you, where, when you are in that place in you and I am in that place in me … there is only One of us.

Namaste. Sanskrit blessing.

A man's true wealth is the good he does in the world. Beauty is eternity gazing at itself in a mirror. But you are eternity and you are the mirror.

Kahlil Gibran.

Be at peace whatever your situation and know that you had to make this journey and regardless of your circumstances however dire they might be, this is the instrument upon which you are being invited to learn. Within the ego centred illusion we represent a highly distinctive form that receives and processes on two basic levels; the natural Universal Consciousness or Source Energy and the corrupted manufactured energy that is internalised and is of the ego that is of ourselves.

Our brains did not create consciousness for one simple reason – consciousness created our brains as part of the instrument that allows us to function in this dimension. That same consciousness is contained in the particles that make up the cells of everything, including every cell in your spacesuit.

Consciousness is one step away from Oneness; from all there is, from God. Consciousness is throughout the Universe. Consciousness is a part of what you are.

'There is still one more degree of realisation … namely that termed in Japanese, 'ji ji mu ge' – 'thing and no thing, no division,' – no division: no separation between things: the analogy suggested is of a net of gems: the Universe as a great spread out net with at every joint a gem, and each gem not only reflecting all the others but itself reflected in all. An alternate image is of a wreath of flowers. In a wreath, no flower is the cause of any other, yet all together, all are the wreath.'

Joseph Campbell.

When ten thousand things become one, then we return to the centre, where we have always been.

Chuang – Tse.

Any place is the centre of the world.

Black Elk.

Ownership

It's very nice to own things and as a result we spend much of our life programmed into wanting, needing and desiring. 'How many toys before you die?' was the legend and the question posed in the 1960's, mindful of the fact that we can only eat so much food, drink so much drink, sleep in one bed, wear so many clothes and collect so many things in any given time.

We are informed that our desires will be satisfied only by aspiration and acquisition when the truth is, once we get what we aspired to and dreamt about we usually discover that it is not enough. We don't own a thing. We may possess the title deeds and therefore in law it is 'ours,' but it isn't really because it only 'belongs' to us in this lifetime, you can't take anything with you; there are no pockets in shrouds – there are no roof-racks on hearses.

Put another way, whatever it is we think we own we are just renting.

As an example let's take the First Emperor of China and his Terracotta Army: Apparently there are 18,000 full sized figures, predominantly soldiers with full weaponry, horses, civic figures including administrators, jugglers and clowns, all there to protect and serve the great man in the afterlife (and obviously construct a similar society that he thought his demise was taking him to, much in similar way that his past life had allowed the greedy, egoic twat to rule over them).

Look, I'm sorry I never met the guy and I am so upset I forgot my own philosophy and am prepared to judge and condemn him, but apparently they have unearthed 8000 of these bigger than life-size figures and they have estimated there are 20,000 more, the site filled with these figures covers 20 square miles. The Chinese have said they know his monumental tomb lies in the middle of all of this and will undoubtedly contain great treasure.

I don't think that's too much of a stretch to believe that anyone with an ego the size of this fella, who had given over massive recourses in manpower to build this monument to greed, (and is prepared to take an army to heaven, hell or wherever he thought he was bound) then he must, I most humbly suggest, have a few quid stuck down his sock, if he hasn't, he's going to be very unpopular with the lads in the afterlife come payday.

The Chinese government states that they have no interest in disturbing the great man. I suppose if, out of respect and mindful of what he represents symbolically to the importance of their culture then fair enough, I begrudgingly get the point.

But I don't believe that is the truth.

We have to assume the Chinese are unlike all other nations and haven't already been into the tomb and skimmed whatever wealth and information lay there first.

This principle could also apply to the tombs of the pharaohs but unfortunately the looters - er sorry - the explorers got in there first. But why not? … and this is just a daft idea, lets get in there and responsibly and with due respect, realise the worth of what lies with the Great Emperor (after all he's had all this accumulated shite for about 2000 years notwithstanding inflation, the dusting bill alone must be horrendous, and if a message comes through from the other side that he wants it all back; then get the risk underwritted at Lloyds and get a book of odds against all this happening at Ladbrokes to cover all costs. (I am singling out Ladbrokes because they once cocked on a nice little treble bet I had on Man United, who scored – but in extra time, so they wouldn't give me my money.)

Anyway, with the fortune that should surround The Great Emperor we could build somewhere really safe in Iraq where the kids could play and we could try and heal them as best as we are able from the diabolical liberties that we have taken with their innocent lives. Let them play, teach them how to learn (not what to learn), give them opportunities of choice, show them how to build renewable sources of power, I bet solar panels would go down a treat. Maybe paints, crayons and musical instruments but avoiding all mention of religion, war and politics, (might also be best to skirt about the fact that we are in their country and that rumour has it that a quarter of all the worlds known oil reserves lie under their feet and that the oil is worth about 100 trillion dollars, give or take a few trillion at today's market value, but hey, can we talk about that when you're a bit older cause then you'll understand? (Well you will never actually understand but by the time you ask the question I will have moved back to America and be dealing with my nervous breakdown).

We could try and throw a bit of love in the mix, I mean it couldn't do any harm, hell is it not the least we could do?

If we could raise a few more quid can we go to Afghanistan and repeat the exercise?

We would feel good about that and when we feel good we don't feel pain, and then we wouldn't need to buy so much heroin from their country to kill that pain, so they wouldn't need to grow it anymore and could produce things like food. That would represent us giving them something back from all we have taken in bringing 'peace' to their country.

If the Chinese mention the small detail of, 'no we can't because we didn't have anything to do with this particular conflict thank you so very much.' Well, we do have other options; we could give the resources to Tibet's children and displaced and the places they (The Chinese Government) have claimed along with the resultant havoc, and to redress the balance we could move onto Fort Knox, Buckingham Palace, swiftly into the Vatican – sorry – there I go again getting all carried away with myself.

Pain

Most people get a fair amount of fun out of their lives, but on balance life is about suffering and only the very young or the very foolish imagine otherwise.

George Orwell.

On this point Orwell made an accurate observation but to overcome suffering we need to become ego-less, but because the ego will distract us by setting up conflicts and separateness, it makes the nature of the human condition such; that all we do is seek to avoid pain.

When we are having a good time, feeling love and joy, we are riding the opposite end of a seesaw and our pain and the source of it is forgotten.

So many of us carry pain and this is why we, in varying degrees, induce ourselves with medications in the form of chemicals.

The deeper our imagined pain, the stronger the medication we need to take, but the pain was put there by the programmers and the same thing happened to them.

Anything introduced to our bodies orally, through breath, through our skin or indeed into our skin via injection, etc, has an effect on our central nervous system. The chemicals that these substances carry alter our mood and our emotions. These chemicals include caffeine, paracetemol, food, cannabis, cocaine, speed and heroin.

We are born as blocks of stone and it is pain that shapes us and erodes us and makes us what we are.

Address to Oxford University graduates. C S Lewis.

Out of suffering have emerged the strongest souls; the most massive characters are seared with scars.

Kahlil Gibran.

'Who taught you all this doctor?'

The reply was prompt.
'Suffering.'

Albert Camus, The Plague

When we resist our fate we suffer, when we accept it we are happy.

We have time in abundance, an eternity to repeat out mistakes but we need only once to correct our mistakes and at last hear the song of enlightenment with which we can break the chain forever.

In your heart you can hear it now, it is the song your spirit has been singing since the moment of your birth.

Nothing happens without cause, the gift of suffering is to bring us closer to God. To teach us to be strong when we are weak, to be wise in the mists of confusion, not to guard what we cannot hold.

Lasting victories are won in the heart, not on this land or that.

Heaven and Earth, directed by Oliver Stone.

Do not take life's experiences too seriously. Above all, do not let them hurt you, for in reality they are nothing but dream experiences ...

If circumstances are bad and you have to bear them, do not make them a part of yourself.

Play your part in life, but never forget it is only a role.

Paramahansa Yogananda. Par-a-gram.

The remnants of pain left behind by every strong negative emotion that is not fully faced, accepted, and then let go of join together to form an energy field that lives in the very cells of your body. It consists not just of childhood pain, but also painful emotions that were added to it created by the voice of the ego. It is the emotional pain that is your unavoidable companion when a false sense of self is the basis of your life.

Eckhart Tolle. A New Earth.

It is said we learn much through adversity however we do not need to have as much adversity and difficulty in life as we very often find. In a fair and even deal with the Universe we might find problems will still come our way but in truth we should consider that our problems manifest themselves because of the way we feel and therefore think, and what we think we will bring to us.

Here in the West, most of us are taught to fear death and as a result when we loose a loved one we feel abject pain. If we could open our minds to the possibility that death is nothing more than a transition and not the end of something but part of a cycle, we would mourn less because we understood more.

Much pain is manifested because we fail to understand. Imagine what life would be like without emotional suffering, there would be no fear, anger, sadness or frustration. We should not look outside ourselves for the solution to our pain because most of our pain comes simply from a futile search for what we think we want.

If we resist or ignore higher wisdom in preference to instant gratification, then our choice will still take us back through what may be a painful learning curve. Our choices can entrap us but at the same time can provide an opportunity to learn.

The choices we make through our subconscious will save us pain because here is where we act with wisdom because we are channelling and open to Creative Consciousness, this is when we allow ourselves to attract people or situations into our lives that will serve our learning and growth and we will do so without the need for pain.

Parents

Children begin by loving their parents; after a time they judge them; rarely if ever, do they forgive them.

Oscar Wilde.

'The fact is that you can't have a good relationship with a girl who hasn't settled things with her father.

All girls' answer as follows: Well, what about guys who don't settle things with their mothers?

That's not as crucial to me, because I'm not looking for a guy.

The thing is that women, if they could look at their fathers objectively, and make an estimate of them, and see where they failed, and forgive them and forget them, they'd be alright. Because they haven't settled things with them, men become the road company of their fathers.

'He never paid any attention to me, either.'

You've got nothing but trouble. The thing is about women is that they don't discriminate. Even though they hate you and think you're insensitive, they won't let on, and they'll marry you and punish you.'

Mort Sahl.

Be nice to your children, for they will choose your rest home.

Phyllis Diller.

Paul McKenna in his book Change Your Life in 7 Days invites us to go further back in our childhood and consider the world of the newborn baby.

'Imagine you woke up one day in a land populated almost entirely by giants. At first you would no doubt be terrified, and the deafening roar of loud noises and the uncomfortable sinking feeling when you fell would stick with you for a lifetime. After a time, you would realise that many of the giants seemed friendly, and that one giant

in particular was taking a particular interest in your safety and well-being.'

Although we are unable to consciously remember being the baby McKenna refers to there is a part of us, buried subconsciously beneath the layers of the onionskin that can. We can also empathise with that babies circumstances and know that inside all of us lives that child. We endure many traumas as we are growing up and under the layers of the onionskin they form compartments or altars. Consciously very few of us can recall our very beginnings but unconsciously it is all still within us and will manifest should our altar be triggered and activated.

McKenna is not necessarily referring to an abusive childhood however we can still relate to the trauma. He further asks us to imagine how we might feel if the giant we had put our trust in one day shouted, threatened or hit us, would you ever feel safe again in the land of giants? As you grow you meet other little people and as a result feel more secure. You swop information and learn the rules that enable you to stay safe. But those rules are ones of conformity, the programmers or giants as McKenna puts it will ensure you do as your told, do not rebel, study, pass exams, gain marks to progress, work, marry and finally complete the cycle by bringing your own small person into the world.

Paul McKenna shows us a treadmill where we have no choice, a life we call it, but is this really living? It gives us profound insight into our own upbringing and just as importantly the upbringing of others. When one considers that even individuals from loving rounded families can fail miserably on the road that lies ahead of them and it also reveals how we create the monsters that walk among us.

Peace

If we have no peace, it is because we have forgotten that we belong to each other.
Mother Teresa.

Peace is constructed not fought for.
Brent Davis.

You don't fight for peace, that's a spin that seems to have stuck. You care, nourish, give empathy, allow and want peace. True peace is not freedom from hassle, it is being unaffected by that hassle.

No one can give peace to you, you can only discover it within yourself.
If there is to be any peace, it will come through being, not having.
Henry Miller.

Peace is not merely a distant goal that we seek, but a means by which we arrive at that goal.
Martin Luther King.

Our instinctive mind yearns for peace and for this to happen we must join with other minds, for that is how peace is obtained. Our programming does not lead us in that direction but the release and deep peace that comes from meeting yourself and your brothers totally without judgment is powerful, because forgiveness creates a picture of a world where suffering is over, loss becomes impossible and anger makes no sense as a result attack is gone.

Everybody today seems to be in such a terrible rush, anxious for greater developments and greater riches and so on, so that children have very little time for their parents. Parents have very little time for each other, and in the home begins the disruption of peace in the world.
Mother Teresa.

Politics

It is an arresting fact of British political life that a Briton can enjoy a national platform and exalted status simply because he is the residue of an illicit coupling 300 years before between a monarch and an orange seller.

Bill Bryson. Mother Tongue.

Those who vote decide nothing.
Those who count the votes decide everything.

Joseph Stalin.

Integrity of 2006 elections cannot be ensured.

The US. Government Accountability Office.

Potentially the subject of politics could take up a great deal of discussion. But this is not necessary because, it does not matter who you vote for the same agenda is always served.

It has been said that politics is show business for ugly people; all masks are ugly because they are a distortion of the truth. To be a politician is to demonstrate the usage of masks, it is the world of the ego and a politician cannot exist without the talent to mask. Somewhere in the dropping of those masks we would have revealed to us the politicians creed, 'we serve others best when we serve ourselves,' and that would be the best we would hope to find, because from there it is all very much downhill.

At grass roots there may well be many earnest bright young people who have signed up to the party for all the right reasons. They might imagine that they want to do good work for those less fortunate than themselves. They align themselves to whichever party is nearest to their implanted belief system in the hope and conviction that they can actually make a difference. These ethics cannot be criticised however the truth is the same in every profession; unless you tow the party line, serve the agenda, do not draw attention to yourself by saying or doing anything that might question the status quo, then quite simply you will not progress.

Presidents and Prime Ministers are not elected they are programmed, groomed and chosen by those that hold the reigns of power. They are the puppets of masters that sit at the very top of what is simply business.

We should in fact pity and forgive our leaders because they are more damaged, directed, controlled and manipulated than we are.

A demonstration of manipulation happened when G. W. Bush was exposed using an earpiece during the Presidential debate. On national television he is clearly show saying 'let me finish,' (before you give me the next answer?). This indefensible lapse would be laughable if it wasn't so concerning. Here we have the former most powerful man in the world being coached, advised and told what to say – and he gives himself away by arguing with 'the voice.'

It is incompetent, fraudulent and very worrying. His manner of speech, his body movements, the bulges in the back of his jacket, suggested further proof of a transmitter, the question is irrelevant as to whether this is a one off or he's wearing one all the time. It is yet another example of all that is wrong with this type of power.

In Thailand it is not advisable to criticise the Royal Family; what a great trick the programmers have instilled into the people. We of course in the free 'unoppressed' West don't have this problem. Well put a uniform wearing person (even if the uniform is dusty and hanging in his wardrobe) in a situation whereby you criticise the Queen or her old Mum for example, and just watch the fury of programming manifest itself before your very eyes.

It's as good as the one in England when a member of one party crosses the floor to join another party because, 'he can no longer tolerate the policies of his present party.' Its all pantomime, and it would be laughable except that we deserve more because we pay the price.

How much longer we can afford to pay, because whilst it might appear to us that there are different policies there simply are not, the same agenda is served by whoever is in power and it always has been this way. We flatter ourselves that in voting for; Liberal, Democrat, Republican, Labour, Conservative … whatever … that our duly appointed representatives will further the promises they made in order to catch our vote. The truth is that they do nothing but pay lip-service to us whilst conspiring to serve themselves – because that is what power does.

Furthermore they do this individually for their own benefit and for the benefit of their 'beloved' party. They may well be enjoying the 'party' but it is we, the electorate who are conned into thinking our 'new member' or newly elected party will actually make some sort of difference.

Politicians share common ground with the rest of us as they operate within a pyramid of power, their position and progress can only be maintained if they serve the agenda. In the thousands of years since the structure of government was first born in the 'democracies' of ancient Greece, polished later in Rome which spawned our democracy and that of America's, imposed upon the majority of the world and most of it's people, it has always been the same. The wealth, knowledge and therefore the power, lies in the hands of the few and those few maintain their position by feeding the masses a diet of fear, lies, guilt and all that other low vibrational garbage, this ensures we maintain their power, on top of that they have the gall to remind us constantly that we are free. (Forgive them – they are programmed). For thousands of years but never more so until recently, we are controlled by a media, government, banking system, schooling, religion and so on, and we witness as our so-called 'leaders,' serve their own agendas in a pretence of unbelievable arrogance.

Knowingly or unknowingly, this arrogance has collectively; seen us perish in our millions upon battlefields soaked with good men's blood for no good reason. It has seen us hock ourselves to the hilt in usury to become slaves to interest payments and consume like there is no tomorrow.

Recessions (the last one was about 19 years ago) go in cycles and are totally manufactured so the banks can sweep up and a few profit while the rest of us burn within the dream that always turns into an abject nightmare.

Nearly at the end of his presidency, Bush announced that every American will pay the equivalent of 2333 dollars per person to bail out the banks and the same announcement was also made to every UK citizen.

The same solution will always be presented.

Who pays every time? – You pay.

There is no money, fuel or food crisis – it's manufactured – it's the advancement of an agenda to further control and subjugate us.

If our political parties and leaders were doing their jobs properly it could not happen, if they can't get it right they should have the decency to stand down and we should try another way but that has never happened.

We have reduced this paradise we call Earth to a wasteland. In the process pouring trillions of our money into largely failed enterprise; civic buildings, millennium domes, nuclear capabilities, wars and space races with little or no accountability.

Corruption exists more now than ever and the numbers and the rewards are so much greater as the system continues its to advance its agenda.

If we were to place one label to most accurately describe our present government in the West, (ie; America, Britain and Europe) the label that would most adequately describe our type of government would be Fascism, welcome to the World – welcome to egocracy.

Politics may not be the world's oldest profession, but the results are exactly the same.

Power

It is an unfortunate paradox that those who hold power are too comfortable to notice the pain of those who are suffering and those that are suffering have no power.

The leaders of nations recognise that the economies of their countries heavily depend on a good relationship with the USA. David Icke in his book 'Tales from the Time Loop' quotes Admiral Stansfield Turner, the former head of the CIA.

> 'Our power is so great, and so unlikely to be challenged for many, many years, that you have to go back to Rome for any kind of parallel. It's a misnomer to speak of the United States as being a super-power. We're a super-duper power, and I don't know if the world has seen one of those before.'

The power extends to much more than the countries economy, security, armaments and shelter fall under the umbrella of shelter from being a friend of such a powerful ally as the United States. As Turner points out, whether your in a bazaar in Cairo or pushing a cart in Shanghai the choice your leaders make in their relationship with America will have a profound effect on your security and prosperity. From a bigger quota for your apples to the funding of a new dam; it pays to be a friend of America.

Few people know of him, yet conceivably hundreds of millions of people are alive because of him; Stanislav Petrov, a retired Soviet military officer is credited with preventing a worldwide nuclear war.

Petrov was a Soviet army officer monitoring the satellite systems for signs of a U.S attack in 1983.

At half past midnight on a cold September night, the whole system lit up and had Petrov responded as his orders stated, to launch a counter attack, millions would have died in the ensuing holocaust. (In a further twist of fate, Petrov was only on duty that evening as a stand-in for another officer).

He chose not to follow orders and instead used the power of his instincts not to respond. Petrov was forced to leave the army and was sent into early retirement; a man who saved millions of lives, who didn't follow orders, suffered a nervous breakdown and was given a pension of $200 a month.

This was how one of the most important and influential decisions of all time was rewarded.

Courage is not the towering oak that sees storms come and go; it is the fragile blossom that opens in the snow.

Alice M Swaim.

When the power of love overcomes the love of power the world will know peace.

Jimi Hendrix

From the perception of the five-sensory human, we are alone in a Universe that is physical. From the perception of the multi-sensory human, we are never alone, and the Universe is alive, conscious, intelligent and compassionate. From the perception of the five-sensory human, the physical world is an unaccountable given in which we unaccountably find ourselves, and we strive to dominate it so we can survive. From the perception of the multi-sensory human, the physical world is a learning environment that is created jointly by the souls that share it, and everything that occurs within it serves their learning. From the perception of the five-sensory human, intentions have no effects, the effects of actions are physical, and not all actions affect others or us. From the perception of the multi-sensory human, the intention behind an action determines its effects, every intention affects both others, us and the effects of intentions extend far beyond the physical world.

What does it mean to say that an 'invisible' realm that is not detectable through the five senses, but that can be known explored and understood by other human faculties?

Gary Zukav. The Seat of the Soul.

The power of consciousness remains our greatest power, people have tried to ascribe meaning to it and define it and never really properly pinned its meaning. It is unknown and unacknowledged by the conventional sciences however this power is demonstrated in evidence all around us. A world exists beyond our five-senses and these principles of energy at work are not theory.

In 1982 Alain Aspect conducted an experiment at the University of Paris and proved that two quantum particles once connected and then separated by vast distances remain connected – if one particle changes the other particle changes and just as remarkably – it changes instantly.

Aspect and his team discovered that these particles are instantaneously communicating with each other regardless of the distance separating them, from a few feet to a few billion miles. This incredible event is one of the most important discoveries of all time, and yet unless you read some fairly obscure scientific journals you are unlikely to have heard of this. The reason the mainstream doesn't talk about this is because they have no explanation for this and it defies the laws of physics.

It might just be, that this unexplained but proven phenomenon demonstrates that the distance between particles is only our perception, that there is no such thing as space and time.

Sure, its pretty heavy stuff but it is awesome heavy stuff.

It is also further evidence that we are connected and not separate, but because this happens outside of our conventional laws of time and space, we don't get to learn about this absorbing and enlightening phenomenon.

We know that powers main attribute is the ability to have it, and furthermore use it in order to receive and respond to impressions from stimuli outside of ourselves.

We are coming to understand that consciousness exists in the smallest of the particles that make up atoms. In a Universal sense, consciousness exists everywhere in the fundamentals of everything that is, or put it another way, our Universe is minded.

This conscious power is in every atom and every cell of our bodies this is the power of mind, it denotes that every single thing in this Universe is alive and connected.

Consciousness is the one and only reality in the Universe.

Programming

You've got to be taught to be afraid
Of people whose eyes are oddly made,
Of people whose skin is a different shade.
You've got to be carefully taught.
You've got to be taught before it's too late,
Before you are six or seven or eight,
To hate all the people your relatives hate.
You've got to be carefully taught.

Oscar Hammerstein II from the musical South Pacific (1949).

You need to tell your loved ones, the little ones in particular, that when they hear
the president talking about Al-Qaeda, Iran and other places, I do so because I long
for peace.

G W Bush.

When we run to the child who has cut his finger and as a result is crying
and staring at it, we are inclined to put a plaster on even though the wound
doesn't deserve one. We may then feel inclined to 'kiss it better,' and with this
action the torrent of tears stops and the crying ceases. What has happened is
that the child's focus has moved away from the incident, the plaster can be
sported with pride as a badge of honour, comfort was called for and received
… all is well.

But what is the 'magic' that heals the finger? Not the plaster of course, it is
the body which has its own mechanism for repair, healing and maintenance. In
the action that we performed we have programmed a child and it is likely that
the same thing happened to us when we were his age.

In a classroom aged about ten I remember asking a question of an Irish
teacher called Mr Kennedy. Perhaps I provoked him in some way when I asked
about whether the battle of Hastings was in France or in England. I remember

Mr Kennedy, who was obviously having a bad day, informing me it was in fact England and saying further while shaking his head, 'there's always one' to the rest of the class. He taught me two things in his one short reply; The Battle of Hastings took place in England and how words can wound and I've never forgotten either. We can all recall how words and actions can wound and often it is not what is said or done but the manner of the delivery and the tone of voice, it is in fact all about attitude.

I remember about the same time with another teacher in another class, we were all asked to write a poem about a postman and the best poem would, we were assured, be published in the school paper which was published at the end of each term.

I was proud that my poem won and took 'Termtime' home to show my father. I showed him my first published work with a flourish and having read it he said, 'it's good, but you couldn't have written it.' I am not judging or condemning him, just using this as an example in the context of the message I am trying to convey to you, because he might also have been having a bad day.

As you go in search for the individuality that is You and your birthright be prepared to be attacked, for the nail that stick up the highest is the one that is the most likely to be hit. In any event and just to create a balance here, I must just stop and tell you at this juncture that I have not written this book from 'page 1' onwards. I have written the main topics and much of what I already had written down and gone back and forth in an attempt to create some flow, make it readable, create some cohesion and only you can say if I have succeeded or not, so might I just mention at this point, how pleased I am to meet you and I am privileged to consider that unless you're doing what I do and are just skipping, *(which is often what I do until I realise I am just being lazy and trying to kind of fast-forward to get to all the good bits and save myself some time)* so when you finally do *(without skipping)* get to this bit, I just wanted to say 'good to meet you,' and if you think I am being sycophantic here I am, it's because I need your attention to consider this following idea – I got back from France right at the end of last year and at that point most of what I have written here, was written.

Now, Uncle Denis, who is my closest blood left on this earth, (my mothers brother and someone I look up to) is a remarkable man of 85 summers and he eats a book just about every single day, he not only reads them but manages to absorb and make sense of them. So having printed this book out and having managed to turn letters on a computer screen into something that I could actually 'touch and feel' and there is a massive difference – like you finally know you have actually done something, so having manifested this into paper form I asked my Uncle if he would be good enough to read it and give me his views (because I respect them and my ego was fragile).

And he said 'yes,' and after three (long) days he phoned me and said, 'I have read it, do you want to call in at my house and pick it up?' and I said I would and got to his house and nervously asked him if he thought it was ok, and he said, 'I have corrected the spelling mistakes *(thanks)*, 'I do not concur with much of what you say on the subject of drugs,' *(totally reasonable)* 'and by the way, I like it – but who wrote it?'

What my Uncle *('who wrote it?')* was saying, was exactly what my Father *('you couldn't have written it')* had said to me all those years ago but from my Uncle it was a complement, a recognition, an affirmation that I was really knocked-out by, it touched me, it helped me, it encouraged me, it made me believe that I might be finally doing something worthwhile – something right. My Uncle said the same thing to me as my Dad did over 40 years ago but with a different attitude because my Dad wounded me and I don't want sympathy from you and I am not having a go at him (remember we have to *automatically* forgive lest we constantly judge and condemn), I am just mentioning it for two reasons;

Firstly – if someone you look *up* to puts you *down* – then forgive him and more importantly – do not at all costs believe him.

Secondly – do not, under any circumstances do this to anyone who might look up to you, (if you can't say something nice say nowt) and if you do speak – then do an impersonation of my Uncle Denis, because you will assist the querient – you or me – to grow).

There exists options; when we are talking to impressionable young people in similar circumstances the following might be an decent example of delivery;

'You have a great use of words and I can see the potential of talent there, but I've noticed that you make the odd spelling mistake, here's a spare spell-checker because I'm like you and I make the odd error.

Instead of alternatives like, 'are you mentally incapable, thick or something?'

Perhaps this would explain my behaviour over a couple of decades when, in another example, I would be driving along, theoretically minding my own business *(such is my world – a safe, warm place full of delusion and denial)* when a car would undertake me and the guy in the back with a snarl on his face sticks two fingers up at me. Now clearly he thinks I've done something to offend him, only I haven't got a clue what that something is.

But the 'old' me would have probably ended up in a chase to the next set of lights and a conversation held at high volume about enlightenment and I daresay at the end of our chat I would not have found a new friend. The 'new' me is different as I view the same incident with an inward shrug and carry on as if nothing has happened.

The guy in the back of the other car has achieved nothing except upset himself and the other occupants in the front of the car and he now has to find another unfortunate victim to vent his spleen. I have not risked life and limb, a heart attack and the unlikely outcome of me securing victory and my day is unaltered.

I have managed to not get involved in *his* drama therefore it has not become part of my reality and in what seems a good deal, his abusive traumatic childhood altars have been activated but mine haven't. So let him go on his way and spoil somebody else's day, month or life. This might all sound a bit simplistic, but we do have a choice and we don't have to buy a ticket to the dance unless it's where we want to be.

I can't believe how long it took me to get rid of that early programming. When I used to react it was simply because there was something lacking in me, not in the spark that was trying to ignite me, because if there ain't no fuel then that spark cannot make fire.

This was because I had a fortress mentality and a fortress mentality is built to protect itself the best way we are able. And fortress mentalities, with there foundations rooted in the ego, are built in childhood because inside every grown up there lives a child and that child can easily surface – especially in the face of adversity.

We were more closely linked with the divine as children. But back then we just took it for granted because we knew nothing else. We had beautiful moments that were filled with love and in those moments we never felt more alive. Although we saw life as beautiful and regarded it with wonder and appreciation, we did not find it extraordinary because our life was filled with these moments. We were in touch with each other and ourselves, then the programming begins and the dance will soon be over.

Children are programmed, broken and domesticated the same way we would treat a household pet. We reward with praise, favour and treats and we punish with withdrawal, criticism and threat.

The dog and the child are 'good' or they are 'bad' and if we are lucky someone is around to reward us when we are 'good' for following the rules imprinted upon us by the parent, guardian, teacher, etc, and so we are taught the principle of how to please – 'come to Daddy, good boy, there's a treat, here's a star, there's a medal.'

We are programmed to wear masks, how to perform, how to 'act.'

If we are acting then it follows we are not being ourselves and it is in our childhoods where we construct the masks we will wear for the rest of our lives.

We are programmed into following our parent's, those we look up to and those that guide and teach us.

Masters waiting in turn to be Misters and then to embrace being Masters.

That's the simplicity of the cycle.

And whilst children may not listen to their parents, they will take after them and will adopt their beliefs because they are small and cannot question. Those of us that do question will find this behaviour risks being rejected, ridiculed, humiliated, ostracised, unloved, with the end result; energy is withdrawn. Thus the child, who is finally broken into this 'reality,' becomes an adult with a judging and condemning attitude to everything externally in 'reality' and internally, with the result that we constantly judge and condemn others and ourselves.

To make matters worse we find ourselves surrounded by similarly programmed people, who are in turn trapped in the same cycle; judge and condemn, and cycles by their own definition do not end unless we realise, recognise and break them.

From the moment I could talk, I was ordered to listen.

Father and Son. Cat Stevens.

And so we are programmed by propaganda, fear of penalties, fines and punishment. We might find that we are being good by compulsion; we are not necessarily being good – by desire.

Control a persons mind and you control them.

Individuals, communities, nations and cultures, are built upon the values and perceptions of the five-sensory personality. And every one of these structures is of our own creation and allows the programming of others upon us.

Our individual and mass values reflect the decisions of our species – to learn through fear and doubt. We are programmed to fear one another, nations fear nations, races fear races and the sexes fear each other. The exploration of physical reality, which is an external power, could have been accomplished in a spirit of cooperation with, and appreciation of, the Earth. Instead we explore with a sense of domination, force and exploitation.

This is the path of our learning, using fear, doubt and worry. Our species has little humility left, there is no reverence, there is little respect, we believe in the advances of our technology and are seduced by the notion that we are in control and yet we are surrounded by incidents that should serve as reminders, that we are not. Take one brick out of our structure and we witness collapse.

Water, fuel, food and money head a long list of indispensable requirements. We are more fragile than ever, more vulnerable to control. We take from one another and the Earth, we destroy forests and oceans and the atmosphere. We enslave one another and we continue to torture, humiliate and murder. If you want the world to become loving and compassionate then you must embrace those qualities as an individual.

If you want to diminish fear in the world, then you must diminish your own.

Through the use of thousands of influences; memes, media, parenting, education, politics and religion, we build outward from ourselves and in the doing create macrocosms of the fear that exists between us. The ripple goes out and affects us all. What is in one is transmitted to all.

How we change is to know we have to change ourselves – there is no other way.

To put the world in order, we must first put the nation in order; to put the nation in order, we must put the family in order; to put the family in order, we must cultivate our personal life; and to cultivate our personal life, we must first set our hearts right.

Confucius

There is no such thing as a mistake however those around us are often slow to forgive but that is the product of programming, if we had a more open view we might just consider that a mistake is simply an opportunity to learn. Any fool can screw up and blow it, I have done it regularly, but coming back builds character and the process is most enlightening.

I don't know if I continue, even today, always liking myself. But what I learned to do many years ago was to forgive myself. It is very important for every human being to forgive herself or himself because if you live, you will make mistakes - it is inevitable. But once you do see the mistake, then you forgive yourself and say, 'well if I'd known better I'd have done better,' that's all. So you say to people who you think you may have injured, 'I'm sorry,' and then you say to yourself, 'I'm sorry,' If we all hold onto the mistake, we can't see our own glory in the mirror because we have the mistake between our faces and the mirror, we can't see what we're capable of being. You can ask for forgiveness of others, but in the end the real forgiveness is in one's own self. I think young men and women are so caught by the way they see themselves. Now mind you. When a larger society sees them as unattractive, as threats, as too black or too white or too poor or too fat or too thin or too sexual or too asexual, that's rough. But you can overcome that. The real difficulty is to overcome how you think about yourself. If we don't have that we never grow, we never learn, and sure as hell we should never teach.

Maya Angelou.

In this predatory society where much value is based on avarice, acquisition, status, and the many ideals we are programmed to aspire to, the outsider is the casualty, the symptom of an ill at ease regime. The development of psychosis in the adult is stimulated because of childhood trauma. Taken down a different path, the individual would not have turned to violence to express his rage and anger.

There are many examples of the outsider, this person alienated from society. When John Lennon wrote the song 'Working Class Hero', he explored these themes of alienation. When his killer was arrested, his was holding a copy of 'Catcher in the Rye' by JD Salinger; this book is similar in its description of the individual's separation and alienation.

The stories are many, the manifestation of fear is endless; from Robert De Niro's performance in Taxi Driver to the shootings in schools and the violence on our streets. What we are witnessing is the result of what programming can do to those that will not, or cannot, accept it. These actions are the results of abject pain locked into our subconscious as trauma. This is the power of manipulation when that trauma is activated, the results of when a dormant alter awakes. This is the influence that some people have over others. There is no place for these individuals in a society that has placed unobtainable obstacles in their way. This is the mindset of those who will perhaps one day snap against the structure and the society that has placed unobtainable obstacles in their way. This is the mindset of those who will perhaps one day snap against the structure and the society that has placed too much of a burden upon them.

This is how we create those people we call monsters.

There's room at the top they are telling you still,
But the first you must learn is to smile as you kill,
If you want to be like them folks on the hill.

Working Class Hero. John Lennon

The world breaks everyone and afterward many are strong in the broken places. But those that will not break it kills. It kills the very good and the very gentle and the brave impartially. If you are none of these you can be sure it will kill you too but there will be no special hurry.

Ernest Hemmingway. A Farewell to Arms.

We are told to not vent anger and count to ten but I could not embrace this until much later in life. But look upon anger as a test, every time you feel it rising in you, ask what is to be learned here? The ego enjoys trouble and builds walls around its programmed beliefs. Watch as others knee-jerk-respond to everything that threatens those beliefs and what they see as interfering with their own beliefs.

Just click the remote to the fabulous Jerry Springer show, (or the guy who has replaced him while Jerry is over here programming us to willingly accept the lie-detector test in our lives, or take a peek if you dare, at the magnificent demi-godlyness that is Jeremy Kyle … *talk about ego – talk about judge and condemn*) if we need prime examples of this behaviour.

We are conditioned in many ways by what we come into contact with. All the master's, in whatever guise they come and whether they are parent's, guardians or teachers, they teach us some of the most vital and profound lessons when we are at our most vulnerable, that is to say in our formative years when we are all little Masters.

Not that I am saying these people are not well intentioned or that they are evil, because as they condition us we should be mindful that they were conditioned themselves in a similar way and so the cycle continues, until we start to question. When damaged people bring up children, (unless they have healed themselves) those people will very likely raise damaged children. Damaged people are not wicked or stupid, but they lack emotional intelligence because they were damaged by their own upbringing.

If a child is told it is insignificant, has no belief in a decent future and is presented with unnecessary fear; that child will usually fail to succeed, will have issues of self-esteem, be more likely to turn to crime, will demonstrate varying degrees of disfunctionality, may have problems with inherent anger and will live a difficult life and usually never get the help they genuinely need, notwithstanding the fact that we have managed to produce, to walk along with many others – yet another tortured soul.

Or to put this into plain English – if you tell him he is a useless twat often enough – it will become his truth.

This will be the message, buried in his subconscious mind; this will be the voice that will chatter away to him wherever he goes and whatever he encounters.

Even if the endless programming we are exposed to is not intentional it still has the same effect. We are subjugated through a system of mind-control to fear and we give away our power each and every time we respond.

One of our missions here is to remember who you are. Perhaps the odd memory in our past will remind us of how the programming worked on ourselves and on others, and in order to remember who we are we need to reduce our egos.

I remember seeing the effects of what a little egoic power did to some of my friends at school – one day they were typical schoolboys, full of daftness and the next the day they were made prefects and they changed. That sly cigarette behind the bike-sheds couldn't happen anymore, because it would mean they would be demoted from their new positions if caught. So, every so often, we smokers had to find another secret location.

When I say smokers, we weren't really, we hadn't adopted the habit yet we were just demonstrating rebellion to each other, being brave and clever (we thought) by doing something we had been told *not* to do, often by people who were smoking as they told us not to, and so we would stand around pulling the guts out of a single Benson and talk shite twice a day.

But where there used to be six of us, now there were five and we had lost a member to the cause, so we couldn't risk the new prefects insider knowledge of our original hideout and we moved to new whereabouts and our heinous act remained hidden.

The results of the marriage in matching and advancing the systems bride and groom – will and programming – can be witnessed in us all; an individual gets a new job or gains promotion and seeks to advance, then one thing will follow for certain, that individual will conform; he will tow the party line and do what is expected of him.

Without these actions he will not progress and the doors to advancement will remain firmly shut. Once a member of the club, his individuality is removed and he becomes part of the whole and melded to whatever hat he is wearing or flag he is flying.

The same dynamics exist in psychological experiments with people divided into two groups; warders and prisoners – then swap their roles over and they adapt and behave exactly the same way.

We are eminently adaptable and willing to use what we believe works best for us, however we are not ourselves when we are acting to suit what it is we think someone else expects of us.

Why do we do this and why have we no right to question?

Because that is the way we were programmed.

Whoever joins an organisation whatever it might be, will most likely sign up with the best of intentions. These organisations are all around us in this over-governed society and they do not celebrate individuality.

You may join the Army or the Police Force or work towards qualifying as a journalist or a political career with all the ideals of good works and the hope of actually making a difference, but you will not progress unless you tow the party line. You have to think with the group and run with the pack and should you chose to think for yourself and foolishly voice your opinion you will be ostracised, ridiculed, continue this behaviour and you will ultimately loose your job.

Then who will work down the mines and serve the top of the pyramid we now all support?

Power tends to corrupt, and absolute power corrupts absolutely. Great men are almost always bad men.

Lord Acton.

I ain't gonna work on Maggie's farm no more …

Bob Dylan.

Questions to provoke thought ...

How many hamburgers are produced when an acre of virgin Amazon rainforest in cleared for cattle?

Did Adam and Eve have navels?

Why is there only one monopolies commission?

Why is 'abbreviated' such a long word?

How is it wrong numbers are never busy?

If it is true that we are here to help others, then what exactly are the 'others' here for?

Pretentious? ... Moi?

If love is blind then why has lingerie proved so popular?

Why do we read left to right yet turn pages right to left?

If work is so wonderful how come they have to pay you to do it?

If you ate a bowl of pasta and then a bowl of antipasta, would you still be hungry.

Where does weight go after you've lost it?

Why is it called after-dark when really it's after-light?

Why be a man when you can be a success?

I have a book in my bedroom about the paranormal, but I don't know how it got there.

Cowardice asks the question – is it safe?

Expediency asks the question – is it politic?

Vanity asks the question – is it popular?

But conscience asks the question – is it right?

And there come a time when one must take a position that is neither safe, nor politic, nor popular; but one must take it because it is right.

Martin Luther King Jnr.

Reality

Beyond childhood most of us learn to keep our minds shut to the possibility that other worlds exist beyond the seemingly solid, deterministic one we accept as reality. We are trained, indoctrinated, to void those aspects of our being that belong to the realms of insight, intuition, spiritual manifestation, and dream. The narrowed consciousness of 'adulthood' is a kind of rigidly defined trance, continually reimprinted on us by the world we have created. If we studied the matter, we might discover that our modern presumptions of rationality rely entirely on second-hand information, on faith in which 'experts' have told us. They have no more basis in 'reality' than a vivid dream or a child's fantasy.

Daniel Pinchbeck. Breaking Open the Head.

All we have to believe with is our senses, the tools we use to perceive the world: our sight, our touch, and our memory. If they lie to us, then nothing can be trusted. And even if we do not believe, then we cannot travel in any other way than the road our senses show us, and we must walk that road to the end.

Neil Gaiman.

The famous motto of the Special Air Service is 'who dares wins.' This elite group of soldiers were the first to adopt the phrase and now Special Forces in nine countries use this as their motto.

Sitting talking the virtual opposite of this famous phrase was voiced by a friend when he invited me to consider, 'who cares who wins?'

No soldier could live by this and neither could most of us because we are programmed to win. Competition and the will to win are important factors in the structure of our society. However for every success there has to be a failure, for every winner there is the prospect of a looser. And a 'looser' in our culture is a defamatory term.

The entire structure we have built seeks direct competition and wants a result that defines the outcome. A man is judged in the material world by what it is he has been able to acquire. A company cannot trade unless it is successful.

That is reality, so we are told.

In truth we hear the word used all the time, 'get real,' 'reality check,' 'in reality,' really? etc. If you are not in touch with reality a psychiatrist might deem you to be schizophrenic, mad, unbalanced. Reality in everyday usage means; 'the state of things as they actually exist.' (Wikipedia). However nothing actually exists except as we have been taught to perceive it.

As children growing up it was the adults around us who trained us, by discipline and repetition to hold our attention in order to learn. By repetition we are indoctrinated to form habits, we learned how to behave in society, what to believe and what not to believe; what is acceptable behaviour and what is unacceptable behaviour; what is 'right' and what is 'wrong'; our tastes were moulded even to the point of what we would find beautiful and what we would find ugly.

Our home, school and all of our interactions with our fellow man all shared something in common; they all wanted our attention and the need for the energy for that attention provides us with and this makes for a superb breeding ground for competitiveness. Almost a justification for being alive, hey! Look at me! I am here! I am special! I have value!

So all the skills of competitiveness are programmed in childhood, when we are innocent, vulnerable and young, it is here where competitiveness is introduced where it is honed and carried forward into adulthood.

We are taught that winning gives us value and meaning but we can only define winning when others lose, so for you to win others must therefore fail.

Before we adopted our present fearful reality we were vastly more spiritual. Our values now place importance upon the physical reality of our five-sense world. The 'survival of the fittest,' appears synonymous with evolution and dominance appears to characterise advanced evolution.

Winning give us value.

Value is an opinion, a belief.

Why do we seek power over one another?

Because of the ego – because we are programmed to do so.

Who cares who wins?

Kenneth Holloway

The jungle creed
Says the strongest feed
On any prey it can
And I was branded beast

At every feast
Before I ever became a man.

Two and a half thousand years separate the following tales, however they tell the same story. They both invite us to consider our concept of reality. In the first, Bill Hicks talks of the World as being similar to a ride in an amusement park. Our minds are so powerful we imagine the ride is real. As the ride progresses it goes up and down, round and round, it's brightly coloured, has thrills and chills. It's very loud and for a while it's fun. Bill goes on to say that some of the people who have been on the ride for a long time begin to question. They start to ask ' Is this real, or just a ride?' Others remember and return, suggesting to others not to be afraid and that this is, after all, just a ride. And we kill those people.

Shut him up, I've got a lot invested in this ride, shut him up. Look at my furrows of worry, my big bank account, and my family. This has to be real. It's just a ride, but we always kill those good guys who try to tell us that and let the demons run amok. But it doesn't matter because it's just a ride and we can change it anytime we want. No job, no savings money, just a choice right now between fear and love.'
Bill Hicks.

The notion of Plato's cave.

Is an incite into the nature of reality. In his model for the human condition Plato puts prisoners who are chained within a cave, they face the back wall of their prison and cannot turn around, they see nothing but shadows cast upon the cave wall, reflections from the fire projected for the onlookers to make sense of.

Because they have been bound from infancy they see nothing unusual in their situation, if one of them escaped and saw the world as we see it from beyond the cave his mind would not grasp the so called reality he now found himself in.

If he returned to the cave and told his former fellow prisoners of his findings, he would be ridiculed, alienated and repelled.

This is a story that has been much analysed on many levels but it demonstrates how the prisoners accept the shadows on the wall, cast by the puppeteers who hold them captive, as their reality even in the face of one of their own returning to offer them enlightenment.

We can draw several conclusions from this famous story but the uncomfortable picture that we are being shown is that we ourselves may well be like the prisoners held in the cave, we watch and learn from projections and reflections just like the shadows on the wall of the cave, we share the idea that reality is what we witness and what we are told.

The cave is representative of the human skull and we are urged to consider – do we live within our heads or do we seek to break out and involve ourselves in the big picture?

Once again we are being offered a blue pill or a red one.

Humankind cannot bear too much reality.

T S Eliot. Burnt Norton.

Universal Creative Source Energy, pure spiritual energy, God, soul or whatever title we could concur upon: there is something within us that gives us life then this is Consciousness.

It creates throughout the Universe and it flows through everything, it designed us, shaped us and formed us and it continues to flow through us unless we block it.

Consciousness is also manipulated by others, most usually unintentionally, but manipulated all the same. Where Consciousness is knowingly manipulated is in the magic we discussed earlier.

Our concepts of size, shape, distance and form, just to name a few are divisions of our conscious perception and form our view of the Universe. As individuals we therefore see ourselves as living in the 'real' world and these concepts cause limitation and the idea of sense and self reinforces that belief.

Our bodies are not dense solid masses they are vibrating forms, the physical body we perceive is subject to illness, the aging process and ultimately death, it is not you because it is not real – it is your perception – your reality.

Our being is in a body and that body is part of everything else.

You are a being of light.

The higher you vibrate the better you feel and at some stage negativity cannot affect you because it isn't present, it doesn't exist.

This condition would accurately describe an enlightened being.

If we could truly realise our being; as the processor of Consciousness then the Universe would appear less 'real.'

Because we are programmed and indoctrinated throughout our lives, we imagine that we see the world as it is, with our eyes; this conclusion then forms our reality. However the light that we see in order to make sense of our reality is reflected back from the objects that we see. This light is passed through the lens of our eyes and hits the retina as an upside down image.

After some chemical operations carried out by cones and rods, this vision becomes an electrical impulse. This impulse is then sent into the nervous system to the back of the brain. The brain now disseminates and makes sense of this flow and converts it into meaning.

The physiology of vision is extraordinary, our eyes see the world upside down and it is our brains that make sense of the data.

Our eyes are delivering light and we are interpreting that light and so when someone says, 'this is 'real' because I saw it with my own eyes,' they are in fact deluded, what we actually see is a copy, a replication, a conversion, a belief.

Our brains are working to make sense of different electromagnetic waves that are delivered at different amplitudes and frequencies. What reaches our brains is the energy from those waves and we call this light. As our brains interpret this energy/light they do so by measuring the different frequencies and as a result we 'see' colour.

And here is another sobering thought; there is no colour in the world except by our brains interpretation. When we see the green of grass it is because the brain has interpreted the energy that our eye receives and decided it is green.

Our brain interprets smell, sound, taste, touch and sight, these conversions form our reality but the only thing that exists in the brain are electrical signals. Our brains interpret our 'reality' and allow us to make 'sense' of our environment.

Each of our sense organs is adapted to its own type of stimulation, which is in essence the conversion of a vibration. Each of these organs shares one thing in common; they serve to translate an electrical pulse or a vibration to the miracle of the brain, (which is little more than a lump of wet meat, which lives in virtual darkness and weighs in at an average 3 pounds). The brains job is to create what we deem to be *real*.

What is real? How do you define real? If you are talking about what you can feel, what you can smell, what you can taste and see then real is merely electrical signals interpreted by your brain.

The Matrix.

What the eye sees and the ear hears – the mind believes.

Swordfish

Reiteration or repetition

Politicians and leaders use this to great effect. They know that if they continually repeat words and phrases they will become stamped more indelibly upon our minds. This grows outwards and as we encounter others we find they adopt the same concept as they repeat the last thing they have heard or read, until something else comes along that makes more sense. This mentality exists everywhere from the newsreader to the guy in the pub.

In an address entitled 'The Statesmanship of Business and the Business of Statesmanship,' Dr Glenn Frank uses repetition in these words;

> 'We are no longer a small nation; we are a large nation
> 'We are no longer a simple civilization; we are an increasingly complex and technical civilisation
> 'We are no longer an agricultural nation alone; we are an industrial nation as well

Robert Ingersol demonstrated repetition with the following speech;

'A little while ago, I stood by the grave of the old Napoleon – a magnificent tomb of gilt and gold, almost fit for a dead deity – and gazed upon the sarcophagus of black Egyptian marble, where rest the ashes of that restless man. I leaned over the balustrade and thought about the career of the greatest soldier of the modern world.

I saw him walking upon the banks of the Seine contemplating suicide, I saw him at Toulon; I saw him putting down the mob in the streets of Paris; I saw him at the head of the army in Italy; I saw him crossing the bridge of Lodi with the tricolour in his hand; I saw him in Egypt in the shadow of the Pyramids; I saw him conquer the Alps and mingle the eagles of France with the eagles of the crags; I saw him at Marengo, at Ulm and Austerlitz; I saw him in Russia where the infantry of the snow and the cavalry of the wild blast scattered his legions like winter's withered leaves; I saw him in Leipzig in defeat and disaster – driven by a million bayonets back upon Paris – clutched like a wild beast –

banished to Elba. I saw him escape and retake an empire by the force of his genius. I saw him upon the frightful field of Waterloo, where Chance and Fortune combined to wreck the fortunes of their former king. And I saw him at St Helena, with hands crossed behind him, gazing out upon the sad and solemn sea.

I thought of the widows and orphans he had made, of the tears that had been shed for his glory, and of the only woman he had ever loved, pushed from his heart by the cold hand of ambition; and I said I would rather have been a French peasant and worn wooden shoes; I would rather have lived in a hut with a vine growing over the door and the grapes growing purple in the rays of the autumn sun; I would rather have been that poor peasant with my loving wife by my side, knitting as the day died out of the sky, with my children about my knee and their arms about me, I would rather have been that man and gone down to the tongue less silence of the dreamless dust than to have been that imperial personification of force and murder.'

The power of words and the manner of their delivery. It is said that the pen is mightier than the sword. Although if it came to a straight shot, I'd rather be attacked by a biro wielding maniac than a sword wielding Shogun warrior in a bad mood.

Religion

Every faith in the world is based upon fabrication. That is the definition of faith –
acceptance of that which we imagine to be true, that which we cannot prove. Every
religion describes God through metaphor, allegory and exaggeration, from the early
Egyptians through modern Sunday school. Metaphors are a way to help our minds
process the unprocessable. The problems arise when we begin to believe literally in
our own metaphors.

Angels and Demons. Dan Brown.

In the 2001 National Census, there were 170 religions in Britain. I will go on
to list a few of the larger ones. I don't pretend for one moment to be an
authority on religion but we are all witness to its effects.

I have found from what little I do understand about the subject, that when
one looks at each religion how similar it is to the next. This perhaps is not
surprising as in the case of Islam, Judaism and Christianity, all three religions all
emanated from the same place and indeed from the same man, Abraham.

If we do have to have religion, can we just not have an amalgamation of
them all? Ideally without people telling us what do, just providing us with
information while we form our own conclusions, allowing each of us to
experience enlightenment. This unification would lead to a far greater degree
of like-mindedness; it is the separateness of each person within a religion that
allows those that control us to lead us into conflict with one another.

If you genuinely are a Christian, then your heart should break as much for
the loss of a child in Iraq as one from your own parish. If we bought into this
concept, perhaps the next conflict we are coerced to support could be prevented
and therefore could not happen.

Every single soul on this planet has exactly the same currency … the same
viability and the same value; it's just that we are programmed to believe
otherwise.

George Bush, Barack Obama, the Queen or the Pope might consider themselves to be the most powerful people on the planet, (remember we give them their power and value by acknowledging their office and existence). They have no more value to me than a child of Afghanistan, Iraq, the continent of Africa or wherever. We may never know that child's name but he has the same birthright to a quality of life, the same quality as you or me.

Going to church does not make you a Christian anymore than standing in a garage makes you a car.

The Noah story as told in Genesis exists throughout the World. The Epic of Gilgamesh is possibly the oldest written story on Earth, found on clay tablets in Ancient Summeria, it tells of the King of Uruk who ruled around 2700BC and the deluge. In the Bible we are told of a similar story, even down to the dove being released. Ancient flood myths abound and are so widespread we can take the view that this event actually did take place.

Judaism, Islam and Christianity were born in the Middle East and all contain the same story. Indeed the more you look into Christianity the more you realise that we took most of it from earlier belief systems. All religions have an inner core of knowledge and at this top level secrets dating back to the Middle East are held.

Schools of initiates, the highest level of the respective priests can trace their knowledge back to ancient Egypt, to the lands we now know as Iraq and Iran that were then known as Babylon and Summeria. The inner level controls the outer levels by symbology, secrets and awareness. The inner levels of priesthood will give us the promise of God and access to Him but always only through them.

The Bible

Much of the information gathered together to form the Bible was passed by word of mouth. As what was written was translated many times as a result, the original was diluted, altered and changed.

In 553AD the Byzantine Emperor Justinian called a meeting of the Ecumenical Church Council and in an effort to preserve and increase his power, virtually rewrote the Bible. Changes included that all but a couple of mentions of reincarnation be taken out.

Religion can assist us all to get to God however according to the priests, vicars, rabbis and so on, we can only get to God via them.

The King James Version of the Bible has, according to the enlightened historian Arthur Findlay, at least 36,191 errors in translation.

All religion changes and develops, if it did not it could not survive.

The early Catholic Church came to be organised under the three authorities of Rome, Antioch and Alexandra, later Constantinople and Jerusalem were added.

It has become the world's largest religious body and the head of the church is the Pope who is based in the Vatican

The Catholic Church is supposed to hold half its equity inside the walls of the Vatican City. Rare paintings, sculptures, devalued jewels, priceless books, gold bullion and real estate deeds. Estimates a raw value of around 50 billion dollars. I wonder if Gods house was supposed to be so richly opulent whilst so many of its followers are so impoverished?

> *'The Catholic Church in 2000 spent one hundred and eighty three million dollars on trying to support struggling diocese worldwide.'*
>
> Universi Dominici Gregis.

Buddhism

Buddha died at the end of the sixth century BC. He did not claim divinity, he recognised that we all have within us the seed of enlightenment.

The story of prince turned prophet. His name was Gautama; he became Buddha or 'The Enlightened One'. He had a life of great privilege but he felt there was more to life and walked away from his life of luxury, leaving behind him his family, palaces and the life he had known.

After sitting under a tree meditating inwardly he became enlightened and achieved a state of bliss. The demon Mara visited him and told him to stay put and told him to enjoy his newly discovered state and not to spread the word as no one would believe him. But another two gods Brahma and Sakra begged him to spread the word. For the next forty-five years Buddha travelled covering all over India to preach his message.

Basically he said that in this world of suffering, only one thing remained the same and that was Dharma or the truth on living right. Only right living can free us from pain.

According to Buddhist tradition everything in the Universe, a drop of water, you and me, a tree, a thought or a molecule are all sankharas. The Buddha taught sankharas are anything that is put together or puts itself together. Another word for sankhara is Nirvana.

Buddhism is not really a religion it is more a system of belief. A Buddhist monk does not take a vow that binds him to this system and he is able to walk away at any time.

I have seen men who are great pillars of their churches in other religions perform good works on a Sunday and then take total liberties with other peoples lives for the other six days of the week. I have found a Buddhist is a Buddhist for seven days of the week, living by an ethical code. War is practiced by all religions in the name of their respective gods. They will fight and die in the name of god. A Buddhist cannot wage war and a Buddhist cannot kill anything.

I am not saying that to be a Buddhist is 'right' because it might not be right for you but I have to say a world without war would be a fantastic start. Just imagine all the resources that go into arming, defending, attacking each other, the billions wasted while we lie to ourselves that we are right and 'they' are wrong – the manufactured enemies we always seem to manage to create. Just imagine … without war we could feed the world, give every person on the planet a life and use the rest to go into space and seed other planets and not call it 'the space-race,' … like it's some form of a futile competition where a few win and the rest loose. We could put all of our massive resources of wealth and knowledge together as one and not only survive … but thrive.

With less demands made upon the planet it will manage to heal and survive, because make no mistake this planet will survive, the zillion-dollar question (used to be a million but there's been *so* much inflation) … is … will we?

Will this Eden, this paradise, that we have managed to turn into a spoil heap for our own ends be able to sustain us for much longer, that is the all-important question? This then is our only answer and it is our only salvation.

If we could actually stop cutting down rainforests and stop obliterating species of animals, we could care for the animals that live with us and just take what we need rather than what we want. The only real cost on the balance sheet would be the deprogramming of all the former soldiers in the world who have to be broken before they are trained to kill.

The corpulent egotistical power brokers, spin doctors and politicians that seek war would also be casualties of this new way of thinking but we could build somewhere nice on the moon for them so they could not be robbed of the folly of conflict and they could then set about fighting one other.

A Buddhist monk was strolling in Central Park in New York. He notices a hot-dog stall and asks the vendor, 'please make me a hot-dog and put everything on it.'

The vendor hands the Buddhist monk the hot-dog and takes his money. The monk stands waiting for a while and then asks for his change.

The hot-dog vendor replies, 'ah change, now that comes from within.'

Buddhism has the characteristics of what would be expected in a cosmic religion for the future: it transcends a personal God, avoids dogmas and theology; it covers both the natural and spiritual, and it is based on a religious sense aspiring from the experience of all things, natural and spiritual, as a meaningful unity.

Albert Einstein.

Hinduism

The common religion of India based upon the original Aryan settlers as expounded and evolved in the Vedas, the Upanishad's, the Bhagavad-Gita, etc. Hinduism has an extremely diversified character with many schools of philosophy and theology.

The typical Hindu conception of history is based on an overall view of the Universe. The great Hindu epics paint a vivid picture of a race of ancient god like beings who had access to flying machines and explosive devices 'brighter than ten thousand suns.' The ancient source of all esoteric Hindu texts are called the Book of Dzyan, this book describes creation in a sequence of unfolding sounds, linked to geometric symbols.

'Presence of the soul is perceived by its consciousness. According to Bhagavad-Gita, all living entities are soul proper. When the soul leaves the body, then it is called death. That means death is a transmigration of soul from one body to another body (Bhagavad-Gita). Soul transmigrates from one body to another body based on their Karmic (performed deeds) reactions.'

Wilkipedia.

The many forms of Yoga come from Hinduism. The practice of yoga is to reunite the individual self with the absolute or pure consciousness. The word yoga means literally 'joining.' The practitioner of yoga is taught to seek union with pure consciousness liberating the spirit from all sense of separation. To achieve this higher consciousness is to be freed of all sense of the illusion of time and space. Yoga teaches as a guide for the individual showing that it is only our own ignorance or inability to distinguish between the real and the unreal, that ultimately prevents us from the realisation of our true nature.

Hinduism is reputedly the world's oldest religion, it brought to the world the idea of the chakras. A chakra is seen as a spiral of energy. There are seven main energy centres, known as chakras or wheels, throughout the body. The chakras resonate with the seven colours of the prism, or the rainbow.

There are in all 300 or more minor energy centres in the body and it is these centres that acupuncture works upon to release and balance the energy that flows through our bodies. Each of the colours of the spectrum vibrates at a different wavelength and so each colour has its own particular energy.

Our entire bodies absorb colour not just by the eyes, as discussed earlier the energies of colour have an effect upon us at all levels. Every cell in our body needs light energy, and colour affects us on a physical, spiritual and emotional level.

Gnosticism

There is no scholarly consensus on how to define Gnosis or Gnosticism. The subject made the headlines when a collection of thirteen ancient containers called codices containing over fifty texts were found in Egypt in 1945. Our history shows a liturgy of book burning over the ages. As civilisations have risen and fallen the conqueror generally suppresses, absorbs or eradicates history and replaces it with their own.

History is written by the winner, is a sobering thought.

The story of the Gnostics is worthy of its own investigation but the gospels (translation meaning 'good news') were thought to have been destroyed during the early years of Christianity. These scriptures included the Gospel of Thomas, the Gospel of Philip and the Gospels of Mary.

The Gospel of Thomas was not included in the Bible as his words were at odds with the agenda, but he became one of the principle saints and founder of the system declared by Pope Leo XII to be the official Catholic philosophy. Bearing in mind Thomas was one of the twelve disciples this seems odd.

Another Apostle Philip was excluded from the Bible as well and the fact that he appeared to have been held in high esteem by the Gnostic Christians may have been the reason.

Peter was crucified upside down and according to records it is possible that John was the only one of the twelve disciples to die of natural causes.

Judaism

Abraham the famous biblical figure, is the founding father of the three largest world religions. These three faiths; Judaism, Christianity and Islam are able to trace their roots back to Abraham and his lineage.

The important historical figures behind these three religions, Moses, Jesus Christ and Muhammad, were all direct descendants of Abraham. It is considered that Abraham was born almost 4000 years ago in a place called Ur, which is in the south of modern Iraq. At the age of 99 Abraham had a son Isaac, Abraham's faith was tested by God in the famous biblical story and he was asked to sacrifice his son, Abraham was stopped from doing this by an angel and a ram took the boys place as an offering. Isaac was the father of Jacob and Esau. Jacob became the father of twelve sons, who became the ancestral fathers of the twelve tribes of Israel.

Judaism is one of the oldest religions; the Jews believe that God appointed them to be his chosen people in order to set an example of holiness and ethical behaviour to the world.

Kabbalah is accepted by some Jewish people and rejected by others. Kabbalah refers to a set of esoteric mystical beliefs and practices that form an alternative to traditional Jewish interpretations.

Kabbalah is regarded by its followers to be part of the study of Torah. Torah is the study of the law of God, and Torah is the name given to the first five books of the Hebrew Bible, which is also the Christian Old Testament.

Sikhism

Sikhism has a following of some 20 million people and is ranked as the world's fifth biggest religion. The greater Punjab region in North West India is the historic homeland of Sikhism although large communities of Sikhs can be found throughout the world. The Sikh faith began around 1500AD when Guru Nanak began to teach a faith that was distinct from Hinduism and Islam.

> *The core philosophy and message of the Sikh religion can be understood in the beginning hymn of the holy Guru Granth Sahib.*
> *There is one supreme eternal reality; the truth; immanent in all things; creator of all things; immanent in creation. Without fear and without hatred; not subject to time; beyond birth and death; self-revealing. Known by the Guru's grace."*
>
> Wikipedia.

> *"Deep within the self is the light of god. It radiates throughout the expanse of His creation.*
> *Through the Guru's teachings, the darkness of spiritual ignorance is dispelled.*
> *The heart lotus flower blossoms forth and eternal peace is obtained."*
>
> Guru Amar Das, Majh.

Sikhs believe that God is inside all of us.

Islam

The religious faith of Muslims, based on the word and religious system founded by the Prophet Muhammad and taught by the Qura'n, the basic principle of which is absolute submission to a unique and personal God, the Arabic word for God is 'Allah.'

> *"The word Islam derives from 'salam,' which means 'peace,' but in a secondary sense 'surrender.' Its full connotation, therefore, is the peace that comes from surrendering one's life to God."*
>
> Huston Smith. The Illustrated World's Religions.

> *"Muslims number 1.61 billion making it the second largest religion in the world after Christianity. Muslims believe that God revealed the Qura'n to Muhammad, God's final prophet and regard the Sunnah (the words and deeds of Muhammad) as the sources of Islam. They do not regard Muhammad as the founder of a new religion, but as the restorer of the original monotheistic faith of Abraham, Moses, Jesus and other prophets."*
>
> Wikipedia.

Muslims seek to live in accordance with God's laws and in the doing bring themselves closer to God. Their practices include prayer, fasting, charitable works and pilgrimage, all in an effort to meet this goal. Muslims recognise all the prophets that the Christian and Jewish adherents would identify with including; Adam, Noah, Abraham, Moses, David, Solomon, John the Baptist and Jesus.

Tao

Tao cannot be expressed but it can be known, in this respect it is a philosophy.

Tao is where we hear the familiar term in the West of 'Yin and Yang,' where every action creates a counter action or a reaction. When Yin and Yang are balanced there is harmony, Yin represents the feminine and Yang the masculine.

It is estimated that there are about 20 million followers.

The Taoists fundamental aim is to become at one with nature, the Universe and all that surround him.

Taoism is as mystical a belief system as we are likely to encounter, it is recognition of a force that flows.

An approximate translation of Tao means 'the way.'

Taoism is believed to have been founded by Lao Tzu who was a contemporary of Confucius. Lao Tzu left a record of his teachings in a book called the Tao Te Ching, it is one of the most spiritual books ever written.

Its adherents continue to grow throughout the world and its areas include acupuncture, herbalism, holistic medicine, meditation and martial arts.

I am one of the least qualified people on the face of this earth to speak on the subject of the individual world religions.

All that has been shown here is a cross section of the religions that most of the peoples of this world subscribe to. There are many more and many tranches of each. I have no views or opinions whatsoever on each individual religion and if your religion, your faith or belief system enables you to find happiness, peace, love and joy, then please let me make myself clear – good luck to you – follow your joy.

However as a generalisation and taking religion as a whole and in its entirety, that is another matter because in my view religion separates us.

I am not saying that the millions of people who attend churches, mosques and synagogues (or wherever people meet to worship) are not for the most part, perfectly decent folk.

Much of what goes on by religious people all over the globe is good and constructive work, but what I am asking to look at is the bigger picture and every religion justifies everything in the name of their 'one' god.

That is not reverence that we are giving, but power to the *idea* of a god.

It is not our belief that we are expressing because we are acting predominantly on what we have been told.

At a part of our lives where we had no choice we are programmed into a set of belief systems that will, by their very nature separate us from our fellow man and as a result, when asked to call upon your religion you are showing loyalty – *not* belief.

You had no more say in the choice of your religion than you did in the selection of your given name.

The same is the feeling indoctrinated into us of Queen and of Country; of patriotism. What Englishman's heart does not swell to the National Anthem?

(Crap song, I agree with Billy Connolly when he suggested that the foot-tapping theme to the Archers should replace it).

And if your surrounded by raging Scots, just start singing 'Flower of Scotland,' and you will render them immobile, upright and they will all start singing.

Our beliefs go deep but are they accurate, do they serve us well?

Surely a true God allows each of us to seek and find.

The believer in the 'true' God knows that; Jesus, Mohammed, Buddha, Allah, Zeus, Vedas, the Great Architect, Brahman, Yahweh, Hayyi, Shang Ti, E'lo-I, God, Adonai, Elohim, Kyrios, Achelois, Apollo, Aphrodite, Concordia, Dionysus, Hotei, Chalchiuhtlicue, Kukulcan, Aten and the many of other names that we give to our Source – is all one and the same thing – we are all One.

'You're not free if you follow a religion, you live in an observation ward.'
Aleister Crowley

So if you imagine that there is a benevolent white bearded God sitting on a cloud up there, then the question follows and we are therefore urged to ask; are we really doing ourselves justice, did the architect of this magnificent Universe design us to perform the way we do? It is my humble suggestion that we have taken a wrong turn somewhere because we are not living the lives we were designed to live.

'Live the dream,' so the advertisers tell us, it is my submission we should all of us – *that is every single individual on the planet* – be living the dream and we have abundant resources to do just that.

Everything in existence is a manifestation of Consciousness that most of us call God. When David Icke was ridiculed on the Wogan show, this for me is what he was suggesting; If we come from God then we are a part of Him and when we die we return to God, then we have completed a cyclic journey.

We are all, every single one of us, the sons and daughters of God, whatever name we ascribe to Him.

We are vibrating forms of energy, of light and of sound.

We broadcast and we receive.

We are affected and we cause effect.

And for every cause there is an effect and behind every cause is Consciousness.

Along with religion comes the notion of evil. Whatever that particular religion dislikes will be evil. And the chief figure that carries this burden is a made up figure, an assemblage of other mythical figures, (as in Santa Claus or Christopher Columbus for example).

He goes by many names, Satan, The Devil, Old Nick and a hundred more.

His presence in religion serves to remind us of the consequences of doing anything 'wrong.' He was after all we were told, a fallen angel who disobeyed God, and disobedience is most unhelpful in religion.

The first thing we do with a person or people with whom we seek conflict is to demonise them; gossip, make others believe they are a threat, a cheat, a liar, make them ugly, make them dangerous, these are the tools of propaganda and we make enemies of others by the use of this.

Get the fear in early and the scars will heal but those hidden, buried wounds will remind the injured of the fear.

Although it is not the only reason, religion has been the single largest factor in causing entire cultures to commit atrocious crimes against one another, crimes such as theft, torture, genocide, etc.

As long as we continue to divide ourselves into boxes there will never be peace on Earth and we will never progress to becoming true spiritual human beings. We place ourselves in an elevated position above animals and we consider ourselves to be civilised, and we search back in time to trace our ancestry.

If we are to believe in the Darwinian form of evolution; that life evolved by the survival of the fittest and in tiny steps of change. We then seek for the process of when apes became ape-like men, then when ape-like men became who we are today. Both naturalists and scientists talk of the 'missing link' and still we search without success. Maybe there isn't one, perhaps we are still evolving; possibly we are yet to become what it is to be truly human.

When you consider how little we use of the brain and the 96 per cent of DNA that scientists call 'junk,' it might be time to see if we could use more of it properly.

It's there, we have proven it, we just need to connect.

And that, I submit will be when we further evolve.

Karl Marx saw religion as 'the sigh of the oppressed creature … the opium of the people, which made this suffering bearable.' Much said here detracts and criticises religion. There are benefits to following any religion and they all teach morality and invite us to be better people; better toward each other and ourselves. All religion gives many people values, ethics and a sense of structure in their lives. There are millions of people all over the world who follow a religion or a belief system; the vast majority of these people are living decent lives, it is the arrogance, control and separation that religion causes that I have a problem with.

It has been said that the greatest social evil is religion. It is responsible for more death, destruction and poverty than anything we could ever invent to replace it. It is a cancer spread by supposition and by lies and it starts in the classroom where children, who are in no position to evaluate the rubbish of a belief system that will later divide them and may well lead them all the more readily to war and to killing.

It has been the way since before records began. It is an appalling deceit played out for all of modern history.

'Don't seek God in temples. He is close to you. He is within you. Only you should surrender to him and you will rise above happiness and unhappiness.'

Leo Nikolaevich Tolstov.

'If a person catches just one fleeting glance of the joy and bliss (of God), it will compensate him for everything he has to suffer.'

Meister Eckhart.

Why not let people differ about their answers to the great mysteries of the Universe? Let each seek one's own way to the highest, to one's own sense of supreme loyalty in life, one's ideal of life. Let each philosophy, each world-view, bring forth its truth and beauty to a larger perspective, that people may grow in vision, stature and dedication.

The religions of humanity should be a unifying force, for all the great religions reveal a basic unity in ethics. Whether it is Judaism, Catholicism, Protestantism, Buddhism or Confucianism, all grow out of a sense of the sacredness of human life. This moral sensitivity to the sacredness of human personality – the Commandment's; not to kill, not to hurt, not to put a stumbling block in the path of the blind, not to neglect the widow or the fatherless, not to exploit the servant or the worker – all this can be found in the Bibles of humanity, in all the sacred books. All teach in substance: 'Do unto others as you would that others should do unto you.' There is, then, a basic unity among the great religions in the matter of ethics. True, there are religious philosophies which turn people away from the world, from the here and now, concentrating life-purposes on salvation for one's self or a mystic union with some supernatural reality. But most of the great religions agree on mercy, justice, and love – here on earth. And they agree that the great task is to move people from apathy, from an acceptance of the evils in life, to face the possibilities of the world, to make life sweet for one another instead of bitter. This is the unifying ethical task of all the religions – yes, of all the philosophies of humankind. There is no need to force our own theological points of view upon one another or to insist that the moral life grows out of final, absolute authority.

Algernon Black.

While I know myself as a creation of God, I am also obligated to realise and remember that everyone else and everything else are also God's creation.

Maya Angelou.

I don't try to imagine a personal God; it suffices to stand in awe at the structure of the world, insofar as it allows our inadequate senses to appreciate it.

Albert Einstein.

Most people have a fairly rigid set of beliefs, not just about religion but just about everything. When presented with a new experience we immediately make a decision on whether we like or dislike it. For example, we have our favoured foods and when given something we have never tried before we will quickly make a judgment: even if that judgment is 'no thanks, its not for me.'

Everyone following a religion had no choice; we were indoctrinated and programmed into it and this is shown to be true in that whilst there are exceptions to most things, relatively very few people go on to change their given religion.

It might also be helpful to realise that in a world where many doubt the existence of anything we cannot; touch, hear, taste, smell or see; that all religions depend on the fact that nothing revealed by the five-senses can prove nor disprove it.

This could also be said of God Himself, however I believe that within our core we are aware of His power. Universal Consciousness, Source Energy or whatever of the many names that we attribute to Him, we ourselves are part of that and therefore we are all fragments of God.

Everything is a fragment of God, it's just many of us follow Him through the structure and regime of religion.

We can all appreciate why we act this way but surely we can ask if this is the *right* way.

Unfortunately to believe in any god implies individuality however it is the illusion of separateness from oneness that creates our reality.

A Rankin

By the way, if you have heard this old joke then I apologise but it's earned me the odd chuckle over the years.

Did you hear about the agnostic, dyslexic, insomniac who lay awake all night worrying about whether or not there was a dog?

The old adage declares, 'never discuss politics or religion,' it is a tip that will stand us all in good stead. For many people a religion offers a sense of belonging, the idea is like an extended club with loyal and true followers. However looking into any single one of the religions, and one comes up with the conclusion that there are factions within that religion that further divide its adherents.

Some years ago in conversation with a Jewish friend I asked the significance of what Christ meant to him within his religion. He told me that within Judaism, Christ was regarded as a prophet and did not hold the same significance that Christians have of him as the Son of God, the Messiah.

When you go within Judaism, Christ represents a variety of things to all the many factions that make up this one religion; for some Christ is a symbol of oppression for some he is the subject of derision and for others he is the Messiah. We find this throughout each and every religion; the followers have some varied and often very hostile differences within them.

Ironically we can often find that between different major religions, more theological ideas that are concurred upon than there are within the one religion itself. Which is perhaps where we might start, that is to say focus on the parts we can concur upon and make less of what we can't. What we are not told as we are growing up is that the Bible, the Koran and the Torah are based on the same events, they tell the same story about Abraham and his family past and present. We are not taught that Christians, Muslims, Jews and Freemasons are all born of the same stock, the same bloodline, because if we were perhaps we could find some peace between us all.

When it comes down to the bible we very often find that it is a matter of interpretation as to what beliefs are formed.

It might be more difficult to find two people anywhere in the world to agree on the many subjects and questions that religion pose and accept that as long as it is around we are destined to disagree with one another.

Disagreement is not the way forward.

Reputation

We make meet someone for the first time and we know absolutely nothing about them but we are automatically scanning them to gain knowledge. This is of course quite natural as it is in our interests to know something of the person we are encountering.

As with many objectives there is much going on especially in the first encounter, both consciously and unconsciously. It is perhaps more interesting to have a blank canvas that is to say, no prior incite into this person because then we are provided with the luxury of forming our own opinions.

However if you have been given opinions from others about the person that you are meeting for the first time, then one of the major factors will be one of reputation. By its own definition, reputation precedes us. But it really should only be taken a guide, because very often, the opinion that was given turned out to be wrong and this was possibly because the informant was wrong, misinformed or had his own agenda.

Speak as you find, is a decent yardstick to use because of several reasons; you are by proximity, more fit to evaluate than the informant as you have direct contact and your own ideas. The informant may well have had duff information by another informant. We do have an inbuilt radar that automatically scans new experiences, when this radar is operating correctly we can look into another person and approach them without preconceived notions, without fear using our powerful instincts, our senses, (not just the five-sense ones) our feelings are vitally important.

We will make adjustments and alterations through the knowing or the exposure we have with the other person and it is likely that we will, in time, discover things about the person that we don't like, aspects that will alienate us towards them but if, through the knowing we find the positives, the things that draw us toward this person, then should we focus upon what we like, we may find ourselves able to form a relationship with them on whatever level we seek.

Look round at those we know now, those we have relationships with, those family and friends we now call 'ours,' there are many things; traits, opinions, habits, the way they sometimes behave, that we don't necessarily like but we don't break our bonds with them and if we occasionally do when there is a flair-up, we usually feel poorer that they are not in our lives because there now exists distance between us.

I remember ranting onto a close friend of mine about some injustice I felt had been meted out towards me by a mutual friend, this is the ego at work as it always is; he said '*this*', he '*did that,*' – the usual insecurity projection crap.

My friend enlightened me with one simple sentence, but like all profound wisdom it packed a powerful punch. As I looked to him for some measure of support; some sign he understood my own selfish, self-inflicted and imagined pain, he asked me a simple question, 'David, is he 51 per cent?'

'Oh yes,' said I, halted in mid-emptying of spleen.

Now I am nodding and saying, 'Yes he's 51 per cent,' as I remembered how fond I was of the person that I was badmouthing.

'Well as long as the he's 51%, that's fine, that is enough.'

And my friend is right, (only if we are going into percentages here, he's about 100% right and I am about 100% wrong).

Who the hell am I to judge and condemn?

And yet our emotions take us down that slippery slope constantly unless we are mindful, it is such rubbish, it is so negative, damaging and unconstructive and we are programmed to do this. Judge – condemn – so negative and such a waste of energy.

With some people you just have to admit, you gave it a shot but you vibrate so differently you are just not going to be able to construct, sustain or maintain any bridges between you and you have every right to withdraw, you are both at different places in your spiritual evolvement, but you do not have the right to try and hurt that individual with the poison that is gossip.

Gossip is just people blowing a lot of hot air and expressing their opinions in an attempt to steal energy from the recipient of their gossip.

The best that can be achieved during the expressing of your opinion to another person as you spit your spite is it that you might create an ally and alienated him towards the object of your angst, a man who he previously might have thought differently of.

If you achieve your objective neither of you will feel very good about the experience.

Perhaps the adage should be changed from 'speak as you find' to the more instinctual 'think as you find.'

'*As long as he's 51%.* (Now there is pure wisdom.)

G Robson.

Same story ... different names.

Summeria ... Babylon ... Egypt ... Greece ... Rome ... Europe ... Britain ... America ... the World.

Romulus and Remus were twin brothers who founded Rome. Their mother was a virgin priestess Rhea Silva and their father was Mars the God of war, (sound familiar?).

Romulus killed Remus spawning this most violent of societies and setting the tone. Romulus founded the Roman Legions and the Roman Senate and so began a history of treachery, sun worship and (dependant upon your view) civilisation or barbarism.

Rome, built by genocide under successive Emperors who without exception deemed themselves Gods and Sun worshippers.

Genocide was the technique that extended the Roman Empire throughout the world. Reduce all resistance and absorb the rest into your own belief system, impose another set of belief systems, soon it will all be forgotten and remember as you serve us, you are free.

Where did the fabulous Holy Roman Empire fail?

It did not fail it came to England.

Along with the Roman Invasion came the obvious imposition of their will. Between 43 and 410AD they ruled Britannia. It was then seen to fail and return to its base in Rome.

The British Empire subsequently employed similar ethics and tactics and spread itself throughout much of the world. Conquering or 'discovering' vast tracts of land as it applied its principles.

In America it appeared to flounder and fade but in actuality it was simply transposed by the bloodlines, the carriers of the baton who took it forward and formed the United States of America.

As far back as we can go there is indisputable evidence of Sun worship depicted in culture. This is hardly surprising if we are to believe the story of those who went before us.

People who lived under the Sun and the stars were understandably consumed by them.

One of the most ancient symbols is the cross of the zodiac, where the sun passes through the 12 houses in 12 months. A cross splits the 12 constellations. The upright of this cross represents the winter equinox and the crosspiece of this cross represents the summer solstice. The cross divides the 12 signs and months into 4 sections or the four seasons, each holding three of the horoscope signs.

The solstice and equinox are represented by two pillars that stand in all freemasonic temples, all important government buildings and originally in Solomon's Temple, these pillars are known as Joachim and Boaz and they represent dualism, black and white, good and evil, the need for two in the world, human progression needs two feet, for us to reproduce we need two sexes.

Ancient people were much more involved with the sky and with little interference from pollution and artificial light, the night skies were much clearer than the skies we witness in the present.

Encoded into their buildings and demonstrated in surviving writings, the people of the past worshipped the Sun as the bringer of light and of life and they worshipped the Sun as a god.

They demonstrated in all aspects of their culture, the ability to measure time with incredible accuracy. They followed the cycles and even knew of planets that we have only recently discovered.

Another name for the three stars in Orion's Belt is the three kings, they line up precisely to the birth of the Sun on the horizon.

Horus was born of a virgin birth, adored by three kings, became a teacher at 12 years of age, was baptised, Horus was the Egyptian son of the Gods, Orion and Isis.

He was the sun of god, from where we get the Son of God.

Born on the 25th of December in 3000BC.

The lion or the sphinx represents Horus; born 5000 years ago he takes his name from the horizon.

Translated horizon means, 'Horus has risen,' and is also where we get the name for hours.

We get the word sunset from Horus brother, his name was Set. Each and every day Horus would defeat Set symbolically on the horizon at sunrise, and every night Set would defeat Horus to bring in the night.

Duality was represented by the two brothers struggle against one another, dark versus light and good verses evil. Set was the keeper of the underworld.

According to tradition three kings arrived to adore the baby Horus and they had followed a star to find him.

In the sky is the large constellation of Orion, you find it in the northern hemisphere, in England the figure stands virtually upright late in the year and in its middle lie the three stars known as Orion's belt. As the mill of the Universe turns slowly around you can see the three stars making up the belt align perfectly and on the 25th of December they point to the brightest star in the night sky. This star is Sirius, (the star in the east) if we follow the three stars of Orion's Belt to Sirius they point at the place on the horizon where the sun will rise. This then is the birth of god's sun at the winter solstice. The 25th of December.

Horus had 12 disciples, performed miracles, was also known as the Lamb of God, he was betrayed went onto be crucified, was dead for three days and then resurrected.

Pick any area throughout the world and find the same story repeated over and over again. Attis, born in Greece around 1200BC, born of a virgin on 25th December, crucified, dead for three days, resurrected. Krishna, born India, 900BC, born of a virgin birth on 25th December, star in the east, performed miracles, was crucified, was resurrected. Mithra, born Persia 1200BC, born of a virgin December 25th, had 12 disciples, performed miracles, was dead for three days and was resurrected. Dionysus, born 200AD, king of kings, born of a virgin on 25th December, miracles, crucified, resurrected. The list goes on and on in case you want to check this out here are a few more; Krishna of Hindustan, Jao of Nepal, Bali of Afghanistan, Indra of Tibet, Baal and Taut of Phoenicia, Zoroaster and Mithra of Persia. Crite of Chaldes, Odin of Scandinavia. Salivahana of Bermuda, etc.

The New Testament Gospels are overloaded with Sun worship plagiarised from much earlier times.

Sun worship is encoded into every cathedral and every church ever built. Take your pick from a multitude of earlier stories of resurrection; in Persia they had the Saviour and he suffered to save the people. In Egypt they had Horus, the son of the Sun God, and his story was similar. In India they have Krishna, the list is enormous.

The virgin birth story of Jesus is another example that is told in much more ancient times. Anyone who was anyone was born of a virgin – Alexander the Great, Asclepius, Plato, Dionysus, Hercules, Minos and Miletus to name a few.

The belief that a god-king was killed and resurrected is at least 5000 years old. Osiris was killed by Set, a sort of Egyptian Satan, who dismembered the body and scattered it. Isis, the female consort of Osiris reassembled the pieces of his body and reunited them (all except his penis). Then fanning the breath of life into him resurrected him. (Just as God breathed life into Adam).

The founder of Rome, Romulus was said to have been born of a virgin birth and after being killed he appeared to a man named Proculus. Every king, queen or emperor who has lived has claimed divinity.

This deification (elevation to the status of a god) is most helpful to the individual because the power of a deity or god maintains their position.

A king or queen is not saying they have a direct connection with god … they are symbolising that they are god.

Shaman

The name 'shaman' started in the language of the Evenk, a small group of hunters and reindeer herders in Siberia. Shaman has become the generic term to describe wise men all over the Earth. Shaman translated means 'one who knows.'

After rooting out its shamans and destroying its visionary traditions, the modern world relied upon artists and poets to create pallid and shallow simulations of what had been lost. From Shakespeare to Spielberg, William Blake to Joseph Beuys. In the modern world the artist took over the role of Shaman. We have even corrupted the word and now talk of shamanism, there is no 'ism' at all, no doctrine, no world shamanic church, no holy book to refer to and no priests to tell us what is right and wrong, what is good or bad.

In a world that we have modified, altered and changed we find ourselves lacking and cut off from Oneness. This was the world that the role of shaman kept people linked to and in touch with, and they knew of the cycles and flow of the Universe. These enlightened beings could break down the mysteries of our matter-based existence and show us of the divine, they could cure the sick and commune with nature, they understood Consciousness and the route back to Oneness.

Now, and much more so in the material West, we have largely become disconnected from Source – from Oneness.

Those that have inadequately replaced the role of shaman such as our doctors, teachers and priests now largely deal with the symptoms of a problem and rarely if ever with the cause. According to the Journal of the American Medical Association, the leading cause of death in America is heart disease, next is cancer but alarmingly death through medical treatment comes in at third place.

Everything in nature is alive and we find ourselves cut off from this cycle of activity with the results that our lives have less meaning and identity.

Shamanic logic begins with the belief that the soul can leave the body, not just as a part of our demise but during dreaming, altered states and dancing. To shaman the plants are teachers; by ingesting plants they take the spirit or the properties of the plant within themselves and journey not from a deviation of what we call reality but to true reality, which in an ordinary state of consciousness remains hidden to us. Their drug taking is not part of an alienation and rejection of society, but a means of integration with others. Imagine the same insights being offered up to our present day leaders and what an unlikely but massively attractive proposition.

'Come on George sit down here by my side, put that gin and tonic down, here let's have a drink of this Ayahuasca,' – later – much later – a bit later still – 'well George how was your trip?'

'Pretty darn good David, most interesting, I mean did you know we are all One separated only by our own manufactured perceptions – those properties of the ego and as a result we have become trapped within our boxed off minds – that are both perceiver and creator – hey cancel that war, shut the banks, gimmie a phone I want to tell my controller to inform Obama's controller, someone tell whoever I'm married to I wanna a big veggie-burger for my tea, jeez I feel so much better, now just you watch this golf shot.'

Years ago as a child growing up I learned of the witch doctor. This powerful man or woman intrigued me because he could heal the sick or curse the healthy. I was fascinated that this person could put a spell onto another person in the tribe and actually kill him if it was his wish.

Later I understood that other names for the witch doctor could be medicine man, sorcerer or magician, but that the best identifiable name has become 'shaman' and the role and power of this individual was far more than the limited information I was able to gather. I came to realise that Shaman existed all over the world and in every society they played a vital role for thousands of years. Wherever cultures of people were, shamanic people existed.

The white-mans intervention has broken this chain of highly enlightened spiritual people. Shaman still exist but they are scattered far and wide, once the more advanced of them communicated with one another all over the planet. Within the tribes of wherever they lived they were held in high esteem.

They were the people who we inadequately replaced with priests and mercenaries. We force fed the natives of everywhere we took, with our religion because we wanted to do them good or that was in any event the excuse … we just knew better and it was proven to be an effective way of guiding the people to become what we had become – 'civilised.'

As we separated them from their belief systems in order to enforce our own, the shaman had no place in the new structure. The shaman would take you in altered states to God and the divine if you so chose, but from now on the native indigenous population on whichever continent we enforced our presence, were instructed that they could still get to God but you had to go through the priest in order to access Him.

Our justification was the fact that at the time these savages were worshiping the wrong idols, running around half-naked and ripe for conversion. That is after we saw who the survivors were after we fought in an always uneven fight, to overpower the people.

The agenda has always been the same, conquer, divide and rule, civilise the population, educate the children, force feed them our religion, our politics, our belief systems and absorb them as fully as we are able into our ways and our society.

Then, in what has always seemed to be a pretty poor deal, we go in search of all the bright and shiny marbles this part of the world might give over to us; the things upon which we place value, the things the programmers have made us think we want; mineral wealth, diamonds, gold, silver, oil and we get a cheap labour force to do all the heavy work to go with the deal.

The natives are put to work and get to make the conquerors wealthier whilst they remain poor and cut of from the old ways of their lives that generations before them had previously enjoyed.

We cannot put right the wrongs of the past but we can change how we progress now. If we amalgamate this entire world with its massive, unbelievable amounts of wealth and distribute its resources a little more evenly, what comes out the pipe at the other end is mind-blowingly healthy.

We have the resources to really make a difference and we would feel so much better doing so much good, and we would in the process, pay back a debt that will otherwise never be paid.

The other bonus to us would be to rid ourselves of the parasite of fear that is instilled in us.

Aldous Huxley experimented with mescaline in the early 1950's, interest in shaman has grown steadily since then. In the late 1960's Carlos Castaneda wrote extensively on his exploration of reality through his teacher and guide, the Yaqui Indian, Don Juan.

Shamans drummed and chanted to heal people, they proved for thousands of years what we are just beginning to understand, that vibrations are the fundamental consciouss force in the Universe.

Cymatics is the study of wave phenomena a science pioneered by a Swiss medical doctor and natural scientist, Hans Jenny (1904-1972).

For 14 years he conducted experiments animating inert powders, pastes and liquids into flowing forms and structures. He used pure vibrational tones within the audible range, the same patterns found throughout nature, art and architecture, to build structure and form. What he demonstrated was a physical representation of vibration and how sound manifests into form through the medium of different materials.

Dr Jenny's demonstrations give us profound incite into our Universe. He shows the principles that inspired the ancient Greek philosophers to the present day.

His experiments on one level demonstrate the beauty of form and the visual evidence of showing how matter responds to sound. But on a deeper level he allows us to recognise that we too are a part of this same complex and intricate vibrational matrix.

The aborigines have a belief that God sang the Universe into being. Sound has a direct measurable effect upon matter, it affects us and everything in the Universe. Take a look at sacred geometry and cynamatics to learn more on this fascinating subject.

Spin

Now dependant upon your viewpoint there are many ways to look at spin. I suppose the optimist might say, it is the power of having a positive perspective in life. On the other hand the pessimist might say more simply, that it is lying.

We are not retreating; we're just advancing in another direction.

General G.S. Patton.

For me 'spin' is the 'spin' word for telling lies when you know they are lies in order to promote your own agenda.

And there is a distinction here: immoral or amoral? An immoral person has low or corrupt moral standards, or in other words they know it's wrong but they do it anyway whereas an amoral person has no concept of the rights and wrongs. For example; babies are amoral while spin-doctors are immoral.

Spin practitioners are sometimes called spin-doctors. They seek to control the spin of a situation in order to show you the side and direction they want you to view as favourable. So we don't invade a country anymore instead; we liberate its people. We don't fight a war; we fight for peace. When our guys shoot our guys, it's more acceptable because its 'friendly' fire … and there will always be casualties in war. The uniforms in the streets (after we have slaughtered the population and reduced the cities to rubble) are peacekeeping. And because they are keeping the peace in tanks, this helps the lads get around and spread the word. Later in the endgame the peacekeepers will protect the construction army that rebuilds the city and guard the oil-pipes and derricks.

And if it's all so great, glorious, right and proper then why is it more American soldiers have taken there own lives as a result of the horror they have witnessed, than have actually died by the actions of the enemy?

Eighteen American war veterans kill themselves every day. One thousand former soldiers receiving care from the Department of Veterans Affairs attempt suicide every month. These figures would have not come to light if it were not for a class action lawsuit brought by Veterans for Common Sense and Veterans United for Truth on behalf of the 1.7 million Americans who have served their country in Iraq and Afghanistan.

Stress

If we are here to learn through experience then the deal must be that we must continually keep an open mind. We cannot keep an open mind if we are in fear of some impending doom or stressed about our present situation- if you have fallen on your backside into a fire at that point the meaning of life will not be what you're thinking. The simple wish to save your life will prevail.

Here is a two-step formula for handling stress.

Step 1: don't sweat the small stuff.
Step 2: remember, its all-small stuff.

Anthony Robbins.

Worry drains the mind of power, it has been calculated the average person runs about sixty thousand thoughts through their heads every day. Furthermore 95% of those thoughts were the ones you had the day before.

This is the tyranny of impoverished, inward thinking because most of these thoughts are negative. We adopt bad mental habits and become captives of our past dwelling on failed relationships, financial problems and bad childhoods for example.

Being stressed is draining. Our brains are about 3 pounds of mass and we use $1/100^{th}$ of 1% of our mental reserves.

About ten years ago the doctor told me my blood pressure was high. He put it down to lifestyle, which, I suppose, covers about everything. It was no real surprise to me, lack of hard exercise in recent years, smoking, too much salt, too little salt and so on. That and the fact that I don't 'do' stress very well and am inclined to vibrate badly when I subject myself to it. So I left the surgery clutching a prescription and after a visit to the chemists I had managed to swap a piece of paper and a tenner for a bag of pills. I duly swallowed the pills for a month or so and in a conversation with another doctor who is a friend; I learned that there were better and more effective pills available.

So at the end of my first course I returned to the doctors surgery for another prescription and I asked to see the doctor who prescribed me the tablets in the first place. Pleasantries exchanged I asked if I could change the tablets to the one's that I had been recommended.

'Ah, yes,' he nodded sagely, 'they are the ones I put my father on.'

'Well' says I, 'if they are good enough for your father, they are good enough for me.'

And pursuing the subject I asked, 'if you prefer these tablets and you know that they are clearly better, why did you not just put me on these in the first place?'

'Because these ones are more expensive,' came the reply.

So this little story should just remind us all that it's not really about health; health comes at least second to money and profit.

It's *always* about the money.

Unless of course I am being my usual silly old cynical self, I mean for all I know the Cheapo Drug Corporation PLC (we sell the tablets that will bring your blood pressure down. However you will slowly break out in open sores, faint once a fortnight and never get another hard-on) went and kindly took my doctor and his wife on a nice Caribbean jolly to educate him about the benefits of the drugs he peddled me.

They're all at it.

A B Solomon.

Suicide

In the year 2000, approximately one million people died from suicide: a 'global' mortality rate of 16 per 100,000, or one death every 40 seconds.

In the last 45 years suicide rates have increased by 60% worldwide. Suicide is now among the three leading causes of death among those aged between 15-44 years (both sexes); these figures do not include suicide attempts up to 20 times more frequently than completed suicide.

Mental disorders (particularly depression and substance abuse) are associated with more than 90% of all case of suicide; however, suicide results from many complex socio-cultural factors and is more likely to occur particularly during periods of socio-economic, family and individual crisis situations. (e.g., loss of a loved one, employment, honour).

World Health Organization.

A guy walks up to the lady behind the counter in a library and asks,
'Do you have any books on the subject of suicide?'
'Yes we do' she replies.
'Well can I borrow a couple?' he enquired.
'No — sorry but you can't.' She said.
Crestfallen he asks 'why not?'
'Well,' she says soberly, 'because you won't bring them back.'

J Knox

Surveillance society

Big Brother is watching you.

George Orwell. 1984.

George Orwell's big brother society has arrived. Cameras that are everywhere silently watch us. The police, politicians and many of the populous say, 'it's not a problem, why should we worry, if you're behaving yourself, you have nothing to be concerned about.'

All well and good, another bomb gets defused or detonated and we cry for more cameras, more surveillance. They are, after all is said and done, there for our benefit ... or are they?

The push continues for more cameras, identity cards, and a database containing our DNA. The justifications of these onerous implications are voiced on a regular basis, the 'if you are not doing anything wrong why worry?' cry being the favourite.

If these expensive implementations help catch the wrongdoers then that has to be good. There is however little evidence to justify the costs against results.

The Echelon Project, according to reports, attempts to capture staggering volumes of satellite, microwave, and cellular and fibre-optic traffic from all over the world. There are masses of satellites orbiting the earth now and the vast majority are looking inwards not outwards. The Echelon project is just one of the many projects that use satellite and other highly sophisticated technology forms to watch and monitor us.

Echelon collects vast amounts of voice and data communications and processes them through filtering technology. The project intercepts radio, satellite, telephone, faxes and email communications, in other words, virtually all forms of how we communicate are filtered anywhere in the World

This massive surveillance system apparently operates with little oversight and the agencies that purportedly run Echelon have provided few details as to the legal guidelines for the project.

Echelon is supposedly based at Menwith Hill, near Harrogate, in North Yorkshire (UK).

Probably the most advanced 'Listening Station' in the world, ironically overlooking the beautiful scenery of the Yorkshire Dales.

Geoff Richardson.

In a report produced by the United Space Command, entitled 'A Vision for 2020', General Howell M Estes III states. 'Globalisation of the World Economy,' will continue with a widening between the 'haves' and the 'have not's.' The aims of the U.S.Space Command – dominating the space dimension for Military operations to protect U.S. interests and investment. Integrating Space Forces into War fighting capabilities across the full system of conflict.'

A leading judge says everyone in the UK and every visitor to the UK should give DNA samples to be recorded on the National DNA database.

BBC News 24. 05 September 2007.

Cops with helmet cameras, the DNA database, automatic number plate recognition, CCTV – all these technologies have been slyly introduced: imagined future benefits are played up while the very tangible, immediate costs of lost privacy are airily discounted.

I am told by Merseyside Police - the first force to buy a drone- that the flying spy has been 'a great success and people feel they've reclaimed their parks.'
Has the drone's footage been used in evidence to prosecute or arrest anyone? No. Not much of a success then.

If police forces were directly accountable to the people they serve, it's doubtful that we would have agreed to such a costly blanket surveillance- whether drones in the sky or cameras on every street corner- without the solid facts to persuade us of its necessity. But when the only person that the police have to please is the Home Secretary, then citizens' rights are irrelevant.

Times Online. Heather Brooke. 4th September 2007.

Fears that the UK would 'sleepwalk,' into a surveillance society' have become a reality, the government's information commissioner has said.
Richard Thomas, who said he raised concerns two years ago, spoke after research found people's actions were increasingly being monitored.
Researchers highlight 'dataveillance', the use of credit card, mobile phone and loyalty card information, and CCTV.

Monitoring of work rates, travel and telecommunications is also rising.

There are up to 4.2 CCTV cameras in Britain – about one for every 14 people.

But surveillance ranges from US security agencies monitoring telecommunications traffic passing through Britain, to key stroke information used to gauge work rates and GPS information tracking company vehicles, the Report on the Surveillance Society says.

It predicts that by 2016 shoppers could be scanned as they enter stores, schools could bring in cards allowing parents to monitor what their children eat, and jobs may be refused to applicants who are seen as a health risk.

bbc.co.uk November 2006.

We are living in a surveillance society but our data protection laws are not up to the job.

Ed Mayo, National Consumer Council.

The personal details of 600.000 people interested in joining the Armed Forces have been lost after a laptop belonging to a Royal Navy officer was stolen, the Ministry of Defence said last night.

The latest data loss incident involving a Government department is potentially the most serious as recruits to the Armed Forces are targets for terrorists.

The laptop was stolen from a vehicle parked overnight in the Edgbaston area of Birmingham a week ago but the theft was only made public last night.

Des Browne, the Defence Secretary, is expected to appear before MP's next week to explain the theft. It follows the loss of 25 million child benefit records and the details of three million learner drivers in the past few months.

Robert Winnett. The Daily Telegraph. 19.1.08

More than 51,000 innocent children have had their DNA samples lodged on a national police database – more than twice the figure previously admitted by ministers. The children, including 30 under the age of 10, have had DNA swabs taken even though they have never been charged with or cautioned for an offence.

This lengthy article goes on to list and summarise its findings as follows; On the database.

5 per cent of Britons have DNA profiles held by the police.

24 per cent of those on the database who have never been charged with committing a crime are from ethnic minorities. This is three times their relative proportion in the UK population.

£300m has been spent on the project.

3 million samples are on the database.

40,000 samples are added each month.

139,463 people on the database have not been charged or cautioned.

4.25m samples will be added to the database by 2008, according to predictions by the Home Office.

0.35% of all the crimes detected by police in 2004/2005 came about as a result of using DNA samples.

51,000 samples on the database were taken from children never cautioned or charged.

The Independent. 22 Oct 2007.

Police used to actually have a reason to stop us, there had to be some justification. The forms they filled our then were called 'pace 1,' search forms. New moves give new powers; the new 'encounter' forms enable those recorded upon them to be fed into the police CIS data system. Thus for evermore that person has recorded data, even though they have only been stopped by the police. Children who might have been nothing more than playing football in the street are recorded on this system.

In England we presently have a police force of one tier, however to bring us in line with the rest of Europe moves are presently afoot to change this. We are about to be introduced to a two-tier level of policing.

One of the police forces grievances is about the government reneging on agreed terms of pay rises, this is a manufactured situation, the police will demonstrate unrest and can make life difficult for the government, but they cannot legally go on strike.

In an unprecedented move the people who control our government are engineering (Brown, Labour or Cameron, Conservative; our next Prime Minister, it does not matter what their names are; the same agenda is always served) the government to take the police on and aggravate them further into a reaction.

A handful of police in England have been told to prepare for war, not on some foreign shore, but a war of civil rebellion or at best civil unrest.

As a result civil enforcement powers are being increased. Some traffic wardens have been issued with three new cards, the first one is to show their authority, the second is a 'pace' card, in order they might assume the same power as the police and will be enabled to arrest a person and read them their rights, the third card is the right to enter a dwelling.

In the next box down of 'importance,' we have the guys with the blue bands on their hats; the Community Officers or Chimps as they are called in police circles. 'Chimps' stands for – 'Can't Help In Most Police Situations.' This is a little unkind and a tadge disrespectful but it is also soon to be inaccurate, because soon the Chimps will assume similar powers to the police.

Traffic Wardens will be disbanded and Community Officers will merge with them and bingo we will have our two-tier police force, just like we do in the rest of Europe.

Incidentally, just in case you're concerned that there will be no one to issue parking tickets, please let me alleviate your worry; local councils will have loads of new recruits on scooters driving about slapping more and more tickets on more and more cars.

I bet that's a weight off your mind.

When the police react to their derisory pay offer we will all be able to see the value of our 'new' police force.

Fantastic how it works isn't it? Divide and rule, a walk in the park, though naturally we will have to be careful in the parks, because those that police them, such as private security firms, will also be given increased powers and everyone will have to do their 'job' with vigour and gusto because … well … their jobs will depend upon it.

Please excuse me a second, I've got the dustbin police at my door … phew … no … its OK … we can all relax again, I thought for a second they had a warrant for me leaving my bin out for three minutes longer than was the law, it's alright they didn't catch me this time, they were just looking for a member of 'the Special Vehicle Police Unit'; those officers who ensure your car is parked within quarter of an inch of the curb … apparently one of them had dropped his tazer gun.'

At this juncture we might be forgiven for wondering why we haven't heard of all these new moves. The reason we haven't is because they do not want us to know.

The same applies to the following little wake up call.

As the New World Order speeds up its agenda we will be subdivided into four basic units,

America will merge with Mexico and Canada as the respective countries remove their boarders and will be called the North American Union; the new currency is called the Amero.

The African Union is well on its way, as is the soon to be formed Asian Union and as we are aware, the done and dusted European Union.

Atop this pyramid will be the missing capstone representing the illuminated ones, the all-seeing eye, those who hide behind the curtains … welcome one and all to the New World Order.

'We shall have World Government, whether or not we like it. The only question is whether World Government will be achieved by conquest or consent.'

Paul Warburg. Council on Foreign Relations and architect of the Federal Reserve System, in an address to the U.S Senate 17th Feb. 1950.

'We are grateful to the Washington Post, the NY Times, Time Magazine, and other great publications whose directors have attended our meetings and respected their promises of discretion for almost 40 years. It would have been impossible for us to develop our plan for the world if we had been subjected to the lights of publicity during those years.

But now the world is more sophisticated and prepared to march towards a world government.

The supra national sovereignty of an intellectual elite and world bankers is surely preferable to the national auto-determination practiced in past centuries.'

David Rockefeller, Private Banker, Council on Foreign Relations.

'Power corrupts: Absolute power corrupts absolutely.'

Lord Acton. 1834–1902.

'Students at a secondary school in South Yorkshire are being tracked by microchips sewn in their uniforms as part of a trial.

The radio frequency identification system monitors pupils' movements, and automatically logs their attendance on the teacher's computer. It can also alert teachers if a student is likely to misbehave.

The trial involves 10 students in whose uniforms this chip was embedded about eight months ago.

Being used at Hungerhill School in Doncaster presently, the chip connects with teachers' computers to show a photograph of the students, data about their academic performance, and whether they are in the correct classroom. It can also restrict access to areas of the school.'

Dailyindia.com/ANI

The fashion of using lie detector tests started in America. We now have it here most noticeably on the Jeremy Kyle show, now we have been introduced to this Jerry Springer type show, which feeds on the psychosis of the individual and works towards the abject humiliation of those on the stage.

Everyone gets a laugh as these people bare their lives, their emotions and their fears to the amusement of the viewer.

In case the very earnest, finger-wagging, judgmental Jeremy does not accept the stories of those he seeks to humiliate for our delight, he then has at his disposal a lie detector test. As usual we believe that the liar should be exposed and anyone telling the truth has nothing to fear.

Now conditioned to find this an 'acceptable' form of entertainment we wait until after the break and for the adverts to end and the 'truth' to be told.

How can we witness the pain of fellow human beings and call it entertainment?

Jerry Springer 'Nothing but the Truth' has arrived, yet another conditioning factor in our acceptance of what is about to be brought into actuality in society; more programming to enable us to accept the use of lie detectors

Naturally we will accept the arrival of the lie detector and we will comply with being put to the test, but of course this will never happen …

Lie detector traps for benefit cheats.

Thousands of benefit cheats will be exposed by lie detectors installed on phone lines. According to the next article many councils are buying a new hi-tech phone system that can reveal those who are lying. The computer software scans the caller's voice for increases in stress levels.

> *City chiefs in Birmingham- who run Europe's biggest benefits programme – are to start using the software from next month in a bid to save £20million lost through fraud every year.*
>
> *The other 400 councils in England and Wales are expected to follow next year after trials of the Voice Risk Analysis system in Harrow, north-west London, saved £110,00 in just three months by nailing 173 council tax and housing benefit fraudsters.*
>
> *And Whitehall chiefs hope the system will help stamp out the nationwide plague of fiddling which cons British taxpayers out of 700 million a year.*
>
> The People.co.uk by Andrew Gregory. 16 Sept 2007.

All kind of waves pass through us, all on different frequencies, radio waves, microwaves. The reason we have to turn on the TV or the radio is that these devices have receivers that translate the transmission into a form we can see and hear.

We humans don't need an 'on' or an 'off' switch, we are 'on,' in some way shape or form, all of the time.

We are both receiver and transmitter.

Is it pure conjecture to think that this massive campaign to make us accept microchips in order to find our dogs, to monitor our children, and to finally accept what is the clear agenda, chips for all; a fully micro-chipped population, so that we can all feel safe?

We accept micro chipping at our peril. It should concern us that the news keeps harping on about the benefits of vaccination against all ills, flu jabs, measles, etc.

Vaccination is a great way of giving us a microchip and we are being sold the idea of in the usual style, bombarded with the fear of what will happen if we don't and what easier way to do it than through vaccination?

We would not then have to be programmed, all that would have to happen is a signal would be beamed to affect our mood, the fear could be instilled at a distance by a centralised computer.

If you doubt the technology exists then please appreciate it is with us now, just pick up the phone and ask Sky to activate your viewing card – *not* the card three feet away in your next door neighbours house, no the card you ask them to activate and *only* that card, the precision technology that allows you to watch certain channels such as movies or football, because someone somewhere unblocks your tiny card, is one and the same as sending a signal as precise, targeted to the microchip in your body.

We wont even get to decide what sort of mood we want to be in, it will be decided for us.

Teaching
... more of our Masters

I was walking Luna our dog at the beach. She was about four months old; she is a German Shepherd about a third grown and small for her breed. There were a group of fifty or so children and four or five teachers at the exit to the beach as we finished our walk. I had tried to get her onto her lead but she was ignoring me in favour of this new distraction.

As I kept trying to catch her I noticed most of the children had seen her but were not paying much attention, they were happy building sandcastles.

But one teacher in the centre of the group had gathered three of the children into her skirts and was showing real signs of distress. As I got a little closer I caught Luna, who was still a distance away from the group, as I put her on the lead the good lady teacher shouted at me, 'can you not keep that dog under control?'

She was really upset and the three children had bought into her drama looked upset as well. Her arms sheltered them like a mother-hen, she was vibrating badly and her little chicks felt her tune.

I apologised and called to her explaining the dog was 'just a pup and honestly no problem.'

'Can you not see the children are upset?' she called back.

Well truth to say, I could.

Everyone else was just happy being at the beach, but teacher mother hen's little firm were busy getting programmed with fear.

As I walked passed them, I apologised to her again and smiled, but all I really wanted to do was say, *'why not teach them how to learn, not what to learn,'* but I didn't.

So perhaps it is me that is finally learning, at last.

A conditioned reflex is learned, either through negative or positive stimuli. The fear of snakes is a learned reflex, as young children who would play with snakes and other reptiles with innocent fascination are soon taught to fear by example or stimuli i.e., a mother screams and pulls her child away from a harmless garter snake, reinforcing the gesture with a statement such as 'you could have been bitten!'

www.ivanpavlov.com

Look at how we react if our favourite band changes its style. One of the greatest frustrations voiced by many singers and bands over the decades has been the cry, 'they just want us to play the old stuff.' We don't like change and we are therefore resistant to it. We are programmed against change.

Those three children at the beach that day may well grow up with a fear of dogs, the seed of that fear was planted one sunny day at the sea-side. That was the day that they learned in school that you should be fearful of dogs.

Of the good lady teacher – I don't know her motivation – she was very likely programmed herself by perhaps a fearful mother.

I would bet there were no dogs in her household as she grew up.

I might be wrong, she may have had a dog that mauled her one day and that dog might have been a small German Shepherd, possibly the dog had to be put to sleep – it broke her young heart.

Whatever her story is I will never know and I am not judging nor condemning her for her actions.

However, whatever the cause of her reactions might have been, she had not come to terms with them and as a result her problem was projected onto her pupils.

She couldn't have just wanted someone to cuddle – it was too warm a day.

Principal Skinner: 'That's why I love elementary school, Edna. The children believe anything you tell them.'

The Simpson's.

It is more constructive to teach and guide children to be aware instead of beware. If you grasp a nettle it will not sting you, if you brush against it, then it will.

We all have both the choice and the karma to take one spiritual path or another, and I would encourage you from the bottom of my heart to follow with complete sincerity the path that inspires you the most. Trust in intuition because whilst our intellect is useful it is something our culture depends upon. Programming promotes the intellect as an achievement awarding prizes along the way as we pass or fail to reach goals. There are no lessons, no exams for anything resembling intuition, which is the key to knowing.

When we are attuned to intuition it will guide our intellect to seek and find true wisdom.

We cannot teach people anything; we can only help them discover it within themselves.
Galileo Galilei. (1564-1642).

Education is an admirable thing. But it is well worth remembering that nothing that is worth knowing can be taught. Were we able to sit in different classes around the world we would quickly understand that the young are taught propaganda as a matter of course.

Ask a teacher in Russia, China, England and France who invented the telephone, tarmac, the toothbrush, the internal combustion engine or the light bulb and so on, you will get very different answers.

But that's what we are taught by grown-ups in school and that's what will cause heated debate, fisticuffs or worse at the pub-quiz in thirty years time – if we're not mindful.

A very wise teacher was educating a group of kindergarten children when all of a sudden a strong breeze blew into the room two ugly frauds called Doubt and Ignorance. The mindful teacher said, 'now children if you ever lose the truths creation has evolved in you, these two illusions will fill your mind with confusion. That will bring disorder and discredit to your life on earth.
Little Jimmy stood up and asked, 'How can we lose our truths Miss Solomon?'
'By forgetting who you are.' She tenderly replied.
Michael Levy. Forever Wise.

Written proudly on the side of a school bus, which belongs to one of the schools in our region, is written the following delusion;

'*Individuality, Independence, Imagination.*'

An admirable piece of propaganda aimed at every loving parent that wants the best for their child.

It is lacking in one word, because it should read,

'Individuality, Independence, Imagination --- *removed*.'

The school could consider just the one word and be nearer the truth, and I offer this up purely because times are tough and want the institution to make savings on the horrendous cost of paint.

The word is 'Indoctrination.'

Theory of conspiracy

Just one of those coincidences – nothing to worry about.

On Radio 5 live on the 7th of July 2005 the following conversation took place. This was the day when three trains and a bus were bombed killing 56 people and injuring many more.

On that morning an anti-terror exercise just happened to be going on as well. Peter Power of Visor Consultants Emergency Management said the following live on air, '*At half past nine this morning we were actually running an exercise with a company of 1000 in London, based on simultaneous bombs going off at precisely at the railway stations, where it happened this morning, so I still have the hairs on the back of my neck were standing upright.*'

The reporter then says, '*So, lets get this quite straight, you were running an exercise to see how you would cope with this and it happened while you were running the exercise.*'

Peter Power responds, '*precisely.*'

On the 16th of May 2004 Panorama screened a programme discussing a mock attack on three trains and a road vehicle. It was almost a preparation account of the attack that followed.

Blair at the time was under increasing pressure to maintain troops in Iraq, the terror attack arrived with impeccable timing, when the dust had settled the public were ready once again, to accept the government's desires. And the war on terror continued, it is not a war *on* terror, it is a war *of* terror, as is pointed out in a very insightful and interesting study about the events surrounding 7/7. The web site shows clips of the Panorama film. It shows an interview with Peter Power discussing the mock exercises, and it goes into details such as the ownership of the company who controlled the cameras at this atrocity, strangely they were all switched off at the time.

It also makes a calculation against the odds of a mock exercises at precisely the four places where the attacks took place.

The probability of the 7/7 2005 drill and attack coinciding without being planned to coincide in a ten-year period is one chance in; 3,715,592,613,265,750,000,000,000,000,000,000,000,000.

The website is. www.conspiracytheoristclothing.com

'Conspiracy stuff,' is now shorthand for unspeakable truth.

Gore Vidal.

Do you remember how we rejected Genetically Modified (GM) Food?

Well strangely now we have food shortages, this is not only an excuse to put prices up it is also an opportunity to bring in what we don't want, what we previously rejected … so wait for it … it's just around the corner, the solution to food shortages is … GM food.

The largest manufacturer of aspartame (which is the most widely used sweetener in the world) is Monsanto they also make Genetically Modified Food.

Now lets just take a breath for a second and remember aspartame and its effects and why we now should think we want something when we clearly don't.

Jeffrey Smith has written a book called, The Seeds of Deception, his meticulously documented facts leave no doubt about corruption and massive injustice on a grand scale.

The following are some of his findings;

Rats fed GM corn had problems with blood cell formation. Rats fed GM soy had problems with liver cell formation. The livers of rats fed GM Canola were heavier. Pigs fed GM corn developed false pregnancies or became sterile. 12 cows fed GM corn in Germany died mysteriously. In a feeding trial, twice the number of chickens died when fed GM corn. The 'promoter gene' in GM crops was found inside rat organs after they ate a single GM meal.

The promoter, which switches on inserted genes, might also; switch on dormant viruses. Over produce allergens, toxins, or carcinogens. Promote genetic mutations.

In the Philippines, thirty-nine people living next to a field of GM corn developed skin, respiratory, and intestinal reactions while corn was pollinating. Blood tests showed that the Philippino's also had an immune response to the pesticide that the corn was engineered to produce.

This food is affecting our health in ways we can only imagine.

Most people will not make changes in their diet or demand that changes be made because they are restricted by economics and lifestyle.

The exposé 'Seeds of Deception,' reveals how industry manipulation and political collusion – not sound science, allow dangerous genetically engineered food into our daily diet.

Company research is rigged, alarming evidence of health dangers is covered up and intense political pressure applied.

Jeffry Smith goes on to say that scientists were offered bribes or threatened, evidence was stolen, data was omitted or distorted. Government employees who complained were harassed, stripped of responsibilities or fired.

Laboratory rats fed a GM crop developed stomach lesions and seven of the 40 died within two weeks. The crop was approved without further tests.

When a top scientist tried to alert the public about his alarming discoveries, he lost his job and was silenced with threats of a lawsuit. Internal memos by FDA scientists, warned of toxins, allergies, and new diseases that were all ignored by their superiors, including a former attorney for Monsanto.

Industry studies were designed to avoid finding problems.

The FDA withheld information from Congress after a genetically modified supplement killed nearly a hundred people and disabled thousands.

Eating such experimental food is gambling with our health.

On May 23, 2003, President Bush proposed an 'Initiative to End Hunger in Africa' using genetically modified foods. He also blamed Europe's 'unfounded, unscientific fears' of these foods for thwarting recovery efforts. Bush appeared convinced that GM foods held the key to greater yields, expanded U.S. exports and a better world. His rhetoric was not new. It had been passed down from president to president, parceled and delivered to the American people through regular news reports and industry advertisements, the usual programming.

The message was part of a master plan that had been crafted by corporations determined to control the world's food supply. This was made clear at a biotech industry conference in January 1999, where a representative from Arthur Anderson Consulting Group explained how his company had helped Monsanto create that plan.

First, they asked Monsanto what their ideal future looked like in fifteen to twenty years. Monsanto executives described a world with 100 percent of all commercial seeds genetically modified and patented. Anderson Consulting then worked backwards from that goal, and developed the strategy and tactics to achieve it. They presented Monsanto with the steps and procedures needed to obtain a place of industry dominance in a world in which natural seeds were virtually extinct.

The more we learn of the injustices in the world the more we become angry. We cannot fix anything that has happened.

There is one thing we can fix and that is ourselves.

By changing the way we think our emotional levels can rise, as we rise we get better at seeing more, we become lighter … truly en-lightened.

Not giving our attention to these injustices and wrongdoings that lie in the past is not irresponsible.

Conspiracies are a way of life and as long as people want to take advantage of other people then conspiracy will prosper.

Children conspire with one another to play a joke on each other in the playground, the dressing room of any sports stadium in the world is the scene of conspiracy, where teams huddle together to outwit one another, in our courtrooms the very word 'conspiracy,' when attached to the actual crime can and often does, result in a heavier sentence than the actual crime being perpetrated and of course governments have conspired against each other … and the electorate … for as long as there has been government.

The dirty word that conspiracy has become is defined, as being shrouded in secrecy, secrecy breed's theory, theory breed's speculation and the cycle never ends.

Conspiracy is inevitable, the truth however is essential and truth is the enemy of conspiracy.

My recommendation is not to ever become a conspiracy theorist.

It will batter your head. Even the phrase does not stand up on its own merit.

Conspiracies exist and are perpetrated against us every minute of every day but unless the full facts are available to you, and they never are, then you are left with what the phrase suggests and that is theory. As soon as the question of an occurrence is posed the tag is deftly placed and that person becomes a 'conspiracy theorist.'

Conspiracy has been made into another one of those dirty words that undermine the status quo and the questions that should lead to a viable enquiry for the truth remain unanswered.

I am not suggesting that we should not demand the truth to be told about something as heinous and wicked as the events of 911 or the other disgusting acts perpetrated by the informed manipulative few against the innocent many, however when can we recall the last time anyone was brought to account? Yes of course there are patsies but for the *real* culprits, it simply never ever happens.

Inquiries, debates, court trials and so on are all shams and those that head these structures are usually, knowingly or not, manipulated into the verdicts that are reached. Certainly something will happen along the way to protect the truth from entering the public domain.

Wherever man has been in the pursuit of profit there will be those who conspire with others to take advantage of their fellow man. Most of all the research, learning and struggle you make to understand the mechanics of a conspiracy will leave you embittered, untrusting and downright angry when it comes down to man's inhumanity toward man.

It is my advice to save yourself from having your energy robbed in search of a truth that will never be found … and *if* found … would never be told.

If one day the impossible happened and the true culprits of 911 or 7/7 were revealed then we have to ask ourselves what would really happen? A few people would get locked up in jail, there would be media frenzy, a head or two would roll, newspapers would sell, the ratings would go up, questions would be asked but nothing would really change.

Because as soon as we had cut off one of the many heads of the serpent, another would grow – others would take their place.

As is our usual practice, we would be treating the symptom and not the actual disease. We as individuals need to change ourselves and see these daily occurrences for what they are; forgive those that trespass against us and remove them from their positions of control and power by collectively seeking an alternative. That alternative stares us in the face; we just need to think and therefore vibrate differently.

Did man land on the moon? The astronauts, NASA, and most of the population would say a resounding 'yes.' But as shown in a recent documentary and based on other information it would appear inconclusive.

Billions of taxpayer's money had been spent on 'the space race.' The people of America were urged by government and media to win by getting their people there ahead of Russia. Like two bullies in a playground this was what we were supposed to believe.

Therefore whether they did or whether they didn't becomes academic but of the motives behind the mission, that as they say is another matter. Could all of the money and manpower have been put to some better use is a question that can only be answered according to each individual's viewpoint. But we do deserve the truth, and for many of us the truth seems to be rapidly becoming extinct.

There is of course the word of the astronauts but again they could have been tricked, they may have lied or been brainwashed into the belief they had been there. The whole episode could have been manufactured on a Hollywood back lot; it is unlikely we will ever know. The one thing that is for certain, after so much investment, failure was not an option.

As with all occurrences you can weigh up the pros and the cons and still not form a conclusion, the only point perhaps is to try and enjoy the journey, because the side-effects of your enquiries presents the opportunity to learn.

Freemasons, the Illuminati, Scull and Bones, Hellfire Club, Reptilian

Humanoid Shape-Shifters, SARS theory, the Protocols of the Elders of Zion, The Lavon Affair, Vril Society Conspiracy, Aid's conspiracy theories. The Bilderburg Group, The Council of Foreign Relations, Men in Black, the Three Secrets of Fatima, the New Orleans disaster and the breaking of the levies, the Tsunami, the Pakistan earthquake, Global warming, Global dimming, The Philadelphia Experiment, The Roswell UFO incident, Area 51, Crop Circles, The Hollow Earth Theory, Satanic ritual abuse, TWA Flight 800, the Veri Chip, Chemtrail theory, water fluoridation, the Waco Siege, the Oklahoma City bombing, Diana's death in the Alma Tunnel, 911, the London Bombings – Britain's 7/7, Pearl Harbour, the Gunpowder plot, Mind Control, all wars, governments control of drugs, the Shag Harbour incident, the Madrid train bombings, eugenics or population control, vaccinations, the deaths of; David Kelly, John F Kennedy, Robert F Kennedy, Malcolm X, Martin Luther King Jnr, Archduke Franz Ferdinand, Marilyn Monroe, Benazir Bhutto, the list is as endless as it is onerous and of course serious investigations should be made, the problem is that the findings always remain inconclusive and the truth stays buried.

All of these crimes against humanity share one thing in common and we return to the 'who benefits' question?

Who benefits by a killing, a massacre or a war, it certainly is not us; the powerful benefit and like all clever criminals they stay far enough away from the scene of each crime to remain untouchable and unfortunately it has always been the same. The true perpetrators are never brought to account.

It will always be this way, as long as we the people allow our fate to lie in others hands. The only way to change the future is to act now. If this does not happen then history is destined to repeat itself as it has done many times before.

With or without man's influence but certainly because of our mindset; a comet will arrive or the polar ice may melt, the sea levels will rise, the earth will get pulled out of kilter because of other planetary alignments, we will suffer one or more catastrophes resulting in mass extinction. There may be survivors who will repopulate the earth because it has happened many times before. (The story of Noah exists everywhere in the World).

Alternatively perhaps a new breed will rise from somewhere else in the animal world and replace our niche.

If aliens do arrive in spacecraft perhaps we flatter ourselves that they would choose to communicate with us, it may well be they would choose a more benign life-form, the dolphin for example with its seven senses, assuming that we haven't already annihilated them.

The other option is that life may start anew with the reseeding of the planet by some extraterrestrial life delivered on a comet.

At some stage we must draw a line in the sand and say that for at least 5500 years we have got it badly wrong.

Only the way each and every individual on the face of this planet can hope to change the future and we could do it instantly, would be to think and therefore feel and act differently.

Every single spiritually advanced human being who has ever walked this earth has shared the same agenda and in the process has fulfilled the same role and worked in the same way; they spoke the truth, had had little or nothing by way of possessions, they gave unconditional love, they were healers, teachers, prophets and they invited us to view the world differently and treat each other with respect and they led their lives by example to their fellow human beings – and we killed them.

Whatever we focus upon is brought into actuality. I have never seen a UFO but millions of people all over the world swear that they have.

I have never seen the Loch Ness Monster but there are many who would risk their reputations by saying they had looked into Nessie's eye.

Do these and other mysteries exist?

They certainly do for those that have witnessed them. Millions of people will agree on the 'realness' of something whilst millions of others will regard that same something with distain and dismiss it with contempt.

As discussed before, reality is not necessarily shared in common agreement; your reality and someone else's may be very different. What we make our reality is what we think about.

What we think about will be brought into actuality to us because this is a basic fundamental and powerful law of the Universe.

As long as there are toxins in our food and water and poison in our minds then cancer will be around.

As long as greedy people allow houses to be built around electrical-pylons and we radiate our sore heads with mobile phones, our bodies will have to fight against what we subject them to, for many this will result in emotional and physical ailments and a lowering of our bodies defence mechanisms. Our immune system, which is already flat out busy coping with the poisons we ingest, when called upon to work beyond its admiral capabilities can be beaten.

However I wonder how many less cases would be manifested if we just stopped having to hear about them *all* the time.

If someone believes that something exists then it does, because for them it is real and we have no right to ridicule them. The question that we should be asking is does that something exist *because* we believe in it and because we think about it.

14% of the American people believe in UFO's: that is a staggering 42 million people. If those 42 million people were to stand in the darkness in the middle of the desert in Arizona would it be surprising if a UFO showed up? I don't think so; I think that without doubt if one person can bring an event into their reality then several people can make it happen, this then is the same principle as the power of prayer.

And this is also a similar dynamic to Uri Gellar's experiment when he famously conducted a trial to start people's old and broken clocks. Gellar has since told the world he is an illusionist however thousands of people responded to his experiment by announcing that their timepieces began to function after attention was once again focused upon them.

Reasons abound, including the idea that the clocks began to work again because they had been disturbed or warmed in the hands of the thousands that held their dead timepieces at that time and on that day. Or were there other benign forces at work here and was it the power of asking and of believing that enabled so many of those timepieces to start working that day?

All that manipulation of energy is the same conscious stream that we are all part of.

I am content with that knowledge but I don't care for the manipulation of it when it enslaves, entraps and manipulates me to think and act against my better judgement in that uncomfortable and very costly gap that exists between consciousness and unconsciousness.

You cannot solve problems with the same level of consciousness that created them.
Albert Einstein.

You must be the change you want to see in the World.
Mahatma Gandhi.

Tradition

A tradition is much like a habit, but a collective habit. We have accepted it; we act within it automatically and are usually not particularly mindful of it. Tradition could be described as a meme.

Monarchy is steeped in tradition and one of the defences for those that support the monarchy is the fact that they bring in tourist money, which helps our economy. (Personally, I think Buckingham Palace would make a lovely playground for disadvantaged children, imagine games of hide and seek would last all day).

The public flock to see the changing of the guard, get there pictures taken with the sentries, realise they can smile at the sentry but he is not allowed to smile back, that kind of thing, it's a bit like porn in that you only really want to see it once (a man at the bus-stop told me) I mean I doubt they save up all year and come back to see them again.

Now I don't want to get into another rant about the monarchy, but I heard the other day it takes one black bear to make the Busby that the guardsman wears on his napper and I was just thinking, could we all write a letter into Her Majesty and ask that the next time they are ordering new busbies could they not please just make them out of something that doesn't have to die?

Beliefs are handed down through custom, government, religion, and the law depend heavily upon tradition. Within those bodies the ego thrives and lives happily, growing in power constantly. The longer the time passes the more factual or traditional it becomes.

Traditions by their nature are rarely questioned; they are an accepted way of acting. There is little or no room in tradition for mindfulness.

Tradition by its definition, abhors change; tradition remains the same and depends upon continuity. All traditions are invented and all tradition incorporates power. Kings, governments, priests invent tradition to suit themselves and legitimise their rule.

However we assume that a tradition goes back in time so far that if the tradition that is being enforced upon us must have existed for hundreds or thousands of years, so we accept very often the unacceptable when it comes to tradition.

Many Scots wear kilts as part of their tradition, it is important that each clan wears its own tartan and displays it in a demonstration of pride and loyalty. It is an assumption that this is an ancient ritual steeped in antiquity. But the kilt is a recent creation and was never the national dress of Scotland. Kilts were a product of the industrial revolution and did not start life as the traditional national dress of Scotland.

(Do *not* under any circumstances discuss this in *any* pub in Glasgow).

Even defining the word 'tradition' contains irony because, as it is interpreted today, it is in fact a product of the last two hundred years. In mediaeval times there was no generic notion of tradition. Although customs and tradition existed everywhere there was no call to use such a word. Therefore the idea of tradition is in itself a creation of modernity, which directly opposes the thought of tradition as being around forever.

Whilst it is true that some traditions associated with religion have been around for hundreds of years, pure tradition is rare, for a tradition to survive it very often has to be adaptable and tradition and change do not make a good marriage because one is inclined to devalue the other.

Judges formally adopted wigs in 1685; the wig allows a degree of anonymity from criminals. Tradition depends heavily on symbology as part of its practices. Christmas for example is traditional.

I heard it said that if alcohol were invented tomorrow it would be banned, its consumption is now part of our culture … it is a tradition.

Our computer keyboards evolved from typewriters, the style of these keyboards is the now widely accepted QWERTY layout of keys. However QWERTY was not invented to help, it was invented to hinder. In 1873 American typewriters kept jamming because of the speeds at which typists could write. Now universally accepted, the QWERTY keyboard was introduced to radically slow typing speed down.

Which is a pretty good example of one of the many traditions that makes absolutely no sense.

Truth

The truth is such a valuable commodity it is normally to be found, fortified by a boundary of lies.

G Keating.

Truth is the most valuable thing we have. Let's economise it.

Mark Twain.

Bigotry tries to keep truth safe in its hand: with a grip that kills it.

Tagore.

A lie can travel halfway around the world while the truth is putting on its shoes.

Mark Twain.

Truth does not change although your perception of it may vary or alter drastically.
John and Lyn St-Clair Thomas. Eyes of the beholder.

Truth is the most valuable thing we have. Let us economise it.

Mark Twain.

Bigotry tries to keep truth safe in its hand, with a grip that kills it.

Tagore.

If you tell a lie big enough and keep repeating it, people will eventually come to believe it. The lie can be maintained only for such time as the State can shield the people from the political, economic and − or military consequences of the lie. It thus becomes vitally important for the State to use all of its powers to repress dissent, for the truth is the mortal enemy of the lie, and thus by extension, the truth is the greatest enemy of the State.

Joseph Goebbels, Propaganda Minister for the NAZI party.

Men stumble over the truth from time to time, but most pick themselves up and hurry off as if nothing happened.

Winston Churchill.

In times of universal deceit, telling the truth will be a revolutionary act.

George Orwell.

All truth passes through three stages.
  First, it is ridiculed,
  Next it is violently attacked,
  Finally, it is held to be self-evident.

Schopenauer.

If it hurts to tell the truth. Suffer the pain and rejoice.
  Truth gives the greatest happiness, but it can also inflict the greatest pain.
  Fear of hurting another leads to the truth being withheld.
  This leads to greater pain, the only way to avoid pain is to always have the truth told.
  Truth is like a multifaceted diamond. Each human being holds a facet of truth within the human experience. All humans collectively collect a truth that embraces each of the individual truths on the planet. No one truth is superior to another, and all truths are necessary to make up the collective whole.
  Truth can be difficult or easy. Truth is always the most difficult thing, and at the same time, the easiest. For ignorant and egoistic people it is the most difficult thing to know, and for those that are inquisitive and have a burning desire to know, it is the easiest.

Maitreya Ishwara.

The inner truth cannot be realised unless the ego dies. 'The ego is the greatest obstacle on your path towards the truth. The ego has no real existence of its own, for the mind and the ego are false. At present we are under the impression that the mind and the ego are our friends, but they are only misleading us, taking us away from our true nature. The mind and the ego have no power of their own; the source of their power is derived from the Atman, our real existence. The Atman is our true master. But we are presently being controlled and misguided by false masters, namely the mind and the ego. Not only do they delude us, they also cover the face of our real nature, know this and try and come out of the limited shell of your mind and ego. The seedling cannot emerge and grow into a large tree unless the outer shell breaks and dies. Likewise, the inner truth cannot be realised, unless the ego dies.'

Mata Amritanandamayi.

Real truth is not cheap. It requires the total transformation of all your individual systems. And this is much more arduous than the booby prize of intellectual understanding and continued suffering.

Maitreya Ishwara. New Dawn.

If you tell the truth you don't have to remember anything.

Mark Twain.

The search for truth is an honest searching out of everything that interferes with truth. Truth cannot be lost, sought or found. It is there, wherever you are, being within you. However truth can easily be recognized or very often go unrecognised.

The absolute truth is that which does not contaminate you; it simply provides you with power. As soon as we are asked what the truth is we are being invited to give our version of it, to define it. This is dangerous territory as it is a biased version in a similar way to those old stalwarts, good and evil.

Truth can be defined as that which cannot harm anyone.

The only genuine truth is the truth that unfolds in you – it is personal.

There is no 'one size fits all' truth that we can all embrace. Those that are inclined to believe that there is will usually be the promoters of their own version. They will fight to preserve this egotistical illusion and present the truth borne of their own ignorance and agenda.

Many differences start with those who believe unequivocally that their personal truth is right.

Follow your truth.

Things ... that separate us ...

Flags
Ages
Uniforms
Religion
Rank
Snobbery
Elitism
Cults
Clubs
Guilds
Hatred
Time
Job titles
Sport
Politics
Labels
Medals
Anything ending in 'ism,' (apart from Shamanism ... which isn't really a word).
Passports
Boundaries
Boarders
Exploitation
Beliefs
Space
Colour
Ties
Masks
Grasping
Envy

Fear
Greed
Class
Gossip
Did I mention boxes?
And many other things, but only because we allow them to.

And finally the biggest problem – the star of the show and we return to the ego – because every one of these things are the manifestation of it.

Things ... that might be true

When you are waiting for the bus and someone asks, 'Has the bus come yet?'
If the bus came would I be standing here?

Billy Connolly.

You do not make the grass grow by pulling it.

You can take what you're given or you can get what you take.

Those without swords can still die upon them.

You can't direct the wind, but you can adjust your sails.
Tough times never last, but tough people do.

Tom Pascoe.

When your Mum and Dad have had an argument, try to avoid her brushing your hair.

Do not ask your three-year-old brother to hold a tomato.

Why does Miss Universe always seem to come from earth?

A person, who is nice to you but rude to the waiter – is not a nice person. (Put another way – you can tell a lot about a person's character by how they treat people that they don't have to treat well).

There are three ways to get something done; do it yourself, hire someone, or forbid
your kids to do it.

Monta Crane.

Life is a bit like a shit sandwich. The more bread you have the less shit you have to eat.

Frank Holmes.

Put your hand on a hot stove for a minute, and it seems like an hour.
  Sit with a pretty girl for an hour, and it seems like a minute. That is relativity!

Albert Einstein.

Everyone is kneaded out of the same dough but not baked in the same oven.

Old Yiddish proverb.

Why does our royal family have no royal blood?

You cannot help the poor by being one of them.

Abraham Lincoln.

Always end the name of your child with a vowel, so that when you yell the name will carry.

Bill Cosby.

If it's sent by ship then it's a cargo, if it's sent by road then it's a shipment.

Dave Allen.

Give a man a fish and he eats for a day. Teach him how to fish and you get rid of him all weekend.

Zenna Schaffer.

Work like you don't need the money,
Love like you've never been hurt,
And dance like no one's watching.

The books that the world calls immoral are the books that show the world its own shame.

Oscar Wilde.

Everybody thinks they have a sense of humour – including those who haven't.

Tears are God's way of paying you back for what he has taken.

We all not only could know everything. We do. We just tell ourselves we don't to make it all bearable.

Neil Gaiman.

When the faith of the healer in healing is stronger than the disbelief of the recipient, then healing occurs.

Dr Wayne Dyer.

Never trust a man who speaks well of everybody.

John Churton Collins.

There is one thing stronger than all the armies in the world, and that is an idea whose time has come.

Victor Hugo.

Whatever you can do or dream you can do. Begin it. Boldness has genius, power and magic in it. Begin it now.

Gothe.

Time

Time is vicious when you take it for granted.
Time simply exists to stop everything happening together.

Procrastination is the thief of time.

Edward Young.

Voltaire the famous Frenchman was a dwarf in body and a giant in intellect.

In his Zadig, a Mystery of Fate is found the following question put to Zadig by the Grand Magi:

'What of all the things in the world is the longest and shortest, the swiftest and the slowest, the most divisible and the most extended, the most neglected and the most regretted, without which nothing can be done. Which devours all that is little and enlivens all that is good?' ...

Here was Zadig's answer,

'Time.'

'Nothing is longer since it is the measure of eternity.'

'Nothing is shorter since it is insufficient for the accomplishment of your projects.'

'Nothing is slower to him that expects.'

'Nothing more rapid to him that enjoys.'

'In greatness it extends to infinity.'

'In smallness it is infinitely divisible.'

'All men neglect it; all regret the loss of it, nothing can be done without it.'

'It consigns to oblivion whatever is unworthy of being transmitted to posterity and it immortalises such actions, as are truly great.

Time is man's most precious asset.'

'Time stretches between a present and a future that have no objective reality. Time is a convention of thought and language, a social agreement

'In other words, time exists because we say it does?'

'Exactly,' so she whispered. 'Time is like a film of your life that consists of separate frames passing in front of a lens. Each frame is where you exist, in a present moment, but the frames appear to move. You can project your mind into what you call the past or the future, but you cannot live in any moment other than the present.'

Dan Millman. The Laws of Spirit.

To live in the moment … this moment … is the only thing you can possess, this is one of the most precious pieces of knowledge we can acquire. We should remember that we invented time and like many human notions such as language and mathematics; it is just another way of enabling us to understand and ascribe value to the meaning of a world in which we live.

There is an assumption that time is linear, that is to say it is an onward going concept that stretches out in front of us.

We are taught in school and onwards that when we look back in time everything is a natural progression, that we have evolved to this point and stand at the head of civilisation, this then becomes an understandable concept however there are many clues and much evidence to suggest that those who preceded us had knowledge which even today we fail to grasp.

Time is our invention, another tool we deploy to enable us to try and understand the way things are. Time is purely our concept and we are absorbed by it. Time is a notion, a belief it only exists because some of us agree upon it.

Animals know nothing of time however we are consumed by it as our minds flick back and forth to the memories past and into the unrevealed future; like the fly on the end of a fisherman's line, we live in the irrelevant, insular past … or the future … a place within our mind. (Which when we get there will not be how we imagine it, because it will have become the present).

The past and the future is of the self – of the ego – within our minds – it isn't you.

Acknowledging and living in the present, this moment, now, with little or no thought of past or future is the road to enlightenment.

To be or not to be, that is the question.

William Shakespeare

The compulsion arises because the past gives you an identity and the future holds the promise of salvation, of fulfilment in whatever form. Both are illusions.

The Power of Now. Eckhart Toille.

Trouble

Every fight is a food fight when you're a cannibal.

Demetri Martin.

More often we are worried about some impending trouble that never happens. As mentioned earlier, we get what think about whether we want it or not. So we should concentrate on what we do want and forget about what we do not want. (Remember the old adage; *be careful what you wish for it just might happen*).

That is why those that want to control us need us to vibrate badly at a low frequency. All negative emotions blind us and therefore prevent us from getting to the place where we should be. Our search is for a return to where we came from and this is why we want to love and be loved.

According to the oldest and most respected wisdom held in ancient beliefs our emotions are the language that Consciousness understands, through emotion we vibrate at a resonance that is translated. If our feelings are lower and towards fear we attract more of what it is we fear, if we feel higher up the scale with positive emotions such as compassion and forgiveness rising towards love, then we are attracting … asking for … bringing to us … what we love.

Experiencing joy and love becomes enlightening and we can rise up the scale of emotions and the entire Universe becomes a different place. I know what trouble is because every morning when I woke up it was on the pillow next to me. But it was only there because of the way I was thinking and behaving. I was quite simply allowing it and attracting it.

When you stop from reading these words and put the book down, as you move on you will not be able to recall most of what is written here, it does not mean these words have gone away somewhere. You are altered because like every experience however insignificant or massive, you are changed.

Perhaps you will think of a film you loved and are frustrated you cannot recall a piece of dialog that you were drawn to. Well the news is; it's in there somewhere it's just a question of can you dig it out?

We don't forget anything, we might not be able to recall something but you experienced it and it changed you even if the change was small.

Usury

Money lending, debit, credit, chucky, HP, finance, etc.

There are many words and applications for money lending; that is charging interest on money being lent.

A banker is a fellow who lends you his umbrella when the sun is shinning but wants it back the minute it begins to rain.

Mark Twain,

But no matter how pretty a dress they put on it, it is usury (doesn't it sound like a dirty word?) and it produces dirty money, filthy lucre and we will do anything to obtain it, we are programmed to do so. The institutions know this and thrive upon this meme.

Bill Bryson wrote something along the lines that it seems in the Western World, many of us are in a headlong rush to get to the sunny slopes of Mount Greedy, his observations sum up our dilemma and a consequence of this results in heavy borrowing.

Debt becomes a form of slavery locking us into to the system. The banks as a result own everything in our lives.

For example; we want to change our car for a newer one. We leave our house, which is mortgaged to the bank and drive our car, which has finance on it to the dealership. The car dealership has a mortgage on its premises, the car you buy will have a stocking loan on it, you part-exchange your financed car, which the dearer will settle and take out a new finance agreement to purchase your new car.

The dealer then pays off your finance, and pays off his finance. Everywhere your feet have touched and your eye has fallen is financed to the banks and upon every transaction interest is finding its way back to them.

Consider that Britain and America was built on a system of debt and credit; this system was introduced by the Templars who became the Freemasons.

This system financed government and military expansion on a global scale as we in Britain painted the map pink.

Massive recourses to expand and upgrade the military were instrumental in defeating the population of whichever country we chose.

All of the recent wars have had both sides financed by the same people. That is, the arming of both sides and the rebuilding of the country that we conquer.

Usury is *the* best business in the World. Forget about everything else. Do not even consider all the other possibilities because they all dance to the same tune; diamonds, oil, property, prostitution, alcohol, a car franchise or a corner shop.

Everything mentioned requires stock, personnel, premises, rents, leases or mortgages. Everything mentioned requires expenses and is hassle. The hassle is not worth it and the expenses are offset against profit and in the process they reduce profits.

We turned the corner in 2004 when more money was spent on 'credit' (read debt) cards than was spent by cash. And this is where we are being forced to go, into a cashless society and the ramifications for this should concern us because they give more control to those that do not have our best interests at heart. In Britain alone there are now more credit cards then there are people. In the near future the banks intend to dispense with cheques.

In Britain it began with William of Orange who was placed on the throne of England to further the agenda. William (well I'll be a Dutchman) became our new sovereign ruler of England, Scotland and Ireland in 1689. Converting from his Dutchness he became William III, and in 1694 he signed a charter with the primary objective of forming the Bank of England. This international banking system now virtually controls the economies of 178 nations. The Bank's prime aim is to fix interest rates; it acts as the government's banker and manages the country's foreign exchange band gold reserves. It has a monopoly on the issue of banknotes in England and Wales and is instrumental in Scottish and Northern Irelands issue.

Usury was invented by the Knights Templar, this monastic military order was formed at the end of the first Crusade with humble beginnings rooted in poverty and as it rose to power (good old St Bernard and the 'Kill Them All Firm.' … bless) it had the backing of Popes and the collective European monarchies. The downfall of the Templars came when the then King of France Philip, turned upon the Order.

We have talked about the Orders rise to power and it was this power that brought them down and the knights were forced to jump from one horse to another. Their costly lesson learned, from this time they would never be seen in the world again, after the treachery of Philip they would never risk being so exposed again. Having found whatever they found under Solomon's Temple, the nine knights concluded their treasure hunt and went into empire building mode.

Bernard of Clairvaux preached powerfully on behalf of these Christian warriors and built them into an order that rivalled his own Cistercians.

Their subsequent rise to power is well documented; they controlled banking, commerce, and building and had the world's largest fleet of ships.

Young men from wealthy families all over Europe, flocked to join them and in the process pledged their inheritance to the cause.

It followed that Europe's most powerful families would pledge their assets as collateral for loans made from the Templar bank.

King Philip owed the Templar's both money and his life; massive loans he could not repay and his life had been saved when the Templar's rescued him from the mobs of Paris.

Philip asked to join the order and was refused; he coerced the Pope to condemn them and to defeat the order but his ultimate aim was to grab their treasure however he failed, (the Pope later retracted his condemnation). This was before that fateful day, recorded throughout history, as Friday October 13th 1307, when the armies of France attacked Templar headquarters and arrested hundreds of knights.

Before that day The Paris Temple, (which was formerly the headquarters of the World's only bank) many of the Templar's had been tipped off as a result the treasure housed in these and other repositories was taken to the port of La Rochelle. It was there it was loaded onto Templar ships and disappeared from history. The fleet sailed in a number of directions, certainly some found their way to Portugal and survived as the Knights of Christ, some to Malta, the islands and mainland of Scotland, North America, Ireland, England.

When Robert the the Bruce stabbed his rival to death in Greyfriar's Chapel, England's King Edward excommunicated him. Robert the Bruce allied himself with two important bishops and several nobles and proceeded to crown himself King upon the Stone of Scone. Robert went into hiding as Edward sought his demise, many Scots lost their lives to the more organised English armies, however came the Battle of Bannockburn and things were about to change.

The Scots appeared to retreat and the English army followed as a fresh force of Knights appeared, the day was saved for the Scots and they won their most famous war for independence.

This day, which remains sacred in Templar tradition was June 24th namely St. John's Feast Day.

Robert the Bruce was of Norman lineage. His family fought in the 1066 invasion, as were the Sinclair family (formerly St. Clair). Since these French families were instrumental in the founding of the Templar's perhaps these widely held beliefs are true.

In 1398, Henry Sinclair of Roslyn, a Scot with French Templar blood flowing through his veins, led an expedition to North America; Henry's voyage took place ninety-six years before Columbus. In Newport, Rhode Island, the Templar's built an octagonal chapel; it was modelled after the Holy Sepulchre in Jerusalem. The only other similar chapel was built in Orkney, Scotland, where the Sinclair family ruled. They went on to build Roslyn Chapel in 1439.

The Chapel was built 56 years prior to Columbus 'discovering' maize (corn) and aloe in the 'New World.' The building stands outside Edinburgh in Scotland, it is a dark and eerie place but carved into the stonework are the unmistakable images of maize and aloe cactus.

Masons and other construction workers from all over Europe built this complex chapel which is a replica of Solomon's Temple. The descendants of these Templar's and their allies would become the Freemasons and were employed by the Sinclair family. Upon James II ascendancy to the throne, he decreed the Sinclair family to be the hereditary guardians of the Freemasons.

Now we need to step forward in time and return to William III and those that hid in the background as a result of the events nearly two centuries before, those that carried the baton of bloodline, those that would never be usurped by anyone not even a king.

The dynamics had changed and those few men now appointed kings, chose popes, ran the money system and as a result controlled the world.

These are the people who pass the baton; the same people who require us to work in their mines of their 'New World Order,' these men are of the bloodline that control us today.

The practice of usury employed by the issuers of credit, was in William III's time, both illegal and dishonest. The bankers knew that William in order to retain his position and in fact his life, needed to keep the Stuarts at bay to prevent them from returning to the throne. He also needed to impose his will upon France. He therefore needed to raise an army but for this he needed money.

William's need for money enabled the Bank of England to force him to make legal its dishonest practice. The deal was simple, William would receive a loan of £1,200,000 at 8% interest and he in turn would grant the Bank the right to issue bank notes … as claims on the same assets loaned to the government to raise its army … it was also allowed to lend out those notes and collect interest on them.

Ok, lets just recap, draw our breath and revue. This is how all wars are instituted and furthermore – if the – 'all matter is energy reduced to a lower vibration,' bit mentioned earlier contains the meaning of how we work in the world, then this deal is paramount in how we now find ourselves prisoners in that material world.

Money is a thought process, simply an agreed meme that has a value over which we have no say but it represents energy and our want to control it.

Only this story is how it controls us.

As time would pass the government would have to pay back the loan plus the interest. The Bank was not concerned how this would be done, either the money would be borrowed from somewhere else or the populous would be taxed.

The Bank of England was now the proud possessor of government debt for the first time in history; it had become the ruler of government. Having lent money that did not exist to William, the Bank discovered it had some £36,000 in assets left. This was deemed a reserve and under the new rules it issued £550,000 in bank notes.

This was then as it is now; a bank may lend ten times what it has on deposit. Only they tweaked it up a bit given their new charter from the King, instead of ten to one (of nothing) they went with over fifteen to one (of nothing).

The Bank 'created' money, printed it with its 'promise to pay the bearer' and by 1696 had added £1,750,000 of its own notes to the amount of money throughout the nation it now controlled.

The Bank of England originated national debt for the government, taxes for the citizens, unlimited ability to create money from nothing and all because it had been engineered, that a man who would be king wanted to retain power and wanted to lead 'his' people to war and so began the blueprint for the rest of the modern world and we became pawns in the game.

The workers/consumers will even sacrifice the lives of their own flesh and blood if it means keeping the rich fat and happy because the rich have promised them that some day they can join them at the table!

But that day never comes, and by the time the working stiff has this figured out, he's in an old-age home spewing a lot of mumbo jumbo about authority and taking it out on the aide who is just trying to empty his sorry bedpan. There might have been a more humane way to spend his final days, but the money that would have financed that was spent by him on all that fantastic AOL Time Warner and WorldCom stock – and the rest was spent by the government on that outer space weapons system that never did quite seem to work.

Michael Moore. Dude Where's My Country?

In every banking swindle every one knows that some time or other the crash must come, but every one hopes that it may fall on the head of his neighbour, after he himself has caught the shower of gold and placed it in safety. Après moi le deluge … is the watchword of every capitalist and of every capitalist nation. Hence Capital is reckless of the health or length of life of the labourer, unless under compulsion from society.

Karl Marx. Capital. 1867.

In America the Federal Reserve was created in 1913-1914 in order to bring stability to the economy and yet every major crash, and that includes the Great Depression and our present recession can be attributed to the Federal Reserve.

Originally there was a system of national banks in the USA but then a consortium of 12 privately held banks got together and formed the Federal Reserve Bank, an entity that is not part of the US government. These banks then purchase notes from the US Mint for printing costs and lend them out through member banks charging interest. The Federal Reserve came into being after its supporters paid for the Presidential campaign of US President Woodrow Wilson.

Wilson signed the bill that transferred US currency to twelve regional private banks; Wilson later regretted his decision saying:

'I am a most unhappy man. I have unwittingly ruined my country. A great industrial nation is controlled by its system of credit. Our system of credit is concentrated. The growth of the nation, therefore, and all our activities are in the hands of a few men. We have come to be one of the worst ruled, one of the most completely controlled and dominated governments in the civilised world. No longer a government by free opinion, no longer a government by conviction and the vote of the majority, but a government by the opinion and duress of a small group of dominant men.'

In the 1930's, President Roosevelt confiscated gold and handed it to the Federal Reserve. At the very moment when Americans have needed to protect their wealth the most, gold was confiscated from American citizens and given to a conglomeration of private banks.

As the bill for the Federal Reserve was being considered, a few politicians spoke out against its creation saying it was *'the strangest, most dangerous advantage ever placed in the hands of a special privilege class by any Government that ever existed.'*

The Federal Reserve makes no secret about the scam they are perpetrating, the Boston section of the Federal Reserve Bank said:

'When you or I write a check there must be sufficient funds in our account to cover the cheque, but when the Federal Reserve writes a check there is no bank deposit on which that cheque is drawn. When the Federal Reserve writes a cheque it is creating money.'

The Rothschild Brothers in London said in 1863;

'The few who understand the system, will either be so interested from it's profits or so dependant on it's favours, that there will be no opposition from that class.'

Henry Ford said

'It is well enough that people of the nation do not understand our banking and monetary system, for if they did, I believe there would be a revolution before tomorrow morning.'

And that is the problem, very few people understand the system. It is obviously not taught in schools and even some financial analysts and fund managers really have no idea how the system works.

Inflation is often defined as rising prices when in fact inflation occurs because of the expansion of the money supply.

Often they link inflation with the economy doing well, saying, *'We should raise interest rates as the economy did extremely well this month but we don't want inflation to get out of hand.'*

I believe that banking institutions are more dangerous than standing armies. If the American people ever allow private banks to control the issue of their currency first by inflation, then by deflation, the banks and the corporations that will grow up around (the banks) will deprive the people of all property until their children wake-up homeless on the continent their fathers conquered. The issuing power should be taken from the bank and restored to the people, to whom it properly belongs.

Thomas Jefferson.

Each and every time a bank makes a loan, new bank credit is created – new deposits – brand new money.

Graham F Towers. Governor, Bank of Canada. 1934–1954.

A bank is a place that will lend you money if you can prove you don't need it.

Bob Hope

Once the American people understand that they have been robbed blind and that the money they thought was being used to run the government is actually being funnelled, in a manner that would make Enron's frauds seem paltry, to the vaults of a few private banking institutions, the people will wake up and join the million man petition for a redress of grievances. The power is with the people, but unless the people use that power it remains dormant. We haven't awoken enough people to their proactive power as the respiratory system of the Constitution and the government. In order to make the government submissive to the will of the people, the people must be educated.

Citizen Spook

We are robbed in the name of the law, laws we are programmed to obey, for us to behave any other way would be treason, heretical, blasphemous, mad, criminal, bad, etc. The agenda is simple. The New World Order is well on its way to maturity. We are aware of some of the changes that the machine spits out as we go about our daily lives. We catch a little here and there, fragments of news, conversations with others. We now have started to realise where we are headed, to some it is obvious, much of it is hidden from us by our own distractions or the information is corrupted or is not in the public domain.

I have no idea who coined the phrase ' it's not in the public interest,' but it's a corker. In case the other side should find out about our technology? So you're going to back down on that one, because if you question what is and what is not 'in the public interest,' you are unpatriotic; you do not love your country and you are promoting all sorts of heresy and treason.

Its similar to the Pope really; those fantastic door-shutters when the heat gets hot. One question for the religion where the bigger and sillier the hat the more powerful the position, one simple question. 'So Holy Father, how about letting those places on earth that want birth control have it? So that millions of people on the face of God's earth could still have a bit of fun sexually with each other and as a result maintain bonds but not more unwanted children, you know just so we don't have people all over the planet dying before they are three years old from the wickedness, the horror and the deceit of poverty. Because for them it really is a matter of life and death?'

But you just know the answers going to come back 'no.' And if God's representative here on Earth was pushed into giving a definitive answer here is the door-shutter, 'no my son it cannot happen and I cannot give you the reason why because God revealed it to me.'

Belter, superb, 10 out of 10. Full marks for whoever thought those one's up – lets all get back to a dream of a better world – and dream on long because as long as – 'God revealed it to me,' and 'it's not in the public interest,' are about, change can never be brought into actuality.

The process by which banks create money is so simple that the mind is repelled.
John Kenneth Galbraith. Economist.

The powers of financial capitalism had far-reaching plan, nothing less than to create a world system of financial control in private hands able to dominate the political system of each country and the economy of the world as a whole … their secret is that they have annexed from governments, monarchies, and republics the power to create money …
Prof. Carroll Quigley.
Tragedy and Hope: a History of the World in Our Time.

Banking was conceived in iniquity and was born in sin. The bankers own the earth. Take it away from them, but leave them the power to create money, and with the flick of the pen they will create enough deposits to buy it back again. However, take it away from them, and all the great fortunes like mine will disappear and they ought to disappear, for this world would be a far happier and better world to live in. But, if you wish to remain the slaves of bankers and pay the cost of your own slavery, let them continue to create money.
Sir Josiah Stamp, Director of the Bank of England.
Appointed 1928 and reputed to be the second wealthiest man in England at the time.

Well we could all just turn up at our bank tomorrow and ask for our money. I would want to be at the front of the queue, because I would bet my life, halfway down the line the cashiers would be saying, 'we've run out of money.'

The unthinkable has already happened in the fiasco of the events surrounding Northern Rock, and this bank (that will finally end up nationalised along with all the rest, controlled by the men who control the government) will *appear* to fail only to be absorbed into the World Bank, which is all part of the agenda.

As with all of the structures of government and financial institutions one should disregard the names they go under, as you climb the pyramid those that hold the real power meld into fewer and fewer names. All these institutions, which also include the stock market, are showing their real muscle these days as we accelerate towards the agenda, the world of the New World Order.

Watching how famous names like Northern Rock, Merrill Lynch and Lehman Brothers (in one year LB's shares have fallen from 65 dollars to nothing) become casualties and are swallowed up for a few cents on the dollar.

In August 2008 England registered over 70,000 house sales, according to figures August 2008 saw 1700 house sales recorded. As Bradford Bingley 'fails' and becomes nationalised we have seen the engineering of a list of lenders reduce to little more than a handful of main mortgage lenders.

It is an engineered situation, streamlining into a world bank has never been more obvious.

Bush instructed every American citizen to contribute two thousand three hundred and thirty-three dollars to the failed system; his electorate. Brown needs everyone in the UK to pull up billions in a similar scam. So Obama's going to save us with hope? Obama works for Wall Street, he is the puppet of financiers, they all are.

Look at our leaders the next time you watch the Programming at Ten and ask are we prepared to believe they and their colleagues came up with this solution? They are puppets immersed in ritual, blinded by power, trapped in fear, consumed by ego, serving the agenda and controlled to the hilt. Do not make the mistake of loathing them, they are more controlled than we are, and don't make the mistake of thinking that we can rise up and violently beat the system because that is what the agenda is prepared for, we simply need to change our minds. Until we do the agenda will be served and we will continue our sleepwalk to perdition and subjugation.

OK, congratulations to the handful of men who have given the people of America, most of Europe and this entire country, no choice whatsoever in bailing out enterprise that they had no part of … who wins? … they win … they always win.

Right now it's cheap acquisition time as those that own the game clean up. Someone's bad is someone else's good or to be accurate; a lot of peoples bad is a few peoples good.

The entire financial system is changing as it wobbles, the pace has never been quicker as institutions crash and become absorbed for a fraction of their value. If it really mattered one could say capitalism is discredited, but if you did that you would be forgetting that it does not matter what title is placed above the door or upon the belief system, whatever the ideology because when you own the system … you own the game.

Permit me to issue and control the money of a nation, and I care not who makes its laws.

Mayer Anselm Rothschild. Banker.

The New World Order in essence is about; a cashless society, a World Bank, a

World Army, a micro-chipped subservient population, eugenics deployed to reduce the populous, cameras installed 'to solve crime' however they are really there to monitor us.

Only normal behaviour that serves the agenda will be tolerated, any expression of individuality will be addressed; consume, work, obey and embrace your place in the matrix, it happening, it is upon us and we were coerced, seduced and programmed to create, participate and perpetrate it ourselves.

The world is governed by very different personages from what is imagined by those who are not behind the scenes.

Benjamin Disraeli. 1840

The real truth of the matter is that a financial element in the large centres has owned the government since the days of Andrew Jackson.

Franklin. D Roosevelt. 1933.

The mystery religions of ancient Sumerian, Babylon, Egypt, Greece, India and Rome helped lay the foundation for occultism, (meaning hidden knowledge).

One of the earliest writings giving reference to occultism is the Egyptian Book of the Dead, a compilation of rituals explicitly describing methods of torture and intimidation (to create trauma), the use of potions and the casting of spells and hypnotism, this ultimately results in the total enslavement of the initiate.

These have been the main ingredients for a part of occultism known as Satanism, throughout the ages. During the 13th Century, the Roman Catholic Church increased and solidified its dominion throughout Europe with the infamous Inquisition.

Satanism survived this period of persecution, deeply entrenching itself under the veil of various esoteric groups.

In 1776, a Bavarian Jesuit by the name of Adam Weishaupt was commissioned by the house of Rothschild to centralise the power base of the Mystery Religions into what is commonly known as the Illuminati, meaning 'Enlightened Ones.'

This was an amalgamation of powerful occultic bloodlines, elite secret societies and influential Masonic fraternities the object being, to construct the framework for a 'New World Order.'

The outward goal of this New Eden was to bring forth Universal happiness to the human race. However, their underlying intention was to gradually increase control over the masses and become masters of the planet.

It was that simple.

If we have a world army, who will that army fight? Does it follow that the New World Army PLC would therefore exist to repel alien attack from the outside or it would exist to subjugate us, the citizens of this brave New World.

The final hurdle, the acceptance of compulsory microchiping will be a breeze, we will call for it, we will have become used to the carrying of identity cards, to retina scans, of lie-detectors (thanks Jerry, cheers Jeremy, nice one Lorraine), fingerprint id systems, streets and roads covered from every angle with silent sentient watchers. Loads of official wearing uniforms with different ribbons on their hats, waiting to pounce (such a similar word to ponce) and earn their wage by taxing your every mistake.

And still people will still say, 'well if you're not doing anything wrong, then what have you got to worry about.'

I honestly don't know what you might think about this but I am going to be straight … I don't fancy it one little bit (and at the moment and for the foreseeable future I am really going to try and not do anything 'wrong'). Your wrong and their wrong are not one and the same.

I wouldn't even fancy it if I trusted the people who were advancing this clear agenda. How can we trust them? There is no honour and there is little accountability. Prime Ministers and Presidents lie to us from our TV screens yet still keep their jobs and still remain to tell us that we're off to war and we are free. It is remarkable as much as it is unbelievable, these people are supposed to be our elected representatives, to serve the people who chose them. It does not work like that anymore; we have become more and more subjugated, more and more governed.

I wish our leaders no harm, be they Brown, Bush or Barack, King or Queen … whatever their names, whichever puppet is chosen for the role.

I cannot wish them harm though I may despise their actions and the agenda … we are all One and therefore it follows you cannot hate another human being.

They are us … you are me … **we are all one consciousness experiencing life subjectively.**

So just to be clear, because I have probable upset a few people on these pages and I don't want to be misunderstood anymore than is necessary; it is a bloodless revolution I seek and if we raise ourselves above the fear and start to feel love rather than hate we will once again know heaven on earth.

And all we need do is change our minds.

Value

Value is nothing more than a matter of opinion.

Paper is poverty, it is only the ghost of money. It is written on our paper 'I promise to pay the bearer on demand,' but what is the value of this paper? As has been made clear by recent events it is nothing more than a stranger's promise and opinion.

A pile of gold has no value compared to a loaf of bread if you are starving and if you were dying of thirst you would give all you owned for one drink of water. Money does not exist; it's a meme, an agreement upon which we collectively agree to value, in these uncertain times we might ask; where has it all gone? It hasn't disappeared we are going through a process of more control as its value becomes adjusted and its availability limited.

Something only has value because we place worth upon it. This may not be monetary. If you are an Elvis Presley fan your most precious possession might be a signed autograph of him, but to someone on the other side of the world who has never heard of him it is worthless. A locket containing a few of the hairs from your much loved grandmothers head, for you personally might have great value as it is a personal reminder of fond memories, but is has no value to anyone else.

The value of a relationship is a process we all deliberate on and we should deploy a degree of empathy with those we have relationships with. When we ask what we need from our partners for example, have we truly considered the price they have to pay in meeting our requests?

Everything has a price. Everything costs something,

Even drawing breath; we need to exhale. Look to nature it always finds balance. We should try and find balance. As we live we discover the price and that price is the value we place upon the object of our desire. It is astonishing where we are prepared to place blame if we have struck out in a direction only to discover the enormity of the price we are left to pay. It is our fault if we did not account correctly. The Universe does not rip us off; we simply failed in our judgment because the vehicles of valuation are our mistakes. If we accept responsibility for the position in which we now find ourselves, then marry this to the recognition that we brought ourselves to this point; we can then form closure on what was, upon reflection, an opportunity to learn. Therefore a lesson has value.

How often do we utter or hear said, 'What are *they* going to do about it?' The likely-hood is not very much as '*they*' do not honour our goals and may not even be aware of them. This then is how we give away our power. We must raise our individual and collective consciences, change our thoughts and values which will change our behaviour and in so doing make for a better future.

> *You are what your deep, driving desire is.*
> *As your desire is. So is your will.*
> *As your will is, so is your deed.*
> *As your deed is, so is your destiny.*
>
> Brihadaranyaka Upanishad.

Programming sees to it that we grow up believing that to give is to lose but the best amongst us know that to share or give away increases the intrinsic value of what it is we are imparting. That it is energy we are giving and that energy is represented by a person giving of his time or in an meme such as money, however this act of benevolence is only valued by our perception of it.

If we use our programming we are acquiring through ego and so we seek out the specialness of our desire, inform ourselves we had to sacrifice for its acquisition, and then worry in case someone takes it away from us. We pay heavily for this mindset and we invest much in its protection and whether it's a person, an object or an idea the illusion of the conclusion we have formed is that this energy is ours.

Giving is receiving and this action liberates us because it stops us competing, fighting and struggling and instead of grasping for the power of acquisition and the dubious results this brings, we share and impart and in the doing empower ourselves. Once you become empowered the objective that you previously sought; approval, affection, specialness, security and attention, you now become the source and everything that you previously wanted you now supply to others.

It is said that nature abhors a vacuum or a void and the results of your benevolence is that you find you are overly compensated for whatever it was you imagined you had parted with. This action is not about generosity or enlightenment and it is nothing to do with right and wrong, this has nothing to do with anything other than the fact that we are all One.

A cynic is a man who knows the price of everything but the value of nothing.
Oscar Wilde.

Nothing real can be threatened.
Nothing unreal exists.
Herein lies the peace of God.

A Course in Miracles.

Violence

I think we ought to raise the age at which juveniles can have a gun.

G.W.Bush.

9/11 gave the Bush people carte blanche to carry out their extreme agenda – and they didn't hesitate for one moment to use it … They've used the war on terror to justify everything from tax cuts to Alaskan oil drilling.

Ronald Reagan.

If the atrocity of 911 had not happened then it would have been difficult to take forward the 'war on terror.'

Billions would have been saved on defence and security upgrades. And the religious war created to ostensibly smash Islamic countries and steal oil, would have been so much harder to sell to the people of the nations who took part.

'Fighting for peace', sounds a catchy political statement that has hung around a while. The politicians use it, soldiers use it, and people in conversation use it. 'We are fighting for peace and this war is a just war. Sure there will be casualties, but in the end we will prevail and peace will be achieved.' This is superb in theory; eliminate a few of the opposition for the ultimate benefit of the many. But it is only a theory, because in all of history (recorded, distorted or made up), this has never been achieved.

Fighting for peace is like screwing for virginity.

George Carlin.

War will disappear only when men shall take no part whatever in violence and shall be ready to suffer every persecution that their abstention will bring them.
It is the only way to abolish war.

Anatole France.

Violence is created because we are programmed to think violence.

If you are under the age of 25 you might never have heard of Mary Whitehouse. But as I grew up in the 1960's and 70's Mary was forever in the news and became a household name in Britain. She was a campaigner who sought to rid us of pornography wherever it was broadcast and was a persistent thorn in the side of many. She took it upon herself to litigate and censor any production she felt was overstepping the mark, from nudity to bad-language. She went too far in many people's views, even to the point of saying that violence in cartoons would corrupt the young. However she felt it her mission to rid our young and impressionable minds of anything she thought offensive.

I thought she was a proper pest we could well do without, I mean I was an adolescent, I wanted to learn new swear words and much more importantly I was desperate to see the undraped female form. If Mary was denying me access to the wonderful world of ladies breasts and buttocks then I could only feel the world would be a better place without her.

The imposition of censorship comes with all sorts of debate and everyone has an opinion and where does censorship begin and end in what is supposed to be a free society? I flatter myself that I have an open mind but I appreciate, for example that young children should not see scenes of extreme violence.

Mrs Whitehouse really opened herself up to ridicule when she suggested that Tom and Jerry were bad for children as they were subjected to the sight of scenes of violence. I thought, as many did, that this was absurd, this famous cat and mouse pair was pure fantasy and it was ridiculous to censor what was clearly supposed to be amusing. I ended up really disliking this busybody's presence on the planet, but I think differently now. I have little idea about what Mary's motivation was, but want to develop why I think that certainly when it came to violence she had a point. We have television, films, music videos, video games, computer games all showing violence. In the case of computer games we actually are involved in the violence, inter-reacting to shoot our enemy down in a pool of blood.

In America it is estimated that a child will watch an astonishing 19,000 hours of TV by the time they finish high-school, much more time for example than all their classroom hours put together since they started in first grade.

By eighteen years of age they will be witness to an extraordinary 200,000 acts of violence, including at least 40,000 senseless acts of murder, with every hour of prime time TV continuing to expose them to at least 6 acts of violence.

It is also estimated that the average American citizen aged sixty will have given over a quarter of his life to watching TV.

In The United States we have as violent society as there has ever been. The land of the free; where there is more imbalance within society than any other, the land of the haves and have-nots ... the have yachts and the don't have yachts ... but the price for subjugating millions of your citizens with the tools of fear are there for all to see; violence is manifest everywhere.

America incarcerates it citizens and those of other nations with utter contempt for the individuals concerned. It executes with relish a never-ending conveyor belt of human misery and two wrongs can never make a right.

For every one of its population the government locks up or kills, is demonstrated a failing on behalf of that government.

Did any single one of those responsible ... as they put another needle in a bad mans arm ... ever stop to think ... what would this man's fate might have been if he had had a chance; had he not been brought up in an environment where abuse and violence was part of life, where every place his young eyes fell; in the home, on the TV, outside the home ... everywhere?

Violence begets violence, you become what you fight; the cycle can only be broken by those who withdraw from violence. Where the young and impressionable are influenced to admire the use of violence by John Wayne or Arnold Schwarzenegger in a movie as a solution to a problem, or we walk the dark seductive pathways of the latest shoot'em up computer game as a distraction, then we become accepting of and are more likely to embrace violence.

The rampant gun culture rooted in its bloody past and the never-ending diet of fear will produce violence and we are groomed to become accepting of it.

This then is the price we will pay; this is the programmer's hypocritical legacy ... violence ... fear ... from the horror of shootings in schools ... to the massacre of innocents in lands far away.

Hate multiplies hate, violence multiplies violence, and toughness multiplies toughness.

Dr Martin Luther King Jnr.

The steady diet that children and young adults are exposed to clearly has severe consequences. Seeing someone die for the first time in your life has a profound effect upon you, seeing your $40,000^{th}$ is by comparison a walk in the park. Outwardly it may appear we are desensitised toward violence but should we be so accepting of it? Surely to be programmed by violence is to feel some empathy with it.

We get what we think about especially magnified when we dwell upon it.

We are affected by everything we encounter because the way our brain functions and most of what we encounter is flooding into our unconsciousness. At any given time we are processing a mass of data and our five-senses cope brilliantly, but the information we are trying to process and make sense of is beyond calculation. Light, sound, colour, noise, taste, smell … all have to be processed and translated; we have no option as we transit through our lives. It is yet another example of the miracle that is *you*.

Our vibrational level is affected by what we are asked to process, if we are relaxed with friends or family in a trusting environment we can feel love, we are allowing.

A simple act like arranging a bowl of flowers enables us to lose ourselves for a few moments and step back and admire the arrangement we made. I am aware to many people this might sound 'soft' however that is simply because most of us men are conditioned to be macho, and we become macho because of fear. Fear of what others might think, fear of criticism, fear of anything that threatens our beliefs, fear of attack, fear of being taken advantage of in a predator based society and so we wear the mask of hardness, the veils that prevent us from expressing ourselves.

I did it for years, it is false, it is not real, I don't want to do it anymore and I have nothing left to prove to anyone else. All I have left from those times are the scars that pepper my body both inside and out. Violence achieves nothing, everyone looses, the only logical argument for violence is the threat of it; we have more nuclear weapons than you have, so don't start with us. I am stronger than you are so don't pick a fight with me because you will get beaten.

Yes, okay for those that live with violence, the impending threat of it might be justified in that it prevents conflict and therefore it is prevented from occurring, that however is its only weak justification because it is still bullying, it is still intimidation, whether it be little Johnny (doesn't he take after his Dad?) in the playground pressurising geeky Tommy for sweets … *or else*. Or the joint forces of America and Britain, demanding what they want from a small country … *or else*. And what is programmed into us as individuals, putting more and more of us in fear manifests itself throughout the masses. If we had no thought of violence then it just could not happen.

When we feel fear we generate a vibration transposed as an energy field, whatever our emotional condition we are broadcasting, this is what we call vibes. When we vibrate with fear or any of its bedfellows such as anger, rage, jealousy, guilt, aggression, etc; this is what we are asking of the Universe. The Universe is benign, there really isn't a God sitting on a cloud above us issuing thunderbolts to the wicked (and if he is – he needs a bit of target practice).

A diet of violence to induce fear is ours for the taking unless we resist and choose another way and we can change it in a heartbeat simply by thinking differently. This is a basic law of the Universe for as long as long as we are fed violence we will manifest it, as long as we consume animals that have been reared and killed inhumanly we will manifest the vibration of their misery; '*you are what you eat.*' As long as we are prescribed drugs, drink chemicals, absorb toxins, live in an environment where we are bombarded with electrical based (unseen by not unfelt) waves, we will lower our defences against functioning right, thinking right and doing right.

How much longer are we prepared to go down the path we are on? How much more of it can we take? How much longer are we going to use our energy to guard what we cannot hold and how much longer are we prepared to let our power and our potential sleep?

What we devote our attention to it follows that we give our energy to. In this respect thoughts, chanting, toning, prayer, healing, interaction with others are all the same … a focus of attention.

When we give our emotions the thought of violence it follows that we manifest violence. The terror starts within us and emanates outwards sending a clear message, every single emotion starts within us and affects our world, and it does not have to be this way.

It is so simple, the truth that many of us have forgotten; if we love we emanate and spread love, if we hate the same thing happens. Don't blame the programmers, most of them have been doing it for so long they don't even realise they are doing it anymore.

We have to change how *we* feel as individuals and the walls will tumble down. If those that seek to control us can no longer make us feel fear they loose their power.

The very least that they deserve is redundancy because it will help them see the truth … there is *nothing* to fear.

War

Those at war with others are not at peace with themselves.

William. Hazlitt.

'Over there are some civil war veterans. Iron flags on their graves. New Hampshire boys had a notion that the Union ought to be kept together, though they'd never seen more than fifty miles of it themselves. All they knew was the name, friends – the United States of America. The United States of America. And they went and died for it.'

Thornton Wider. Our Town.

If war produces one thing it produces many cemeteries, and in cemeteries there are no enemies.

The worst barbarity of war is that it forces men collectively to commit acts against which individually they would revolt with their whole being.

Ellen Key.

It is curious that physical courage should be so common in the world and moral courage so rare.

Mark Twain.

Beware the leader who bangs the drums of war in order to whip the citizenry into patriotic fervour, for patriotism is indeed a double-edged sword.
It both emboldens the blood, just as it narrows the mind.
And when the drums of war have reached a fever pitch and the blood boils with hate and the mind has closed, the leader will have no need in seizing the rights of the citizenry.
Rather, the citizenry, infused with fear and blinded by patriotism, will offer up all of their rights unto the leader and gladly so.

How do I know?
For this is what I have done.
And I am Caesar.

Julius Caesar.

And since then until now, nothing has changed. Nothing will ever change as long as we fight for war instead of allowing the want of peace.

The world it would seem, is as insane and out of kilter as it was two thousand years ago and in fact it's worse because we have found even more ingenious ways to kill each other and we have made killing an acceptable form.

However there is one important difference to then and now; we have never been in a better position to actually do something about it.

Those who cannot remember the past are condemned to repeat it.

George Santayana.

War does not determine who is right, only who is left.

Bertrand Russell.

Naturally the common people don't want war: neither in Russia, nor in England, nor for that matter in Germany. That is understood. But, after all, it is the leaders of the country who determine the policy and it is always a simple matter to drag the people along whether it is a democracy, or a fascist dictatorship, or a parliament, or a communist dictatorship. Voice or no voice, the people can always be brought to the bidding of the leaders. That is easy. All you have to do is tell them they are being attacked, and denounce the peacemakers for lack of patriotism and exposing the country to danger. It works the same way in any country.

Hermann Goering. Hitler's most loyal of supporters. One of the primary architects of the Nazi police state in Germany and the Holocaust.

All wars are civil wars, because all men are brothers.

Francois Fendon.

All that is necessary for evil to succeed is for good men to do nothing.

Edmund Burke.

Whenever you are in conflict with someone, there is one factor that can make to difference between damaging your relationship and deepening it. That factor is attitude.

William James.

A soldier will fight long and hard for a bit of coloured ribbon.

Napoleon Bonaparte.

Terrorism is war by the poor, and war is terrorism by the rich.

Peter Ustinov.

The pioneers of a warless world are the youth who refuse military service.

Albert Einstein.

Patriots always talk of dying for their country and never killing for their country

Bertrand Russell.

Are you righteous, kind, does your confidence lie in this?
  Are you loved by all?
  Know that I was too.
  Do you imagine your sufferings will be less because you loved goodness – truth?

From the film, a Thin Red Line.
Spoken in voiceover emanating from a dead soldier.

The English were about to fight a battle, one of the battles in the Hundred Years' War the date was 25th October 1415 (Saint Crispin's Day). The armies at Agincourt were those of the English King Henry V and Charles VI of France. Some historical reports of the battle say that the English had odds against them of five to one. Word of the French superiority had filtered back to the rank and file soldiers and they were not relishing the fight. King Henry stood on a hay cart and delivered the following incredibly inspirational speech.

Many of the English archers (who had a massive influence on the outcome of the battle) had dysentery and diarrhoea, legend has it that they dipped the tips of their arrows in their own contaminated faeces so that the wounds inflicted on the French would infect. War is a dirty business and that's all it is – business.

(Of course Henry V didn't really say these words, they were penned from the imagination of Shakespeare).

'No my fair cousin Westmoreland if we are marked to die, we are enough to do our country loss.
  And if to live, the fewer men, the greater share of honour,

Gods will I pray thee wish not one man more

Rather proclaim it Westmoreland through my host.

That he which hath no stomach for this fight

Let him depart – his passport shall be made, and crowns for his convey put into his purse.

We would not die in that man's company that fears his fellowship to die with us.

This day is called the feast of Chrispian – he that outlives this day and comes safe home will stand at tiptoe when this day is named and arose at the name of Chrispian.

He that shall see this day and live old age will yearly on the vigil feast his neighbours and say tomorrow is St Chrispian's.

Then will he strip his sleeve and show his scars and say these wounds I had on Chispian's day.

Old men forget – yet all shall be forgot. But he'll remember with advantages what feats he did that day.

Then shall our names familiar in their mouths as household words, Harry the King, Bedford and Exeter, Salisbury and Gloucester, Warwick and Talbot. Be in their flowing cups freshly remembered.

This story shall the good man teach his son.

And Chrispin Chrispian shall ner go by from this day to the ending of the World! But we in it shall be remembered.

We few we happy few, we band of brothers – for he today that sheds his blood with me shall be my brother – be he ner so vile – this day shall gentle his condition.

And gentlemen in England now a-bed shall think themselves accursed they were not here.

And hold their manhood's cheap whilst any speaks that fought with us upon Saint Chrispian's Day!'

William Shakespeare. Henry V.

So there we have it – it's official – the royal edict; be proud to die for your country, it's totally fine to kill another mother's son because our fight is the 'right' one, the justifiable one. Fight long and hard because hatred will dispense with more of those we have decided to hate, if you survive the bloodbath you are about to be involved in you will be a hero back home for the rest of your natural, it's thoroughly advisable to programme your son so that he too is instilled with patriotism, belief and passion for the next war, which will be just around the next corner … *err no* … sorry I can't tell you who it is you will be fighting … they haven't actually told me yet, anyway … where was I? Oh yes, today you're fit to be my brother, tomorrow you go back to serving me … the agenda … and those that control me … anyone who disagrees is a traitor … we don't like traitors … anyone not here is a stinking coward … we don't like cowards … right lads get stuck in.

It was a pack of lies then and it's a pack of lies now.

They wrote in the old days that it is sweet and fitting to die for one's country. But in modern war, there is nothing sweet nor fitting in your dying. You will die like a dog for no good reason.

Ernest Hemmingway.

War dehumanises us and we speak of those we have made our enemies as if they inhabit a different moral Universe. War enables enemies to view each other as less than human beings.

I read a while back that a country can be judged on its level of civilisation by the way it incarcerates its criminal population. It should also be judged how it wages war. Where there used to be standing battles it is unlikely there will ever be one again. War is now a different dynamic; those who institute and wage war do so from a distance with weapons of mass destruction.

There is no honourable way to kill, no gentle way to destroy. There is nothing good in war. Except its ending.

When a crime is committed and the police arrive to investigate, the prime suspect is always the person who will benefit from what has occurred.

So who benefits from war?

War profiteers depend mainly on government contracts. At the same time governments need an excuse for spending the enormous amounts of money required, for example, 'national security', 'peace forces,' 'the war on terror.' It follows that if war profiteers depend on government contracts then they need to be in positions to influence decision-making. Throughout the years they have positioned themselves to have massive political power within government.

The way this works is for the individuals to move between government and corporation. This has become known as the revolving door – a former military general or a member of a defence ministry moves to a corporation that manufactures weapons. They then become defence contractors, taking all knowledge of both sides of the fence. The reverse applies when say the head of a weapons manufacturing corporation moves to a government defence body. They then become influential in who gets what in a contract.

There are many examples of the revolving door. Dick Cheney being an example, when he went from being the Secretary of Defence to the CEO of Halliburton to Vice-President of USA.

Just to mention two in the UK; Julian Scopes is BAE Systems' most senior political lobbyist and a former MoD civil servant, Scopes is reported to have retained his all-area pass to the MoD, where he could easily view confidential information. BAE has not confirmed or denied whether other senior members of staff have similar access. In another case Lord Inge, Chief of Defence Staff from 1994-1997, became Non-executive Chairman at Aegis Defence Services.

Heavy lobbying happens when companies have an official role in making policy and contract decisions.

Examine the European Union to see how this works. For many years the arms industry tried hard to influence Brussels's decision makers, promoting the concept that a strong military Europe needs a strong arms industry. While drafting the text for the constitution the European Convention's working group on defence invited a number of 'experts' to give advice on what should be included in the treaty text. Three of the thirteen experts represented the interest of the arms industry: Corrado Antonini, president of the European Defence Industries Group. Anthony Parry from BAE Systems and Jean-Louis Gergorin from EADS. The message of a strong European arms industry for a strong military Europe was there.

A similar situation exists in the USA with the Defence Policy Board, which was created in 1985, made up of 30 plus representatives of industry, technology and military contractors. The Defence Policy Board meets four times a year to advise the Secretary for Defence on what weapon systems to buy, what countries are 'threats' where they need a 'pre-emptive strike', what country should they occupy. For example, in 2006 the Defence Policy Board includes Jack Sheehan who was in the US Marine Corps, General in NATO, and Supreme Allied Commander in the Atlantic who left the military and became Senior Vice President at Bechtel. Bechtel is one of the largest contractors groups in the world, and has one of the largest contracts in Iraq to work on its 'reconstruction.'

In many countries war profiteers can legally donate large sums of money to political candidates in turn they expect their loyalty when votes come up for weapons systems. Of course bribery also takes place. In the US there are many instances of Congress voting for contracts that the Pentagon has not even asked for, but the corporation has a 'special friend' in Congress who has pushed the defence contract through.

Weapon manufacturers have become so powerful that they can tell the government what they want and don't want. BAE Systems (formerly British Aerospace) has told the UK government that if they do not buy from them they will pull out of the UK and go to the US. According to the US

Department of Defence, BAE Systems (they dropped the word 'British' to become more trans-national) was the Pentagon's seventh largest supplier in 2005. The companies claim that they leave the moral decisions to the government, and they are 'only doing their patriotic duty' by responding to what the government needs.

War profiteer are not only those that benefit from the arms industry, but also those that impulse military action and elaborate strategies to profit from war.
The Broken Rifle. Sept 2006.

During the 119 years between Napoleons defeat at Waterloo and the founding of the Bank of England. England was at war for 56 years, most of the rest of the time we were either rebuilding after it or preparing for it. The few who prospered were the bankers, since they are now the most powerful people in the world and throughout history, it is these same bankers who have financed both sides in every single conflict, they control the politicians who justify the reasons to go to war and the media that drip feeds us with validation, misinformation and propaganda.

War is a business and in business having an interest in your competitors firm is ironically known as a conflict of interest.

Military men are just dumb stupid animals, to be used as pawns in a foreign policy.
Henry Kissinger.

The Battle of the Somme
On the first day we lost nearly 60,000 men with the dead numbering almost a third of them. It remains the worst day in the history of the British army. The Somme was a joint French and British operation, and during the four-month offensive the British suffered 420,000 casualties, the French nearly 200,000 and an estimate put the losses of German soldiers at about 500,000.
Both of my grandfathers fought in on of the bloodiest battles of the First World War but they never talked about their respective versions of the Great War, it was not until late in their lives that I was told. Unlike many of their friends and comrades they had lived to tell the tale, but no … they never talked about it.

I remember how moved they were by Remembrance Day when the fallen are honoured and now I realise, a little, what an effect all this must have had upon them.

'*They shall not grow old, as we who are left grow old;*

Age shall not weary them, nor the years condemn.
At the going down of the sun and in the morning.
We will remember them.'

L Binyon. For the Fallen (1914)

Wonderful words, they touch my heart and I fight with tears whenever I read them, they convey loss, give respect and invite remembrance and they solemnly acknowledge the sacrifice of hundreds of thousands of good men lost to the long dead silence of the past.

Remembrance of that waste, their sacrifice and that horror is a right and proper thing.

But in addition our minds should remember which wars in history were really worth fighting? What triggered them? Why are they allowed to begin? What action of the ego made them start; stupidity, greed, anger or wickedness?

The old men that start them and run them from the safety and luxury of home play no part in the battles, but they are resolved to send other mothers sons to fight with other mothers sons. We should not tolerate this and then by ending it, before it starts, seek some measure of comfort in its absence rather than in its being. Let's allow the men with rampaging egos, who seek very different agendas; more power, more control, more money, more glory and more revenge, let those who want war let them go and find it amongst themselves, if it's what they really want, I doubt even a punch would get thrown such is the substance of bullies.

The cause of war is fat old egoic men, ugly faiths and the desire for power, the lust of control, false propaganda, lies and deceit, constructed programmed bigotry, money and acquisition.

We would be well served to remember this the next time we are called upon.

That I feed the hungry, forgive an insult, and love my enemy – these are great virtues. But what if I should discover that the poorest of the beggars and most impudent of offenders are all within me, and that I stand in need of the alms of my own kindness; that I am myself the enemy who must be loved – what then?

C G Jung.

I think now, looking back, we did not fight the enemy; we fought ourselves. The enemy was in us.

Platoon. Oliver Stone.

Water

Apparently we are about 65% water and a cow is 74% and yet we view ourselves as solid.

We can only drink a small fraction of all the water on earth; the rest is poisonous because of the salt it contains. Although there is just over two teaspoons of normal salt in a litre of seawater confusingly there are other chemicals we call salts. Seawater is strange in that if we drink it we would be poisoned and yet it is the same as what we sweat and cry.

Estimates pronounce that the earth is 3.8 billion years old. The same amount of water has been around throughout that time; nothing added nothing taken away. Most of the Earth's water is undrinkable. If a large bucket of water were to represent the seawater on the planet – an eggcup would represent the amount of water locked in ice caps and water is continuously recycled as a result of evaporation driven by solar energy. This cycle is estimated to consume more energy in a day than that used by humankind over its entire history.

About 70 percent of freshwater goes into irrigation but in some places half or more of it never reaches the fields because of leaks and evaporation. Irrigated land in the developing world is expected to increase by 20 percent and water withdrawals for irrigation by 14 percent in the next 25 years, since irrigation increases the yield of most crops by 100 to 400 percent.

It takes, 1,000 times more water to grow food for an individual than to meet that person's needs for drinking. It takes one cubic metre of water to produce a kilogramme of wheat. And it costs 90 US cents to desalinate a cubic metre of water, making sea water an unlikely source for food production. Regions that are pumping out ground water faster than aquifers can be recharged include the Western United States, Northern China, Northern and Western India, North Africa and West Asia.

Some of the world's freshwater resources are simply disappearing. They include the Aral Sea, which covered 68,000 square kilometres in 1960 and has since lost 60 percent of its area and 80 percent of its volume; Lake Chad, which has shrunk to about one fifth of its former size in 40 years; and the Colorado River, which no longer reaches the sea in the dry season.

UNESCO. The New Courier Oct 2003.

There are 1.3 billion people in this world who do not have access to a glass of clean water.

RWE/Thames water is England's worst polluter and its debt-choked corporate parent makes for a toxic combination. Liquid thinking? That's what the water giant prides itself on. The trouble is if not properly contained, liquid tends to leak and it makes a big mess.

German owned RWE AG made its name in the energy sector but through acquisitions, it's now a leader in the water industry. RWE is the parent company of Thames Water, a British water company fully owned since 2000, RWE controls more than 600 subsidiaries, and Thames Water serves as the operational manager of RWE's international water business including the management of U.S subsidiary American Water Works. Thames water serves 70 million people across the world with water and wastewater services.

RWE's combined operations have earned a spot at number 78 on the global fortune 500 list, higher than any of the other private water companies. Fortune lists RWE's revenue as 50.9 billion dollars, with an annual profit of 2.657 billion dollars. Or, in other words, a revenue equal to the *combined* gross national income of Armenia, Burundi, the Central African Republic, Chad, the Republic of Congo, Croatia, Eritrea, Guinea, Haiti, People's Republic of Lao, Kyrgyz Republic, Lesotho, Malawi, Mauritania, Moldova, Mongolia, Mozambique, Namibia, Nicaragua, Niger, Papua New Guinea, Rwanda, Sierra Leone, Tajikistan and Togo!

RWE's annual revenue is equal to the combined income of the 153.2 million people in these countries.

Not only is Thames water known for its remarkable pollution record – it has missed its targets to fix water leaks in London three years running. More than 250 million gallons of water are lost daily. This is enough to supply 500,000 homes. A £2 billion plan, "Thames Tideway", to fix sewers owned by Thames Water, was scrapped in August 2004– raising fears of returning to "the Great Stink"– a not so memorable period in 1858. The plan would have cost an extra £40 per year. Instead, Thames water initiated a hosepipe ban in London and warned of fines for any household that violated. Thames Water also reduced water pressure to avoid further pipe breaks, forcing homeowners to install pumps to use their showers.

Water bills levied by the company rose by 99 per cent during the decade following the 1989 privatisation of England's water systems. In 1995, Thames Water slashed investment in infrastructure by £350 million, but the reduction in expenditure only benefited shareholders.

Thames Water and parent RWE push infrastructure cost on consumers instead of taking responsibility for repairing the leaking pipes with its massive profits. Thames Water's true consumer interest is to suck as much money as possible into the corporation, to increase its profits and leave investments dormant as long as possible to record sky high profits. While Thames was financially squeezing consumers and refraining from fixing the leaks, Londoners were told to conserve- London's Mayor Livingston asked Londoners to refrain from flushing if just taking 'a pee.'

www.citizen.org/cmep/water/

Water may well become the future currency of the world.

G Scofield.

It is only a matter of time as our most precious asset becomes scarcer. Prepare the next generation for water tokens. All you will need to buy them is a retina scan or a transmission from the microchip in your head, your thumb will be placed onto a red light that scans you for your fingerprints or activation by your personalised microchip will institute proceedings. By the good grace of the New World Order you will then be allowed to pay for your monthly ration. You won't hand over any money of course, money will not exist anymore and the computer will credit your allowance.

There will be no resistance to this 'normal' behaviour – it is being programmed into us right now.

Words ... provoking thought

Kill one person and you are a murderer
Kill many and you are a conqueror.

Fascism is Capitalism in decline.

Lenin.

'He always wanted to know what was over the next fence and as he got older the fence got a little higher.'

The words of the father of David Hicks
a Guantanamo Bay detainee.

For every action there is an equal and opposite reaction.

Isaac Newton.

For every thought or action there will be an effect.

We are what we think, having become what we thought.

Light cannot be seen, it can only be known.

Walter Russell.

We have been chosen, by fate or providence or whatever you wish to call it. As far as we can tell, we are the best there is. We may be all there is. It's an unnerving thought that we may be the living Universes supreme achievement and its worst nightmare simultaneously.

Bill Bryson. A Short History of Nearly Everything.

The fact that we view ourselves at the head of a linear development and we head in prowess and success as the best and highest form of life we are aware of is great for our morale as a species. But if some event occurs in the future to eradicate us from the planet, leaving behind nothing but cockroaches and bacteria, then there is a justifiable argument to say these organisms were actually more successful than us.

Our image of the World is little more than light being converted by the brain.

If you only walk on sunny days you will never reach your destination.

A M Johnston.

An old Indian woman found a snake frozen.
    She picked up the snake and gently put into her bag.
    She reached her home and placed the snake near her fire.
    The warmth from the fire slowly brought the snake back to life.
    The woman opened the door to her house and showed him the door saying.
    'Go … be a snake.'
    The snake crawled towards the woman's door halted and bit her.
    As she lay dying, the woman asked the snake, 'why did you bite me?'
    The reptile replied, 'Because I'm a snake.'

You only needs two tools in life … WD-40 to make things go, and duct tape to make things stop.

G. Wellacher

The strong take from the weak, but the smart take from the strong.

I think we are drawn to dogs because they are the inhibited creatures we might be if we weren't certain we knew better. They fight for honour at the first challenge, make love with no moral restraint, and they do not for all their marvellous instincts appear to know about death. Being such wonderfully uncomplicated beings, they need us to do their worrying.

G B Evans.

Clones are people two.

We do not receive wisdom, we must discover it for ourselves, after a journey through the wilderness, which no one else can make for us, which no one can spare us, for our wisdom is the point of view from which we come at last to regard the world.

Marcel Proust.

Even in these days of 'girl power', there is no such thing as studdess. In any event girls whether you want it or not you have always had power over us mere men, you just allowed us to think we had it.

I walked into the barbers to get my hair cut and there was no one in the operations end so I wandered through to the back room.

Four girls broke immediately from their conversation like I had caught them doing something naughty, sensing I was onto something I asked.

'What was I interrupting?'

'Oh,' said Cathy, 'just talk of you men.'

'Really?' I said, 'now that it's just you and me can you please just tell me, how you get away with – all you get away with?'

Cathy's Irish blue eyes sparkled as she shared 'the secret' with me.

'You see David, the truth is that it's us girls that bring you men up.'

You cannot beat a revelatory moment like that. There are good men who have gone before me – they have been born and they have died and they have not known this simple truth.

You woke every day with nothing to worry about. This is possible. We live in an abundant World and there is room on this planet for every single individual to share abundance. We have however, given away our power to those who seek to govern and control us. We should be mindful that it is we; the masses that hold this pyramid of power aloft and by our collective conscience could therefore bring it down.

We could start a revolution from our beds.

John Lennon

X-rated

Univited Communcation?

Now I can't tell you where and when I got to know about this one – I feel like I have bared enough of myself in this book (beware ego alert). But I distinctly remember that this was *not* one of the things they told me as I was growing up.

A friend of mine, who shall remain nameless (because we haven't yet discussed the amount of money I want for my silence – so this – just like the subject, is a somewhat sensitive area), following advice, went to get his prostate checked.

Now for those of you that don't know, the prostate is a small walnut shaped gland that is most easily accessed through the anus. The medical profession tells us men that we should get it checked out every few years after we turn 50.

So my friend duly attended his appointment in his local hospital and was asked to assume 'the position' while a very attractive nurse (which cannot have helped the ensuing situation), stuck a very well lubricated finger up his bottom in search of the aforementioned prostate gland.

My friend, Paul Smith, 51 years of age, of 17 Acacia Ave (just kidding – I told you we haven't agreed terms), recounting the story my friend then mentioned that he immediately became the possessor of an erection like he hadn't seen since he was 14ish – an erection of such proportions that he was proud of for a millisecond until he remembered the circumstances that he was in.

The kind nurse reassured him that this occurrence was only natural, not at all unusual and she had seen it all before.

Thirty years ago, the same guy and another friend had to share a bed in a hotel. They had ordered two rooms and both these guys were considered firmly heterosexual and they were both married with families. The hotel was full and the best they could do was offer the lads one bed to share, one guy took it philosophically and was content to share, the other insisted the hotel put a sheet of marine ply down the middle of the bed thus preventing any unintentional man contact during the night, which incidentally passed without further incident.

Thirty years on and now he knows two facts – marine ply keeps two friends separate but a well-lubricated finger can change your world.

Things that also rank as X-rated are the things that are censored from us as we are growing up.

We are programmed to win and censored from how to handle defeat, so perhaps we are mistaken in wanting to win so much, maybe if the massive importance we place upon winning was placed somewhere more constructive we would have at our disposal an enormous amount of energy, and with this energy we could help to gain a balance in the World.

Wouldn't it be nice if instead of taking endless queues of hundreds of thousands of hopefuls, people who stand very little chance of winning a competition and bask in a brief moment to obtain what we are programmed into - this thing we call celebrity, fame and approval and are judged by people who are the real financial winners? At the end of these programmes having witness one 'winner' they, along with all the other contestants will have been exploited, and all those tens of thousands of 'losers' will be broken and likewise used to amuse. Why can't we let the people in those queues know that if they were all able to express their talent and discover without the falsehoods of aspirational wanting - to just 'die' if they won and perish, fade and die anyway if they lost, what else might they do with their lives?

Because to teach is to demonstrate.

So what if at the age when we make that extremely difficult transition from master to mister like Martha Lucia Espinosa who at this age around 15 was studying and teaching seminars on neo-Gnostic principles, which were based on three creeds:

The death of the ego self, rebirth of the real self, sacrifice for Humanity – that is to teach the first through the experience of the second.

Not for a second am I suggesting that as master morphs into Mister would the fully programmed child we have made want to study the simple truth of how to live a loving, abundant, constructive, healthy life by simply understanding and living by the above tenets, of course most of them would reject such folly, but it is only because by the tender age of 15 they are filled with other ideas, concepts and beliefs – they understand self and violence, hypocrisy and mask wearing, they seek competition, fame, fortune, celebrity and aspire to all the values we have groomed them to admire.

But just where do all the losers go?

Contrary to popular belief and despite what the films we watch teach us, there is no belief worth killing for and there is no cause worth dying for, the only reason we seek glory in either of these falsehoods is because we have been instilled to think they have value.

As the song says – you've got to search for the hero inside yourself. The hero is in you and not 'out there' somewhere, when we worship idols that's precisely what we are doing, being idol – projecting our lives onto someone else and not fulfilling our own genuine potential. Fear has won us over, we are being too lazy to try or more accurately, we just don't stand a chance, not a snowflake in Hells chance, of being a hero and have reluctantly fallen to the power of programming, and if we could take all those children and give them the tools to all be heroes the world becomes a different place.

You

If you really put a small value upon yourself, rest assured that the world will not raise your price.

Take care when you look at your face in the mirror in the morning. For the face that looks out of the mirror should be a pleasant face and although you may not see it again until tomorrow, others will.

The spirit is the reality that endures, I am spirit, and I endure, the tenant of many fleshy tenements.

There is only one 'I' in the world because all the rest are you's.

Whether you think you can or you think you can't – you're probably right.
                                                        Henry Ford.

Optimists and pessimists will be born and will die the same, but they will have led very different lives

Life is a gamble against terrible odds … If it were a bet you wouldn't take it.
                                                        Mark Twain.

If you have not considered how special you are it is about time you did. Consider some of the odds against you being here and realise you are a miracle in form.

You read these words clinging to the Earth whilst hurtling through space at 66,000 miles per hour. Your father produced in one emission, enough sperm to fertilise most of the women in Northern Europe. One of those sperm fought a battle with millions of his travelling companions to be first to penetrate one of your mother's eggs. You are a winner just by being alive.

The world is most consistent, it was here before you arrived and it will still be here after you have decided to leave, what you make of it all in the interim while you're here is what is important.

How you think – your emotional set point – will attract what you think about. This is your blank canvas before programming hits you.

You are a bright and shinning star, don't let anything or anyone try and dull your light, you have value, you are a miracle that beat incalculable odds to be here.

Go take what is yours.

We are not human beings, we are humans becoming.

How much longer are you going to let your energy sleep?

How much longer are you going to stay oblivious to the immensity of yourself?

Don't lose time in conflict; lose no time in doubt – time can never be recovered and if you miss an opportunity it may take many lives before another comes your way again.

Bhagwan Shree Rajneesh.

All esotericism teaches is that in order to go up you have to go down, and no one understands what this means: to get more you must go down. And to get less you go in the same way as you always go- you're Being transmits your life. If you have nothing at the present that satisfies you completely, it is because of the state of your Being, and you will never get what you want as long as your being is tuned into that wavelength.

You have to change yourself to get new influences, and changing yourself is always 'getting rid of yourself' …

If you try to increase yourself as you are, you will only become worse than you are at the present. The development of Real Will consists of feeling new influences.

Excerpt from Psychological Commentaries on the Teachings of Gurdjieff and Ouspensky, by Maurice Nicoll. M.D.

The reason why we are disenchanted with ourselves is because we entertain in the depths of our psyche, a kind of vision – an anticipated vision of what we could be, if we would be, what we might be.

Sufi master, Pir Vilayat Khan, in a lecture 10.10.1983.

In my own notes I had at first labelled this defence ('The Jonah Complex'), the fear of one's own greatness or the evasion of one's destiny or the running away from one's own best talent … it is certainly possible for us to be greater than we are in actuality.

We all have unused potentialities or not fully developed ones.

It is certainly true that many of us evade our constitutionally suggested vocations

... so often we run away from the responsibilities dictated (or rather suggested) by nature, by fate, even sometimes by accident, just as Jonah tried in vain to run away from his fate.

From The Farther Reaches of Human Nature. Abraham Maslow.

If you're having a tough time in life and seek inspiration, I would urge you to read a small book, 'The Greatest Miracle in the World,' by Og Mandino. According to accounts of his life he was the stereotypical down and out alcoholic. At the age of 35 both his wife and child had left him, depressed and seeing no way forward he went to a gun shop to buy a gun and end his life.

In the store he realised he could not quite afford to buy the gun and decided to live a little longer, at least until he could afford it.

He worked, taking any job he could find and started to spend more and more times in free libraries where his appetite for consumption of the thousands of self-help books replaced his need for alcohol. In one of these libraries he found the book that would change his life, by W. Clement Stone called, 'Success Through a Positive Mental Attitude.'

Og Mandino's life changed by adopting Stone's philosophy and he began working for his mentors insurance company. Within a year he was promoted to sales manager and formed a sales team, which broke all previous, company sales records. He took a week off work and rented a typewriter. His mother had told him that he would be a famous writer one day and the dream of writing had never faded from his heart. In 1976, Mandino resigned from sales and wrote full time and he was invited to lecture. He produced 'The Greatest Salesman in the World. He died in 1996 and his books still sell by the thousand every year.

'The Greatest Miracle in the World' is a short story and Og acts as an intermediary, a channel, between God and You.

We are all in the gutter, but some of us are looking at the stars.

Oscar Wilde.

No matter what our age, each of us longs to remember who we truly are. Each of us longs to finally come 'home.' Going down through the layers is not the only way to tap into and directly experience the peace and freedom that is your Source. There are so many other ways that can take place in every moment of your daily life.
My experience is, once you've had a full awakening to this that you really are, Source keeps nagging you. It just won't leave you alone! Once you've journeyed home, home keeps beckoning you again and again. Truth keeps calling you into itself,

until finally you fall so in love with it that you're not willing to do anything that would take you away from it.

Brandon Bays. The Journey.

A human being is a part of the whole called by us Universe, a part limited in time and space. He experiences himself, his thoughts and feelings as something separated from the rest, a kind of optical delusion of his consciousness. This delusion is a kind of prison for us, restricting us to our personal desires and to affection for a few persons nearest to us. Our task must be to free ourselves from this prison by widening our circle of compassion to embrace all living creatures and the whole of nature in its beauty.

Albert Einstein.

Each time a person stands up for an ideal, or acts to improve the lot of others … he sends forth a tiny ripple of hope, and crossing each other from a million different centres of energy and daring, those ripples build a current that can sweep down the mightiest walls of oppression and resistance.

Robert F Kennedy. (1925-1968)

No one is useless in this world who lightens the burden of it for anyone else.

Charles Dickens.

'Come on in, and try not to ruin everything by being you.'

As Good as it Gets. Mark Andrus.

Yesterday is but today's memory; tomorrow is today's dream.

Kahlil Gibran.

To know the sweetness of the Infinite within us, that is the cause, the reason, the purpose, the only purpose of our being.

Nicholas of Cusa. (1401-1464).

Some type of consciousness had to be present in that single microscopic cell to develop into a foetus, create all the organs, the tremendously intricate brain and your spinal cord, and all the other incredible complexities of your fully formed body. Spirit was within you at the moment of conception, and then it divided that one cell into two, and then divided each resulting cell again and again until, in the short space of approximately 280 days, you emerged comprised of some 63 trillion cells. And every one of those cells, from first to last, contains Spirit; just as every cell of your adult body still contains the Consciousness Power of the Universe. Consider for a moment the great wonder of this!

Marta Hiatt. Mind Magic.

A man's life is what his thoughts make it.

Marcus Aurelius.

You have to leave the city of your comfort and go unto the wilderness of your intuition. What you'll discover will be yourself.

Alan Alda.

You are who you are because of where you have been. The experiences that you have subjected yourself to have resulted in making, you, who you are.

The past is written and unchangeable, the future is open to scepticism and romance, all we possess is this moment, this moment is called NOW.

So it doesn't matter; if you're rich man, poor man, beggar man or thief, all that we own is right NOW – this moment – the present.

We should try and use it wisely.

Remember your past is written so don't live there, the future can only be affected by what you now.

'Some people walk in the rain whilst others get wet.' I love that one, again I can't remember the author and I got it from somewhere way back when, but remembering to walk in the rain and not think about it in a negative way is a guaranteed way to feel so much better. You know the feeling and it is a good way of measuring your emotional set point – how you are feeling, what you're thinking about and therefore what you are manifesting and drawing to you.

The penny dropped for me and realisation dawned soon after hearing this old adage. I was walking the dog wishing I was somewhere else, I was probably going to be late for where I thought it was I wanted to be next – getting soaked – getting stressed and vibrating badly. As we turned around on our hurried walk, I hesitated and admired the trees, the leaves were shinning brightly as the rain had touched them, all around seemed clean and new and the thought of nature and its beauty was therefore allowed to enter my stressed head.

I looked at the dog and smiled inwardly, had another word with myself and lifted my emotional set point a couple of notches. All of a sudden I got it – we were still walking in the rain – the world had not altered – but I had. We need to remember to practise this often so that it becomes habitual. I try, but admit to forgetting too often.

There are three perceptions of the self; how we think others see us – how they really see us – and how we really are. The irony within this is that, we can only be who we really are, because there is little or nothing we can do about the first two.

The next two quotes confirm and develop this idea;

The highest courage is to dare to appear to be what one is.

John Lancaster Spalding.

To thine own self be true.

William Shakespeare.

When you get what you want in your struggle for self,
And the world makes you king for a day.
Just go to the mirror and look at yourself,
And see what the man has to say.
For it isn't your father or mother or wife
Who judgement upon you must pass.
The fellow whose verdict counts most in your life
Is the one staring back in the glass
Some people may think you a straight- shooting' chum,
And call you a wonderful guy.
But the man in the glass says you're only a bum
If you can't look him straight in the eye.
He's the fellow to please, never mind all the rest,
For he's with you clear up to the end.
And you've passed your most dangerous, difficult test
If the man in the glass is your friend.
You may fool the whole world down the pathway of life
And get pats on your back as you pass.
But the final reward will be heartache and tears,
If you've cheated the man in the glass.

The Man in the Glass. Dale Winbrow (1934).

A little more about You.

On certain easily accessible levels we know who we are. You know your name, your age, who your relatives are; you know what you like and what you don't like. These symbols make up you. Whilst these tags, labels, tastes and desires might represent you, they cannot give the full picture nor tell the entire story.

In the matter-based environment in which we live we search for identity. We are also inclined to search for the identity of others in perhaps what is an attempt to measure and compare ourselves.

We scan and are scanned by those we know and those we meet. People watching is a fabulous tool, an incite into trying to discover what makes others tick and in the mirror of that experience we will very often discover something new about ourselves.

One of the reasons we watch soaps, reality shows, gossip with one another, read papers and those glossy magazines, for example, is to gain incite into the lives and identity of others. But we know this is not the whole story, the story of *you* cannot be told by your tastes, your desires, your wants needs and requirements.

Know thyself – now that is a tough one.

But the ability to know yourself is available. Just as the ability to know someone else is impossible, we can gauge and measure someone, we can love them for what we know of them and perceive them as being, but very often we fail to know them and we fill that space with massive amounts of assumption. When our love goes wrong and it invariably does, it is because we have dropped the masks that the ego made when we thought we could find ourselves made whole – made One – by another human being, a person we thought we loved and in the doing forgot how much we required of them – for comfort, sex, self-esteem, money, so your Mum would stop asking … when are you going to settle down? – So your Dad will stop telling you that you will die lonely and alone – to escape your environment – for a better life together – because you would be more together – together, because she said she would leave you if you did not commit – then she said if you did commit she would never leave you – because she filled your heart?

Trust and respect is built based upon tradition and both these qualities are constructed because of our personal involvement or because of hearsay.

We all know of stories of what we considered to be great relationships between a couple, who may have raised children and spent half a lifetime together, for one of the partners to walk away from the relationship and disappear leaving the other partner to ruminate and perhaps state 'I thought I knew him.'

The businessman who comes home from work and murders his family,' he just snapped, even he doesn't know why' said one of the neighbours, 'he seemed such a decent man.'

The elderly mother presented with the evidence of her beloved meek and mild mannered son, who it transpires is mass-murderer, the initial denial and the pain of realisation that she too never knew him.

The ability to know yourself is available according to the world's great spiritual traditions. They all state that below the threshold of ordinary consciousness there lies a different self. A bright immaculate identity that is the true nature of the individual.

By peeling away the false ego constructed layers, as one would the layers of an onion our true Creative Source and the authentic You can be revealed however this is a quest that only you can make.

We entered this material realm as that pure Creative Consciousness tainted only with the elements of ego and we leave this material world with this indefinable entity that we have come to call our soul, this part of God.

As we grow from birth to death we are programmed, just as we programme ourselves with false individuality.

Much is sealed away from our immediate awareness by walls constructed in the mind by the earlier programmed experiences of our lives and the portals to knowing are guarded by our emotions who act as doormen and resist our 'access to all areas.'

Is that why we all want to be VIP's?

As long as the egoic mind is running your life, you cannot truly be at ease; you cannot be at peace or fulfilled except for brief intervals when you obtain what you wanted, when a craving has been fulfilled. Since the ego is a derived sense of self, it needs to be both defended and fed constantly. The most common ego identifications have to do with possessions, the work you do, social status and recognition, knowledge and education, physical appearance, special abilities, relationships, personal and family history, belief systems, and often also political, nationalistic, racial, religious, and other collective identifications. None of these is you.

The Power of Now. Eckhart Tolle.

If you can accept that your body is not a solid but a mass of vibrating atoms, then it is the body that is your spacesuit that allows you to survive in this matter-based dimension.

Then what is the essence of soul, which is housed in the body?

The nearest description to describe the metaphysical aspect of soul might be that it is made up of three components;

Spirit – giving us access to the divine life force.

Mind – the creative and formative principal by which we, should or could build with the life force.

Will – the aspect that gives us individuality and the freedom of allowing us to create.

The YOU that is You causes separateness, our own bodies that define us in turn enable this separateness. Without our bodies we return to Universal Source Energy with a desire to return to Oneness via spirit – we are all One Consciousness experiencing life subjectively – you are me and I am you and only our ego prevents us from accepting this and keeps us from this knowledge.

Zimbardo Dr P.

Dr Phillip Zimbardo, an eminent psychologist ran what became known as the Stanford Prison Experiment. In 1971, a group of volunteers were divided equally into prisoners and warders. Using classic prison ploys aimed at dehumanising the prisoners, the experiment soon degenerated to the point where it had to be abandoned. The study given over to this experiment has been extensive and reveals many interesting dynamics about the nature of the human condition.

One of the most interesting of these dynamics is the roles played by 'normal' young men and their responses that affected them to the extent they demonstrated how many of us respond when asked to perform certain roles.

It is a demonstration on many levels but indicative of how easy it is for 'good' men to perform with evil intent.

'It wasn't until much later that I realised how far into my prison role I was.' Zimbardo observed in retrospect, 'that I was thinking like a prison superintendent rather than a research psychologist.'

Zimbardo went on to say, 'less than 36 hours into the experiment. Prisoner no.8612 began suffering from acute emotional disturbance, disorganised thinking, uncontrollable crying, and rage. In spite of all of this, we had already come to think so much like prison authorities that we thought he was trying to con us – to fool us into releasing him' – furthermore, the Zimbardo 'guards' were escalating their abuse of prisoners in the middle of the night when they thought no researchers were watching and the experiment was off. Their boredom had driven them to ever more pornographic and degrading abuse of the prisoners. This included middle-of-the-night strip searches, making the prisoners clean the toilets with their hands and tripping them when they walked past. It demoralised the volunteers so thoroughly that they lost all sense of the artificiality of the project.

The article above was extracted from The Guardian (16th October 2001), it described how the BBC was planning to re-run the Stanford Prison Experiment as a Big Brother type game show called 'The Experiment.' The article went on to say:

None of this could possibly happen in 'The Experiment,' insist the organisers. 'Zimbardo set up his experiment rather naively says Holmes. 'He didn't understand what he was getting into. Some of the worst excesses happened because there was inadequate supervision of what was going on inside. We have been able to reap the benefit of what he did, to design something that's a little more stable, a little safer. We're certain it will be more controlled.'

It was announced in late January 2002 that 'The Experiment' had been called off.

Stone walls do not a prison make, nor iron bars a cage.
Richard Lovelace 1618 – 1657.

These words may make fine poetry but the reality of our lives demonstrates that we are all incarcerated inside the structure we now find ourselves housed within. The Stanford Prison Experiment was supposed to last for two weeks and was called off after six days. The participating college students whose role were guards, became sadistic and the students who played the part of prisoners became depressed and showed signs of extreme stress.

The participating students had answered an advert calling for volunteers to partake in an experiment in the study of the psychological effects of prison life. The organisers chose 24 college students having eliminated candidates with psychological problems, medical disabilities or a history of crime. These 'normal' men were then separated arbitrarily into two groups by the flip of a coin, they then became either guards or prisoners.

The prisoners were arrested and confined by the police in Stanford County Jail and then taken into custody in their new role as prisoners. Realism was sought for as each of the men wore chains on their ankles and given an identity number, the dehumanisation stopped at shaving the men's heads as in many jails and in the military, but the men had to wear stocking hats on their heads.

The 'guards' remit was to do whatever they thought necessary to maintain law and order in the prison and to command the respect of the 'prisoners.' The guards all wore the same khaki uniforms and dark mirrored sunglasses. Dr Zimbardo said the idea for the glasses came from the film, Cool Hand Luke, he wanted the guards to hide their eyes and prevent their emotions from being read.

Boss: *'Luke. I'm just doing my job. You gotta appreciate that.'*
Luke: *'Nah – calling it your job don't make it right, Boss.'*
Cool Hand Luke. Donn Pearce and Frank Pierson.

By the end of the study the prisoners had disintegrated both as a group and as individuals. They had become in the space of a few days, much like genuine prisoners of war or hospitalised mental patients. The guards had won control of the situation and the blind obedience of each prisoner.

Dr Zimbardo mentioned one final act of rebellion. Prisoner 416 was newly admitted as one of the stand-in prisoners. Unlike the other prisoners who had experienced a gradual escalation of harassment, the new inmate experienced a more full-blown experience upon his entry. The 'old-timer' prisoners informed him that quitting was impossible, that it was a real prison. Prisoner 416 reacted by going on hunger-strike to force his request to leave. The guards failed in their attempts to get him to eat and they threw him into solitary confinement for three hours, even thought the rules stated one hour was the maximum.

He still refused and instead of becoming a hero to his fellow prisoners was seen as a troublemaker. The head-guard then exploited the situation by giving the prisoners a choice, he would release 416 from solitary if they gave up their blankets or they could leave him there all night.

The majority chose to leave 416 in solitary.

Two months after the experiment, Dr Zimbardo interviewed prisoner 416, remember this was *just* an experiment that lasted for only six days, these are his words;

'I began to feel that I was losing my identity, that the person that I called Clay, the person who put me in this place, the person who volunteered to go into this prison – because it was a prison to me; it still is a prison to me. I don't regard it as an experiment or a simulation because it was a prison run by psychologists instead of run by the state. I began to feel that identity, the person that I was that had decided to go to prison was distant from me – was remote until finally I wasn't that, I was 416. I was really my number.'

The Stanford Prison Experiment turned average college students into broken passive prisoners and sadistic overbearing guards, it remains a classic demonstration of the speed and severity in which roles can overwhelm ordinary people.

You do not have to look far to see this same dynamic work in our everyday lives.

Dr Zimbardo quotes a genuine prisoner who wrote to him from inside a Ohio penitentiary, after being in solitary confinement.

'I was recently released from solitary confinement after being held therein for thirty-seven months. The silence system was imposed upon me and if I even whispered to the man in the next cell it resulted in me being beaten by guards, sprayed with chemical mace, black-jacked, stomped, and thrown into a strip cell naked to sleep on a concrete floor without bedding, covering, wash basin, or even a toilet … I know that thieves must be punished, and I don't justify stealing even though I am a thief myself. But now I don't think I will be a thief when I am released. No, I am not rehabilitated either. It is just that I no longer think of becoming wealthy or stealing. I now only think of killing – killing those who have beaten me as if I was a dog. I hope and pray for the sake of my own soul and future life of freedom that I am able to overcome the bitterness and hatred, which eats daily at my soul. But I know to overcome it will not be easy

Rehabilitated? Well now, let me see. You know, I don't have any idea what that means … I know what you think it means. To me, it's just a made up word, a politician's word so that young fella's like yourself can wear a suit and a tie and have a job. What do you really want to know? Am I sorry for what I did? … There's not a day goes by I don't feel regret. And not because I'm in here or because you think I should. I look back on the way I was then. A young, stupid kid who committed that terrible crime. I want to talk to him. I want to talk some sense to him. Tell him the way things are. But I can't. That kid's long gone. This old man is all that's left. I gotta live with that. 'Rehabilitated?' that's just a bullshit word. So you go on and stamp your forms, sonny, and stop wasting my time. Because to tell you the truth, I don't give a shit.

The Shawshank Redemption. 1994. By Frank Darabont based on the story 'Rita Hayworth and Shawshank Redemption' by Stephen King.

Involved in the lucrative and big business of caging and incarceration, the United States is in the midst of the biggest prison building boom in history, with $37 billion dollars spent in recent years and $5 billion still in the pipeline. The prison and jail populations have tripled since 1980, and according to the 1990 census, prison cells are the fastest growing category of housing. One in 250 Americans is in a correctional facility. The United States has the highest incarceration rate in the industrialized world, and imprisons blacks at a rate four times that of apartheid South Africa.

Politicians constantly campaign about tougher laws, harsh sentencing, more prisons, want to escalate executions and raise the subject of violent juvenile crime.

The US has 2 million of its population in jail, which represents a quarter of the worlds prison population. The notorious three-strikes rule sees some inmates doing life terms for non-violent crimes, in company with murderers and psychopaths.

The animalistic image of gang youth as 'super-predators' fuels the fear vehicle in the anti-crime rhetoric of politicians. In a radio address, Presidential candidate Bob Dole used this racist image: 'Unless something is done soon, some of today's newborns will become tomorrow's super-predators – merciless criminals capable of committing the most vicious acts for the most trivial of reasons.'

A new generation has grown up since The Stanford Experiment ended so abruptly, but if we are to think things have changed we should cast our minds forward to the events at Abu Ghraib prison. The soldiers or guards were ordinary men and women who were caught up in a similar culture of prisoner abuse seduced by their power over their fellow man as demonstrated by the leaked photos of Sergeant Joseph Darby. In the few years that have passed since he showed the world photos of the abuse of prisoners by the guards, he has been hailed both hero and villain. He sought protective custody and now lives in hiding, threats to his mother and wife forced them to move from their places of birth and out of their homes.

These and similar abuses continue to occur as we have recently witnessed in the horror of places like Iraq, Afghanistan and at Guantanamo Bay.

Final Thoughts

A man who becomes a Freemason goes through an initiation ceremony that goes so far back in time no one can say when it began. In a ceremony that is older than religion, a master who wishes to become a Freemason stands before his Master, he is hooded, (hoodwinked) there is a noosed rope around his neck (Masons call it a cable-tow which became the modern day tie). The point of a sword is pressed against his chest over his quickly beating heart. He has been stripped of most of his possessions; he is left with his body, his intellect, his underpants and most significantly, his emotions. If he proceeds without permission he will perish upon the point of the sword, once the ritual initiation is over, his passage is complete. He has symbolically died and is reborn; he is reincarnated, altered, changed and initiated.

I stress again, I am not having a go at Freemasons, they like all the rest of us are trapped in a pyramidal structure where only those at the very peak are aware of the reality that has been constructed, of its workings and how to manipulate energy. As mentioned, our leaders have been altered, their software reprogrammed in a series of accepted rituals, medals, approval or disapproval, beliefs, all set in place and tested before earning the right to move ahead to the next phase, the next degree. They are puppets consumed with ego and the seductive lust of power, they are the scapegoats and they are the manifestation of a greater power by magicians who enable their control. For that reason alone we have to forgive them.

Every single one of us has been initiated through ritual and every ritual deploys the same end; the individual master may only become a Master through the commonly held thread of fear. So why fear? Because fear is our baseline, it is where we are at our most vulnerable, at our weakest, where our traumas are made deep in our subconscious, where we become possessed into worshipping the wrong ideals, the wrong gods. Fear, which is so powerful an instrument that when activated it enables our imprisonment. Fear; a largely unfounded emotion because in the unlikely event that what we fear happens, then it never happens the way it said on the tin.

Religion informs us to purify ourselves. However the washing away of our sins is a guilt trip because we are not guilty of anything unless we allow ourselves to believe it, we can only believe we have been guilty of something if we have been negatively programmed. We then do guilt and we do it by projection onto others, when we don't we turn inwards, and are inclined to hurt ourselves in a variety of ingenious ways. The reason for our projection is that we are looking at ourselves. What we don't like in another person is our guilt at what we fear in ourselves. Those that walk around angry with people are simply angry with themselves; this is true of all emotions. Experiment with this and as an alternative try forgiving them, to practice quantum forgiveness is not only to forgive those that trespass against us, it is to forgive ourselves, it is to forgive You. If we all knew we deserved and were entitled to have an abundant joyous, loving, life and were able to fully grasp this, we would have at our disposal one of the keys to life; if you hate anyone you hate yourself, if you love someone (unconditionally) you love yourself. We become confused because of the magic of the programming that imposed our beliefs. We find aspects we are repelled or drawn to in others simply because of how we feel about ourselves. That's why we are complicated, stressed and fearful over our inner conflict; the source of so much pain. However that pain is imagined, it isn't real, it is represented because we have made a decision as to what is we like and do not like and we therefore constantly judge and condemn.

To regain our power and mastery we need to understand that our thoughts guide our emotions, our emotions are how we feel, our feelings dictate how we vibrate and how we vibrate will find a matching vibration in Consciousness. When our essence, our spirit, finds a match, as a result our thoughts/emotions/feelings/vibration, have married to whatever we are asking for. Our emotions hold the key to unlocking our power. Our emotions are not who we are, but they will bring to us what we are emotional about and provide a chance to learn. Our emotions move us up and down the scale between fear and joy many times a day. What wave we choose to ride is ultimately our choice and we had that choice as we were growing up as masters until the Masters removed it. Remembering what we have forgotten would allow us to function on a more even playing field, if we were more left to our own devices, free to make choice rather than be bombarded through the many communicated manipulators that control and imprison us as we have discussed on these pages.

Our emotions are transmitting and receiving by the use of our DNA, that magical helix deep within us is calling to Consciousness, and because of our mindset much of the time we are summoning into our reality that which is of no benefit to us. In fact it is to our cost as it empowers our enslavement.

We will never meet anyone who has not been subjected to radical initiation and alteration, as long as we live in fear we never will, because in fear we are attuned to the wrong frequency, shut down and lost in the abyss. The drugs we consume, be they prescription or otherwise are all counterfeit, but they allow us to quell our imagined pain and in some cases perform a genuine solution in penetrating the veil of this reality and reveal to us that we are all One. Remove our egoic pain and guilt and the veil falls away, we see how much more joy is available to us. We can still ingest mind-altering substances safely, or dance into a trance, endure a breakdown or catharsis, suffer a sudden shock, experience a near death experience. We can get there through deep states of meditation or through ecstatic sex with one another; (but that's *not* using sex in a demonstration of power that one individual can have over another, which unfortunately represents most sex in many places throughout the World). All these things and more can enable our visitation to other realms. And it is here we discover and confirm that when we act with love in our hearts, we really can create some fascinating alternative options.

Baptism, a knighthood, your entrance into the Hells Angels, the boy scouts, the bull fight, the fox hunt, marriage, the entrance to the Lodge, your first football match, the school prefects passage, the boss, the boardroom; all change the individual. We live in a variety of boxes and to maintain their existence we have had to adapt and change in order to sustain our beliefs. Change comes by absorbing the cause and continuance of whatever war we are watching whilst in a trance like state.

Most adults and children's programming through, sport, advertising, in fact everywhere we turn, we are told to believe there must be a winner. In truth virtually every programme fired from Lucifer's dreambox indelibly informs us that we all must come out top. Have we lost so much on the way that we need others to judge us for approval? What obscenities do we commit to our bodies and our minds because of the virus of low self-esteem? In the numbers game it follows that in fact most of us are losers.

With no disrespect to my Jewish friends, when they cut that little bit off the end of your tally-whacker then that must smart a tadge. Children all over the globe endure other similar trauma-based rites of passage. Walking the maze at Chartres, covering the ground of any city, every church and cathedral all built precisely to Solomon's manipulative design, wearing that ring, sporting that tie. OK perhaps you think I'm going too far; how does wearing a tie transmit fear? It symbolises slavery; it declares your status and you go onto make judgements with friendly or opposing ties. (On this account we should invade Tie-rack).

We are highly sensitive and yet we still deny. What is occurring? What do all these traditional accepted habits and rituals share in common? You're in a state of fear and at a subconscious subatomic level you're having DNA tweaked. And at the risk of ridicule, (well hell we've come this far) your vibrational level is being reduced, your in free-fall towards being less of a human and more of a reptile. You will therefore accept further ritual, be less empathetic to all other living things, you may love your own children and think you know love but you should love all children, without exception and condition. If you don't accept this observe those who have adopted a child, because they have overcome that obstacle in a demonstration that proves the definition of love.

Reptilian downloads are cold blooded, habitualised, organised and regimented, they need power over others and are close minded. Reptiles should not be condemned; I just fervently don't want to become one of them. 'Go ahead reptiles get another blue pill into you.' My apologies for the ridicule, I am not criticising you because this is the reality you have chosen, but you know different, you know better, and I am reminding you of that simple truth.

We all know the remedy is love. Everything we do is a call for love but because of programming many of us look for it in the wrong places, with the wrong agenda and in the wrong people. Love is not the love of specialness, of individuality, worthiness, and approval, want, need and requirement. Love is not the love mentioned in the latest pop song or movie that moves your emotions. The genuine article is the love that You are, the love that you came from, the love that you feel when the masks are down. Love does not separate, it unites in empathy, love does not judge and condemn it quantumly automatically forgives, I apologise for repeating this several times, but our lives would vastly improve were we to embrace this truth. We will all return to love, part of you still resides there, you know this in your core. Every experience we encounter on this journey we call life moves us nearer or further from love.

Let's all begin to understand our individual power, summon love back into our lives and change this World in an instant. To do that we need to dispose of fear and his bedfellows and only that can be enabled when we rid ourselves of the root cause of these malcontents. Fear (the ruler of the kingdom of negative, debilitating, emotional states) is communicated to us everywhere we turn and triggered because we were programmed as we were growing up. The antidote is love and every artist, poet, musician, scribe and shaman has alluded to that, every person on this planet knows it deep down, it is written in every uncorrupted scripture throughout all religion. Many of us have either chosen or been coerced into forgetting this simple truth, but not one of us is lost. Time does not exist in the realm of whom-so-ever you choose to call your god, and your god waits forever for your return to him, to Oneness. When You return to Oneness this Universe, this reality, this life that you have chosen to experience ends, (which is a reverse of the Big Bang). To be found is a blissful, perfect place, a place we dream about but a place we are incapable of fully understanding whilst locked into this matter based 'reality.' This heaven, where neither time nor space exists, awaits you, but I won't be able to tell you when we get there, *'see … I bloody well told you so!'* … because when we meet I will be without ego and so will you. In the interim, enjoy your journey child of god.

All is well.

The much vaunted theory of relativity promotes the view that everything that exists in the material world is measurable and is therefore predictable, in relativity movement is continuous, determinate and defined. In quantum theory the opposite is true this is why most scientists have favoured the theory of relativity choosing to ignore quantum theory, as both theories are incompatible and contradictory.

In the 'reality' of relative theory … you, your cat, your favourite armchair and any one of the stars in a distant galaxy are independent objects that have no way or very limited ways of communication through our five heavily programmed senses. In the metaphysical domain of the quantum there is instant communication and that communication exists because there is no separation. This is compatible with much in Eastern philosophy and religion, the material world being Maya, defined by being nothing more than an illusion, and although we are programmed to think that we are solid physical beings moving through a physical world, this is also an illusion. As we have talked about this is also the realm of the shaman, but most importantly it should be the domain of us all and had we not been propelled down the path in the development of our intellect and the building of our ego, but instead shown the way of instinct, Oneness and enlightenment, the simple truth is our lives would be very different. This wonderful, joyous, loving way of being is I suggest, also contained within the roots of all Western religions that is before they were rewritten to conform us and to control us.

Physicist David Bohm believes that Aspect's remarkable findings, (discovering that under certain circumstances subatomic particles can instantaneously communicate with each other regardless of the distance separating them) implies that objective reality does not exist, that despite the way we perceive it we are limited and that the Universe is one colossal and magnificent hologram. To understand why Bohm makes this assertion, we must first understand a little about holograms. A hologram is a three-dimensional photograph made with the aid of a laser. To make a hologram, the object to be photographed is first bathed in the light of a laser beam. Then a second laser beam is bounced off the reflected light of the first and the resulting interference pattern, which is the area where the two laser beams mingle, is captured on film.

When the film is developed onto a plate, it looks like a meaningless swirl of light and dark. But when an additional laser beam illuminates the developed film, a three-dimensional image of the original object appears.

The three-dimensionality of such images is not the only remarkable property of the hologram because if we take the original image and cut it into ever decreasing halves the image is still preserved or in other words, every part of a hologram contains all the information possessed by the whole. This property of the hologram provides us with an entirely new way of understanding the Universe. Western science has taught us that the best way to understand a physical object is to dissect it and study its respective parts as if the parts will answer the whole. A hologram teaches us that some things in the Universe will not conform to this and certainly a hologram is one of those things.

Bohm believed one of the principles in understanding Aspect's remarkable discovery shows that subatomic particles are able to remain in contact with one another regardless of the distance separating them but this is not because they are sending some sort of mysterious signal backward and forwards, but simply because their separateness is an illusion. He argues that at some deeper level of reality such particles are not individual entities, but are actually extensions of the same fundamental One thing.

To enable people to better visualise what he means, Bohm offers the following illustration.

Imagine an aquarium containing a single fish. Imagine that you are unable to see the aquarium directly and your picture of it comes from two separate television cameras, one pointed at the aquarium's front and the other at its side. As you watch the two television monitors, you would assume that the fish on each of the screens are two separate entities. The cameras are set at different angles therefore each of the images will be different. But as you continue to watch the two fish, you will eventually become aware that there is a relationship between them. When one turns, the other also makes a slightly different but corresponding turn; when one faces the front, the other always faces toward the side. If you remain unaware of the full scope of the situation, you might even conclude that the 'two' fish must be instantaneously communicating with one another, but this is clearly not the case. This is same as the observation we made earlier regarding birds, bats, or fireflies, these seemingly separate entities act as one however they act as separate to us only as the programmed observer.

This, says Bohm, is precisely what is going on between the subatomic particles in Aspect's experiment. According to Bohm, what we assume is a faster than the speed of light connection between subatomic particles is really telling us is, is that there is a deeper level of reality that we do not understand, a more complex dimension beyond the one we are attuned to that is similar to the aquarium. And, he adds, we view objects such as subatomic particles as separate from one another because we are 'seeing' only a portion of their reality. Such particles are not separate 'parts,' but facets of a deeper and more underlying unity that is ultimately holographic. Therefore the Universe is in itself a projection, a hologram and this in part was the allegory of Plato's Cave.

These are the findings of other experiments we have discussed which enhance this theory and would explain a multitude of the things we presently cannot explain, and if we try to embark in discussion with many others we encounter we face rejection, dismay, and ridicule, well I don't care any more and I intend to wear my invisible 'I am a mad wizard badge' with pride!

David Bohm was a genius and clearly thought outside the boxes that many of us have allowed ourselves to be restrained and constricted by, unlike many geniuses he was eminently respected, furthermore he was generous with his findings, he explained that a thought is a system that not only includes thoughts and feelings, but it includes the state of the body; it includes the whole of society – as thought is passing back and forth between people in a process by which thought evolved from ancient times. Understanding his work is vitally important to mankind, his words will echo long after his passing and as he so beautifully said; 'suppose we were able to share meaning freely without a compulsive urge to impose our view or conform to those of others and without distortion and self-deception. Would this not constitute a real revolution in culture?'

If the apparent separateness of subatomic particles is illusory, it means that at a deeper level of reality all things in the Universe are infinitely and constantly interconnected and communicating with everything else.

The electrons within a carbon atom in the human brain are connected to the subatomic particles that comprise every fish in the sea, every other heart that beats, and every star that shimmers in the sky.

Everything interpenetrates everything, and although human nature may seek to categorise, box off and segregate all the various phenomena of the universe, all these things are by necessity artificial and all of nature is ultimately a seamless, timeless web, Consciousness, a Matrix or whatever name we chose to ascribe to it.

In a holographic universe, both time and space could no longer be viewed as fundamentals. Because concepts such as location break down in a universe in which nothing is truly separate from anything else, time and three-dimensional space, like the images of the fish on the TV monitors, would also have to be viewed as projections of this deep order.

At its deeper level reality is a hologram in which the past, present, and future all exist simultaneously. Allowing, for the sake of argument, that the hologram is Consciousness or the Matrix or whatever word we pin onto the web that connects everything in being and that has given birth to everything in our Universe, the bottom line is that it contains every subatomic particle that has ever been or will ever be, every configuration of matter and energy that is possible, vibrating at different frequencies, from snowflakes to stars, from us humans to light. It should be seen as a sort of cosmic warehouse of all that there is. We in turn are processors of this Universe and dependant on which setting we are attuned to is paramount to what we are capable of receiving and transmitting, if, for the many reasons we have discussed in this book, we are (for a variety of those reasons) blocked and stilted from operating on as wide a possible bandwidth (such as programming, ego construction, chemicals and unnecessary manufactured fear, manipulative architecture, media propaganda etc.) then it follows we are less than we are. We witness coincidence, synchronicity, have gut feelings, know instinctively there is so much more, crave for wholeness, make genuinely serious attempts to find our other halves, when an adjustment in our software to operate on the same bandwidth as the sages, mystics, shaman, and enlightened beings that have walked this earth is all that is necessary, and as I trust I have demonstrated on these pages those very few people who have held this power have withheld it from us because they would loose that power, the remaining people such as the shaman, or 'w-holy' people have either been silenced by eradication or their messages have been corrupted to further subjugate and control us.

Bohm stated that we have reason to assume that his super hologram will contain much more, or as he puts it, perhaps the superholographic level of reality is a 'mere stage' beyond which lies 'an infinity of further development.'

Bohm is not the only researcher who has found evidence that the Universe is a hologram. Working independently in the field of brain research, Stanford neurophysiologist Karl Pribram has also become influenced to consider the holographic nature of reality.

Pribram was drawn to the holographic model by the puzzle of how and where memories are stored in the brain. For decades numerous studies have shown that rather than being confined to a specific location, memories are dispersed throughout the brain.

In a series of landmark experiments in the 1920s, brain scientist Karl Lashley found that no matter what portion of a rat's brain he removed he was unable to eradicate its memory of how to perform complex tasks it had learned prior to surgery. The only problem was that no one was able to come up with a mechanism that might explain this curious 'the whole in every part' nature of memory storage.

Then in the 1960s Pribram encountered the concept of holography and realised he had found the explanation brain scientists had been looking for. Pribram believes memories are encoded not in neurons, or small groupings of neurons, but in patterns of nerve impulses that criss-cross the entire brain in the same way that patterns of laser light interference criss-cross the entire area of a piece of film containing a holographic image. In other words, Pribram believes the brain is in itself a hologram.

Pribram's theory also explains how the human brain can store so many memories in so little space. It has been discovered that in addition to their other capabilities, holograms possess an astounding capacity for information storage by simply changing the angle at which the two lasers strike a piece of photographic film, it is possible to record many different images on the same surface. It has been demonstrated that one cubic centimetre of film can hold as many as 10 billion bits of information.

Our uncanny ability to quickly retrieve whatever information we need from the enormous store of our memories becomes more understandable if the brain functions according to holographic principles.

Indeed, one of the most amazing things about the human thinking process is that every piece of information seems simultaneously correlated with every other piece of information, which is another feature of the hologram. Because every portion of a hologram is infinitely interconnected with every other portion, it is perhaps nature's supreme example of a cross-correlated system.

The storage of memory is not the only neurophysiological puzzle that becomes more understandable in light of Pribram's holographic model of the brain. Another is how the brain is able to translate the wave of frequencies it receives via our senses (light frequencies, sound frequencies, and so on) and into the world of our perceptions. Encoding and decoding frequencies is precisely what a hologram does best. Just as a hologram functions as a translating device able to convert an apparently meaningless blur of frequencies into a coherent image, Pribram believes the brain also uses holographic principles to mathematically convert the frequencies it receives through the senses into the inner world of our perceptions.

An impressive body of evidence suggests that the brain uses holographic principles to perform its operations. Pribram's theory, in fact, has gained increasing support among neurophysiologists.

Argentinean-Italian researcher Hugo Zucarelli recently extended the holographic model into the world of acoustic phenomena. Puzzled by the fact that humans can locate the source of sounds without moving their heads, even if they only possess hearing in one ear, Zucarelli discovered that holographic principles could explain this ability.

Zucarelli has also developed the technology of holophonic sound, a recording technique able to reproduce acoustic situations with an almost uncanny realism.

Pribram's belief that our brains mathematically construct 'hard' reality by relying on input from a frequency domain has also received a good deal of experimental support.

It has been found that each of our senses is sensitive to a much broader range of frequencies than was previously suspected.

Researchers have discovered, for instance, that our visual systems are sensitive to sound frequencies, that our sense of smell is in part dependent on what are now called 'cosmic frequencies,' and that even the cells in our bodies are sensitive to a broad range of frequencies. Such findings suggest that it is only in the holographic domain of consciousness that such frequencies are sorted out and divided up into conventional perceptions.

But the most mind-boggling aspect of Pribram's holographic model of the brain is what happens when it is married with Bohm's theory. For if the solidity of the world is but a secondary reality and what is evident is a holographic blur of frequencies, and if the brain is also a hologram and only selects some of the frequencies out of this blur and mathematically transforms them into sensory perceptions, then our present objective reality ceases to exist and our physical world is confirmed as an illusion.

We are really receivers and transmitters floating through a kaleidoscopic frequency, and what we extract from this sea and translate into physical reality is but one channel from many extracted out of the superhologram.

This striking new picture of reality, the synthesis of Bohm and Pribram's views, has come to be called the holographic paradigm, and although many scientists have greeted it with scepticism, it has galvanised others. A small but growing group of researchers believe it may be the most accurate model of reality science has arrived at but traditional institutions are extraordinarily slow to accept change especially when that change alters previously believed and programmed views. Many are starting to believe it may solve some mysteries that have never before been explainable by science and even establish the paranormal as a part of nature.

On reading this it would appear that I am a Buddhist. I am not (I would take it a compliment if anyone accused me of being one) but I empathise more with the views of Buddhism than the alternatives. It is impossible to wage war as a Buddhist and if its followers have only got this point right, then it should serve as an example to us all. They offered up no more than token, passive resistance to the Chinese who have taken over the part of the world where many of them live. Their new masters have even imposed their own Lama to replace the exiled Dali Lama who is their spiritual leader and a most remarkable man.

I looked right into the belief system of Buddhism and spent time visiting various retreats throughout England. In particular I have visited a beautiful monastery outside Newcastle a few times and as bizarre as this might sound, the light in these places seems softer, more diffused.

The monks come from all over the world and I have had the privilege to sit and talk with many of them. I have found virtually every Buddhist monk that I have engaged has a peace and calmness about them, in their eyes is a serenity that one rarely finds in the outside world. The monks never preach about their beliefs and they do not castigate any of the other world's religions.

You come to Buddhism in your own time and in your own way, there is no pressure. Similarly a monk does not have to stay within this belief system, there are no vows and he is free to walk away at any time.

In the desert in a cave there lived an elderly and reclusive Buddhist monk. He was rarely seen and few had spoken to him in the years he had lived in the cave. Every morning he would sit and contemplate in a meditative state high up on the side of the cliff near the entrance to his cave.

It was a beautiful vantage point but difficult to get to as he had to climb up a steep eighty or so metres to gain access to his home. This did not trouble the monk because he hardly ever needed to leave the place.

Three travellers had heard about the hermit monk and his profound wisdom so they journeyed the two kilometres from the nearest village in the hope of seeing and engaging him. They sought some enlightenment from him and had curiosity in talking with a man who had given over his life to living this way.

The walk did not take long and soon they reached the bottom of the cliff face below the monks cave. They saw him as they neared him; he was sitting cross-legged, as still as the rock ledge upon which he sat as he looked out to the east.

As the men drew near they knew better than disturb his stillness, so they sat on the ground and talked quietly amongst each other until the old man stirred himself. He pulled himself to his feet, brushed himself down and peering over the ledge he bowed to them in acknowledgement and wished them all 'good day.'

The three travellers called back to him, returning his complement.

'We have walked to see you because we have heard about you as many have, and we wondered if we could do anything to help you?' said the traveller's spokesman.

'No, but thank you I have everything I need, but you are most kind.' Said the monk bowing his head slightly.

'We have some water would you care for some?' said the traveller.

'No, no thank you,' said the monk pointing towards the rocks, 'there is a spring up here just around that corner and the water from it is most pure, in the years I have been here it has never gone dry,'

'How do you get food, we have some are you not hungry?' asked the traveller.

'No,' said the monk,' thank you but every night I lower down a basket on a rope and when I pull it up every morning there is food in it.'

'Well, that is both wonderful and remarkable,' said the traveller,' but what would happen if it was empty when you pulled it up?'

To which the monk replied, 'in all the time I have been here – that has never happened.'

This story shows some of the aspects of Buddhism and we can all learn from this. We can be more trusting of this Universe and more mindful of others. We don't need to have loads of 'things' that need dusting, guarding, paying for, watching and worrying about.

We can just take a chance, break from habit and strike out in any direction, if your mind is right you will be just fine and conversely if it isn't then your going to be exposed to what you need to learn, but you and only you can allow it. It requires courage but the rewards will manifest and the journey will make sense at some stage.

When we think right, the right things happen.

We must walk consciously only part way toward our goal and then leap in the dark to our success.

Henry David Thoreau.

You can do anything you want in life providing it does not hurt anyone else and is appropriate to you.

A Rankin.

How should we therefore conduct ourselves in order to lead more meaningful lives? What is the philosophy should we adopt? We could try and dissolve the ego, which contains the social masks we wear to protect ourselves and to get the bright and shiny things that we think we want. Dissolving the ego gradually (and do not underestimate the battle - I lose it every day) will bring us closer to one another and lessen our separateness and begin the process of the recognition of Oneness that we are.

We could clarify the real meanings of the word love, perhaps think of another communicative symbol to discern between conditional (I will love you if you behave in a certain way), special (look at me, am I not wonderful?), romantic (you complete me because I am incomplete without you) and the very different, unconditional love ... that is the love that we are, the love we seek, the love we yearn for and are compounded to return to.

There are many other words that should be redefined, words that have opposite meanings – master, magic, drugs, crime, reality and so on.

We could allow children to learn different values, instead of programming them to be obsessed with specialness, and communicating to them that they must be unique, famous, prettiest, fastest, a winner, the very best, because this is an egotistic trap to lure us into separation and the belief that we are different. Within our ego reality we are urged into the segregation that separation brings with it, from all this falsehood we classify each other as being better or worse by this preposterous form of judging, we are completely at odds with one another by these dehabilitating ideas. When we allow our ego to enforce the thought that we are special it becomes the instrument ... the hand that builds our reality and manipulates how we see our world, a world that we have constructed.

We are aware the donkey never gets the carrot and that there is no pot of gold at the end of the rainbow however most of us live our lives reaching for a prize we will never obtain. You are the author of your reality and when the pen we use to write with is the ego, we live separate, fearful existences. We judge and condemn because we believe that we are different, better, more talented, more beautiful, winners, superior or the reverse of these things where we have accepted some are better and some are worse. When we finally come to accept that everything is inclusive, undivided, whole and all is One we become less self-centred, much more objective and our cynicism and critical view of the world dissipates and we become liberated, freed of our programmed ego.

We could stop propping up the pyramid so well illustrated by Icke. This pyramid encapsulates us all as we support it, the names change however the structure is always the same, call the names whatever we choose, in the construction of the boxes we have made to separate us from one another;

Democrat, Labour, The News at Ten, whites and blacks, money, monarchy, religion, males and females, us and them, the government, the judiciary, the army, the police, any football club, Hollywood or the FBI, these names and the millions more we have thought into being can be put into one word – they are egocracies – they are the kingdom of the ego.

We cannot advance whilst the vast majority of us are either in poverty, fearful, stressed and separated, coerced into various stages of dis-at-ease, of conflict and depression.

Every known civilisations has risen and fallen but all have been replications of themselves, Summaria, Babylon, Egypt, Greece, Rome and now us – and the extension of us – which is the US of A.

The same education and programming, same belief systems, same politics and religion – however it is packaged – whatever pretty dress they put upon it, the only changes that were ever implemented for improvement was for the few to control and therefore to live off and prosper from the many.

And that these leaders who have passed the baton down the generations for about the last – say – 5500 years, have always ultimately got it badly wrong, and for the price of their self-promotion, their delusion, their lust for power, their lies and their deceit (always the ego) – we have always picked up the tab.

We, who have given away our power to those who ultimately have no accountability; to the politician, priest, president and banker, to the celebrity, the King and the Queen, we give them power and it is our prerogative to also remove that power (attention = energy).

It is not titles that honour men – it is men who honour titles, but those men are few and for the most part we will never know their names but we recognise them when we meet them – they care for their fellow man, they ask for nothing, they heal, they give love unconditionally, they teach by example, they are humble and compassionate, they are priceless and they are exceptionally rare.

These are the qualities we need to aspire to, these are the gifts that we need to place value upon and give admiration to – this is something we are not doing very well at the moment.

Which is why we witness the same cycles for 5500 plus years; boom and bust, feast and famine but above all fear – always the fear – the fear that we are somehow less than they are, the fear they know more than we do, the fear of stepping outside the box, the fear that has controlled us from then until now.

As I hope has been demonstrated on these pages, fear is the witchcraft that is practiced upon us. Every single act perpetrated against us, has been delivered through the instrument of fear, who pays? – You pay – every single time.

Abolish fear from our minds and the world will become in one heartbeat, a different place in which to live.

I reckon 'they' have been given enough time and perhaps it should now be our turn to return to Eden.

All we have to do is want it and love is the answer and that capability - the want to love - the acceptance of love - the thought of love - changes our vibrational level and we allow the right things to happen.

All it takes is for us to use our minds.

This would reveal a world we only hear about through the veils and mists of times long ago, through fairy stories, myths and fables.

Was there really a time in a place far away, an Atlantis or an Eden, and were those times very different than now?

Did people live for hundreds of years because of their lifestyle and mindset, did those people live in a world without conflict, was there love in abundance in their lives and did they have loads of opportunity to give to whatever pursuit they chose?

A lack of fear, a life that did not involve going down the mines everyday, a life without the ingestion of chemicals, programming and fear; where work was something you did because you were helping someone rather than chained to subservience for a wage, a wage which gets fully paid back with buttons on in order to fund the lifestyles of materially richer people who we will never meet and who care nothing for us.

Did those ancient people with open minds connect better to Universal Consciousness and communicate telepathically with one another thus negating the need for speech? When they placed their feet on the ground did they scarcely leave a footprint such was the extent of their individual and collective enlightenment? Did those people live in harmony with the animals and did those animals as a result have no fear of them? Was it possible that those ancient minds knew far greater technology than we do now, (or certainly have very different technology)?

Was it possible those ancients harnessed the power of their clearer minds to move the massive rocks demonstrating that we really can move mountains, as they constructed what remains of buildings we have since discovered, answering all the questions we cannot answer despite what all the 'experts' say.

Our limited view of history gives us hints as to how life might have been however is it really important to know of how different life may have been in these mythical, magical but perhaps not imaginary paradise's?

An idea might be not to dwell in the past but to live in this moment - the present - and know with clarity what we are capable of and to try and achieve what perhaps has never fully been done before, and together and as One build this utopian world.

Certainly in the archives of history there is firm evidence to the contrary of what we have been told. In the peoples of the many civilisations we know of who went before us, there are signs and in every day life all around us there exists the evidence. We see it in others and in their creative work, we glimpse it when we receive it and when we are thinking right we give it - it is simple - it is love.

When we practice forgiveness; because we understand as best as we are able that forgiveness is a feeling that vibrates with love, rather than the programmed conditions we all have to endure to some extent or another.

Programmed into fear, rage, guilt, jealousy, blame, frustration, hatred or any of the low vibrational emotional conditions born of the ego, where we fall deeper into the dense and cold embrace of others who control us, where our spirit endures but cannot grow and cannot thrive.

When we can, individually and collectively, stop judging and the automatic process of condemning that is compounded to follow, only then can we escape the matrix, or in other words this dream of a 'reality' that we have created, and then we do not have to come back because we have broken the cycle and our journey is complete - we don't need a body anymore - we are fully enlightened and as a result become matter-less.

As we used to repeatedly judge and condemn, we now practice forgiveness and become more and more aware of when we are doing it, therefore it follows that we become mindful, this then allows us to practice being in the present and to be.

Only by repetition can we allow this to become automatic or habitual; it is tough because we are undoing years of deeply entrenched programming and habitual behaviour. If this in itself is not difficult enough, there is a double-whammy because we also have to deal with the ego and this is a massive fight because the ego wishes to maintain its identity and it will fight long and hard to find energy and present us with an endless stream of 'problems.'

It follows that during the process of our enlightenment that the ego will fight for its survival and be sure, any and all of our problems come down to the ego but remember it's not real, its nothing more than a manifestation of our mind, a projection like the images in Plato's Cave, it is of our own doing and of our own perception.

In a series of encounters the programmers constructed our sense of self when we were children and in the process formed layers like the skins of an onion, as we slice through that onion there may well be tears but we loose nothing and gain everything.

Our creative nature breaks through and blossoms when we reduce or forget our ego, this is the place where instinct subdues intellect – this then is a state of grace. This is where we are given insight and demonstrate our creativity and this is how we can be sure of how much more exists beyond the programmed self - quell this ego identity and witness your natural self.

By diminishing this sense of self we peel apart the layers of the onion upon which the ego feeds and inside is to be found You.

The real you that came here at the beginning of your life before those layers, those masks were made.

So yes, drugs and chant and dance and dream may reveal to you the nature of the Universe - the place you have in it and the fact that we are all One, but only momentarily, to really reveal YOU is to live in the absence and without the falsehood of time - in the present - I repeat - in this moment; all you can own, everything you possess - be still on this - be mindful of this - be at peace with this - meditate on this - and you will find YOU - and you will love what you find.

So we are presented with a choice - when we absorb a blow, someone criticise us, someone we love does not love us back, when we are asked to queue at the Post Office, when we get cut up on the road, when we don't get what it is we think we want, when we turn on the news and all the other millions of other potential pitfalls that we are presented with. We seethe and we boil, we worry and we fret, but it all comes down to a straight choice - we judge and condemn or we simply forgive. When this process is automatic and becomes a habit we cease to judge, when we cease to judge we cease to condemn.

And when we achieve this the ego has been subdued and we find escape from this matrix we call 'reality.'

And then again - please forgive me - you may want to stay in the matrix but I ask you, was life really meant to be 'the daily grind?'

I hope I have demonstrated how our DNA is receiving and people who control us can manipulate broadcasting information, but transmissions when we are unblocked can receive messaging from the more benign Universal Consciousness Channel. However when blocked or tampered with we receive messages via symbols, patterns and directions which are not necessarily to our benefit.

This then is what quantum physics demonstrates; that this life we call 'reality' in a matter based dimension is a frequency we are locked into through our five senses and the programming we endure, the world of the sub-atomic, which we are just beginning to scratch the surface of, should be one of the major things we are taught as we are growing up, but to date we are largely denied, we are told it does not fit, even the genius of Einstein had a problem with it on many levels, because we now know that electrons can travel faster than he said they could. Everything in nature and that includes ourselves, shares information as it communicates instantly, not faster than the speed of light – instantaneously. We are attuned to everything and we tune ourselves in not through intellect but through instinct and imagination. Consciousness flows at a subatomic quantum level, we are part of that soup of vibration, the ancient Greeks called it 'the ether,' some call it the matrix, but throughout this book I have called it Consciousness because it is minded and knowingly or otherwise we manipulate it.

Inside the world of quantum physics are to be found the answers we seek, how everything including thought, is communicating and therefore affects everything else and this why we must not view ourselves as solid but as different grades of energy. Solid, liquid, gas, atomic, sub atomic, etheric and super ethric, these seven frequencies (like the piano keyboard) vibrate on different scales and agree to make you, You; an electrically driven, organic, conscious robot and when your done you do not die, this is a fallacy, your consciousness passes to a different frequency of existence.

The world beneath the atom is understood by the very few, it is the world of the shaman and the magician and for the most part they have been the puppets of those who have controlled us for 5500 years, Consciousness has been accessed and thereafter manipulated to put us in slavery, by a handful of people sitting behind the curtains pulling the strings of others who in their turn pull others strings in a pyramidal structure.

These are the alchemists, the dark wizards of the present day; these are the people who manipulate Consciousness.

In this beautiful Universe where Consciousness is everything and is in everything there is absolutely nothing to fear, but in this matter-based dimension that we have chosen to inhabit, we can see how magic - the manipulation of energy - occurs.

We should object to such manipulation especially when it hinders our truthful destiny and denies our proper birthright.

The expression goes, 'if you always do what you've always done then you'll always get what you've always got.' We deserve more than we have; more lives of quality and equality and the ridding ourselves of all unnecessary fear and separation would be a massive step in the right direction.

We will always show concerns for our future and those we care for and love, but concern is a natural motivational emotion especially when an individual has hope, when the society we live in can offer up solutions to the problems that naturally occur. But when hope is unlikely and help is improbable, people in essence will either resort to desperate measures or become frightened, depressed, cut off and insular.

The price of these different reactions leads people to become none-contributing members of society and if we were to do a head count we can count those people in their billions.

As long as we continue to think and act the way we do, we are destined to witness the same cycle repeated constantly as it has been for every generation past.

The only way we can enable ourselves for change is by changing ourselves. And we can only change by the way we think.

We can think as we are programmed to do, in a series of dramas about our sense of self as we play the same tape repeatedly to ourselves. The situations change and the circumstances alter but the results are the same because our minds are run by the ego, and when we communicate with ego the way we were programmed to do we are obsessed with 'I,' 'me' and 'mine.'

The ego is not interested in truth it is interested in survival and growth, in a quest for self-preservation it feeds upon all the low emotional states such as fear and what fear births which is anger, and anger can be directed inwards or outwards but the results are the same – damage and destruction and so it follows that our ego then enables us to perform in ways that are dysfunctional leading us into behaviour such the urge to be special, violence and delusions of grandeur.

Beyond this dream of separation at the higher vibrational levels separation matters less and less until finally it ceases to exist.

There is only one reality; there is only One and we are both a fragment and a part of One, we cannot understand this in separation because we create dualism which enables opposites of varying magnitudes.

It suits those that prosper from us to have the structure that we have, there is a massive proportion of people whose wages are paid by the public purse to judge us and condemn us. Government and their agencies, the aptly named judiciary, the police, the armed forces - all around us we find these structures all fighting to justify their existence. Indeed the system survives and prospers because of big business that franchises factors that are enabled to take care of these 'problems' in our society, such as unemployment, crime and the resultant courts and prisons, the security industry, drugs, terrorism, war and so on. On the face of it this is a seemingly outrageous comment but it is not lightly put – people will go to extraordinary lengths to protect their power, to advance their positions, their blind ambitions will stop at little or nothing to protect what it is they think they believe in and what they imagine they cannot live without.

In turn we are programmed to fear all these things and many more which goes on to justify the existence of these energy-sapping delusions. However all these vitally important issues can be addressed. The resultant waste of energy, money and recourses can be put to better use for the benefit of everyone.

It is time to remove the blinkers and go beyond the limited prison of the vibrational zone we are presently trapped in.

The time has come to save ourselves and really have a fantastic time. And don't you dare go feeling guilty about that - I had to mention this because I just felt the tiniest shudder go through our collective consciousness at a sub-atomic level - just then - like a little tremor - please understand; it really is totally appropriate for you to have a fantastic, loving, wonderful, joyous, abundant life - but your not going to get one until you stop thinking you don't deserve it.

We can continue to take the blue pill everyday and we can try and ignore the tirade of fear that constantly knocks at our door, but we owe it to our children to teach them differently for as we know, they are the future.

But that is all children everywhere and without any exception, so as not to become slaves to the machine but to have lives of richness and fulfilment.

It is ourselves we need to work upon, it is ourselves we need to fix, because if we continue to programme as we have done (and has been done to us - so do not go doing the guilt again and beating yourself up) and thereafter, hand our children over to school and religion for the real proper heavy stuff to be placed deftly and deeply in the amygdala and other parts of our memory brain, (can you remember the nightmares?).

In the process of creating this buried pain and resultant guilt we create an altar in some deep, dark and impenetrable corner of our mind and it will release itself uncalled for in later life and be made manifest; as a behavioural problem, an eating disorder, a craving for celebrity and approval, a bad temper, a propensity towards violence, a penchant for drugs, a pain body, an addictive personality, obsessive compulsive behaviour patterns, a depression or malady that will never leave, - and so on - I mean - would it make you feel a little better if I share a secret with you? – I've had the whole lot.

Only we can break the cycle, only we can heal ourselves.

Perfection cannot be found in this reality - in this matter based dimension, because we created a version of it with our minds and we are not perfect, only God is perfect and that's why we yearn to go home, back to perfection, back to Oneness, to sit once again with God from whence we came. But that was before our spirit made the decision to find form, to manifest as matter and to create this reality.

We have the power to reject and find the strength to heal.

For all of the negative energy and the snuffing out of all rebellion that went into the breaking of the child that lives within us, the instinctive talent, unlimited potential and in the doing made us vibrate so badly with fear that we completely forgot what we knew when we first entered this life - that you are connected and came from Universal Creative Source Energy, from Consciousness; God, Allah, the Great Architect or whatever symbol we feel urged to place upon our hero's shoulders.

If for one moment that small and fragile child could just tip a bit out, just a fraction of all that baggage that we have managed to lug around with us for years, always sapping our energy, always distracting and deluding us. And that is also in recognition of the energy we waste in pretending what it is we think our fellow men would need from us in order we might be popular, fit into the 'they seem awfully nice people routine.'

These are the masks we wear; these are the manifestation of the ego.

If we could just tip some of the fear out and find some more room for the good stuff - the Universal Creative Source Consciousness stuff, the energy from whence we all came and the very same Source to which we all return - then the walls of the boxes that separate us would evaporate, grace would be allowed to enter our lives and then we wouldn't have to drop the dishes as we dried them and we could land a fly on the water to lure the elusive brown trout with ease.

(If this last bit means nothing to you - shame on you - you have been skipping again, please go back to section under 'grace').

Heaven awaits us, Hell exists only here on earth in this 'reality' that we have created here on psycho-planet - we are so powerful we can manifest either and we have proven it many times over.

The choices are ours to make and we can change it all in a heartbeat, we only have to ask.

Everyone thinks of changing the world,
But no one thinks of changing himself.

Leo Tolstoy.

There were many who helped me in the writing of this book, many of the names of those I quote allowed me to construct the points I have tried to make.

Those people past and present, I sincerely thank.

My sincere appreciation goes to Annie, to Alan and to Allan; they helped me in so many ways I cannot begin to describe. However I can describe how they made me feel and how they supported me but in one word they - in very different ways brought me joy.

All of this redoubtable trinity I have just named, had sight of this book at about the halfway stage; when one remarked, 'what point are you trying to make, what conclusions are you going to come to?' It is a very valid point and now the book is finished I don't think that I've adequately answered the question. I am not sure I wish to reach some earth-shattering conclusion but I sincerely hope that you find something on these pages that makes you ask questions – different questions to the ones we are presently asking in our lives – in that respect I will have achieved more than I could ask for in the writing of this book

I was out on the town a few years ago, there were about ten of us sampling a few continental lagers, we ended up at a table in a restaurant and were joined by two other people that we all knew.

One of them I have known for many years, due to the lager the conversation was all over the place and we got onto the subject of nostalgia. We were pondering on our pasts and what had brought us all to this point in our lives. I mentioned that I wondered how different my life might have been had I stuck in at school and behaved myself. (Not been a rebel almost without a pause – led a more ordered, disciplined, structured and controlled life and in turn become more subjugated by the programmers).

One of the people that had joined us, a star called David, replied immediately. 'Yes of course you would be different - but you would not be you.' This straightforward but thought provoking statement holds true for us all. You are who you are because of where you have been, the things you have done, the mistakes you have made, your triumphs and disasters, all the lessons you have chosen to experience have all combined to made you what you are now.

You have had choices and sometimes it might have appeared that you had not, but whatever has happened, whatever age you are and wherever you are in the stages of your unfolding and becoming, the miracle that is you goes on and how you feel will play a major role in where you find yourself – which vibrational wave you choose to ride – what state your in.

It doesn't happen yesterday when the summers were longer and the winters were short, it doesn't happen tomorrow when what might be never is the way it will be - it happens now.

Relax, focus on this, focus on now, be happy, be still, be calm … note your breathing, slow your breathing, how your chest moves, feel the air as it flows in and out, celebrate yourself, forgive yourself, know of your power, feel good, smile.

Now that didn't hurt did it? - Go on read it again and feel the love that you are.

It is time to remove the blocks in our minds and to remember our immensity and through the medium of love we can do anything.

The more we act from love than through fear; the more we will be living the lives we were designed to live.

Every situation is a test and you fail when you react badly and you go down the emotional scale because that's what you were programmed to do. You pass the test when you practice quantum forgiveness and don't react and you remain elevated and mindful and towards the realm of love.

Others around us who vibrate the same or in a similar way will amplify our power. And we will draw to us the right circumstances and find the best in people by vibrating correctly. Others will 'get' that you're a spiritual warrior and your vibrations will form a match.

If you can't find a match - stick around because you are about to be tested - the test will become apparent, you learn and you move on.

You can forget something with ease; a face, a fact, an occurrence, but you cannot unlearn a thing. You are who you are because of where you have been. The only thing you can meaningfully change is you, changing yourself now will take immediate effect and will govern what you are attracting into your present and therefore affect your future which in turn will become your present.

All of the situations you have been exposed to have brought you to this point and shaped you and made you the way you are, in fact they define who you are now.

Conversely, you would not be who you are had you not experienced these things. Let go of the guilt and move forward - nothing can stop you.

Contained on these pages are 'The Things I Wish They'd Told Me As I Was Growing Up,' and had I known them life would have been much easier, however that is not the point because I had to live my life to bring me to this point and I had to realise that wherever I put myself provided me with an opportunity to learn. It had to be that way, I am totally responsible because I manifested my reality and this is true of us all - but if - just if - I had understood earlier;

The shiny genius of Bill Hicks. The incisive brilliance of Daniel Goleman. The complete sense of The Barefoot Doctor and his teachings about the Tao.

The astounding conclusions of Jeremy Narby. The compassion and pure and utter sense of Buddhism. The awesome and undeniable truth of the book called 'A Course in Miracles,' and the book that unlocked its wisdom and helped me understand it, 'The Disappearance of the Universe.'

If I had better dealt with my fears and not fought so hard and so long against programming but dealt with it by seeing it for what it is and what it does. If I had been given the chance to appreciate sacred geometry (rather than the many fabrications we continue to be taught in school). If I hadn't got so depressed and angry about all the injustices in the world and realised earlier that what we think we will bring to us and therefore we create our own reality.

I wish I had known how powerful we are and to become even more powerful we need to grow, to love and to be happy because even though we are conditioned to believe otherwise, we are here to create ourselves – literally – you are here to fix yourself, but programming states that's selfish - your only thinking of yourself, but your not because if you fix yourself and progress towards what it is to be enlightened then you can help others fix themselves, and that has to be what it is to be truly human.

I wish I had known that God equals love and ego equals fear, and so I also wish I had understood the masks, delusions and the falsehoods of my own ego.

I wish I had understood why we should never judge and condemn and grasped the undeniable truth of quantum forgiveness and I wish I had listened better when in the presence of wisdom - just when to shut up.

I wish I had been programmed to understand that we heal by realising that everything – every single thing - in human behaviour manifests as an expression of love or as a call for love - but the more egotistical and damaged you are then the more ridiculous this will sound.

If I had begun to learn to meditate earlier I would have saved myself pain but again that's not the point because pain is the instrument that enables us to burn away our impurities.

Just one more thing I wish I'd known; that virtually all the resources (to which ironically we entirely contribute) are in turn used against us to subjugate and subordinate us so that we feel the need to be so severely governed and how we therefore stumble, falsely seduced and become accepting of the rubbish we are compounded to consume every second of every day of our lives – (lest we are mindful) - lives that for most of us are nothing more than an existence and a real hard one at that - in a world that could so easily be changed and become a place where anyone and everyone could be a leader by example and be allowed, without any outside interruptions, to fulfil his destiny and follow without impediment his joy.

And if all you want to do for three or four hours a day is to sort out the big mushrooms from the little ones – then so be it – that's your choice – enjoy – is that not better than the way things are at present? – trapped within a society where the vast majority of us live like mushrooms – kept in the dark and fed shit.

This is not the life YOU were designed to live – you were designed as a god by a god, to process love and joy and have an abundance of whatever you thought into your reality.

This then in part is my story, how I arrived at this point to the believing in what is contained on these pages, but as I have waxed and waned between confidence and despair in the ability to speak my truth, in weaker moments when I believed I might fail I may have demonstrated a lack of confidence as I have used so many others voices, who echo with the power of their wisdom as they talk to us down the ages, but those voices have moulded me and shaped me, and as I fought to understand their meanings their power reverberated thorough me, altering me, shaping me, moulding me – like the work of Hans Jenny or the sound that brought this Universe into being, or the notes that change matter – like the magic I hope I've explained.

I make no apologies for using these great words for as they touched, moulded and seduced me – I pray they touch you.

Your circumstances are altered by the way you think and therefore how feel – but you think what you think – and therefore feel what you feel – because of where you have been – because of who you are. We need to change to make for a better future and having begun to fix ourselves we could do worse than concentrate our efforts on helping the generation behind us, and the bonus is held safe in the knowledge that we would feel so good about it. This would stop the baton being passed and the Grail would be revealed to all of us (not just the lads behind the curtains) this would hinder the programmers and allow the cycle to be finally broken.

I have quoted many people on these pages, some are long gone, others are still around and they have all inspired me to view the world differently. I trust I have appropriated the right words to the right people.

Many of the answers that I hope will help you lie in the wisdom of others contained in these pages. I hope you might be encouraged to research further into these and other people's works and minds.

Our minds can take us anywhere – especially when they're open.

I have nothing but respect for those that can paint pictures with words and so we should encourage the next generation to read and write the right stuff, furthermore we should try to give them everything by way of opportunity to express themselves and be what they would be.

When I criticised the dynamics of celebrity - on both the side of the adored and the adoree - if the next generation were given the opportunity to properly express themselves they would all be celebrities, stars each and everyone of them. If we were all helped to achieve our true purpose it follows we wouldn't need celebrities because we wouldn't need to project our wants and needs onto others and so we would all become the hero's of our own dream. Thus the gap would narrow because those that can express their own talent and the Source it came from are enabled to achieve their own individual self, not the self imposed upon us. To be You and truly who You are is the fulfilment of an agenda-less dream and what is to be a truly spiritual being. The results are we would be less inclined to live our lives through projection onto others - others who only appear to be more talented. This is an illusion - a dream - you can be anything you choose, it can easily be fun again. Real talent is out there in abundance and it is every single person on this planets birthright to have the chance to experience and demonstrate it.

And should you choose - that includes being the most respected sorter-outer of the big mushrooms from the little mushrooms - in all of your entire known Universe.

Individually and collectively our purpose here is to learn and create and in the doing we grow.

You are part of it all - you are a god in human form and creation and growth is a god's job.

Living via the ego and therefore within ourselves, creates the circumstances that inevitably mean that we learn most of our vital lessons through the instrument of pain, but it does not have to be this way. Our mistakes to date have been very costly, to ourselves, to each other and to our environment. That, certainly for most of us in the past, has been the way it has always been, this is what we have drawn to us.

Now is the time to restructure, review and build better lives for ourselves, but we need to break from the chains of constraint that have held us back for thousands of years. The collective rockets of desire we should be sending out to the Universe should be positive, we shouldn't worry about war, interest rates, terror, crime and all the other man-made conditions in existence - we shouldn't focus our minds on these negative conditions - we should simply think them out of existence.

It follows that eradication of these energy sapping conditions would result in a lack of the other negative conditions that we presently regard as natural occurrences.

Having cleansed our minds of fear, of man-u-factored conditions such as war, is it too fanciful to think that most of the rest would start and simply take care of itself?

It isn't 'soft' to love and it isn't weak to abhor violence - it is brave - and if you believe otherwise it is because you're programmed ego is blocking your truth.

The material resources we give over to war alone, if redirected would provide for and heal every single soul on the planet.

If we vibrated nearer to our Source with love there would be no need for all the drugs that the doctors prescribe to our sick society, drugs that bandage but never heal our dis - at - ease.

There would be less need for people to work hard down the mines all week and resurface at the weekend to find dubious release in the distractional seductive arms of drugs like alcohol.

We live in reactive mode, fire-fighting and jumping from one blaze to the next, full of fear and vibrating badly and as a result largely cut off from Source, we need to finally see that this headless-chicken mode is not the way forward.

When reacting rather than pro-acting, we are far more likely and susceptible to quick-fix, do drugs, manifest erratic behaviour, have meaningless sex, go impulse shopping and so on. When pro-acting you will as defined by the law of attraction, bring others to you who vibrate at a similar resonance, which is why 'like attracts like.'

Trust me - just use your magnetic personality.

Whatever your circumstances you must try and find the strength to vibrate well. With our minds open and relaxed the possibilities are unimaginable and our prospects immense.

We are the greatest miracle and we stand atop the heap, whether we earned that right by the fair use of equipment (like our opposable thumb) or by our guile and bulling, is purely a matter for conjecture. It is in the past - it is irrelevant. It is what we do now, in this moment that will portend our destiny; our future is shaped purely by the power of our minds - by our thoughts, our emotions and our desires.

We can fight for war or peace but the two will always create division because the word fight demonstrates disagreement, therefore someone wins while someone looses.

Alternatively we can forget about the entire concept and conflict will disappear.

We could stop ourselves from listening to the programmers who poison our minds and in the process rid ourselves of the melancholy that ails all of us to some extent or another.

Alan suggested to me on reading this; 'beware David you know people don't like to be preached to,' and I accept his sage words however I am going to push the boat out here – the reason I am not preaching is that somewhere deep down inside you – YOU feel that much contained here is truth, and I don't think that I am alone in thinking that we all feel at our best when in the truthful zone.

To be free of any delusion is to know truth.

Truth can be defined as that which cannot harm and to know truth is to be truly free and we all knew this with clarity when we started our journey here on planet-psycho, before we were groomed, programmed and propelled down whatever path to wherever we now find ourselves.

To change the world we only need change ourselves – we can walk in the rain – enjoy the wet - stop defaulting toward fear - rise to love.

I am not preaching, I am reminding - or at least I promise that is my intention and in any event how can I preach anyway? - As I trust we have established - I am completely insane!

In theory life should get better and progressively improve.

We make a mistake, we learn, we grow and we prosper. But what prevents many of us from a constant progression always going upwards and improving ourselves physically, spiritually and emotionally? We ourselves manage to do that, with lots and lots of help from the programmers, those who pass us the baton, those who enable us to vibrate nearer to fear than we do to love.

You are everything and you are made from its substance - the stones you walk upon, the water you run your hand in, all the trees you will ever see, every animal you think you have ever owned, every animal you have eaten, every person you have kissed, every person you have loved, everyone you have ever encountered and everyone you have ever hated - is you.

That's why we are all brothers and that's why we are all One Consciousness.

We vibrate within a small frequency in a vast spectrum and we can alter our frequency by vibrating higher. We call the other parts of the spectrum where we do not inhabit, 'other dimensions.' Our conditioned-self can be made aware of these other dimensions through access such as feelings, hunches, intuition and synchronistic occurrences. We can be taken to these other dimensions by changing our vibrational levels and as a result we gain access to Consciousness through the variety of the methods we practice.

This matter based and very limited spectrum is the place we call the 'real world,' but it is a tiny fraction of what is available. What we refer to as 'real' is a result of programming as we built our egos; we need to awaken from this material level of form.

Religions talk of finding God, but You are god and you and only you can allow yourself to have god revealed to you. You have god within every cell of your body - and if you define that God is good and is love - then it follows that you have the Devil, with badness and hate in you as well.

What will ultimately define you is the one you allow to influence your life.

It is your choice. This then is the eternal struggle. This is how man is capable of great acts of selfless love and yet can still orchestrate and perpetrate the most disgusting and wicked of deeds.

This is how a man can give orders to kill thousands of people in a bombing raid six thousand miles away, and later watch as a cities skies light up as soldier and civilian (people exactly the same as him, as you and as me) are slaughtered half a world away.

On the night when his masters took advantage of their programming and gave him orders to kill innocent children, as they lay warm in their beds. On that same night, that same man kissed his own children tenderly on their foreheads as they lay in their beds and he felt such an outpouring of love for them, that he thought his heart would burst. This is schizophrenic dysfunctional behaviour and this is what egoic power has done to the puppets that shape our world and control our destinies.

We are - every single one of us - capable of all of these acts and dangerous emotions and we readily accept enormous levels of delusion and hypocrisy because ultimately the unfortunate truth remains - the best lies that we tell are the ones we tell ourselves.

The simple truth remains that there is absolutely no difference between those children except they were born in different parts of the world, they are simply separated by space and time which is a total delusion of our 'reality.' We are all One, when you kill someone you are harming yourself and when you love someone you are loving yourself - it is that simple.

What are the consequences of this important soldiers action? What is at stake here to see the truth? That if he didn't follow the order to press the button to slaughter then someone else would? - this excuse is given regularly but it can't be considered a justification. That he would loose his job, his esteem in the community and would bring disgrace to his family name, the uniform and the flag? Because he is a soldier and he comes from a long line of soldiers, their polished, clean-shaven faces radiate from photographs housed in polished frames, displayed along countless mantelpieces or small tables covered respectfully with linen – faces – shiny, clean, proud, uniformed and medallioned, but all of them frozen in images before the horror of war will bend their very souls as they give witness and participate in the dance of man's inhumanity to man.

Could it be that his wife would leave him because he faced a court martial and she couldn't bear the shame? He would likely loose the friendship and respect of his brothers-in-arms, those bonded by similar belief, those who have fought by his side. He would loose the place he calls home.

Are all these reasons justification to kill people he will never meet in a place he will never visit, based entirely upon programmed, imposed and developed beliefs? Just how wrong can we be in our attempts to be right - to guard what it is we think we value – to hold to whatever it is we think we trust?

Unless we begin to question the madness.

You are everything, from the highest to the lowest, it all reside within you - you can create, you can destroy, you are natures greatest miracle - now what will you do with your unimaginable power?

We can continue to live in boxes and wear our masks; we can take short peeks from behind them when we have a few drinks too many or manage to reduce our egos.

The higher we develop the more ego-less we will become and profound humility characterises being beyond ego, 'the meek shall inherit the earth,' is to be humble and will ultimately be the way we can pass through the events that are upon us but we must put aside our personal wants, needs and desires.

A question we might poise ourselves is; are we ready for the transformation? Are we ready to find out? Are we ready to live in the Now? (The 'Now' that Eckhart Tolle presents in his writing) because in this moment - in this present - is all we can ever own - all we can ever truly possess and all we can ever be.

We are urged to do so because Now is where we can find the freedom of a life without fear because Now is to quell the ego.

We can fight for what we believe in and be deluded into the belief that the cause is just or we can see what heinous acts we perpetrate in supporting a programmed belief – our opinion, of what is 'right' and what is 'wrong.'

Know with clarity that you are capable of being anything you desire, but be assured your journey will be easier if your path is filled with truth and love. You can be anything because you are everything.

You can walk with a snarl or a smile and your world will be separately and clearly defined - for what you give, you will get.

The mystery that surrounds the Holy Grail and all the pursuit and desire we have shown for its acquisition, it is with us right now, just where it has always been, right under our noses.

What is it we could possess that would give us dominion and power over both ourselves and the way we live our lives?

The ability to harness how we think and therefore how we behave is the Holy Grail - this is the answer to all our problems - all our maladies - all our separateness - the ability to perform pure magic and create a wonderful life.

There is no 'secret,' it has always been with us - we just forgot what we knew when we first arrived here on our journey, before the programmer's got to us and before we developed our egos; the seed of which we brought with us on our journey, a seed now watered and nourished which grows more powerful and more deeply rooted as we feed it, by the games we play from behind our masks as we practice its power many times a day right here on planet psycho.

At present the real secrets of the Grail are held by the few to influence and corrupt our minds and therefore control our destinies and this is why we find ourselves living the way we do and in turn how we make the world what it is.

As we have discussed there are many experiments that conclusively prove what we are coming to terms with - below the atom in the world of quantum physics we have established that mind affects matter with the result that mind can alter and shape matter, it is an astonishing thought. We are not only denied this knowledge it has been used against us for thousands of years. The ability to perform magic was held in the ancient mystery schools and now exists in the present held in secret societies, where those who assume power over us use it against us.

To a greater or lesser degree we have all become contaminated, subservient. Those who have broken us into their beliefs performed mastery over us, the solution is to regain mastery of the self, because without this we are what many of us have become which is both prostitute and pimp, as we serve the nightmare of our creation - dumber and numbed to fear. As a result we accept our lot almost without question but we know in our core this is not all that there is. We need to stop looking outwards to external programming forces and look inside ourselves and reconnect to Source and we need to trust that Source will flow through us, both individually and collectively, and when we feel right by ridding ourselves of ego and the resultant negativity and fear, then our lives will become awesome and Source will communicate and flow and we will know grace once more.

History shows that those who have worked on the outmost boundaries of creative intelligence and have understood wisdom beyond their experience in this matter-based realm, have reached this place whilst in altered states, in the mind set we presently adopt we can achieve nothing ahead but a repeat of the cycles we see left behind us.

The secret of the Grail lies within each and every one of us, we simply need to believe again - all of us can live lives of abundance, of joy and of love - we just need to allow it.

I have fought with anger, with others and with myself - been seriously depressed and been seriously happy. When Stephen Fry talked about his depression he interviewed other sufferers from all walks of life. He asked them if they could become 'normal' would they push the button that removed their 'problem' or would they choose not to push the button and remain as they were. Almost without exception they elected not to push the button - to remain imbalanced - mad - that is not to be 'normal.'

I wouldn't want to press the button that Stephen Fry refers to either. I will always choose the red pill and I assure you that those that prosper from and control us don't like that at all.

As for those of us who take the blue pill, perhaps it's time to ask yourself – do I want to do this forever?

However whichever coloured 'pill' you have decided upon, my wish is that it works for you on your journey.

My other wish for you is that something in this book might just spark a flame and help you on that journey.

Live long and prosper.

Mr Spock.

And remember to have fun and try not to take it all too seriously - remember it is all an illusion - it is not real - and stop doing fear, and yes - I suppose that's preaching but anyway I got it off my chest and now my ego is replete - thank you for coming with me on this journey - I sincerely wish you well with yours.